VAGABOND POLICEMAN

By Max K. Hurlbut

Copyright © 2013, Max K. Hurlbut
All rights reserved.

No part of this book may be reproduced, stored in a retrieval system, or transmitted by any means, electronic, mechanical, photocopying, recording, or otherwise, without written permission from the author.

ISBN 978-1-625-17287-7

EPIGRAPH

"Not all who wander are lost."

J. R. R. Tolkien. "The Fellowship of the Ring," *Lord of the Rings* (50th Anniversary Edition), Boston (2004), page 170.

CONTENTS

EPIGRAPH iii

INTRODUCTION xvii

I. OWANUX 21
   "Last of the Mohegans": A Family Legacy 21
   The "Live Free or Die" State 23
   The Civil War Drummer's Tale 23
   Soap Poisoning 24
   Tech Savvy but Dumb as a Brick 25
   Radio Daze 26
   "The Thing on the Fourble Board" 27
   Wartime Medicine 27

II. DAD'S LAST SHOT 29
   The Reo Truck 30

III. CALIFORNIA OR BUST 32
   "Red Ryder" Rides 32
   Gorgeous George 34
   Surf Critters 35
   Out of the Past 35
   Grunion or Snipe? 36
   Printer's Devil and Projectionist 36
   Prospecting 37
   Sputnik 37
   Runaway 38

IV. THE BOYS IN WHITE 40
   Freeway Nightmare 40
   The Wino Sting 41
   Meet the Addams Family 41

    The Pike Killer-Coaster 42
    The Wandering Dead 42

V. LAPD BLUE...45
    Testing 45
    Police Academy 47
    Badges 49
    First City Gear..49
    Chief William H. Parker 49

VI. LAPD IN 1960 51
    Communications 51
    Patrol Cars..53
    Weapons 53
    Baton 54
    Hot Sheets 55
    Emergency Lights 55
    Sirens...56

VII. HOLLYWOOD..57
    First Night in the Field 57
    First Felony Arrest 58
    Hollywood Station 59
    No Cause for Alarm 59
    Hollywood Station Layout 60
    The "Computer"...61
    Hollerith File...61
    "Hooray For Hollywood" 63
    The First Year...64
    The Onion Field 65
    Panzer Man 70
    "Make My Day!" 71
    Griffith Park Riots..72
    Hollywood Train Mystery 72
    The Egyptian 74

Beatles at the Bowl	75
Rapatronic Outpost	76
"Imus in the Morning"	76
Celebrity Citations	77
The Great Imposter	78
The Batt	79
The Bat	82

VIII. HOLLYWOOD VICE 84
Greyhound Bus Depot	84
Ladies of Negotiable Affection	85
Occupational Hazard	86
Time-Life Pervert	86
"The Trouble with Harry"	87
Ferndell No. 9	88
Making Book	89
The Chain Game	89
Queer Slang	90
Bizarro Names	91

IX. TRAFFIC ANARCHY 92
Acme Arrives	92
"Frankenstein on Wheels"	93
Pink Status	93
Nemesis and the Freeway Flyer	94
Pursuits	96
Ladies' Night	97
Bubble—Trouble	97
Double–Trouble	98
The Missing Barricade	98
"918 Victor"	99
Disciplinary Action	100
Working on the Railroad	101
Risk Reduction	101
T.J. Hooker	102

X. THE VALLEY AND BEYOND 104
- North Hollywood Division 104
- End of an Era 107
- Van Nuys 108
- San Fernando/Sylmar Earthquake 109

XI. THE WATTS RIOT 110
- 144 Hours in August 111
- The First Day 112
- Night Watch Sweep 113
- Firearms 113
- "Shootin' and Lootin'" 114
- Fire Discipline 115
- The Watts Riot Brick 116
- "Muhammad Speaks" 116
- The Detroit Riots 116
- The Death of America 118

XII. OLD SWAT 119
- "We Have Met the Enemy, and He Is Us" 119
- SWAT Origin 121
- Operations 121
- SWAT Study 122
- The Results 123
- Single-Officer Entry 125

XIII. THE EXPERIMENTAL DIVISION 126
- The Field Command Post in Action 127
- Personnel Investigations 128

XIV. THE SOUTH END 129
- University Division 129
- South End School Dropouts 130
- Off-Duty University Duties 131
- Seventy-Seventh Street Detectives 131

Michigan State	133
Hoodie Terror	135

XV. THE POLICE COMMISSION 137

"Here Come de Judge"	137
The Bird Watchers	139
The Mole Surfaces	139
Politics Prevails	140
The Alphabet Bomber	140
Discipline	141
The Pumpkin Field	141
Skeleton in the Wall	142
The Badge	143
Chief R. Lee Heath	146
Motorcycle Drill Team	147
1984 Summer Olympics	148
Halcyon Days	149
International Police Association	150
Mexican Coronel	151
Paladin International	152
An Epiphany	153
Retirement	153

XVI. NORTH TO ALASKA 155

Kodiak	155
Northern Narcotics	156
SWAT Champs	157
Home on the Bay	157
Pillar Mountain Run	158
Shuyak Island	159
Colt Python	160
The Ghost Ship	160
Bayside Fire Department	161
Al-A-Ga-Zam!	161
Sacred Whale Hunt	163

Northern Holidays 164
Resignations 164

XVII. THE ALEUTIAN CHAIN 166
The Thousand-Mile War 166
King Cove 167
Japanese Internment 167
The Stick 170
Bear-anoia 171
Aleut Justice 172
The "Dark Crazies" 173
The Mayor's Challenge 174

XVIII. THE PRIBILOFS AND PRINCE WILLIAM SOUND 176
Tunnel Town 176
Vagabonds Head North 177
The Bird House 178
City Marshal 180
Eighty-Six List 181
Air Crashes 182
Foot Casts of Snow on Bare Ground 182
Starting the New Year with a Bang 183
Barricaded Suspect 183
State Record Narcotics Haul from Cruise Ship 184
Romance on the Rocks 184
Out of Town by Sunset 185
Rail Ambulance 185
Deadly Glacier 186
Babes as Shields 187
The Pribilofs 188
Last Train to Nowhere 190
Alaska's Picturesque Speech 191
Duct and Cover—A Tacky Heritage 192
Native Cuisine 192

XIX. "THE TOWN TOO TOUGH TO DIE" 194
- Trouble in Tombstone 194
- Salmon to Scorpions 194
- Deputy Criminals 195
- Cochise County Corruption 197
- Twenty Miles From Water & Two Feet From Hell 198
- Arizona Highway Patrol Audit (or) "I Smell a Rat" 198
- Lies, Damned Lies, and Statistics 199
- Devious Dever's Dope Disposal 200
- Holding the BAG 201
- Badges with a Green Glint of Corruption 201
- Restraining Order 202
- The Only Honest Man 203
- The O.K. Corral 204
- Vengeance Ride 205
- A Matter of Justice 205
- Vigilance Committees 206
- The Bisbee Massacre 207
- "Kiss My Six-Shooter" 208
- Rotten Row 210
- Drunk Driving—Horse 211
- POST Certification 212
- Waste of Finite 213
- Speed Trap and No Tickets for Locals 213
- Auto Boot Hill 214
- Mormon Mafia 214
- Blood Atonement 215
- "Cocaine Borane" 215
- Tombstone Silver Badges 216
- Weapons 217
- Tombstone Underground 218
- Special Investigations Team 219
- Tombstone Turmoil 220
- Automobile Seizures 221
- Death of Hidalgo 223

Death of Hudson 227
Border Woes 228
"Fast and Furious" 229
Security Theater 230
FBI Bombs World Trade Center 230
American Kristalnacht 230
Farewell to Tombstone 231
Return to Tombstone 232

XX. THE ARMY 234
Basic Combat Training 234
Conscription 235
"Fire in the Hole!" 235
Military Police 236
Cuban Crisis 237
"De Oppresso Liber" (To Free the Oppressed) 237
"No Obstacle Too Difficult" 238
Green Hell 238
The Mustang 239
Incident at Bragg 240
The Technology Trap 242
Pulling the Pin 242

XXI. ROYAL THAI BORDER PATROL POLICE 244
Thumper 245
The Cause of Conflict 246
Brother Number One in Year Zero 246
Police Aerial Reinforcement Unit 248
Duel 248
The King and I 249
"Lucy's Tiger Den" 250
An American in Thailand and Cambodia 250
"Bridge Over the River Kwai" 250
The Elephant Never Forgets 251
"Born to the Naga" 252

 Bamboo Train to Battambang 252
 Execution by Elephant 253
 Jungle Meet 253

XXII. TAMING THE TIGER 255
 Wind Dummy 256
 Matsu and Quemoy 257
 The Colonel's Daughter 258
 Chinese Food 259
 Crazy Dog Wave 260
 "Uncle Chicken" 261
 Triads 262
 Hong Kong Handover 263
 The DMZ 263

XXIII. UP ABOVE AND DOWN UNDER 265
 Canadian Army North Pole Expedition 265
 Geographic Pole 266
 Magnetic Pole 266
 Border Guards Abandon Posts 267
 "E-Pana" 267
 Down Under 268

XXIV. TEST-JUMPING FOR THE RAF 269
 Problem Solved 269
 Lili Marlene 270

XXV. FLUNKING FRENCH 272
 Battle of Kolwezi 272
 The Two "Surrender Monkeys" 273
 "We Are Here, Lafayette." 273
 La Golondrina 274
 Cinco de Mayo 274
 "March or Die" 275

XXVI. SPRINGTIME IN GERMANY	276
XXVII. SUMMER IN THE SUDAN	278
Democratic Peoples' Republic of the Sudan	278
The Pitfall	279
Escape from Khartoum	281
XXVIII. MBOGO	283
Jailed in Egypt	285
XXIX. BONGO IN THE CONGO	287
Murder for Meat	288
Leopard Men	289
The Whip and Iron Collar	289
Dispatches from the Bush	290
Two for One	290
Track of the Elephant	291
Home Again	293
The Last Safari	294
XXX. THE TAR BABY	296
The Scam Begins	297
The Flawed Generation	297
"Blowback"	298
American Exceptionalism	299
Axis of Empire (or) Roots of Terror	299
Gulf War/Kuwait	300
Like Father, Like Son	302
A Genuine Intel Failure	305
The Tenth Crusade	307
Intelligence and War Crimes	308
Torture	310
Everything You Know Is Wrong	312
Defeat in the Middle East	313
Graveyard of Empires	314

Right and Wrong 315
Generational Gap 316
Lawrence of Arabia 318
"Fire the Generals" 319
The Longest War 319
Iraq Remembered 322
The Undiscovered Country 323
A Matter of Time 323

XXXI. THE SAMSON OPTION 324
The Enemy Within 326
A PROMIS Enhanced 327
Atomic Spies 329
The Samson Origins 329
Master and Servant 331
Control of U.S. Foreign Policy 332
Attack on the "USS *Liberty*" 334
"Cognitive Dissonance" 335
Frummer Friends 336
Teachings of the Talmud 337
"Joshua Fit de Battle of Jericho" 338
Israeli Labor Camps 340
Killing for Women's Rights 340
Ethnic Cleansing 341
Holocaust Denial 341

XXXII. SUZIE'S GOT A GUN 345
Discrimination, Prejudice, and Slavery 346
Minorities 347
Slavery 347
Affirmative Action Wonders 349
100,000 Fewer Arrests 351
Escalation of Force 352
Women in Law Enforcement 353
God Is a Woman 354

Pregnant Police 356
Lowering the Bar 357
Home on the Range..360
Babes in Arms 361
Girls with Guns..361
Women in the Israeli Defense Force 363
The World of Suzie Wong..364
Stand and Deliver...364

EPILOGUE..367

INTRODUCTION

"L.A.P.D.—$489 a month," reads the small advert in the *Los Angeles Times* discarded at the dispatcher's desk of Bowers' Ambulance in Long Beach.

"The year is 1959. I am a driver (earning seven dollars for a twelve-hour shift) while attending Long Beach State College as a full-time geology/mining engineering major. I carry a heavy-class load and my ambulance job allows me to sleep between emergency calls or to do homework."

"I can work fewer hours, make more money, and still attend school," I reason as I send for an application. Upon such whims and crossroads do our fates hang. I enjoy police work—largely problem-solving—and never return to the earth sciences other than as a hobby. I do not even wish to go end-of-watch following a night on the streets, as I am afraid of missing something….a common experience among new policemen.

The first of August 2010 marks my fiftieth anniversary of entering the LAPD Academy. As many years "retired" as in harness. A friend, LAPD Principal Detention Officer Samuel J. Flowers ("Call Box Sam"), suggests it is time to write down our memories—a collection of special moments—before they fade and are lost. The Department of Health and Human Services publishes life expectancy demographics by year of birth—I am projected to expire back in 2000. No time to waste!

I am the crow collecting shiny things—the bits and pieces that color life. You each have your own stories. The gypsy in me leads me off the beaten path. Autobiographical material must contain a natural essence of ego, or falsity can creep in as feigned humility. With that said, my experiences may not be as heroic as yours but simply different. Ambition does not drive me, but I lead an active life blessed (or cursed) by a wide-ranging curiosity.

The years pass and humorous little incidents often seem to outshine the more dramatic ones. I hunt the elephant *alone* in a triple-canopy Congo rainforest so dark I can hardly see the animal as I creep up upon him. But a native's revenge is what nearly nails me. I have a major malfunction in my first civilian parachute jump—into San Pedro Bay off Angel's Gate. I am later to test an experimental parachute for the British Royal Air Force fitted with a simple modification to prevent inversion malfunctions and to save the legs and lives of future jumpers.

I meet kings and cannibals, generals and presidents. I marry the daughter of a Chinese army colonel following a prank organized by an entire company of his soldiers—again involving parachutes. [Hueih-Hueih (pronounced *"Way-Way"*) teaches Chinese classical dance—but her biggest asset is putting up with me].

As a member of the Adventurers' Club and Explorers Club, I know Lieutenant General James "Jimmy" Doolittle (<u>Thirty Seconds Over Tokyo</u>) and (former) rascal Ferdinand "Fred" Waldo Demara, better known to an older generation as "The Great Imposter," then in his final metamorphosis. I visit fellow club member Thomas C. Christian, great-third grandson of Fletcher (the "HMS *Bounty*" mutiny of 1789) on Pitcairn Island. I ride the highest train in the world across the Tibetan Plateau, the bamboo trains of Cambodia, and the southernmost steam "convict train" in Ushuaia, Tierra del Fuego, Argentina.

I rise from private to lieutenant colonel, Army of the United States, as a "Mustang" (an officer directly commissioned from the enlisted ranks). I wander the globe because of a single strange incident at an Army base. Although not in Vietnam, I play a small part in dulling the tip of the Vietnamese spear on the Thai/Cambodian border. I take scientific readings at the North Pole with the Canadian Army. I am arrested in Egypt as a possible "Israeli spy" and am pursued in the Sudan after observations of military activities in the south. I am kissed on both cheeks by the French commandant at Pau and am forever a proud "para-frog." I observe the Legion's deployment to Zaire.

Hollywood Patrol and Vice at the end of the L.A. Noir period and "Golden Era" of Chief William H. Parker are E-coupon rides. Half-a-century later I stumble across the answer to a gangster shooting of one of Mickey Cohen's enforcers. I work detectives, the Freeway Flyers, a "Brushfire" unit in the Watts Riot, am team leader on the first-ever SWAT teams, orders writer for Chief Parker, and more. As captain of the L.A. Police Motorcycle Drill Team we lead the torchbearer into the Coliseum for the 1984 Summer Olympics. LAPD Lieutenant's Badge No. 1 is retired with me. I also prize my detective gold card.

A third career is troubleshooting small police departments in Alaska from the Aleutian Chain and the Bering Sea to Kodiak Island and Prince William Sound. A lone officer must find a solution to drunken bar brawls between fishing boat crews. My wife and I drive the last rail ambulance on the continent through long tunnels also traversed by freight trains. We patrol the "weirdest town in Alaska"—without road access—on skis, snowshoes, all-terrain vehicles, and in kayaks. Sea critters sometimes reduce victims of crime and accidents to skeletons.

I am drawn out of retirement for a final run as City Marshal of Tombstone, Arizona—a department running amok right out of the 1880s. I fire deputies with arrests for rape, narcotics, and homicide. (Who are then hired by the Cochise County sheriff as his deputies!) Two of my four deputies are found shot to death in their cars. I return fourteen years later and the sheriff dies that very day in a mysterious single-vehicle turnover.

Errors are exclusively mine, and I apologize if I have forgotten names or details of incidents you may recall with greater clarity. (Or, that I remember *too* well for your comfort!) My "politically incorrect" views I lay upon a rural New England farm background in the final years of the Great Depression. My roots run deep into the twentieth century. I know Civil War veterans, WWI pilots, train-jumping hoboes, and policemen who crack the heads of anarchists in the early 1900s. They, no doubt, consider me a dumb kid who never experiences life or hard times. Like most of you, however, I evolve from the sheep to the wolf.

Max K. Hurlbut, 10603, LAPD
LTC SF AUS (Ret.)

Chapter I

OWANUX

"Owanux! Owanux!" (Englishmen! Englishmen!)—the sentry's cry that seals the doom of 600 to 700 Pequots (Algonquian: "The Destroyers") trapped in their burning log palisade fort near the present town of Mystic, Connecticut.

The red man is to prove less than noble and the white man less than civilized….The struggle for survival between them is fought without rules along the fringe of a vast wilderness.

"Last of the Mohegans": A Family Legacy

Thomas Hurlbut, my great-seventh grandfather, is a companion of the Mohegan ("Wolf People") Sachem called Uncas. They attack the fort in the early hours of 26 May 1637.[1] Thomas, with about eighty fellow soldiers and an equal number of braves under Uncas, engages in America's first declared Indian war—the Pequot War of 1637.

Those not killed under Sassacus retreat into the wilds of what is now Manhattan to enlist the aid of their allies, the Mohawks. Sanctuary is refused and they are beheaded. The few survivors are sold as slaves into the West Indies.

Their name is taken from them. The Pequot River is renamed the Thames and the town of Pequot becomes New London. They cease to exist as a nation. [James Fenimore Cooper's *Last of the Mohicans* (1826)

---

[1] Max K. Hurlbut, "A Soldier in the First Indian War." (Unpublished dissertation in Military History, Kensington University, Glendale, CA, 1980), pp. 9–10 and 80–96. See also: *Under Lock and Key* (Descendants of Sheriffs and Constables of Colonial and Antebellum America), February 2012, (Vol. 1, No. 2), pp. 2–3.

is inspired by a letter written to Thomas by his commanding officer, Lion Gardener[2]].

Our somewhat peculiar surname is an occupational one, from the English "hurlbat"—a thin fifteenth century all-metal throwing axe sharpened on all four auxiliary ends to a point or blade. This ensues damage against its target of a shield wall or the legs of a cavalry horse. An obvious disadvantage is that, when thrown, the hurlbatter is disarmed and the enemy is in possession of his weapon....

Thomas, Constable of Wethersfield in 1644,[3] is the first policeman in the family. Two Gideon Hurlbuts (father and son) are privates in George Washington's Continental Line. My maternal great-fourth grandfather leads a Troop of Horse to the Lexington/Concord Alarm of 1775.

* * * *

I am born, cap pistol in hand, in Worcester, Massachusetts, in 1939. I listen to Westerns and mysteries on our old Atwater-Kent. The Great Depression lasts through the War. Everything is rationed. We kids do not realize we are poor farmers. Family, not money, determines community standing in provincial New England. Those arriving after the Revolutionary War are *forever* outsiders. (Class today is largely determined by income, not social attributes.)

My folks work while, after chores, I am on hand for the daybreak arrival of the steam locomotive at the Marlborough coal yard. I mingle with hoboes, tramps, and bums. (All beg, but hoboes move and work, tramps walk and loaf, and bums loaf and sit.) It is not until joining the ambulance service and LAPD that I become aware of another class—the wino! They are bums who favor "Thunderbird," short dogs of "Ripple,"

---

[2] This twelve-page letter on vellum is one of only four original documents by participants in the war. It is "lost" for over 300 years. I begin a search for it in the National Archives and Library of Congress. After three trips to Hartford, Connecticut, I find it in a pile of uncataloged Colonial documents in the Watkinson Library at Trinity College.

[3] Henry R. Stiles, *The History of Ancient Wethersfield*, Vol. II. (New York: Grafton Press, 1904), p. 443. I am Charter Life Member #33 of the "Descendants of Sheriffs and Constables of Colonial America."

and various cough medicines. They are often filthy and impregnated with urine, feces, and vomit. The travelers of my youth are dirty from the road/rail and ragged in dress, but drinkers get no handouts. One does not hear of the violence, mental illness, and crimes associated with today's homeless. The occasional chicken disappears, but not your sister or the family cow.

The "Live Free or Die" State

We move from Marlborough to tiny Lochmere, New Hampshire, where a little grocery and gas station ("Cozy Corner") are added to a farm. Our water supply is a hand pump in the kitchen above the well. The outhouse is a two-holer a short stone's throw beyond.

We hunt our deer and partridge and tap sugar maple trees. [It takes over fifty gallons of sap to produce a gallon of maple syrup. The lighter the color, the better the quality]. We grow corn and root vegetables and raise chickens.

I discover a little dry mustard mixed into water can be spooned down the holes of giant "night crawlers." The irritated worm soon emerges. At one and one-half cents a worm to fishermen, I soon have nice savings. Cokes are five cents, but the discarded bottles along the roads can be redeemed for a penny. Change is in silver, and Indian Head pennies are often found in our cash register. The 1943 pennies are zinc-coated steel. I still have some Continental currency from our attic. ("Not worth a Continental" is no longer a valid saying.)

The Civil War Drummer's Tale

My folks caution us to stay away from "Crazy Charlie," a sawmill bum in the nearby swamp. Old Charlie favors the applejack he brews following nocturnal visits to various McIntosh orchards. He sets the cider outside until slushy from the cold. Skimming off the ice leaves behind hardened cider. (Johnny Appleseed is not popular because he brings tasty fruit, but because he provides the ingredients for hard cider.)

Charlie claims to survive the winters by burrowing into warm sawdust piles. [They are known to spontaneously combust, especially following spring rains. Every farm boy has "exploding haystack" stories.] Charlie, in his nineties, carries around a decoration that looks like an early Medal of Honor, but is a GAR (Grand Army of the Republic) emblem. During his lucid intervals he tells detailed stories of his Union enlistment as a twelve-year-old drummer boy and messenger. He claims to survive so many battles that even we kids assume he exaggerates.

Charlie illustrates that even a wastrel has a history. He arrives at our store one day with an enormous freshly-caught rainbow trout—the largest anyone has seen. While he drinks his two beers (in trade for his fish), he tells me his secret.

"Battlefield noise is so loud that drum commands can't be heard," explains Charlie. "I was soon issued a musket and put into the front ranks. Smoke from black powder musket and cannon fire engulfs the field. As soon as men around me start getting hit, I flop to the ground. After the following ranks step over me, I get up and join the rear…." Not so much a lesson in valor, perhaps, as one of survival.

No one, in my recollection, considers Charlie's historical perspective of particular interest, much like today's kids contemplating the stories of the few remaining WWII veterans also in their nineties. I regret not having the sense to ask Charlie more of his times and of the interesting people he knew.

Soap Poisoning

There is an enormous gulf between the public education of today and schooling of the past. I come in at the end of something now lost. Pull up some eighth grade examinations (allowing passage to high school) from the early 1900s to see how you fare. Today's schools appear to be babysitters for busy parents and intended to make kids useless as adults.

A scarred wood paddle, with a half dozen holes at the business end, hangs next to our classroom blackboard. It is not a decoration. We kids mask our secret pleasure in seeing classmates return to their seats with tears streaking their faces. Carrying a note home from the teacher is the kiss of death, as teachers are gods and parents always side with them!

Kids store their shotguns and rifles in the school cloak closet so as to hunt on the way home. "Show and tell" might feature an antique family sword or firearm. We buy cartridges from the local grocery or hardware store without question. School shootings and "drive-bys" are unknown. I do not recall an accidental discharge or a hunting accident. Responsible firearms ownership and handling are considered preparation for the time when one will enlist or be drafted. (Yes, some head north into Canada—not to escape the draft, but to enlist before the U.S. becomes involved.) Home invasions are also unheard of—a foolish thing for a criminal to contemplate in a farm or home where even the girls and women can shoot.

Lifebuoy soap not only popularizes the term "B.O." (body odor) but tastes terrible, as accurately depicted in the 1983 movie, *A Christmas Story*. (Ralphie, in his punishment fantasy for cursing, explains his blindness: "It was soap poisoning!—Lifebuoy.")

One never sees screaming out-of-control kids in public as is common today. Swift and sure punishment greet any such outbursts! Doctor Benjamin Spock, propagating permissiveness and instant gratification, destroys several generations of kids.

Tech Savvy but Dumb as a Brick

Computers and cellular telephones revolutionize education and our entire society. "Twitter" (2006) becomes the younger generations' preferred method of communicating. Its 140-word limit coincides with a plummet in reading comprehension. Few complaints are made, however, as addicts do not notice their decreased brain function.

After school, in my day, is time for chores. Spare time is for the wild things in the woods—collecting frog's eggs, picking lady's slipper orchids and berries, and sledding and skating in winter with no one telling us to "be careful." After supper we listen to *Boston Blackie*, *Challenge of the Yukon*, the *Green Hornet*, the *Lone Ranger*, and other exciting programs of the "mind's eye." I recall my folks approaching a tunnel, pulling to the side of the road behind a line of stopped cars. A Sunday afternoon episode of *Nick Carter, Master Detective* is winding to a close. Reception dies inside tunnels and no one wants to miss the exciting ending.

Radio Daze

The impact radio has upon us is difficult to comprehend today. It develops imagination while television is passive observation. Radio sound effects are subtle and multilayered. *Light's Out* features cleavers striking raw meat and knives slicing heads of cabbage. One of my favorites is frying bacon as Old Sparky electrocutes another felon. People turned inside out and wind howling from *The Hermit's Cave* are steeped in the creepy and grisly. Horses fart when Marshal Matt Dillon (played by William Conrad) rides out of town. When he enters the Longbranch Saloon and calls for Miss Kitty Russell (Georgia Ellis), she yells, "Be right down, Matt—I'm upstairs with a customer!" Scalpings, burning outlaws to death in their hideout, lynchings…and more unfold before our alert ears.

Bad for kids? Wish to compare my generation with yours? Our folks read us *Hansel and Gretel*, where kids outwit a cannibalistic witch and push her into an oven. *Snow White* is in her coffin while her stepmother cooks and eats what she believes is her heart. Jack beheads giants and Sinbad blinds the Cyclops with a red-hot iron.

"The Thing on the Fourble Board"

Mutual Broadcasting's *Quiet, Please!* features a marvelous late-night drama on 9 August 1948. A driller seeks oil a mile deep into a million-year-old formation. In a core sample up on the fourble board,[4] his crew finds a stone finger with a gold ring attached.

Strange accidents happen and partially devoured bodies fall from the fourble board. The driller climbs the derrick and is confronted by an invisible creature that makes kitten-like noises. He throws a can of red paint on it, revealing a beautiful girl's face on a monster's body.

Twenty years pass and the rig is long abandoned. The driller-narrator mutters about putting makeup on this beautiful and haunting creature, and hints at its disgusting eating habits. You, the listener, arrive and are invited in as the driller's dinner guest. He asks you to step inside as his wife is anxious to meet you. You enter the dark cottage and hear quiet mewing as from a lost kitten….

Okay, you have to be there as a kid on a dark and stormy night! Although the voices of my radio friends grow dimmer, they can still be heard in the darkness before sleep. I suppose they are also an awareness that our time, too, is about to pass.

Wartime Medicine

I cut my left knee and it becomes infected. Each week, they hold me down and slice it open to drain and scrape putrefied flesh. No anesthetics such as opiates or novocain. Drugs go to the military, including rediscovered penicillin. I almost lose my leg but recover. Surgery is the only available remedy for infection. My mother gets a lung infection and they cut out her lung. (It's not called the "practice" of medicine without reason.)

Our dentist has a chair with leather arm, head, and leg restraints. He jams in a steel mouth immobilizer gag opener. (I have nightmares

---

[4] This is the narrow platform that runs around the derrick about halfway up. (Two lengths of drilling pipe are a "double," three a "thribble," and four a "fourble"). Also called a "monkey board."

about this for decades.) In later years, I cringe to see Laurence Olivier as Dustin Hoffman's Nazi dentist in *Marathon Man*. (Steve Martin as sadist Orin Scrivello in *Little Shop of Horrors*, however, strikes me as funny.) Pain is a companion of rural life in the 1940s, as it has been for centuries.

Chapter II

DAD'S LAST SHOT

The dismal lives of our farming ancestors are noted by Sherlock Holmes, who comments to Dr. John Watson as they travel by train past farms in Aldershot: "The lowest and vilest alleys in London do not present a more dreadful record of sin than does the beautiful countryside.... Deeds of hellish cruelty, the hidden wickedness which may go on, year in, year out..."[5]

"Albert" Fish, child rapist and cannibal; Edward Gein, Wisconsin farmer and grave robber (who inspires both Norman Bates of *Psycho* and Leatherface from *The Texas Chainsaw Massacre*); and, Bonnie Parker and Clyde Barrow of the "Public Enemy" era are rural twentieth century legends. Rural crime rarely receives the attention of better-publicized big-city events.

Here is my father's tale of rural New England crime:

Max LeRoy Hurlbut is born in 1915 in the north end of a farmhouse split by the Vermont/Quebec border. He gives me a .45 Colt Peacemaker he has bought at a local auction in the 1930s for three dollars. Serial 119691.

Town Constable Old "Dad" Coe can be found dozing on his bench outside the only bank in town. He does not like his cramped little office in the rear of city hall, and he hates paperwork. There is unhappiness in the mayor's office that traffic fine revenues drop in hard times.

My father is in school the morning two men in suits and greatcoats pull up to the bank in a sedan with out-of-state plates. They leave the engine running and pay no attention to the old man in a sheepskin coat dozing in the morning sun. A few minutes later they emerge. "Robbery!" comes a shout from inside the bank.

---

[5] Arthur Conan Doyle, "The Adventure of the Copper Beeches." *Strand Magazine*, 1892. (Reprinted in *The Adventures of Sherlock Holmes*, 1995, Barnes and Noble, NY), p. 301.

The younger bandit jumps into the driver's seat. He turns to see Dad dangling a set of car keys from his fingers. Dad shoots him as he reaches for his pistol-gripped short-barrel shotgun thrown onto the backseat. The second robber stops on the granite stairs and raises a Thompson submachine gun suspended from a shoulder sling beneath his greatcoat.

Dad returns fire and ducks behind the engine compartment as an entire drum of fifty rounds is emptied. (The copper-jacketed slugs become prize souvenirs of the kids.) Then silence. Dad walks slowly around the car, ejecting casings and reloading from his pocket. The bandit is fumbling to fit a second drum carried in a pouch in his coat. Dad says, "You lose," as he fires his last shot into the man's head.

Dad is retired on a modest pension. Although the "man-of-the-day" who saves the bank's money, there is talk he executes the robber after his empty gun clatters to the pavement in surrender. Dad never returns to his spot on the bench and dies in his sleep that winter.

Dad's Cavalry Model (seven-and-a-half-inch barrel) is shipped in 1887 to the Springfield Armory and returned to replace worn parts in 1903, per my Colt Factory Letter. Its ivory grips are apparently added by Dad Coe. Years later, I open a Colt book to find my gun listed as one of sixteen extant "Railway Mail Service" guns shipped by the army to the railway post office to guard express shipments. Western bandits switch from robbing stagecoaches to robbing trains.

The Reo Truck

We have forgotten some of the apprehension that greets the industrial world for many.

Ransom E. Olds gives his name (and initials) to two automotive companies. My grandfather, Edson T. Hurlbut, buys a used chain-drive Reo truck for his Vermont farm shortly after WWI. One day he drives down a dirt path, through a brook, and up the other side of the hill. The chain breaks and the truck, out of control, rolls back down into the creek.

Grandfather, considerably shaken, walks home and returns with his team of horses to drag his Reo back to the barn. Edson never drives again. The truck is still in that barn when I am a kid in the 1940s.

Next to the barn is a stone basement beneath a shed. In the days before air-conditioning and refrigeration, grandfather cuts blocks of ice from Lake Memphremagog when it freezes 30-inches or more. He insulates the blocks with sawdust. The ice lasts all summer. I love to hide here to evade chores.

Chapter III

CALIFORNIA OR BUST

The harsh winter of 1946–1947 finds my father beneath his Kaiser auto during a subzero blizzard in Lochmere, New Hampshire. Radiators are drained every night as no antifreeze is available. Car batteries are disconnected and brought into the house. He lights a small kerosene fire beneath the oil pan to thin the motor oil so the car will start. "I've had it!," he suddenly shouts. "We're leaving for California!" Several weeks later we head southwest to intersect Route 66.

My folks gawk for movie stars at Hollywood and Vine. My eyes fix upon a wondrous mechanical device with moving arms, red and green lights, and a synchronized gong. It is an Acme Traffic Semaphore,[6] the world's first connected system of mechanical traffic devices. The sign on Mount Lee still reads, HOLLYWOODLAND.

"Red Ryder" Rides

"I got a star on my car and one on my chest,
A gun on my hip and the right to arrest.
I'm the guy who's boss on this highway,
So watch what you're doin' when you're driving my way.
You'll know me when you see me 'cause my door's painted white,
My siren a-screamin' and my flashin' red light.

---

[6] While working old University Station at 809 West Jefferson in 1961, I am called to search for a burglar in the cupola atop the Southern California Automobile Club. Pieces of a disassembled Acme are strewn about. The manager later recalls my interest and presents them to me. A date stamp on the case indicates it may be the last one—pulled from the Plaza and North Main in December 1956. Hurlbut, "The Acme Traffic Semaphore." *The Link* (L.A. Police Historical Society), June 1997 (Vol. 8, No. 2), pp. 10–11.

I work all day and I work all night,
Just a keepin' law and order, tryin' to do what's right...."

Jamison "Junior" Brown
"Highway Patrol" (1993)

We roll into San Clemente, a beautiful little town with white stucco houses and red Spanish tile. My dad is promptly pulled over—for driving too slowly—by a short, gruff, redheaded, bantam-rooster-in-uniform named Bruce Crego. We are "warned" by a Southern California legend who also comments upon our similar hair color. To him I am forever "Red."

Crego, born in 1902, is forty-four and running a Signal Gasoline station when Chief Art Daneri recruits him to do something about the traffic and accidents in "Slaughter Alley," a stretch of pre-freeway Highway 101 south of town. Bodies are often strewn about from head-ons. Steering columns—in the days before seat belts and air bags—become spears and steering wheels are cookie cutters.

Bruce (aka "Red Ryder") is not exactly the town's "Welcome Wagon." His record is *350 moving violations in a week!*[7] [Weep, you eight-a-day BCMCs (Big City Motor Cops)]. Bruce works almost every day for twelve or more hours and single-handedly supports the town treasury during tough times. *Time* magazine credits him with the prodigious annual ticket-writing feat of over 5,000 citations.[8]

Bob Hope regularly barbs Bruce on his weekly national radio show, as Hope becomes a recipient of Bruce's keen appetite for law and order. Bruce is often the lone on-duty policeman between San Diego and Los Angeles. The California Highway Patrol—better known as "Triple-A with Guns"—responds only to call-outs at night. Bruce is known among the marines at nearby Camp Pendleton for shooting up their cars during 100 mph chases along the Pacific Coast Highway.

I sometimes ride along with Bruce, also the juvenile officer, in the evenings. He stops a loud and abusive driver for 502 (old Vehicle Code

---

[7] Jennifer A. Garey, *Images of America—San Clemente* (2010), San Clemente Historical Society, p. 71.

[8] "Richard Nixon Slept Here," *Time*, 7 September 1970 (Vol. 96, No. 10), "Nation" page.

section for "drunk driving") whose car bears a Mexican plate with the single digit, "1." The driver demands "diplomatic immunity" as the Mexican Ambassador. Bruce, irritated by his attitude, later explains to the mayor, "I got so tired of his 'diplomatic immunity' I kicked it down the hall and into the cell for the night."

It is my sad duty (and great honor) to give Bruce's eulogy in May 1973.[9]

Gorgeous George

San Clemente is a sleepy town with miles of open fields and beaches. (How quickly this is to change.) Unlike today most kids work. We "haul fish" down the San Clemente Pier. We line up our homemade wagons to await the docking of sports fishermen so as to cart their burlap bags of heavy catches the length of the pier, and then race back for a good spot in line.

Most tips are in the range of a quarter. Wrestler George R. Wagner—"Gorgeous George" (his legal name)—gives me a five-dollar bill. I take harassment from the other kids as he is known for his resplendent capes and exaggerated effeminate behavior which draws crowds to boo him. It is hard, today, to realize how his flamboyant image and showman's ability to work a crowd enable him to become a national celebrity said to establish television as the predominant entertainment medium.[10] George dies at age forty-eight on Christmas 1962. He influences me to take up collegiate wrestling, which favors control over throws, at Long Beach State.

---

[9] Todd Crowell, "Bruce 'Red Ryder' Crego Mourned," *San Clemente Daily Sun Post*, 18 May 1973.

[10] George's entrance, to "Pomp and Circumstance," takes more time than the actual match. His valet throws rose petals in his path and sprays the ring with a disinfectant called "Channel No. 10" ("Why be half safe?"). Once the match begins, George—an excellent freestyle wrestler and holder of the world light heavyweight title—fakes injuries and cheats in every way possible, drawing furious "heel heat." He insults fans ("cheap heat"), calling them "peasants," and creates character theatrics as a cowardly villain. Some of you may recall his Van Nuys cocktail lodge—"Gorgeous George's Ringside."

Surf Critters

We kids get bored awaiting the arrivals of sports fishing boats. We obtain a length of braided 500-pound test line and a large hook. At the halfway point of the original pier is a fish-cleaning trough which empties into the surf line. (No adults question why fish guts never make it to the beach, but we kids know.) We bait the hook with the head of a large fish and toss it off. On every wagon-haul we stop to see if anything is attached to our line. We tie a piece of broomstick to the line to guide the heavy critter down the pier and hand it off to a chum on the beach. We regularly beach ten- to twelve-foot Great White sharks and hammerheads.

This clears the water for a day until Public Works arrives to drag the carcass off to the dump. Even though you are more likely to be struck by a falling aircraft than bitten by a shark, City Fathers are not amused by the complaints of tourists. We are ordered to desist or be eighty-sixed from hauling fish. The heavy hand of government slaps us down at an early age.

Out of the Past

Sixty years later: 25 October 2011. Retired LAPD Detective Edward A. Slattery sends me an e-mail attachment where you click on your state and county to see old "Penny Postcards." I click "California" and "Orange County." Six postcards pop up for San Clemente. The last is a shot of kids "hauling fish" at the end of the pier in 1951. I am pulling my wagon with a load of fish. Ahead of me is my sister Robin (with the fisherman pulling her wagon). I am not aware, at the time, of the photo being taken.

Grunion or Snipe?

Sardine-size California grunion beach themselves to spawn from two to six days after a full new moon, soon after high tide, as early as February and as late as September. The female digs into the sand with her tail and several males wrap themselves around her. We grab the tasty things and bring them home by the bucketsful. My New England cousins are convinced this is just another Wild West snipe-hunt tale.

Printer's Devil and Projectionist

I mow greens and fairways at the local golf course, pump gas and grease cars at my father's Richfield Stations, and run the Simplex carbon-arc film projectors at the "San Clemente Theatre." Nitrate film is phased out in 1951 but still in use for several years (as it is cheaper than safety film).

The film is made of nitrocellulose, also known as "gun cotton, a low-order explosive and propellant. The film occasionally becomes jammed in the projector and the arc-heat of the two carbon rods (creating the light) burns a hole in it. It immediately flashes and is responsible for many theater fires and deaths. Burning nitrate film produces its own oxygen and can burn underwater. It is difficult to extinguish. Our projection booth is lined with asbestos with several large chemical fire extinguishers near at hand.

Sun-Post Devil. I am the printer's devil for the *San Clemente Sun-Post*. I empty the "hell-box" (where discarded lead Linotype slugs are tossed to be remelted into pigs) and set movable type using a composing stick and pica pole [brass ruler that measures inches on one side and ems (picas) on the other. One inch equals six picas or 72 points]. I can still read upside down and backwards.[11]

I run the Heidelberg "Windmill" letterpress. The ambient din of Linotype machine, typewriters, and ancient sheet-fed flatbed press require everyone to shout. A place for work, not for comfort. Our lone reporter is a young

---

[11] Such "talents" can unfold years later. I recently spot a Washington state personalized license plate: 37OHSSV. (Read this upside down.)

Harry W. Lawton who is to write *Willie Boy: A Desert Manhunt*, later made into a 1969 movie *Tell Them Willie Boy is Here*, starring Robert Redford and Robert Blake.

When stories are "spiked" (those deemed unworthy of publication are stabbed onto an upright sharpened metal rod), I rewrite them for practice. My first "scoop" is an interview with a reclusive oldster named Ulysses "Dad" Ryan, who can be found hanging around the old blacksmith shop at Mission San Juan Capistrano. Dad is obsessed with his experience in the Great Dayton (Ohio) flood of March 1913, which kills 428 and destroys over 20,000 homes.

I strike journalistic gold. Dad runs a Baldwin Piano repair shop near the Wright Cycle Company at 1127 West Third Street, Dayton. He supplies the Wright Brothers with the piano wire to build their 1903 Flyer![12] "But let's get back to the flood of '13."

Prospecting

My friends surf, but I roam the hills. I stake two mining claims: one for placer gold in Van Dusen Canyon near Fawnskin, north of Big Bear Lake, and 160 acres of zirconium and scheelite (tungsten) in Cleveland National Forest between Elsinore and San Juan Capistrano. The Forest Service shuts me down over a technical permit matter, or I would be a grammar school millionaire. The mineral is dispersed in loose, easy-to-bulldoze and load-eroded quartz diorite. Quartz diorite is the perfect roadbed material for the Santa Ana Freeway, then under construction.

Sputnik

The Soviets launch Sputnik (Satellite)-1 on 4 October 1957. Its impact upon the Western world is little remembered today. It is the beginning of the Space Age. President Dwight Eisenhower, concerned about our Lockheed U-2 flights and our own Project Vanguard, says Americans should cooperate with them in this International Geophysical Year.

---

[12] Hurlbut, "Capo Oldster at Air Age Birth," *San Clemente Post*, 29 October 1956.

My father owns a Telefunken short-wave radio set. Sputnik broadcasts on a one-watt transmitter at 20.005 and 40.002 MHz. It travels at 18,000 mph in an elliptical low earth orbit. As it passes overhead, it is clearly visible. I time its "beeps" for twenty-two days until its batteries die. It is obviously falling into lower orbit and in fact burns up on 4 January 1958.

I send my observations to the Commies. A postcard soon returns with a picture of Sputnik and Cyrillic writing. I have it translated and it says: "To an Observation Partner of the First Soviet Artificial Earth Satellite in the World; From the USSR Committee for the International Geophysical Year." It is thanking me for my "observations of scientific value." I am looking at it today in my scrapbook.

I expect the FBI to come knocking. Columbia University in New York City (WCKR) broadcasts the beeps of Sputnik to the public. The next morning, the FBI shows up and confiscates the tape, never to return it. It is a major coup for the Soviets and an embarrassment to the U.S. A wake-up call, however, that ends with the eventual collapse of the Soviet Union.

This is an exciting time for those of us interested in the sciences. My brother Jeffrey and I observe an atomic explosion one morning before dawn. It turns night into day—but much more intense. Jeff, a chemistry professor, still speaks of it. We, hopefully, will be the last generation to witness such a man-made release of energy. But don't count on it.

Runaway

Nostalgia isn't what it used to be! I run off to Mexico for three months in 1957 with $100 in my pocket. I travel on third-class busses with the goats and chickens. I do not, yet, speak Spanish but am "adopted" by a group of *braceros* (manual laborers; from *brazo*, "arm") heading south.

A bridge across a river near Culiacan is washed out in a storm. For a peso each (seven U.S. cents), Indians paddle us across rough water in shallow dugouts. We acquire another rickety old bus on the other side and soon stop at a cantina for a cheap meal and a cerveza (which even a kid can buy). My new amigos examine my change…then beat up the bartender, snatch a few coins from the register, and run for the bus. Apparently, I am shortchanged! (An incident I neglect to mention to my LAPD background investigator.)

I sleep outside in my sleeping bag but need to find a cheap room in Mexico City. I foolishly leave my wallet in the room of the Hotel de Cortez and head downstairs—into the middle of a robbery by five masked men. I lose only my pocket knife. They loot the ground floor and carry off the safe.

The police arrive late the next day, but don't bother to question witnesses.

I visit Aztec sites and on to Yucatan to see Mayan ruins. I hitchhike back through Mexico and walk into our house. Some strangers are inside. They know of me and say, "Your parents sold their gas stations and we bought their house. They didn't leave a forwarding address!" I eventually locate them near the Canadian border on Lake Whatcom in Washington State (where they have Mount Baker as an active pet volcano).

I am never again to live at home but tell people, "Some kids run away from home, but my folks ran away from me!" Dad and Mom glance at each other and exchange little smiles.

Chapter IV

THE BOYS IN WHITE

Medical, military, police, and firefighter are careers where your on-scene presence can have a life-changing impact. Bowers' Ambulance of Long Beach hires me as an attendant and driver after they win the City Police and Fire Contract. Bowers' is the first private ambulance company licensed in the city of Los Angeles (the Wilmington Office in 1938). The pay is six dollars for attendants and seven for drivers—total for an entire twelve-hour shift. I study between calls and attend Long Beach State College full time.

The Red Cross trains me as a first aid instructor. We become good at stopping bleeding, splinting bones, and running the new resuscitators, which provide the positive pressure of bottled oxygen to breathe for the patient. It is to be several years before cardiopulmonary resuscitation (CPR) is discovered. Oxygenating the blood does little if the blood is not circulating….

Freeway Nightmare

Heavy fog sometimes reduces visibility to zero on the Long Beach Freeway (then called the Los Angeles River Freeway). One night we respond to a "multiple t/a's" broadcast. I become a "gutter bunny" with the right wheels of our 1959 Cadillac in the fog-line rain gutter. Cars, driving blind, speed past us. The occasional flare-up in the fog ahead is followed by a "whump," indicating we are nearing the massive pileup of over 200 vehicles! No fatalities, but ambulances and tow trucks must be called out as far away as Los Angeles. We request the police to barricade the freeway on-ramps and begin the first of many runs to nearby Seaside Memorial Hospital (1907–60). We earn our seven dollars of salary that night.

The Wino Sting

At the scene of a homicide one evening, I recognize a detective as a drunken patient from several nights before whom we pluck from inside a dumpster. He sees me staring and calls me aside. "You passed, kid." I have no idea what he means until a week later when several attendants are served with arrest warrants for theft. Undercover officers, with loose cash and valuables, pretend to be drunks. Ambulance personnel are largely transients. Some handle temptation by succumbing to it.

Meet the Addams Family

Ambulances with trained crews are expensive. When you travel in rural areas, keep in mind who has stretch vehicles capable of transporting patients—mortuaries! Guess which side of the business profits more, depending upon where they deliver you—the medical transport or the mortician?

A friend works at a mortuary and we sometimes drop by for coffee. (The company is still in business so is not named.) One night he is performing a cremation. After removing the "cremains," he strains the ashes through a sieve and discards the larger bone chunks. He then scoops out a little more ash from a five-gallon can in the corner. "When there does not look like enough remains," he explains, "we add a little from the can." (The can contains the ashes of indigents cremated at county's expense.) This practice no longer exists, as they now use bone-grinders on the portions that fail to burn.

One of the worse things I see is a man intentionally ground up in the treads of a large tracked crane by his wife's boyfriend, the crane operator. Airplane and train crashes also provide a nasty potential. We dread calls to tramp freighters (foreign registered and poorly maintained with no fixed itinerary or port of call). Dark and greasy ships with holds dripping water and slime. Removing an injured seaman from its bowels—up slippery vertical iron-rung ladders and through mazes of hot moving machinery—is some of the most physically demanding work I've done. And tough on those white starched uniforms (which we pay for).

The Pike Killer-Coaster

The Pike, off Long Beach and East Ocean Boulevards, is a 1902 amusement park noted for its "Cyclone Racer," a wooden dual-track roller coaster built out on pilings over the water in 1930. It is the terminus of the "Red Car" (Pacific Electric Railway) from Los Angeles. To the west is a sailors' slum known as "The Jungle."

The "Cyclone Racer" has a 7,400-foot run and exceeds 50 mph on turns. It pushes the limits of coaster technology and is a white-knuckle ride anyone who rides it never forgets. You "race" a second car side by side. Kids sneak in beneath the timber supports as it rains coins and the occasional wallet.

One of the cars, often loaded with sailors, leaves the tracks at the first turn following a slow ascent to the top and fast drop. No one, to my knowledge, survives these occasional derailments. Small repairs are made (to satisfy the permits), and they are back in business. The show must go on. We Bowers' employees and guest nurses get to ride free. The only thing they ask is that we not "bad mouth" their operation.

The Wandering Dead

The Pike's "Walk of a Thousand Lights" features unusual exhibits and oddities like Zuzu the Monkey-Girl. In the "Laff in the Dark" ride, kids roll past a hanging dummy named Elmer, glowing in the dark with florescent paint. Elmer is unrealistic in appearance and supposedly made of fiberglass and leather.

A film crew shooting "Carnival of Spies," an episode of the *Six Million Dollar Man* TV series, knocks off Elmer's arm. Actual bones protrude. Thomas Noguchi, L.A. "Coroner to the Stars," is called. A 1924 penny and a ticket to a Los Angeles "Museum of Crime" are found in Elmer's mouth. The ticket leads to his identification. A bullet is also found imbedded in the carcass.

"Elmer" turns out to be Elmer McCurdy, a mummified outlaw killed by an Osage Hills, Oklahoma, posse in 1911. Elmer robs the wrong train and nets only $46 in loot. His last words are reported as, "You'll never take me alive!" McCurdy is embalmed and sold to a traveling carnival. Price of admission: five cents, to be placed in his mouth. (It is reported he earns more in death than in life.) McCurdy now rests in the Boot Hill section of Summit View Cemetery, Guthrie, Oklahoma.[13]

The ambulance service is an important function and a sobering and responsible job for a young man. I hold Los Angeles County Ambulance Driver License No. 469, which costs five dollars. The only other requirements are a "standard" (basic) first aid course, a City of L.A. "Driver's Permit," and a California chauffeur's license. The pay is so poor, even by late 1950s standards, that trained and experienced personnel continually leave for better-paying jobs.

It is not unusual for the driver to request the assistance of a police officer, or even a bystander, to help perform first aid or to load the gurney—as the new attendant is vomiting in the gutter. They are known to throw down their bloodstained white jacket and walk away from the job in the middle of an emergency.

Bowers' Ambulance is privately-owned and collects its own fees. It is cold to ask patients and distraught relatives for payment. I have had them pencil checks on greasy hamburger bags and paper napkins. (The bank always honors them—a check is simply a written order on a bank for money and has no required format.)

The use of "G-Unit" to describe a Los Angeles ambulance comes from Georgia Street Receiving Hospital—their headquarters from 1927 until 1957, when Central Receiving Hospital opens on Sixth Street at Loma. Early ambulance runs concentrate on a safe and comfortable ride, as little emergency treatment is available upon arrival at hospitals.

---

[13] "Find-a-Grave" Memorial No. 1706. Elmer McCurdy (1880 to 8 October 1911). Several yards of concrete are poured over his coffin to ensure he remains in place.

I love my ambulance service. It is my first job that is not just a means to make money. I actually save lives and rescue people in serious trouble. (I also admit to enjoying the rush of piloting a Code 3 ambulance through nasty traffic—and never putting a scratch on it.)

A doctor or nurse complimenting you for a good bandaging job or resuscitator operation on a difficult-to-maintain airway, or a relative thanking you for saving someone dear to them, makes you forget the long hours and low pay. The red and black "First Aid Instructor" patch on your shoulder is worn with professional pride. I still have contact with two fellow drivers I work with sixty-five years before. Most, long ago, make their last run…and I still miss them!

You see terrible things. People die despite your best efforts. You reach a point of confidence (as with policemen) where you can handle anything. You save lives by being on scene in the first few minutes of an emergency, often during mass confusion or poor visibility, where others are stunned into immobility. Your actions spell the difference between someone dying, becoming a human vegetable, or living a normal life. Holding the hand of one who knows he is in his last moments is something you will take to your own grave.

Chapter V

LAPD BLUE

"Los Angeles County is the most dangerous place in the U.S. to be a police officer….Almost every day of the year a police officer is shot while on duty."[14]

Applying for LAPD is much different sixty years ago. You pay a one-dollar filing fee and are assigned a date for the written exam.

Testing

Written. The "written" is an all-day college entrance exam that counts for 50 percent of your grade. (The oral interview is the other 50 percent.) The math and English portions are especially tough. I am the only one in my class to pass the English exam with a high-enough score to avoid taking a "bonehead English" course at a local college during our year-long probationary period.

Physical Training (P.T.). The "Physical Fitness and Agility Test" is *pass* or *fail*. We run an obstacle course at the academy: over a seven-foot wall, through a maze, and over hurdles, followed by a sprint home.

Three pieces cut from a steel train rail, weighing about 35 pounds each, rest upon an upright T-shaped platform: two on the ground and one at shoulder level. You lift one rail from the ground to shoulder height. Then place the one beside it down. You are graded on the number of rails lifted in eight long minutes. I pace myself and do well in this and pull-ups as I lift loaded gurneys for a living. I do "average" running and poorly on sit-ups and push-ups, but survive.

---

[14] Rebecca Leung, "The Ghosts of El Segundo," *48 Hours Mystery* (CBS), 7 May 2009. The shooting deaths of two police officers in 1957 are solved in 2002 by matching a partial thumb print from the mirror of a stolen car.

Psyche Exam. Psychological Testing includes the "Minnesota Multiphasic Personality Inventory" with "fake bad" scale, intelligence quotient test, and others. In my interview with the psychologist, he asks, "Why did you give classical responses to the inkblot test?"

"Because I admire Herman Rorschach from my college psych classes," I reply. "And because I thought you would prefer me seeing an Egyptian scarab rather than one monkey cornholing another."

He laughs and says, "Get out of here! Next...." (I later realize I am lucky to survive giving this flippant remark.)

Oral Board. The oral board consists of three civilians and a police sergeant. Sergeant Riley W. Maxwell, LAPD's number one fingerprint man, asks the toughest questions: "Would you cite your wife?"

"No, I'm not married. But if I were, I would be the one having to pay the fine. I'd warn her."

His final question is one I will also ask future applicants: "It is the middle of the night with little traffic. A smart-ass kid in a hot rod pulls up to a red light. He looks about and floors it through, mid-phase, in obvious contempt for the law. An elderly man and his wife come puttering through the same light in an old Chevrolet, apparently not noticing it is red. You have only one ticket. Which would you cite, and why?"

I think a moment and answer, "The old man." Riley smiles while the civilians frown and question my reasoning. "The purpose of citations is to prevent accidents. As much as I'd like to nail the idiot kid, he looks both ways and proceeds safely. The old man doesn't see the light and may strike another car or pedestrian passing through...."

I am to later join the 316th Criminal Investigation Division (Military Police) and am surprised to find Riley as one of the agents called to active duty during the Cuban missile crisis. (I am their company clerk.) Riley tells people (as I eventually outrank him) that he has his one chance to get me, but flubs it. We still exchange Christmas cards—and occasional friendly insults—by phone.

Medical. I fail the medical: "Defective vision; right leg 5/8ths of an inch longer than the left; and, insufficient chest inflation." I take time off to appeal. I obtain a doctor's statement that my leg bones are unusually symmetrical;

my vision is 20/15 and 20/22 (over 20/25 in one eye is disqualifying); and, my chest expands to within normal limits.

I return to Central Receiving Hospital. The doctor looks at his colleague's disqualification letter and says, "What does he know?" He approves me without examination. [I am to later learn most applicants are put through this. Civil Service reasons—if you want the job badly enough, you will appeal].

Background (B.I.). Background investigators must speak to everyone I know—and many I do not. Their favorite question: "Who do you know who does not like him or knows things he prefers not to tell us?"

I end up number one of 4,643 applicants.[15] Just 227 of us are selected for the job in 1960.

Police Academy

I am notified of my acceptance to the academy on late Friday afternoon and told to report at 0600 hours Monday. I work a Saturday night shift at the ambulance service and bid farewell to my friends. I quickly pack things into my 1956 International Harvester 4×4 pickup and spend Sunday night in the Downtown Los Angeles YMCA. The academy, above Chavez Ravine (pre-Dodger Stadium) in Elysian Park, is in a beautiful rock garden setting of palm and pine trees between Echo Park and Chinatown to the south. The pride and awe I experience as I walk through the stone gates for the first time remains with me through the years.

On our first quarterly testing, I score the highest academically and the lowest physically. I am assigned to the 0500 hours "goon squad" for early morning physical torture. Others study at night; I run and do push-ups and sit-ups.

P.T. sadist Roy V. Bean shouts, "Take another lap, Hurlbut—you barnacle on the ass of progress!" He and Joseph J. Farrell run us until roughly a quarter of the class fall out, puking. (You run to your limit; to fall out risks

---

[15] L.A. Civil Service Commission "Notice of Eligibility" of 23 November 1959 (and) "Notice of Certification" of 15 July 1960. *LAPD 1960 Annual Report*, page 12.

immediate dismissal.) I will die before falling out. (Several do, bringing an end to the long "Cardiac Hill" runs.)

Being young, I make rapid progress. I am soon toughing out 100 push-ups and sit-ups. I am inspired to run for another forty-five years. (And keep in touch with Bean and Farrell through the decades—very personable fellows, off the drill field).

The academy staff includes Olympic shooter (Rome) John W. Hurst and James E. Dougherty, first husband of Marilyn Monroe.

Lieutenant Samuel L. Posner (of University Division) fills in at the gym. Sam secretly wrestles in the sports arena as the "Masked Marvel."[16] (No work permits are allowed for professional wrestlers as they compete with "civilian jobs.") I wrestle in college and enjoy an advantage.

We practice takedowns along with "choke holds": the bar arm control and carotid holds. The bar arm is a forearm across the larynx, interrupting breathing. The carotid is slipping the bar arm, elbow to the front, so pressure is applied to both sides of the neck, stopping blood flow to the brain. Both result in rapid unconsciousness. [Even those on PCP (phencyclidine—"angel dust"), possessing superhuman strength, need oxygen to continue fighting.] We "combat-wrestle" each other, until one is choked out ("doing the chicken") or slaps his hand down in surrender.

Officer Robert K. Koga teaches us his "Koga Jutsu (Method)"—judo adopted to law enforcement needs which uses an opponent's strength against him. It is to save many of us in the years to come. I am taught a few gun takeaway moves by a retired Seattle Police Department officer, Svend J. Jorgensen (SPD: 1920–50), in 1958. He teaches LAPD officers judo in the late 1920s and remains known to the academy staff.

---

[16] Sam gets an early start: "Sam Posner subdues burly felon with headlock." "Straight Shooting," *Popular Science Monthly*. February 1938 (Vol.132, No. 2), p. 62.

Badges

LAPD uses serial numbers rather than badge numbers to identify officers. [Badges are reissued upon an officer's retirement prior to October 1984. Subsequent badge numbers are permanently retired with the officer "and shall not be reissued"[17].] I am serial 10603 with Policeman (our Civil Service rank) badge #3524. (This number is, conveniently, the inside extension for Records & Identification Division, Wants and Warrants Section.) I later trade it to an Accident Investigation Division partner, William Lesner, as it is his serial number. I retire on 8-5-85 with Lieutenant's Badge No.1.

First City Gear

Our academy class of 1 August 1960 receives the first city-provided revolvers, batons, uniforms, and Sam Browne belts. (A new Colt or Smith and Wesson .38 Special costs about $35.) We are issued Colt "Officer's Model Match" revolvers with six-inch barrels. (Mine is serial 927240.) Later, classes are issued S. & W. K-38s. Personnel and Training Bureau Notice of 18 August 1971 orders all officers with Colts to turn them in for S. & W. K-38s with four-inch barrels. They are then altered to fire double-action only. The city sells our Colts to "Western Surplus," which advertises them for $59.99 in 1972. When I retire in 1985, the city declares my Smith revolver "surplus" and sells it to me for $49.52.

Chief William H. Parker

Chief Parker tells us, "You come from all segments of society and share its attitudes and prejudices. But if you treat anyone with disrespect or unfairness, your ass will be mine....I cannot change your beliefs, but I can change your employment!" (Paraphrased informal talk to recruits at academy range; August 1960.)

Chief Parker takes office during the city's centennial in 1950 and dies in harness on 16 July 1966. Those of us serving during LAPD's "Golden Era"

---

[17] David D. Dotson, Dep. Chief, "Retention of the Official Police Officer's Badge," Personnel and Training Bureau Notice, 18 October 1984.

will never forget these special times when we are a band of brothers united in good works. This is especially apparent to those of us "retiring" to other departments, where badges show the green glint of corruption and officers are half-a-century removed in procedures and professionalism.

Chapter VI

LAPD IN 1960

Most of you are not yet born when these events take place. It may be useful to briefly describe what Hollywood Division is like inside and outside of a patrol car in the late 1950s and early 1960s.

Chief Parker establishes a professional climate, but we are working with officers who come on in the 1920s and 1930s. (I know Chief R. Lee Heath, who signs on in 1904 and retires in 1926.) Officers buy their own guns, sticks, uniforms, and sometimes their very jobs. Their motto is, "You don't disturb the sergeant—ever!" They make frequent Solomon-like decisions and carry a nickel in their shirt pocket to summon help by public telephone.

<u>On Stage</u>. Los Angeles is very different in 1960. City Hall (1928), at 453 feet and 32 floors, is the tallest building (until 1964). Bunker Hill is higher than today and covered with Victorian houses. Engine Company 16 (1904–1962) at 139 North Hill Street charges us a nickel to park in their lot while testifying in court. "Angel's Flight," the 1901 funicular railway, also costs a nickel. The first star in the Hollywood "Walk of Fame" (for Joanne Woodward) is placed in 1960.

Telephone calls go to a dime. The minimum wage is one dollar. Gas is thirty cents a gallon. Hamburgers are ten cents as is the cost for a pound of pre-Cesar Chavez grapes. Dwight D. Eisenhower is president, and "Made in Japan" is synonymous with "cheap." Pacific Electric "Red Cars" run for another year and streetcars until 1963. ZIP codes are three years away, and mail delivery is twice a day and once on Saturday. A postage stamp costs four cents. Dashiell Hammett is alive.

Communications

LAPD uses its prewar 1730 kilocycle AM dispatching system until 1965. Blown fuses are a problem. Citizens (and crooks) pick up police calls on their AM radios. If your police car's six-volt battery dies, the radio reverses polarity; the receiver works but the transmitter rotor spins in the wrong direction.

Transmitters are mounted in the trunk in a metal box. No car-to-car communications are possible. [Parker believes all instructions must come from a centralized control. Chief Thomas Reddin (in 1968) gives us a VHF band (Tac-2) so we can speak with each other.]

The Motorola control head has two knobs: squelch and volume. You turn your radio on, volume on high. Then turn the squelch control clockwise until static is heard. Then back it off to the point of no noise. Turn it too far counterclockwise and the station cuts out.

KMA 367 is our call sign from 20 May 1949 until about 1984. The FCC requires you to give the entire call sign after each broadcast, but we shorten it to "KMA." Your transmitting signal is bounced off the car's roof by the antenna. Your car must be pointed towards the fixed receiver (near the Griffith Park Planetarium for Central and Hollywood) to be effective. Our calls sometimes skip and overpower stations on the East Coast, Hawaii, and once off Attu. (Navy Fleet Tug USS *Sarsi according to the L.A. Times* of 10 November 1945.) The RCMP frequently complains.

We are forever filling out Form 7.14's ("Requests for Radio Repair Service".) You drive to Radio Technical Division at the Main Jail—the only all-civilian division in LAPD—for repairs by Lee Sublette.

A "clear frequency" must be requested for a lengthy broadcast, such as a want or warrants check. These typically take about twenty minutes to return. A pneumatic tube request is shot from Communications to Records & Identification in the Police Administration Building, and then back.

Many are the times we kick loose a suspicious traffic violator to eventually receive a "Code 6 Charles" (dangerous wanted suspect). As your suspect is also listening to see if he is wanted, now is the time to draw your weapon. We also use a "Code 6-W" ["Off the air at 'Winchell's Donuts'"—the only twenty-four-hour coffee stands—manned at night by winos. You watch them closely or sip for a salty taste]. Pursuits require clearing the frequency, which can back-up calls for the remainder of the watch.

The emergency call number 911 is not implemented in Los Angeles until 1 October 1984. Before this, one usually dials "0" for the operator (which returns your dime on pay phones). The emergency number, from 1946 on, is 116. Kids are taught, "When in a fix, dial one-one-six."

Patrol Cars

Our low-bid fleet is 1959 Fords. No air-conditioning, but we finally have heaters. The city is too cheap to invest in alternators. Hit the red lights *and* siren at the same time, and the engine dies from lack of current to the spark plugs. Forget to turn off your radio on a call, and you return to a dead battery and reversed radio. The vacuum tubes must warm up before you can call for assistance or help. We are still generations away from handheld radios and cell-phones. But we are "free" and unsupervised as no future policeman shall ever be. A few get into mischief, but we are imaginative and motivated crime-crushers.

The 1960 Plymouth Savoy with its 318 cubic-inch engine (and tail fins) is a big improvement. Plymouth builds taxi fleets that stand abuse. Engines grow sluggish in 1966—the first year of exhaust emission controls. (Police cars are not exempt.) LAPD believes that power steering does not lend itself to good vehicle handling. Time resolves the issue in 1976 when manual steering is no longer available.

Weapons

We are restricted to .38 special ammo (under 1,000 feet per second velocity) with 158 or 200 grain solid bullets. I carry my .357 Smith & Wesson (.44 frame) with a half-dozen "just-in-case" .357 rounds in a pocket clip. We wear a twin-pouch containing 12 extra rounds on our Sam Browne belt. Many of us keep a box of 50 rounds in a case on the back seat. I have an ankle holster (hand-made by "Lewis Leather" on Sunset Boulevard near the Academy, as no one then sells such a thing) for my three-inch S. & W. five-shot Chief's Special.

Gunsmith George Mathews in Downey makes a "Mathews' Special." He hones the action of my .38 S. & W. "Military & Police" Model 10, lightens the trigger spring, and modifies the hammer. He cuts the barrel to three inches and ribs it. He removes a portion of the trigger guard (but not cutting it completely through), making it easier to slip in a gloved finger. The polished action cycles like glass. Thin Art Kanthack (our academy law instructor) scales make an easy to shoot and to conceal grip.

As I become a little more prosperous, I invest in a S. & W. Model 19 (.357 Magnum) with a four-inch barrel. Angelo Bee (former Browning factory engraver) arrives in Chatsworth in 1975. His engraving and gold-inlaying of this revolver are magnificent. Grips by John Hurst.

The small station armory in Hollywood Division contains about fifteen 12-gauge Remington Model 31 pump shotguns and a few Winchester Model 97s, along with a lone Lefever double-barrel twelve stamped "LAPD" on its stock. Three .45 auto Reising submachine guns (from the USMC) and a lone Winchester .30-30 lever action are also there. (Desk Officer James W. Cannel shoots an escaped wolf from the Griffith Park Zoo with it and says he is still receiving hate mail.) We have few shotguns until after the Watts Riot in August 1965. They are checked out from the change-of-watch sergeant who typically does not encourage this waste of his time.

The average citizen does not realize the policeman's weapons are primarily to protect *him*, not *them*!

Baton

Our twenty-six inch hickory baton (useful for measuring distances at crime scenes) is uniquely LAPD. It has eight long flutes for the grip and a hole drilled nine inches from the handle end. You insert the two ends of a leather thong through this hole from opposite sides and knot each of the protruding free ends. Stick your thumb into the resulting loop of about fourteen inches and rotate your hand so the double-cord wraps around the back of your hand. If someone is able to pull your baton away, the loop is not attached to you. (Now is the time to draw your revolver to see if he can run a thousand feet a second.)

The hole is eliminated in the mid-1960s, and a rubber grommet is used to carry the baton in its holder. This straight-stick baton is replaced by the polycarbonate PR-24 Monadnock side-handle baton. This "sissy" baton is considered an improvement as it strikes with less force. (Just ask Rodney "The Piñata" King.)

Hot Sheets

The Teletype Section of Communications Division prints "Hot Sheets" on light cardboard—columns of stolen or wanted vehicles by their last three digits. They are distributed several times a day. You update the sheet at roll call and insert it into a metal frame mounted on the dashboard in front of a sheet of clear plastic. A small flashlight bulb on a toggle switch lights it from behind. You regularly update it from radio alerts. We snag many a "hot roller." A hinged sheet of aluminum is later attached to the bottom of the frame to be used as a tiny desk. A small flexible lamp provides illumination.

One of the sadder license plate entries is for a Volkswagen owned by one of our Hollywood sergeants. He has a gambling problem and one day fails to appear for work—forever. He is last spotted between L.A. and Las Vegas. We never learn his fate.

I recently find a hot sheet from Tuesday, 6 November 1960, tucked away as a bookmark in a volume of bound *Daily Training Bulletins* from the 1950s. I frame it for my den.

Emergency Lights

The two "tin can" lights (aka "Mickey Mouse ears") are made by S. & M. in Santa Fe Springs, and, from 1958 on, by Trio Sales. (There are three partners.) I am presented, on retirement, with a board containing two lights with a siren in the center by friends in the auto repair shop. They are stamped on top with "Trio Sales, Model T-2, Los Angeles, Calif." Front lenses are red; rear are amber. A simple toggle switch under the dash of a 1959 Ford activates them. In my day, they do not flash.

Sirens

"Federal Sign and Signal" (Illinois) makes most of our pre-electronic, chrome-plated, center-mounted roof sirens. Spinning the rotor and forcing air through the stator ports (little square openings) chews up six-volt batteries. The later electronic sirens do not sound the same, as their wavelengths differ. Mechanical "growlers" are still in use, as their direction can be more easily discerned and they penetrate auto interiors better. Our 1960 sirens are either foot-activated by the dimmer switch on the upper left floorboard or thumb-operated off the steering wheel horn rim.

Running "Code 3" is a coordination task in a 1959 Ford L-car (one-man unit). You must steer, alternately switch the lights and siren (so as to not kill the battery power to the spark plugs), apply gas and brakes, and key the mike to broadcast if in a pursuit. Seamus N. Keenan, one of my new officers, also adds to the mix by drawing his revolver as he closes in on his quarry. He, unfortunately, "keys" the trigger instead of the mike. Although still on probation, he survives by buying a new windshield for his patrol car....

Chapter VII

HOLLYWOOD

"Where men are men—and so are the women."[18]

Academy graduation excitement is high. Forty-one of us survive, including five from other municipal police agencies. One is destined to die in a fire he sets in his bar to collect the insurance and his classmate-partner is sentenced to San Quentin State Prison. Another, with six kids, runs off with his partner's wife, leaving behind her brood of five. Two join the L. A. Fire Department and one the California Highway Patrol.

I am the lone posting to Hollywood Patrol.

A policeman's first assignment is recalled as a magical time by most. You hate to take your scheduled days off as you might miss something. It is also a time of uncertainty, as—for the first year—you can be terminated without cause while on "probation." Those who cannot "cut it" on the streets are cut loose in disgrace—sometimes for reasons not readily apparent.

First Night in the Field

My first partner is old-timer Tommy O. Hutton, 4598, in 6A15 (the Griffith Park car). [The number for Hollywood Division is "6" (the sixth division established); "A" is the "Field Unit Service ID Letter" for a two-man car; and, "15" is Reporting District 615 (corresponding to a Census Tract to enable the gathering of demographic data to compare with crime stats).] There is no formal "training officer" program. Recruits are the third man assigned to a car and work with whichever partner is available.

We are tasked to oversee the American Nazi Party picketing the Huntington-Hartford Theatre [the old Lux Radio Playhouse (1926), 1615 North Vine Street]. They object to a one-man show by Sammy Davis, Jr. The

---

[18] Sergeant Edward L. Callier, 7288, PM watch roll call, Monday, 24 October 1960, 1545 hours, "Officer's Notebook." A few words of welcome to the new kid; with laughter and calls of, "You'll be sorr-eeee!" We run an eight-car plan that night.

demonstration turns out to be a few teenage kids with swastika armbands we must rescue into "protective custody" from an irate crowd.

We "F.I." (field interview) them—complete 3×5 information cards—and call their parents to pick them up.

First Felony Arrest

Several evenings later, Wayne C. Haas, 7791, and I receive a call, "Six-A-Nine. Shots fired. 459 at 2864 Pacific View Trail." This is the home of Detective Sergeant Thomas Hughes in the hills west of the Hollywood Freeway and north of Mulholland Drive. A neighbor (a security guard) sees two burglars exiting Hughes's home, one with the sergeant's .38 Colt two-inch "Detective Special" in hand. Shots are exchanged and the two run into a nearby canyon choked with sagebrush.

Two other PM watch cars respond and a discussion takes place: "Those guys are armed, and you can't even walk through that thick dirty brush. Let's vote (snicker) on who is the bravest policeman here, or, THE ONE WITH THE HIGHEST SERIAL NUMBER." All five turn to look at me.

"All right, all right, I'll go." I strip off my Sam Browne (so it won't get scratched) and stick my revolver in my pants' belt and handcuffs in a pocket. It's not possible to walk upright, so I find a rabbit trail tunnel and crawl down into the canyon. The dust on the sage is heavy and I am soon coated. My wool uniform is soaked with sweat and torn in several places. I reach the bottom and lay prone to rest. It's getting dark and I contemplate crawling back. I then hear scraping noises approaching.

One of the suspects (age seventeen) is startled when he crawls through a bush to find my revolver in his face—and me with a big grin. The sergeant's .38-caliber is in his pocket, with two shots fired. I have the subject crawl ahead of me, handcuffed in front, as the brush is so thick. The other officers appear surprised I actually find and capture someone.

We turn the subject over to felony car 6F4. Wayne has located their nearby getaway car, a 1947 Hudson sedan. The kid is AWOL from the Joseph Scott Juvenile Detention Camp in Bouquet Canyon, Santa Clarita, and has phony ID. He cops-out on his adult partner who walks home to find the two F-car officers awaiting him. I shower and change before returning to the field. My uniform is beyond repair, but the station fund pays half the price for a new one.

Wayne says, "Good job—but we weren't really going to insist on you going down there…." It's my first "big" arrest, however faulty the tactics, and I am happy. Another day in the Big City.

Hollywood Station

Hollywood Division is founded October 1913 and the old station, at 1358 North Wilcox and DeLongpre Avenues, is dedicated in March 1930. It is remodeled in the early 1960s and torn down in 1976.

Change-of-watch takes place in a narrow drive separating the station from Hollywood Receiving Hospital on the south side. Once, while going end-of-watch at midnight, I look up to see two shadowy figures atop the roof of the apartment building across the street. The entire watch runs over and surrounds the place. Two marines from Camp Pendleton are trying to burglarize an apartment and do not notice a police station is nearby. As I spot them, I get to work a few hours longer, booking them and dictating reports. Let no good deed go unpunished.

I work Hollywood for three tours: 1960–1961, 1964–1965 (Vice), and 1969–1971 (AM watch commander).

The public climbs granite stairs and walks through a stone arch doorway to a long mahogany desk. The captain's and watch commander's offices are to the left (north). The desk officer operates the Western Electric two-plug "Gamewell" console, and plugs into incoming PBX (private branch exchange) calls.

No Cause for Alarm

The Gamewell call-box system originates in 1899. Five hundred boxes link patrol and beat officers with divisional desks. All officers must carry a belt loop with a ring containing a call-box key, handcuff key, and chrome-plated brass whistle. These are tucked into the left rear pocket (for right-handers) so they will not jingle. The expensive-to-maintain Gamewell system is integrated with the city "Centrex" (central exchange) in the mid-1970s and rotary-dial phone sets are placed into the call boxes.

Handheld radios soon seal the fate of the call box. Beautiful "Keystone Iron and Steel Works" (973 North Main Street, L.A.) cast iron police and fire boxes, with finials and brass number plates, are hooked from the pavement and shattered. City salvage sells the few undamaged ones for $75. (Mine is number 3325).

NOTE: Call boxes may be black, blue, red, orange, yellow, white, gray, or silver. These color variations make them difficult to spot. A repairman once tells me, "Call box colors depend upon the color of the paint we have on the truck that day."

Hollywood Station Layout

The jail is behind the public desk at the southeast end. At the top of the main stairway, to the right (northeast), is the roll call room with Vice in the corner. The locker room is in the southeast (above the jail) and records in the southwest corner. The small analytical office is in center (midwest), with detectives taking up the northwest corner. The downstairs basement is originally a police garage, but eventually houses the property and coffee rooms at the north end. A steep ramp rises to the alley separating the east side from Engine Company 27, 1355 North Cahuenga, now the Fire Museum.

Jail "trustees," mostly winos sentenced to six months, clean Hollywood Station and man the shoe-shine stand next to the coffee room. They cheerfully spit-shine your shoes for a nickel. Released trustees often take their savings to the liquor store, and, that night, are back in the central drunk tank awaiting sentencing and return to the only home they know. They are "family" and we care for them as best we can. The Trustee Program ends in August 1962.

The "Computer"

Chief Charlie Beck wishes to develop "Predictive Policing" for LAPD by using "technology."[19] Computer analysis will sift data about previous crimes so as to deploy officers where they are the most effective. A good idea, but a little dated.

I occasionally assist Officer William H. Cobb, the Hollywood Division analytical officer, to compile crime stats and predict trends. It is a labor-intensive job involving logs (DFARs—"Daily Field Activity Reports"), crime and arrest reports, F.I.s, and pin maps. (One of our sergeants, Richard J. Long, is the DFAR inventor.) An adding machine and my K. & E. Log-Log Duplex slide rule are our only tools. Patterns of criminal activity emerge and we run to Captain Walter C. Nemetz to enlist heavy deployment and Metropolitan Division to saturate areas for bandits, burglars, and rapists.

One of our successes is a liquor store on Vermont Avenue near the Hollywood Freeway. We predict, on several occasions, the night it will be hit by bandits from the south end. The crusty owner has his own plans. When held up, he opens the cash register and then feigns a convincing heart attack. As he flops to the floor he retrieves a Colt .45 auto—cocked and locked with one up the spout—from a lower shelf. The bandits, eyes on the money, invariably reach for the register.

The owner kills four or five but loves telling his story to the press. The next bandit comes in and blasts him as he falls to the floor in his act. The money is left in the till.

Hollerith File

Next to the teletype machine sets our "computer." It is a most unusual antique wood-case card-sorter using border-punched cards for crime data processing that possibly dates from the late 1800s. It is, I suspect, unique to Hollywood Division. It vanishes (probably scrapped) during the 1962 station remodeling.

---

[19] *Seattle Times*, 5 September 2010, p. A5.

Railroad tickets of the 1880s (called "punch photographs") are punched to describe the passenger, so as to verify that the one occupying the seat is the same originally presenting the ticket. These inspire Herman Hollerith to devise a punch card, from Manila stock, to tabulate the 1890 Census. (The 1880 Census takes eight years to hand-sort; Hollerith's electric tabulator reduces the time to a year.) Storage is a problem, so he makes his punch cards the size of a pre-1929 dollar bill, as cardboard currency boxes are plentiful.

Our cabinet holds thousands of simplified, mechanical, horizontal Hollerith cards. They are perforated along the top edges with holes representing race, tattoos, physical deformities, etc. Suppose you are a detective looking for a one-armed Chinese forger. The tops of the appropriate holes are clipped off when the card is filed. You insert a long steel sorting needle into the front of the drawer through the "amputee" hole and lift. All the cards of those missing arms and legs drop to the floor. Gather them up and insert the needle for "Oriental," followed by "forger." Pencilled on the card is a brief description of the suspect, associates, and past addresses. Sometimes there is a photograph. It is quick and works well for small groups. It is not constantly maintained and updated, however, so eventually loses its effectiveness.[20]

Hollerith's tabulating company eventually becomes "International Business Machines." IBM leases its punch-card technology to Nazi Germany to automate their personnel and census data and the individual skills of their concentration camp labor—all linked to the personal identity cards required of all citizens. (This should be a warning against today's use of Social Security numbers as national identification numbers.)

Those numbers tattooed on the forearms of inmates are "Hollerith Numbers"—an American-inspired idea.[21] The Germans call the offices, located in every labor camp, "Hollerith Abteilung" (Hollerith Department).[22]

---

[20] LAPD uses a specialized Records & Identification Division "Oddity File" on a Form 5.5, "Identification Report." It is broken down into "Monikers, Marks, Scars, Amputations, Deformities, and Tattoos." Any officer can access it by dialing R. & I.

[21] Edwin Black, *IBM and the Holocaust* (2001), pp. 351–365.

[22] The Holocaust Memorial Museum maintains that "during the holocaust, concentration camp prisoners received tattoos only at *one* location, the Auschwitz camp complex"

Jews sue IBM in 2001 claiming American punch-card technology is a big cause of the Holocaust "success." They extort $3,000,000 from IBM's German Division before the case is dismissed.

Black, himself a Jew, notes each of the concentration camps is assigned its own Hollerith Code Number: 001–Auschwitz, 002–Buchenwald, 003–Dachau, 004–Flossenburg, etc., despite the Holocaust Museum's insistence than only Auschwitz uses them. Most inmates, not just Jews, are tattooed.

There is an explanation for this apparent conflict. Israel expands the definition of "holocaust survivors" to those European Jews who are alive during the War, not just those who are in camps. "Survivors" without numbers are NOT camp inmates but still entitled to reparations. An excellent discussion of this scam and resulting extortion of Swiss and German banks and governments can be found in: Norman G. Finkelstein, *The Holocaust Industry* (2000), Second Edition, pp. 151–162.

"Hooray For Hollywood"

Filming permits require the hiring of off-duty policemen for security and traffic direction. The names of officers desiring such employment are entered into a Rolodex file in the Watch Commander's Office. Turn down a job and your name goes to the back of the line.

We enjoy working with the stars of these years. Some take time to speak with us: David Janssen, Steve McQueen, Jack Webb, John Wayne, Clint Eastwood, James Arness, William Conrad…. Others make known their aversion to policemen.

The "Reel" Hollywood. The movie industry likes customers to believe they move West for longer days of sunshine. While partly true, the real story is more interesting.

Lower East Side Jewish crime syndicates steal Thomas Edison's camera and projector patents to shoot more profitable nickelodeon porn films. They burglarize his theatres to steal his equipment.

("Tattoos and Numbers," *Holocaust Encyclopedia*, United States Holocaust Memorial Museum, updated 11 May 2012.)

Edison and his movie "Trust" hire thugs of their own to shut down these pirate nickelodeons. They force audiences from theatres, smash arcades, and set fire to entire city blocks where these shows are concentrated.[23]

Leaders of the notorious "Yiddish Black Hand" (men like Charlie "The Cripple" Vitoffsky, Joe "The Greaser" Rosenzweig, and Gyp "The Blood" Horowitz), assisted by their gun molls (Tillie Finkelstein, Birdie Pomerantz, and Jennie "The Factory" Morris) rain bullets from the rooftops down on the Trust's enforcers. Massive fires destroy Edison distributors' warehouses in the Bronx, Chicago, and Philadelphia. An outraged public forces the police into action to raid the "immoral" nickelodeons.

Marcus Loew of Metro-Goldwyn-Mayer, Carl "Little Lamb" Laemmle of Universal, Adolph Zukor of Paramount, William Fox of Twentieth Century Fox, and the brothers Harry, Albert, Sam, and Jack Warner, flee West.

Lower East Side "Murder, Inc." hit man and charming sociopath Benjamin "Bugsy" Siegel heads the mob's L.A. operation. Through contacts of actor George Raft, he begins extorting the motion picture studios to support his lavish lifestyle.

Siegel and Allie "Tick-Tock" Tannenbaum kill informant Harry Schacter (aka "Big Greenie" Greenberg) in Hollywood in November 1939. This is Murder, Inc.'s first Southern California hit. Siegel is acquitted (because he murders the two wits), but his reputation is in tatters. An unknown assailant empties the magazine of an M-1 Carbine into Siegel through the window of his Beverly Hills home on 20 June 1947. You can say Kaddish for Bugsy at the Beth Olam Mausoleum at "Hollywood Forever Cemetery," 6000 Santa Monica Boulevard.

The First Year

Donald C. Satterlee, 6387, is the next to inherit me. It's a quiet night when he says, "Max, I need to tell you something in confidence." All ears, I ask, "What?" "There's a notorious homosexual working the PM watch."

---

[23] Thaddeus Russell, "Bad Jews, Thomas Edison, and the Invention of Hollywood," *A Renegade History of the United States* (2010), pp. 237–239.

"Who is it?" I reply. "Kiss me and I'll tell you!" I keep one hand on the door handle the rest of the evening.

Don works the slowest car in the division but has the highest recap. (We average a felon a night). We bring in old dark coats to slip over our uniforms and "hink" (lurk) in the alleys. (It's surprising how far the sound of breaking glass travels at night.) We are eventually assigned to Felony Car 6F4 (plainclothes, unmarked car). Don and I correspond for many years until his death in 1998.

The Onion Field

Joseph A. Wambaugh, Jr., is in the academy class (May 1960) before mine. Joe does a good job of covering the execution of Ian J. Campbell in his *Onion Field* (1973).[24] He autographs and inscribes my copy: "To Max— From Ian's friend and mine." Karl Hettinger comes on exactly one year before me.

An accident investigation officer and I are the last policemen to see Ian alive. (Joe does not realize this and does not interview us or Ian and Karl's supervisors.)

Ian and Karl are Marine Corps buddies in Korea. I work with them for several months and we have many little adventures:

* We take a 459 report with a most unusual m.o. (modus operandi). The burglars bring a box of donuts to eat while they ransack. They defecate on the floor and leave a note, stuck into a door with a knife, warning the victim to not call the police. We locate a reluctant witness who sees the burglars depart and gives a description. We eventually identify and pick up the two suspects who are well-known male hustlers and employees of the Vogue Theatre on Hollywood Boulevard.

---

[24] See also Hurlbut, "Classic Copper Capers," L.A. Police Protective League's, *The Thin Blue Line*, May 2009 (Vol. 64, No. 5), p. 29 (and) "The Onion Field Remembered (Update)," *The Daily Mirror* (Larry Harnisch's blog on L.A. history), 25 January 2010.

* Sergeant Rodney Ingram, 3984; 17 Feb 1961: "Officer Hurlbut and his partner, Officer Ian Campbell, working a special plain clothes, high frequency crime area, observed a robbery committed on an elderly female victim. Officers gave chase on foot but lost the suspect between houses. A systematic search resulted in the arrest of the suspect who was perspiring heavily although the night was cold...." [211 PC Booking No. 320076. Taken from 1.27, "Incident Record."]

* Sergeant Edward Callier, 7288; 13 March 1961: "Officer Hurlbut with his partner, Officer Ian Campbell, 10046, while on patrol observe a suspect holding a rifle in the stomach of a victim. Hurlbut alighted from the police vehicle while Campbell requested assistance through Communications. Hurlbut deployed behind a telephone pole, drew his revolver, and ordered the suspect to drop the rifle....

  "Hurlbut, because of his position of advantage, did not immediately fire. The suspect dropped the rifle...The suspect was marching the victim to a vacant lot to shoot him because of a dispute. Hurlbut remained calm under extremely tense emergency conditions. He is commended for his initiative, deployment, good common sense, and excellent judgment which probably resulted in saving a person's life." [Santa Monica Boulevard and Madison Avenue; booking no. 339568; DR 61-439925. Taken from 1.27, "Incident Record."]

* See also "Hollywood Train Mystery" (page 72).

I transfer to Accident Investigation Division, and, on 9 March 1963, Officer Gary E. Kirby and I are working 6T91. Near EOW (End of Watch), we retreat to the downstairs coffee room to complete accident reports.

Ian Campbell and Karl Hettinger, working 6Z4 (a divisional "special assignments" car—not a "felony car"), drop by. They are working "fruit rolls" (politically incorrect term for the street robberies of gays). Karl goes upstairs to consult with detectives on a pending court case. Ian, Gary, and I discuss an incident this very day (Saturday).

Inglewood Officers Kidnapped. Two Inglewood police officers, Douglas Webb and Arthur Franzman, see a white Chevrolet Corvair run a red light at Manchester Avenue and Crenshaw Boulevard. Unbeknownst to them, the two have just held up the "White Elephant Restaurant" at 8420 Crenshaw and taken $2,700. (This story is told in the *L.A. Times* of 10 March, "Fleeing Driver Forces Police Into Cemetery"—Reproduced in Larry Harnisch's blog and is a clipping in my "Officer's Notebook" of this date.) It is also on the teletype for Citywide Roll Calls.

Franzman walks up to the car and is confronted by the driver holding a .45 auto. Webb is ordered, "Drop that gun or I'll blow your friend's head off." Both officers drop their gun belts and are marched into the nearby cemetery and handcuffed to a marble statue, unharmed.

This is one of three similar police kidnapping incidents in the Greater L.A. area in the past month. We conclude the bad guys probably fear the death penalty so have not harmed the officers. Karl returns and he and Ian drive off in their unmarked Plymouth to their destiny at Carlos Avenue and North Gower Street.

Salt-&-Pepper 211 Team. Hollywood at night is the time of the street people. Gregory Ulas Powell admits to committing nineteen armed robberies, four of them with Jimmy Lee Smith. The two are looking for another victim when a red spotlight appears behind them. Powell is driving when Ian and Karl pull over their maroon Ford as a "good shake." Probable cause is the license plate light being out. The real reason is good instincts.

Powell pulls a gun on Ian and turns him around, ordering Karl to disarm or his partner will die. The two officers are captured almost exactly as are the two Inglewood officers earlier. Powell and Smith drive them to an onion field near Bakersfield where Powell shoots Campbell through his upper lip and chest. A cloud passes over the moon and Hettinger runs for his life.

Patrol Bureau Order 11. The Campbell-Hettinger shooting changes procedures on LAPD and within the entire law enforcement community. Commander John "Two-Gun" Powers writes Patrol Bureau Order 11 six days later, which is reflected in today's officer survival training: "Don't give up your gun!"

Karl's surrender of his revolver and subsequent flight (which saves his life) come under intense scrutiny. Karl is forced to appear before fellow officers at roll calls to describe and answer for his actions. It is not pretty!

Chief Parker selects me to be his next driver but takes Karl instead. We do not have a department shrink in these days, and it is an attempt to relieve some of the pressures on poor Karl. Karl is caught shoplifting—an act completely out-of-character—and is forced to resign. He becomes a gardener in Bakersfield, *near that very onion field*! (Why doesn't anyone take notice of this?)

Karl dies, supposedly of cirrhosis. [Two of his supervisors in Hollywood, Sergeant (later Lieutenant) Edward L. Callier and Lieutenant (later Captain) George R. Milemore insist, to their final days, that Karl shoots himself.] Karl is cremated. He is as much a victim as is Ian, just with a slower death.

Smith and Powell are both sentenced to death, but reduced to "life" after court decisions halt executions. Smith is paroled nineteen years later but dies in prison in 2007 after a drug violation sends him back. I write to the "California Board of Prison Terms" in January 2010, as do others, opposing the parole of Powell. I suggest *he* denies "parole" to the two officers and that his actions effectively kill them both. His sentence is for life—let him serve it. Parole is denied. He dies in prison on 12 August 2012.

Powell's Trick. Some years later, an informant, a fellow prisoner with Gregory Powell, says Powell brags of surprising Ian with a gun trick he regularly practices.

LAPD procedure in felony stops is to order the passenger to place his hands out the window, so as to be within view of the passenger officer. Driver is ordered to keep his hands atop the steering wheel (which can be seen through the back window in the high beams of the police car).

The driver is then ordered to place his left hand outside the window (with the right remaining on the wheel) and to open his door using the outside button or latch. As he steps out, he is ordered to face forward and slowly back up, hands in the air, until he is safely out of traffic. He is then 'cuffed and proned-out on the ground for searching.

Powell keeps his piece on the floor, just under the seat behind his right foot. He practices opening the door with his left hand and, as he steps out, slides the gun along the floor with his right foot. His right hand, momentarily out-of-sight of the officer, dips down and he emerges, gun in hand.

Ian and Karl have found their fruit-roll suspects but do not realize it. Few officers, even then, will approach such a suspect vehicle without guns out, held down out-of-sight beside their leg. Flashlight in left hand is shining in the eyes of the suspect. Ian screws up. Powell comes out talking but not shooting. Ian should have blasted him.

Following the Onion Field shooting, Powell steals a car and heads back to Los Angeles. A CHP officer stops him on the Grapevine. He again tries sliding his gun with his foot, but the weapon snags and bounces out of reach, possibly saving the life of the Chippie.

The Rest of the Story. Sergeant Edward Callier, Karl and Ian's immediate supervisor the night of the kidnapping, gives me additional information but asks me to not reveal it until after his death (31 May 2005). Ed's wife, Vivian Fay (retired secretary to L.A. County Sheriff Peter J. Pitchess), eventually mails me the eleven-page "Station Log" of Sergeant Jerome W. Rummel and a two-page report of Officer Johnny Johnston, 10441, Hollywood Vice—on what happens next.

An ex-con spots the abandoned Plymouth at Gower and Carlos—doors open and lights on. He calls Hollywood Station and the watch commander, (the late) Lieutenant Jesse Pistole, responds to the scene. Time is given as 11:00 p.m. for discovering the vehicle. A command post is established at 12:10 a.m. under Pistole and Callier. Units are not assigned search areas until 1:05 a.m. (More than two hours have passed.)

Callier, before joining LAPD, is a policeman in Salinas, California. He stops two armed robbers using a teen to drive their getaway car. The boy alerts Ed that the two are about to shoot or to capture him. Ed is able to apprehend them. Ed is convinced Ian and Karl are victims of such an incident—as also happens in Inglewood earlier this day—and wants to alert LAPD and outside agencies to immediately search for them.

Pistole insists they hold off as the two are probably visiting girlfriends in nearby apartments and such a disclosure will get them fired. Pistole leaves to canvass the area on foot, delaying the search.

Callier, becoming alarmed and against orders, activates a CP and triggers a massive response. Pistole eventually returns and is grateful Ed takes the initiative. At 4:10 a.m., Powell is reported in custody in Bakersfield. It is not known, of course, if a more timely alert will make a difference and save Campbell. It is a serious blunder, however, that is covered up. Two officers' lives are destroyed and Ed spends the rest of his life feeling responsible.

Panzer Man

Our final phase of training is working an "L" car—no partner to cover for you. I enjoy the freedom and ability to make my own cases. Detectives are overburdened and happy to have someone do their own follow-ups and interviews. (It is also a respite from those partners who smoke.) We also serve "greenies." Greenies are warrant notices (on little pieces of green paper) for those neglecting to appear in court. I am busy checking these on Sundays, when people tend to be at home. An easy arrest with minimal paperwork. I keep the jailor busy.

"The Panzer" is mentioned at a number of roll calls. An elderly man drives—apparently sporadically—a dark 1930s car and rams motorists who displease him. The driver often curses his victims in German. We now refer to this as "road rage."

I am eastbound on Franklin Avenue headed for Griffith Park when a motorist frantically waves me over. A large crease runs along the lower left side of his auto and the description of the hit-and-run fits *der Panzer*. He is headed up Vermont and east on Los Feliz, making for the Golden State Freeway or Glendale.

Ahead, I see a 1934 Packard Eight sedan, doing about 20 mph, with some interesting modifications. The front bumper is replaced with a section of train track rail. Two similar pieces are mounted beneath the outer edges of both running boards, braced with supports welded to the frame. He is not some crazed Barney Oldfield, but a well-dressed elderly gentleman who claims to be a retired producer of silent-era films. He is now engaged in punishing those who violate his right-of-way and sense of the open road.

I feel a little badly booking him and impounding his car, thinking this may be me at some future date.

"Make My Day!"

I admit to enjoying the writing of some traffic tickets. Two early favorites come to mind:

* I am returning from court and northbound on the Hollywood Freeway in the Silverlake District. I spot a car dodging in and out of heavy traffic, making numerous unsafe lane changes. I attempt to nudge cars in front of me out of the way with taps on the horn so as not to prematurely alert the offender.

  The violator spots me in his mirror sneaking up on him. He rabbits, using his horn and running on the shoulder or next to the center divider. I now use red lights, horn, and siren taps. As we approach the Cahuenga off-ramp, both in the number one (far left) lane, he suddenly darts across all lanes and down the ramp. His arm extends out the window in a one-finger farewell. No way can I follow him without causing an accident.

  The freeway in these years has a Cahuenga on-ramp to the north across from the bottom of the off-ramp. I glance to my right to see Sydney Suspect reenter the freeway next to me. He is looking back to see if I exit the off-ramp behind him. As his head swivels and he spots me, I wave and smile. He pulls over in surrender. No citation today. A booking for reckless driving and evading. A number of satisfying honks and cheers sound from passing autos as I 'cuff him.

* I chase a speeder up North Cahuenga onto Cahuenga Boulevard East, which parallels the Hollywood Freeway. As we approach Barham Boulevard, I see him watching me in his rearview mirror. It should be a clue to him that I am now braking and falling behind. He guns it. What he fails to notice is that there are (then) two parallel roadways next to the 101. The one on the left enters the freeway. The other dead-ends into a chain-link fence across the road....

"Suspect in custody. Request AI unit and supervisor. No CPI (city property involved)—except 'by influence.'" Yes, he is intoxicated.

Griffith Park Riots

Swarms of black teenagers begin harassing white picnickers in Griffith Park in the Spring of 1961. On Memorial Day, 30 May, they jump on the sixty-eight horse 1926 merry-go-round and refuse to pay because they are "Freedom Riders"—somehow linking their little thefts to the "civil rights" movement in the South. The seventy-five-year-old carousel concession owner tries to evict them and is beaten.

I am working 6L84 when the call, *"Major 415 (disturbing the peace)"* is broadcast about 1600 hours. Responding officers are met with baseball bats and a hail of rocks and bottles. Four are injured. We retreat to the park foreman's office. The crowd is estimated at 3,000 by the *L.A. Times*.[25] My 1959 Ford is turned on its side, oil running out. Two of our four arrestees receive one-year prison sentences, but the disturbances continue on a regular basis. When I return to Hollywood as the morning watch commander in 1969, I am made field commander of the Griffith Park Detail to plan and combat this continuing weekend problem.

Hollywood Train Mystery

Historical Note: In a pre-auto nineteenth century Los Angeles, it makes economic sense to run railroads down city streets. These industrial spurs link shipping with inland manufacturing. Cheap rail access is to have unintended consequences a century later when trains became longer and automobiles rule.

Acting Captain George Milemore receives a call from Public Works that the pavement in the intersection of Santa Monica Boulevard and Highland

---

[25] "75 Policemen Quell Riot in Griffith Park," *Los Angeles Times*, 31 May 1961, Part 1, pp. 1–3.

Avenue is "chewed up" every few weeks. They want someone to bill for expensive repairs.

Ian Campbell and I are working 6X77 (X—an "extra" car) this deployment period and given this low-level assignment. It is especially low priority as Public Works is delaying paving our parking lot beside the receiving hospital.

The intersection is an old Red Car line now the terminus of railroad tracks down the center of Santa Monica Boulevard, ending just before they enter Highland from the west. A night train hauls lumber to the old Bekins Van and Storage warehouse near the southwest corner. The wood is used to build vaults (packing crates). A short spur runs off to the warehouse just west of the intersection.

Our biggest clue is that railroad track and train, but the connection to the deep gouges and broken pavement (now covered with hot tar) is not apparent. No buffer stop is erected at track's end, as it would be a hazard to motorists at night.

We begin staking the intersection on slow nights. The old steam locomotive chugs to the end of the tracks. The engineer reverses the cars onto the siding and the lumber is unloaded. They then pull out and return home in reverse.

We nod off one slow morning but are startled into alertness by a loud metallic slamming noise. An amazing sight! The locomotive is across the intersection many yards off the track. The pavement holds until they reverse the engine. The drive wheels then chew up asphalt until the inertia is overcome.

We hit the red lights and siren—unnecessary as no other cars are in sight. The startled engineer and conductor confess—no Miranda warnings in these days. They sometimes must add an extra lumber car to their train. When they reach track's end, the last car is still too far back to clear the spur switch. They discover they can move the locomotive beyond the tracks as it is linked to the cars remaining on the rails. They feed the train slowly back onto its tracks without derailing.

We write a long-form 15.7, which apparently makes its way through channels to Public Works. Our parking lot is unexpectedly paved. The tracks are long gone, but the spur rails are still visible on my last visit in 1998. Ian and I may hold the LAPD record for train pursuits of fewer than 100 feet.

The Egyptian

"The Egyptian" is a skinny black bisexual pimp with a dozen aliases obscuring his original "key" name. He claims Cairo as his place of birth. (It is Cairo, all right, but Cairo-the-southernmost-city-in-Illinois.)

He dresses well and has a Jamaican lilt to his speech, but reverts to Ebonics with his friends. Adam Safian, our oldest beat man, says he obtains his moniker from turning tricks in the upstairs men's room of the Egyptian Theatre, 6712 Hollywood Boulevard.

The Egyptian does not treat his girls especially harshly other than with occasional outbursts of violence intended to maintain order and cash flow. He eliminates his competition by ratting them out to us. He is the subject of several fruit-roll complaints, but nothing sticks.

A pedestrian waves me over one winter evening and says there are two bodies near the dark intersection of Yucca Street and North Hudson Avenue. I find a middle-aged, out-of-town white businessman seated on the curb. His jacket front is bloody. Beside him is the Egyptian, with four shots from a .25 ACP in his head and chest. He isn't merely dead, but really most sincerely dead. [Apologies to the Munchkin Coroner in the *Wizard of Oz* (1939).] A fancy, engraved little 1908 Colt auto, now empty and blood-covered, is on the curb between them.

The survivor admits encountering the Egyptian in a hotel bar and walking to this street, known for its poor lighting, for a sexual encounter. The Egyptian suddenly pulls a pistol and shoots his victim twice before reaching for his wallet. They struggle and the victim ends up with the gun. Both are now seated on the curb a couple of feet apart.

The businessman hopes someone who can summon the police and an ambulance will stroll by. (This is decades before cellular phones.) Time passes and he is weakening from blood loss. He knows, should he pass out, the Egyptian will grab the gun and kill him. He resolves the dilemma by firing the remaining rounds into the Egyptian.

I suggest, as the recorder of this incident, he might wish to rephrase his statement so as to clarify events. Just another street robbery with shots going off willy-nilly during the self-defense struggle. The Egyptian has his heart weighed against the feather of justice by Osiris, the green-skinned ruler of the dead, and is found wanting. Or, as my report notes, "Suspect in custody—Deceased."

Beatles at the Bowl

I am assigned to Hollywood Vice but given a uniform "Special Detail" as security at the Hollywood Bowl on North Highland Avenue the evening of 23 August 1964. I am partnered with the legendary Marion D. Hoover, who shoots more than a dozen bandits in gunfights during his career.

The Beatles, an innovative and commercially successful rock group, are considered (by many policemen) as noisy icons of the negative countercultural transfiguration taking place in the '60s. Our duties are crowd control and preventing kids from sneaking down from the surrounding hills without buying tickets.

Marion asks me to cover for him for a few minutes. "I need to get the signatures of the Beatles for my daughter Beverly." I am a little amused by this, as they are surrounded by guards and hordes of shrieking preteen admirers.

Marion returns shortly—with the signatures of the Beatles in his officer's notebook. "I located Brian Epstein," he explains, "their manager. Told him I am Mayor Sam Yorty's driver and Hizzoner wants the signatures for his kids."

Marion is in charge of the LAPD detail to protect presidential candidate Robert F. Kennedy at the Ambassador Hotel on 5 June 1968. Kennedy rudely rejects their assistance, as uniformed officers present a "negative image" to his supporters. Marion maintains Kennedy would not have been shot had he been there. A clear case of suicide.

Rapatronic Outpost

I wander the remote Hollywood Hills on slow days. A peculiar building, with helicopter landing pad, is concealed by trees at 8935 Wonderland.

The inhabitants soon become aware of my snooping and reveal themselves. It is a secret, disguised, Department of Defense/Atomic Energy Commission site manned by the USAF 1352d Photographic Squadron. I am cautioned to not mention it or enter it on any paperwork.

The "Lookout Mountain Air Force Station" (1947–1969) takes and processes rapatronic (rapid action/electronic) photographs of atomic explosions, one ten millionth of a second after detonation. Their later cameras take 15 million frames a second. Instead of a mechanical shutter, they use an electronic pulse to regulate a Kerr cell sandwiched between two pieces of polarized glass, mounted in opposition. Their photographs are eerie and stunning.

The site is deactivated and is now a private residence recently listed for $6.3 million.

"Imus in the Morning"

John Don Imus becomes famous as a radio host and lands on the cover of *Time*. Insensitive remarks about blacks, Italians, Jews, and various liberal politicians (especially Hillary Clinton) plague him.

Years before Imus' success, he is a brakeman for the Southern Pacific Railroad. I am after him for an $80 traffic warrant. He successfully evades capture for over two months. His mother on North Hobart Street finally tires of being pestered and gives me his new address of 6315 Willoughby Avenue.

Imus's first wife, Harriet Ann Salamonte, insists he is not home. I stake on the house, however, and see him through a rear window. "Come out, Don. I know you are hiding in there!" He takes his booking with good grace and humor. A nice fellow.

Imus' son, Wyatt, is born thirty-three years later. His publicist requests an "Honorary Marshal Wyatt" certificate from the Tombstone Marshal's

Office, which I mail. I do not speak with Imus and doubt he recalls me from so many years ago.

Celebrity Citations

The motoring public looks upon traffic officers as armed tax collectors.

We prefer to think we are educating folks and preventing accidents. Realizing tickets are expensive and disruptive, we try to "sell" them and leave the violator his dignity and an understanding of the necessity for the process. It is not unusual to be sincerely thanked by a violator.

I decide upon a citation or warning before approaching the driver in most cases. A fellow policeman does not get cited. [If he is an obnoxious idiot, I write a 15.7 (a blank report used for miscellaneous communications) to his chief or CO. Punishment is usually severe—often thirty days without pay for a (then) $12 ticket].

I cite the late "Gunther Toodie" [comedian Joe E. Ross (Joseph Roszawikz) of *Car 54, Where Are You?*], for an improper turn. He demands "police courtesy." Ooh! Ooh! (His signature expression). A most unpleasant individual (who later records, "Love Songs from a Cop"—very hummable). I also stop my future landlord, character actor Vaughn Taylor, and allow him to escape with a warning.

I pull over Terrence "Steve" McQueen for speeding on Mulholland Drive but do not cite him. He drives fast but with skill and control. He is not a public danger, but has a reputation for "baiting" police officers into mountain road pursuits. His good attitude helps. I find we both ride 650 Triumph TR6 "Trophy" bikes. (We also hate the Lucas Electrical system on them, forever vibrating parts onto the roadway.)

Connections. There is something to Frigyes Karinthy's 1929 belief that the world is shrinking and only six acquaintances separate us all. Or is life the aimless collision of billiard balls?

A friend and fellow member of the Adventurers' Club, Loren Janes, is McQueen's stunt double from 1959 until McQ's death in 1980 at age fifty. Most believe it is McQueen—as "Bullitt"—who hurtles down Taylor Street in San Francisco and sideswipes the black Charger at 90 mph on the Guadalupe Canyon Parkway. No, Loren is driving.

Loren, in turn, is a close friend of Matt Nelson, son of teen idol Eric "Ricky" Nelson. I take a 459 report from Ricky and his football-player roommate in 1960, where he loses several of his gold records. Ricky is not popular in Hollywood Division as he sucker punches an officer. (His dad, Ozzie, gets the charges dropped by the city attorney.)[26]

The Great Imposter

The priest administering the last rites to McQueen in Mexico is another friend and member of the Adventurers' Club, Ferdinand Waldo Demara (no. 916). Fred is best known as "The Great Imposter."

Fred masquerades as Benedictine and Trappist monks, an editor, a cancer researcher, lawyer, deputy sheriff, psychologist, prison warden, and others. He steals the credentials of a Canadian doctor and reports aboard a destroyer during the Korean War. He operates on sixteen combat casualties, including a Korean officer shot in the heart and lungs and not expected to live. While orderlies prep the patient, Fred disappears into his quarters where he quickly skims a book on thoracic surgery.

All recover and Fred is decorated by the navy and Korean government. This generates publicity in his "hometown" of New Brunswick, where the real doctor practices. They allow Fred to quietly leave the country.

Fred, in clerical garb, sits with me during our Thursday night club dinner meetings. He tells me he has a "photographic" memory and simply bypasses years of study.

I ask, "Are your present duties as the chaplain at Good Samaritan Hospital in Anaheim just your latest impersonation?"

Fred replies, "Those I work with do not recognize me or know of my past, except for my superior." (Fred is now considerably overweight.) "I've always been religious and have found my true home. As to my past," he says (with a little wink, smile, and in a convincing Clerow "Flip" Wilson impersonation), "the Devil made me do it!"

---

[26] Also mentioned in Kristen Paglucci, "Travelin' Man: The Life and Music of Ricky Nelson," *Newark Classic Rock Music Examiner*, 17 February 2011.

Fred dies at age sixty of diabetes and a heart attack, following the amputation of both legs. We mourn a delightful companion who does not tread the beaten path in life.

The Batt[27]

Meyer H. "Mickey" Cohen is in prison the summer of 1951.[28] Anthony Brancato and Anthony Trombino, members of Cohen's mob (with totals of forty-six arrests and seventeen convictions) rob the Flamingo Hotel's lay-off cash room of $3,500. A Beverly Hills bookmaker happens to be present and recognizes the Two Tonys as the ones who previously rob him.

Jack Dragna, Italian gambling competitor of gangster Cohen, orders the Two Tonys hit. They are shot to death by someone in the backseat of their auto, parked on Hollywood Boulevard on 6 August 1951 [a scene in *L.A. Confidential* (1997)]. LAPD suspects the Battaglia brothers are involved but has little evidence. Jimmy "The Weasel" Fratianno later joins the witness protection program and confirms he is one of the shooters and the other is Charles Battaglia.

John L. "The Batt" Battaglia and his brother, Charlie Batts, work their way up the New York Bonanno mafia family the old-fashioned way—by using a baseball bat to break the arms and legs of those not paying "insurance" to keep their businesses from being bombed or burned. Refusal is not an option.

Capo di Tutti Capi (Boss of Bosses) Giuseppe "Joe Bananas" Bonanno, sends the Battaglia brothers to L.A. to look after the "family" business. This is where I enter, stage right, for my minor role.

"6L1—Ambulance shooting at 2912 Nichols Canyon." I find The Batt rolling on the floor with a bullet in his gut. He claims he accidentally shoots himself, but then recalls he scrawls a suicide note: "I shot myself.

---

[27] Originally told as "The Two Tonys": Hurlbut, L.A. Police Protective League, *Thin Blue Line*, April 2011 (Vol. 66, No. 4), p. 24.

[28] Chief Parker's antipathy towards Hebrew school dropout Mickey Cohen is not because he is Jewish, as some charge. It is because he is a criminal. It is true, however, that Parker believes the Jewish community shelters an inordinate number of his critics.

I don't know what came over me." No powder burns. No gun. Blood is (largely) mopped up. I cut his shirt and bandage the wound. (G-units can be slow, and I have lots of practice patching holes as an ambulance driver.)

"Forgive my skepticism, Sir." (Yes, I speak this way.) "But aren't you due in court Monday for a special federal grand jury indictment alleging your involvement in organized crime?" Even hurting—and fibbing like a snake—The Batt is courteous and a gentleman.

While awaiting the ambulance and detectives, I wander about. I find a .38 Smith & Wesson two-inch "Chief's Special" deep inside a kitchen drawer. Cylinder splatter and odor indicate it is recently fired twice, but the two casings and one cartridge are missing.

Patsy, the beautiful and decade-younger wife (a former Las Vegas showgirl), is in another room with a ferocious German shepherd named Cherokee. Patsy refuses to speak, so I go about picking up a couple of shopping bags full of betting markers near the telephone. (The Batt is known as "Bookie to the Stars".) I bet (pun intended) that many of his customers call in wanting payoffs for their winning combinations, as he no longer has any records—an occupational hazard for an arrested bookie.

After relocating Cherokee to a closet, I arrest and handcuff Patsy for 245 PC (ADW). It is obvious this is a "family dispute" (with the emphasis upon "family"). I still marvel at the numbers of Hollywood and downtown detectives who respond. Followed by FBI and Treasury agents. Ad (Administrative) Vice and Intel seem especially pleased with my collection of markers. I spend another entire watch on OT. [No pay in these days; just "comp" (compensatory) or "white time" (on white slips of paper) that is tossed out when you accumulate over ten days on the books.]

I anticipate a 1.27 ("Incident Record"—a 3×5-inch thin sheet, where minor commendations are recorded in your divisional package). Really good deeds warrant a larger 15.7. Instead, the very next day (Sunday), I am on the transfer teletype to old University Division at 809 West Jefferson. "Just routine," says Captain Walt Nemetz, who is having difficulty suppressing a smile. I am soon to depart to play soldier and do not know the disposition of the case: 61-550757.

L.A. Noir to Lumineux. A half-century passes and I chance to read an issue of an Oregon electric company journal.[29] It says Johnnie C. Bennett (Batt's old alias) self-publishes a book on his early life in Hollywood, mentioning his mother shoots his father. Bennett, a child actor, complains his father, skillful with a mob bat, borrows $40,000 from him but never returns it.

I write to Bennett. ("Hey, I jailed your mom!") He sends me his book, *Mafia, Cowboys and Cocktails* (2008). He promises to pass my best regards to his now eighty-year-old mother, who remembers me without rancor.

Patsy shoots The Batt as he is running around on her. The DA refuses to prosecute her because of Batt's conflicting stories. Batt goes to the federal pen for extortion and not paying taxes on his bookmaking business. (Something to do with large numbers of betting slips multiplied by years of unpaid taxes on estimated proceeds. Ha, ha.)

The Batt dies of a heart attack at fifty-two. Charlie Batts is escorted into the desert and never again seen. (Bennett believes he is tortured and buried.) Bennett's book (pages 108 and 109) reproduces an article in the *Los Angeles Examiner* of 29 October 1961. It names me as the arresting officer and source of the conflicting statements by the wounded "victim" (who is prosecuted) and the shooter (who is freed).

I leave L.A. in 1985 after purchasing a fifth-floor jail door from the old Main Jail (Lincoln Heights), which closes on 4 July 1965 (and reopens, briefly, for Watts Riot arrestees). The door now guards my den up here on the Canadian border. Bennett wants to see it, as it is the very door that hosts Patsy that weekend so many years ago.

My friend and Hollywood partner, Steve Hodel, writes of *his* father being the serial killer of Elizabeth Short, the "Black Dahlia." Bennett has a mafia dad in the L.A. Noir period. Mine is running a Richfield gasoline station and not taking bets or whacking competing station

---

[29] Debbie Schoeningh, "Member Spotlight: Hollywood Ending," *Ruralite Magazine*, March 2010, pp. 28–29.

operators. (At least, I do not believe so). Some of us come from such mundane origins.

The Bat

I make lieutenant on 21 September 1969—and back to Hollywood as the AM watch commander. I arrive early each evening to suit up, check the station, and speak with the PM watch commander before preparing for roll call. A jail check comes first. (More internal police problems originate in jails than anywhere else.)

White-haired slender old-timer Eugene Solesbee likes working inside, so the PM watch commander, Robert Wachter, has him on jail or desk duty. Divisional jails are temporary detention centers to facilitate booking offenders and quickly returning officers into the field without long runs to the central or main jails downtown. Detectives arriving in the morning can more easily interview and process prisoners. A routine jail wagon or bus arrives each watch to transport excess prisoners downtown for court or longer detentions.

Solesbee tells me the only unusual case is a "psycho" who tears up our lone padded cell. He has committed no crime other than creating a disturbance. As we walk the line of cells, a strangely muffled scream can be heard, punctuated by "thumps."

A mesmerizing sight unfolds at the east end. The cells are large cages with bars across the top. Suspended upside down from the center bars is a gagged and strait-jacketed man. He resembles a huge white bat as he swings back and forth like a pendulum striking the sides of his cell.

Solesbee explains prisoner transport refuses to take the prisoner downtown as he is too loud and abusive. Even in restraints, he is able to bite off the rubber-fabric wall coverings. I order him cut down and summon Dr. Nick Famularo from the receiving hospital next door. Diagnosis: "Crazy as a loon."

G-6 straps him to a gurney and heads to Unit 3 (the psychiatric ward) at L.A. County General Hospital, Boyle Heights, for a seventy-two-hour observation period. From there he is confined to the thirteenth floor jail ward, where he is 'cuffed to one of their bed frames pending release. Not too satisfactory a system, but better than simply turning him loose, which is now done if he is not considered "a danger to himself or to the public."

Lieutenant Wachter is far less concerned than I, and a tad irritated that I "take over" his prisoner before official change-of-watch.

Chapter VIII

HOLLYWOOD VICE

"Suspicion often father of truth."[30]

Glitz and sleaze coexist in an uneasy balance in Hollywood Division. Vice acts upon the "three C's": citizen complaints, commercial activity, and conspicuous behavior.

The movie business continues to attract an endless supply of runaway boys and girls who, unable to support themselves on the streets, fall victim to sexual predators. A decade before Canadian flight attendant Gaetan Dugas becomes notorious as "Patient Zero" for AIDS, Hollywood Receiving doctors speak of opportunistic infections and immune system diseases common only in Hollywood. They suspect something is amiss in the gay community.

Greyhound Bus Depot

My initiation into Hollywood Vice takes place in the sordid Greyhound Bus Station men's room, 1409 North Vine Street, two blocks east of Hollywood Station.

Sergeant Donald L. Erath instructs, "Just lean against the wall near the urinals. If someone gropes your private parts or asks you to engage in some unnatural act, this is 647a PC (lewd conduct in a public place). Tap twice on the wall and I'll come running."

A young man enters and stands a long time at a urinal. He turns and smiles. I smile back. The door suddenly flies open and another young man enters to announce: "I am a police officer, and you two fags are under arrest for faggotry!"

---

[30] Warner Oland as *Charlie Chan at the Race Track* (1936).

The man at the urinal cries, "I can't go to jail, Officer, how else can I handle this arrest?"

"You are in luck," says the policeman. "Our jail is very crowded tonight and I am authorized to accept your bail. It is $150. How much do you have?"

Urinal boy starts sobbing and says, "I only have $100." "All right, we'll accept this reduced amount. How about you, Red?"

"I didn't do anything wrong," I reply. "Why are you arresting us?" "Pay up and save yourself a big fine and prison time where they will wait for you in the showers every day."

I produce my three-inch .38 Chief's Special and my ID. "I have a badge, too, but it doesn't look like yours. Up against the wall, you two! You are under arrest for impersonating a police officer and extortion."

Two thumps on the wall and Erath and I hook up my arrestees. They are two marines on a weekend pass from Camp Pendleton working their "second job." The shore patrol escorts them to the brig to await their courts martial.

Ladies of Negotiable Affection

Street walkers, massage parlors, and by-referral-only hookers with their own apartments come to our attention. Prostitution (647b PC) involves the elements of sexual services in exchange for payment. Prostitutes, thus, can be male or female. (Elegantly made-up women sitting on bus benches are often not women and not waiting for the bus.) Streetwise hookers,[31] wise to an entrapment defense, will try to get the john to bring up price. It is, otherwise, just a legal "act of love."

We sometimes follow a prostitute and her customer to her apartment. When he emerges, we "squeeze" him a little to later introduce one of us as his referral. Many cooperate because they are married and somehow get the idea that if *they* are also arrested, their wives will find out. Not a glamorous side of police work, but an activity generating millions for organized crime and feeding the drug trade.

---

[31] "Hooker" does not refer to the Civil War general of that name, but is used in the 1820s for the notorious concentrations of prostitutes around Corlear's Hook (later Crown Point) in Manhattan. It is an important navigational landmark for 300 years.

Occupational Hazard

Drivers pull over to proposition pedestrians on streets as Selma Avenue, known world-wide.

Defendants include military chaplains and assorted clergymen. Teachers and professors are well represented. High-ranking military officers and the occasional policeman are captured. Danger exists as arrestees can have much to lose. Those with teaching jobs and security clearances are reported to their agencies. Homosexuals, at this time, are considered susceptible to blackmail and are, thus, security risks.

Our partner is nearby and we don't get into cars before the arrest. To prevent a panicked response, I find it is best to grasp the driver's arm and say something like, "Don't be alarmed, but I am a police officer. Let's talk about it." You turn off the ignition and handcuff the arrestee before the surprise wears off.

Time-Life Pervert

I am standing at Selma and Cherokee Avenues on 31 July 1964. It is a time of few arrests because of a sensational photo-essay, "Homosexuality in America," in the 26 June issue of *Life* magazine. The crew rides with Hollywood Vice for months and details how to conduct a conversation with a stranger so as to avoid arrest.

A red Alfa Romeo pulls up and the driver says, "Come with me and suck my cock." No coy arrest-avoiding conversation. The defendant is Andrew David Kopkind, correspondent for Time-Life News Service. I confiscate LAPD Press Card 143, as well as ones for LASO, the CHP, and San Francisco PD. (Booking number 294257.)

I ask Kopkind why he comes on so strongly, as he is one of the authors advising caution on the street. "I don't recognize you!" he cries. (He fails to notice that LAPD vice officers work only an eighteen-month tour—to avoid the temptations that cause past departmental scandals.)

Deputy Chief James G. Fisk calls to express his amusement with my arrest. (He is unfavorably quoted in the article.)

"In January 1966, *Time* magazine declared: 'Homosexuality deserves no encouragement, no glamorization, no rationalization, no fake status as minority martyrdom...and above all, no pretense that it is anything but a pernicious sickness.' When one of *Time*'s reporters, Andrew Kopkind, was arrested for (wanting) sex with a man in...Los Angeles, in 1964, the publishers of the magazine told him he would have to 'become straight' or he would lose his job. They sent him to a psychiatrist who tried to teach him how to meet women on airplanes."[32]

I still feel badly about this insensitive disposition that costs Kopkind his job. There is viciousness, but also sadness, in this lifestyle. I teach classes on prostitution and homosexual offenses at the Academy Vice School and am an early proponent of greater tolerance. This is not a popular view on the LAPD of the early 1960s.

"The Trouble with Harry"

Defenses to "disorderly conduct" charges include: the act is not lewd, mistake of fact and law, homophobic law enforcement, "trying the officer" ("Isn't it true, Officer, that you are the one who groped my client?"), entrapment, and that the location is not truly public and there is no one to be offended. (An officer's "peace" cannot be disturbed.)

What most defendants fail to realize is that the city attorney will drop their first lewd conduct arrest to "trespassing" or other minor offense upon a plea of "guilty." Attorneys imply they have influence with the C.A. and (for a hefty fee) can get the charge reduced. (They must otherwise register as a sex offender under 290 PC.) The client will not even have to undergo the embarrassment of a court appearance (where he might observe what actually takes place).

Short (five-feet four-inches), flamboyant, and effeminate attorney Harry E. Weiss—a legal giant and gentleman—captures much of the lewd conduct business. His fedora and cape are elegant, but a century out of fashion. He

---

[32] David (Smith) Allyn, *Make Love, Not War* (2001), p. 149.

"cops out" 95 percent of his clients. Of the few (usually with priors) he defends, he simply asks the officer, "Tell us what happened?" The court listens to the client's defense and Harry rests. Most are found guilty.

Harry also handles officer divorce cases for a flat $150, no matter how complicated. He is missed.

Ferndell No. 9

Ferndell No. 9 is an outdoor Griffith Park restroom that attracts 647a's like flies. After PM roll call we often head here to stroll the trails until dusk. On a warm June afternoon, Officers William "Steve" Stevens and Charles "Denny" Humphry chase a large black man through the brush on a steep hillside when he refuses to submit to arrest.

My partner, Carens "Mel" Melton, and I run to assist. I am farthest away and veer off on a small trail. The suspect, running downhill, bursts through the bushes above me. I dive to avoid a collision. He cannot stop and I contact him below the knees with my shoulder. He goes airborne and lands with his neck in the fork of a tree. He is still and appears dead.

The others arrive and we extricate this huge man from the tree. He has a pulse so we cuff him. He soon awakens and we have a battle controlling him. We belt his legs and it takes four of us to carry him to our car.

Evenings are taken up with ABC violations. We visit Aunt Charlie's (1642 North Cherokee–from *Charley's Aunt*, a popular 1890 transvestite play and a 1941 Jack Benny movie), an S/M (sadomasochism) leather bar called The Gauntlet (1210 N. Highland), The Vieux Carre (1714 Las Palmas—"Old Square," the French Quarter in New Orleans), and others.

The bartender at the Red Raven (7013 Melrose) catches me—despite a standing-room-only crowd—sipping water from a beer bottle I have smuggled in. "You must be Vice," he says, "too cheap to buy beer."

"No," I reply. "I don't like beer, but enjoy the company."

I then tip him three dollars. He is later unpleasantly surprised to find his first observation is correct.

Making Book

I am partnered with James D. "Smokey" Stover on days. I get haircuts and shaves at "Dave's Barbershop" on Vine Street. (We have a 3.18 vice complaint, which must be cleared in thirty days.) I memorize bets being accepted. We stake on newsstands and follow men buying scratch sheets to nearby telephone booths to observe the numbers they dial.

We stiff calls to bookies and, when a bet is accepted, kick in the door to prevent the destruction of evidence often recorded on flash paper. Your partner, picking up the phone, is further proof the call went through to the proper address.

Advances in telephone switching technology make it difficult to know where the physical telephone is located. One of Smoky's talents is repairing doors kicked at wrong locations. No one asks the question: "If gambling was illegal at the track, would horse racing even exist?"

We run a phone number and it comes back to an apartment at the "Blair House," 445 North Rossmore, in early February 1965. Terry Pierce takes a running jump and boots the door above the knob with both feet. He bounces off. The bookie has replaced the wood door with one of steel. We employ our "Key to the City," a lead-filled pipe with handles. The booms are deafening and the door dented, but still it holds.

The back room door is eventually opened by a known bookie who inquires, "Yes, Officers?" His employees are seated around a table sipping coffee. Telephones are yanked from the walls. We reconnect the wires and start recording incoming bets—good enough evidence for a booking. Fines are around $25, but the real loss to the syndicates comes from savvy customers later claiming winning bets. A bookie welshing on a bet is soon out of business or worse.

The Chain Game

I lean back against a pine tree in a portion of Griffith Park known as Box Canyon on 27 August 1964. A man, dressed entirely in black leather, is approaching across a clearing. It is dusk but I can see he is wrapping the ends of a small chain about both fists, as one would hold a garrote.

Ooh, ooh! I think. *This is a fruit roll and he believes I'm the fruit.* I step behind the tree to free my revolver from its ankle-holster. The man detects my concern, as I peer around the tree at him, and says, "Don't be afraid. I'm Phillip and I just want to play a little game of 'chains.' I know you'll like it."

"I admit to being a little intrigued and more than flattered," I say. "But before you step any closer, tell me how this game is played."

"First, we each get a hard-on," says Phillip. "Then we wrap the ends of this chain around our dicks and have a tug-of-war. You'll really like it!"

"That's lewd enough for me, Phillip. You are under arrest!" I signal to my partner, Donald G. McWhirter. Don books him while I type the report. (Booking number 315698.) Sergeant Erath must sign as approving supervisor, but suspects it is one of our little jokes to which he has recently fallen victim.

"Here, Sarge, hold the chain; it's still warm and sticky."

He won't touch it but goes into the jail to question our arrestee. He soon returns shaking his head and saying, "I've been on this job too long."

Queer Slang

Slang rapidly changes, especially in the "gay" community. ("Gay," before I come on the job, does not mean "fruity".) "Queer" is more popular than "gay" or "fag" (faggot).

A couple of terms from the mid-1960s that are now dated:

"Auntie" is a homosexual over thirty. A "bog queen" frequents public toilets. A "friend of Dorothy's" is a reference to being gay. (Dorothy being Judy Garland's character in the "Wizard of Oz".) "Twink" is a cute, boyish male. A "snow queen" is a black man who prefers white males. "Nellie" means effeminate. Police officers are referred to as "Millie," "Tillie," or "Mae."

Polari. The gay subculture of the 1960s uses words of polari, an Italian/British cant brought to the U.S. by waiters, circus and theatre performers, and servicemen serving in the U.K. "Punch and Judy" street puppet performers have long conversed in it. Many borrowings in polari come from Romany and Yiddish.

"Ajax" (adjacent to or nearby), "bitch," "drag," "hoofer" (dancer), "naff" (dull, awful), and "rough trade" (a potentially violent sex partner) have entered the mainstream. Polari is intended to communicate in a manner outsiders do not understand. It also serves to identify themselves to others. When this secret language became somewhat public, it fell into disuse. It seems to be undergoing a revival. We learn to converse in Polari.

Bizarro Names

The meanings of proper names change over the centuries. Some change theirs, as do movie stars, to seem more mainstream or acceptable.

We book a Peter Lorre, Jr., who says he is the son of the actor. He bears a remarkable resemblance to actor Peter Lorre—but eventually reveals he is an imposter who legally changes his name to take advantage of the resemblance. The real Lorre wins his case in L.A. Superior Court but dies a few months later—and the impersonation continues.

Filipino names in Alaska canneries—like "Joker," "Jejomar" (a combination of Jesus, Joseph, and Mary), and even Hitler—are not uncommon. There are many Batmans, Robins, and Superman. My wife's Chinese sisters are Yueng-Yueng (coin-coin) and Ping-Ping (apple-apple).

I read of a fellow who legally changes his name from Christopher Garnett to KentuckyFriedCruelty to protest chicken abuse. In Alaska, I encounter an Inuit with the last name of Everybodytalksabout. Hollywood arrestee Frank Lala is not a particularly unusual moniker. His middle name, however, dooms him: Trala.

Chapter IX

TRAFFIC ANARCHY

Captain Sidney E. Mills is amused to receive a note from an army private predicting the collapse of Accident Investigation Division without the expertise of said soldier. AI is a specialized uniform division with a long waiting list. Applicants must have five years in patrol to apply and be evaluated in the "upper ten percent." I am released from active duty and on Transfer Order 5 of 13 February 1963.

Acme Arrives

Post World War I traffic in the Central Business District of Los Angeles is approaching gridlock. The solution in this new age of science and technology is thought to be mechanical. The Acme Traffic Signal Company at 621 Marsh-Strong Building convinces the city they can move and coordinate heavy traffic by the world's first connected system of traffic devices.

Acmes have a large green and red light. (Seven-second all-red intervals precede the later yellow three-second caution light in tri-light signals.) Folded into the case are two semaphore arms swinging out to read "STOP" and "GO." A gong sounds at each signal change, which annoys nearby residents. Birds sometimes nest in the slot. Right-turning trucks take out the arms.

The Acme monopoly ends in 1931 with the arrival of the tri-light. Acmes and tri-lights have metal hoods attached during WWII to shroud their visibility from aircraft at night. This shading is found to also enhance their daytime visibility.

"Frankenstein on Wheels"[33]

Those traveling in Bangkok, Beijing, Mexico City, or Rome have an understanding of traffic anarchy. Traffic signals and two-way lanes are mere suggestions. LAPD is experiencing 330 traffic deaths a year by the late 1930s. A "traffic investigation detail" of twelve men and two cars is established in September 1937. It becomes "the leader in follow-up investigation of hit-and-run accidents and all other types of investigations involving traffic injuries and deaths."[34]

Street Cars. Mythology says old Red Cars are killed off by General Motors to force people into automobiles. The truth is that people simply abandon them for the convenience of their cars. I recall many complaints of trolleys snarling traffic. We also have "trackless trolleys" (electric busses) powered by overhead wires but with tires.

Pink Status

New AI officers are called "pinkies." Until deemed qualified to work alone and handle any traffic situation—and then tested and interviewed to verify it—your name appears on the daily deployment board on pink paper. (Sergeant Philip S. Rivera evaluates me and I am off "pink status" on 17 April 1963.)

Legendary Criminologist Ray H. Pinker, our instructor on the Drunk-o-meter,[35] also teaches the new Breathalyzer School. We train at Reeves Field (the old Terminal Island Naval Air Station) in Harbor Division to drive in pursuits and to determine speed from observation of vehicles. We study accident reconstruction, photography, and the determination of speed

---

[33] Inspector R. C. Combes, "Frankenstein on Wheels," *The Guardian*, L.A. Police Revolver and Athletic Club, 1937, pp. 77 and 199.

[34] Arthur W. Sjoquist, "Traffic," From Posses to Professionals, Thesis: California State University, Los Angeles, 1972, pp. 154–56.

[35] A portable breath tester where the subject blows into a rubber balloon attached to a tube of purple liquid (potassium permanganate in sulphuric acid). The bleaching of the color indicates the concentration of alcohol present in the breath. A simple high school chemistry titration.

from skid marks. We will never again fear (as do most patrol officers) being assigned a confused and complicated accident call.

Luther "Mac" McCormack and I bag so many "deuces" (intoxicated drivers—taken from section 502 of the old California Vehicle Code)—that we are assigned to the "Deuce Car" from 0115 to 1000 hours. (It is surprising how many impaired drivers are present in heavy morning traffic.)

Caticide. The "major objective symptom" of one driver south on Main Street from Seventh is that he swerves into the northbound lanes to run over a poor cat. No other traffic is present. He blows a 0.02 percent blood alcohol and performs a flawless FSE (field sobriety exam). He is a light drinker, but judgment is affected before physical abilities. (It does not improve his case that both Mac and Max are cat owners.) We expect him to present a defense of "I was not intoxicated but just do not like cats." He, instead, pleads "guilty."

Another defendant blows a 0.44 percent b.a. His driving is not that erratic, aside from constant little road corrections. (At this time, 0.40 percent is on the chart as "lethal".) He has almost twenty priors, but is still licensed to drive….

Nemesis and the Freeway Flyer

FT (freeway traffic) 88 rockets down the Pasadena Freeway[36] at 90 mph and transitions to southbound on the Harbor Freeway. (If you think 90 isn't fast on the Pasadena, you've never driven it.) We practice this run often in the early morning hours. Apparently, so does the Corvette we are after. He is awaiting us at the Marmion Way on-ramp. He waves an arm out the window in a middle finger salute. The rear end dips and he makes his run like a pro. He is "Nemesis" with a covered license plate, who recently challenges several AM interceptor crews.

I am driving this early March morning of 1964 and academy classmate Dale E. Waaler is broadcasting our pursuit. (No red lights and siren, which

---

[36] The Pasadena Freeway (Arroyo Seco Parkway/CA 110), built in 1940, has six ten-foot lanes (two feet less per lane than other freeways). Original speed limit is 40 mph. The smaller Plymouth is thought to be a better choice of Interceptor for this run.

can confuse other freeway traffic.) We are strapped and caged into Shop 19803, a 1962 Plymouth, our oldest freeway interceptor. It is a heavy road-hugging machine with reinforced frame. Motor transport superintendent Ray Wynne drops in a new 350-hp engine fitted with three double-barreled carburetors with extra vents, Ed Iskenderian ("Isky the Camfather" of Gardena) racing cams, stabilizer bars, double-welded oversized wheels, special sintered metallic brakes, and other improvements. It guzzles 100-plus octane Richfield "Boron" gasoline, which allows a high-compression ratio in the V-8 engine. (Strangely, Wynne uses 20-weight engine oil in the transmissions without problems.) We replace tires following every pursuit.

At two-thirds throttle, only one carburetor sucks. (The accelerator controls carb air intake, not gas flow, drawing the proper amount of fuel into the airstream.) Carbs numbers two and three cut in, and our speedometer needle now lays on the max mark of 150 mph. On-ramps flash by like picket fence posts. The tail lights of the Corvette slowly recede into the light fog drifting in from the Harbor. We reluctantly—son of a bitch!—admit defeat and shut down our pursuit.

Sergeant Edward H. Hannum [aka "Sniffer" for his uncanny ability to detect if accident drivers are HBD ("have been drinking")] soon requests our presence at an all-night drive-in restaurant off the Harbor Freeway. Sniffer strikes again.

Interceptors run roughly at slow speeds, and our Plymouth is snapping and popping from our long run. The Sniffer's black-and-white is parked next to a red Corvette, also snapping and popping. It's driver is a grinning off-duty AI officer we shall call Ernie B. Ernie is my former roommate in Hollywood Division.

Chief Parker is, fortuitously, out of town. So Ernie retains his job following a six-month vacation without pay. Ernie is still with us at the time of this writing. He is in the final stages of Alzheimer's and no longer chuckles at his short career as "Nemesis." Drive with God, Ernie.

We train at the Pomona Fairgrounds and Reeves Field. Initial interceptor training is OJT. I must first do a stint on 6TL87—a one-man car to handle traffic accidents on the Hollywood and Harbor Freeways (down to Vernon Avenue), 2345 to 0830 hours. This frees the Freeway Flyers to concentrate on enforcement duties.

I largely attribute my modest driving skills—and never having a traffic accident in over thirty-five years in harness and in scores of pursuits, as well as in sixty years on the road—with the patience and training of these early interceptor crews.

The freeway interceptor program ends 1 October 1969 when state law gives the CHP jurisdiction over freeway enforcement.

Pursuits

The demise of the street car brings smog (a portmanteau of smoke and fog), traffic, and a scofflaw culture to L.A. The freeways are its stage. Witness highly mobile criminals like O.J. Simpson. [Why isn't he stopped and proned-out like any other murderer, guys? You make life difficult for the rest of us.] The average L.A. motorist spends about ninety-three hours a year on freeways, seething in tie-ups.[37]

KTLA's "Skycam" encourages rabbiting at all costs, even when all hope for escape is gone. When interviewed from their cells, most say they believe they will not be caught and anticipate telling their friends of their "great escape." Pursuits tap into the primal and lizard-brain, driving reason aside. Chases embody freedom, speed, and escape.

No PIT (pursuit intervention technique) maneuvers for us. We have too few cars and a preventable t.a. means days off without pay (in a number equal to damage costs).

SigAlerts. SigAlerts (named for Gene Autry's Golden West Broadcasters' executive, Lloyd C. Sigmon, 1955) are called in by officers to announce major traffic problems or other emergencies. The

---

[37] Tad Friend, "The Pursuit of Happiness," *New Yorker*, 23 and 30 January 2006, p. 65.

switchboard activates a tone and the policeman's message goes out to all radio stations.

One of the first SigAlerts creates a jam of monumental proportions. A self-propelled Budd Rail Diesel (the "San Diegan") derails after leaving Union Station on 22 January 1956, killing thirty. So many doctors, nurses, and sightseers head-in that police and ambulances are blocked. Fistfights between police and reporters prompt Chief Parker to appoint Inspector Edward Walker as our first press relations officer.

Ladies' Night

An occasional female joins our "100 mph Club." Over ninety is an automatic booking for "reckless driving" and a trip to Sybil Brand Institute for Women (1963–1997) at 4500 East City Terrace Drive in Monterey Park. The walls are painted "pretty pink." Much nicer than our previous light green female jail on the fifth floor of the Main/Lincoln Heights Jail.

Bubble—Trouble

Horace is an elderly dignified gentleman, who, every morning, develops the accident and DUI photographs we take with our Graflex Miniature Speed Graphic/Army Signal Corps surplus cameras. They have a spring-back into which we insert a cut-film holder containing two 2x3-inch exposures.

Horace boils into the office of Captain Sid Mills with the latest outrage. Some unknown AID policeman is using the cameras to take lewd or suggestive pictures…usually involving naked females or clothing store manikins in lewd positions. The intent appears to be to irritate poor, staid, easily-offended Horace.

Captain Mills appears at one of our PM roll calls. He passes around several amusing photos of "Bubbles," a heavy Central Division prostitute known for her enormous breasts and friendliness towards uniformed policemen. Bubbles is sprawled, supine, across the hood of a police car. The shop number of the car and license plate are taped over. She wears only a traffic officer's white hat and a gun belt.

"Any of you know who took these pictures?" asks Mills.
"No, Sir!," shouts the watch, almost in unison.
Mills then asks Officer Ronald P. Kiser to step forward. Mills says, "Look closely, Ron. What do you recognize in this picture?"
Ron replies, "Oh, crap!"
Bubbles's holster is a "clamshell." (Pushing a release button in front of the trigger releases a spring which flips open the entire side, allowing a faster draw.) Ron is the only officer in the division wearing this holster...despite its prominence in the later *Adam-12* television series.

Ron apologizes to Horace and all is well again in Scientific Investigation Division's fourth-floor Photo-Lab Land. Ron works for me, ten years down the line, in the Police Commission. He is my most competent detective sergeant and an outstanding enforcement team leader, but remains the first one I question when some clever practical joke strikes down some pompous command officer.

Double–Trouble

Jose A. Quintero and I light-up a pickup truck on Sunset Boulevard for erratic driving. In our headlights we see the passenger and driver exchange places several times. We order them out. They are identical twins: Terry and Larry McKee. We have no idea who is driving as each says it is he. At the station, they blow almost identical blood-alcohol readings. We resolve the dilemma by booking them both! Terry appears in court and cops out.[38] Larry is released.

The Missing Barricade

Deputy city attorneys know to never ask a question when they do not know the answer. They are sometimes overwhelmed with cases, however, and neglect to properly prepare, going to trial "cold."

---

[38] *Citizen News* (Hollywood) and the *Modesto Bee*, p. B-8, 19 March 1964.

A motorist, after dark, runs into a sinkhole resulting from a broken water line. A simple report. I write "CPI" (city property involved—the roadway) across the top of the report and check one photograph taken. The driver has not been drinking and is transported to Central Receiving Hospital for minor injuries. I impound his car, still nose down in the big hole, for safekeeping.

Several years pass and I receive a subpoena on a civil case against the city. The issue is city liability for not adequately lighting and barricading an obvious hazard.

The plaintiff testifies he drives into an unlighted hole. A Department of Public Works supervisor counters that barricades and kerosene lanterns are in place. He cannot understand how any sober motorist could possibly drive into them. He offers into evidence a photo of lights and sawhorses in place around the hole.

I leave public seating and approach the city attorney at the defense table to whisper a warning and to request a brief recess. He impatiently waves me away. The plaintiff's attorney has taken notice. He calls me to the stand and asks if I have anything to add to the case.

I testify that, upon my arrival, the motorist is still in his auto. No lights or barricades are present. My flash photo substantiates this. Public Works scurries to the scene and sets up their barricades after the accident. I remain at the scene to guard the hole until this is accomplished.

The CA apologizes to the court and to the plaintiff. He thanks me, in private, for a lesson-learned. A most gracious response.

"918 Victor"[39]

AI partners Robert R. Kendrick and Richard A. Wegner enlist me in what at the time sounds like a fun project. In retrospect, it is one of the crazier and more dangerous things I am to ever attempt.

We head to Torrance Municipal Airport after work at daybreak on 8 February 1964 to make our first parachute jumps into the waters off Angel's Gate Light in San Pedro Bay. They borrow some parachutes and rent a

---

[39] "Violently Insane Person." L.A. sheriff's radio "Tens-Code."

Cessna 172 "Skyhawk." We notify the Coast Guard and Harbor Patrol so they will not think an aircraft has gone down when parachutes are spotted. A small boat will release a dye marker as the signal to jump and be on hand to pull us out of the water.

It is cold and overcast. Kendrick and Wegner decide not to jump but will head to the harbor to assist in the boat. I have come this far and will go.

The pilot reaches 3,000 feet, and we spot the green dye marker. I exit the plane. The 'chute, unbeknownst to us, has a "sleeve." It holds the canopy and slows the deployment sequence to reduce the opening shock. It malfunctions and wraps around the canopy like a barber pole, preventing it from opening.

I look up and realize the sleeve must be unwound. I have a reserve 'chute but do not pull it as it will probably just become tangled in the mess above. I reach up and start unwinding it. The wind pulls the end from my hand and it unwinds itself. The opening shock at terminal velocity of about 120 mph tears off my sneakers. The others say my canopy deploys about 150 feet above the water. I hit the water almost instantly. A close call.

I decide, if I am to ever do this again, to go "airborne" in the army so as to do it right. I eventually make many water jumps, during which you activate a quick-release and slip from the harness as you enter the water. You do not want your canopy or equipment to drag you down.

Disciplinary Action

LAPD discipline can be both harsh and peculiar. My only sustained complaint in twenty-five years occurs when I run afoul of an AID policy. We earn no paid overtime or extra compensation for working unusual hours or holidays. We put in requests for personal days off, but are at the whims of our watch commander and his deployment schedule.

Someone becomes ill or injured or some incident requires heavy deployment, and we must work. We handle a terrible accident on the Harbor Freeway one night with several fatalities. We acquire over eight hours compensatory overtime, which places me over the ten-day maximum. No leeway exists on the schedule for a day off.

Lieutenant Robert Tucker calls me forward in freeway roll call to read my 1.27 Incident Record: "Officer Hurlbut failed to keep his accumulated overtime under the ten-day maximum as outlined in Item 6 of the PM watch policy...." No mention of the manslaughter filing or excellent investigation—this is expected—or devotion-to-duty for working another shift without pay. (Hoots and laughter). Even Tucker winces. Discipline, not justice, is the issue. My penalty is forfeiture of the one and one-half hours over ten days; thus, restoring balance to the LAPD universe. I request a transfer to Hollywood Vice.

Working on the Railroad

Ernie B., on his suspension from interceptor duty, obtains a job as security to guard mail cars and cargo for the Southern Pacific Railroad at the Taylor and River Station Yards. I join him, especially at Christmas and other busy times. The pay of five dollars an hour—cash—is good.

Transients are occasionally injured or killed, so much of our work is evicting trespassers. It's a pleasure to see a good engineer and brakeman kiss cars together so gently that the coupling is heard as a "clink" rather than a slam. The old link and drop-in pin coupling is the origin of the saying: "It's so quiet you can hear a pin drop."

I am told of a worker pinned between two rail cars as they slam together. The coupling is made inside his abdomen. He is still alive as blood does not leak out and its pressure is maintained. They call his wife for a final "good-bye" before uncoupling him....Deaths happen this way in a yard, but I've always suspected "calling the wife" is the product of an urban legend.

Risk Reduction

Modern technology creates risks inherent in the complexity of these very systems. A series of minor failures can cascade into a catastrophic one, as at Three Mile Island Nuclear Power Plant in 1979. We also have a tendency to compensate for lower risks in one area by taking greater risks in another.

The automatic braking system (ABS) is a marvelous invention that should reduce accidents. It does not. Drivers instead use their enhanced safety to drive faster and more recklessly without increasing their risk of an accident. This is probably why more pedestrians are killed at marked crosswalks rather than unmarked ones. They compromise the "safety" of a marked crosswalk by being less vigilant.

Sweden, in the late 1960s, switches from driving on the left side of the road to the right. Traffic fatalities, expected to skyrocket, drop 17 percent (for a year) as people compensate for their unfamiliarity with the new traffic pattern by driving more carefully.

T.J. Hooker

Thomas Warren Hooker also graduates from the academy in 1960. He is awarded the Medal of Valor in 1962 for saving people in a burning building on West Thirty-eighth Street. We work together in AI. Tom's partner is later shot and killed in front of him. Tom makes sergeant and retires after twenty years to become a security guard.

I introduce my bride to the academy range staff in July 1982. They allow her to shoot the combat shotgun course. We see that William Shatner is filming a *T.J. Hooker* episode (no. 5, Second Season) on the athletic field.

Shatner waves us over and says this is "Big Foot" (shown 30 October 1982). He graciously poses for a photo with my wife, which she still treasures. He delays filming to chat until we notice the concern of his now idle crew.

Tom, noting the similarity of T.J. Hooker's background (divorced, his partner shot in front of him), states the character is patterned after his career. (The show's creator, Rick Husky, denies this but the news picks up on it.)

Tom's third wife, Joy, and his adopted son—who previously serves ten years for bank robbery—are convicted of setting their house on fire to kill Tom and collect the insurance. The two rescue the family dog, but not Tom. Tom, almost blind, on dialysis, and with heart problems, is fifty-eight. His doctor says they should have waited a month. Tom will then be dead of natural causes.[40]

---

[40] Ann W. O'Neill, "Hero Officer's Murder Tale Stranger Than Fiction," *Los Angeles Times*, 18 July 1993.

Chapter X

THE VALLEY AND BEYOND

I transfer to Planning & Research Division after my Hollywood Vice tour.

A day of written examinations on the English language, followed by an interview with Captain Henry H. Bertch, Jr., our old CO at the academy. Two questions only: 1. What is your favorite book on the language? [Answer: Strunk and White's *Elements of Style* (1918)] and, 2. How would you word the motto of the Manuals & Orders Unit, if we had one? [Answer: "As many words as necessary; as few as possible"]. I get the job.

Writing orders for Chief William H. Parker is an honor. It is also an exercise in frustration as the OIC, Lieutenant Jack L. Eberhardt, demands that no questions or ramifications go unaddressed. (Jack masters Bislama, the Creole language of Vanuatu, in one week!)

Officer James Annes, my partner, is in charge of the Dexter Pullen Memorial Library, a chronicle of past orders. It is named for the late Dexter Pullen, a city engineering clerk who retires after forty years with no known accomplishments. I take the sergeants' exam; Jim defects to the FBI.

I tie for fourth place on the sergeant's list of 277 and am appointed on St. Patrick's Day, 1965. Captain Bertch calls me into his office. Together, we walk to Personnel Division for my new badge (number 696) and ID card, and then to the city clerk's office at city hall for swearing in. Bertch snaps a Polaroid of me, right hand raised.

We retire to the Police Administration Building, eighth floor coffee room, for a light lunch. Bertch tells me of his remembrance two decades earlier of the cold LAPD promotional process when he makes sergeant. I shall never forget this dear old man.

North Hollywood Division

Off to Sergeant's School and obtaining a teaching credential, followed by a loan to Internal Affairs Division.

North Hollywood Division morning watch is quiet. We often deploy two cars: one in the north and the other in the south. This means, when anything goes down, our chances of confronting it are good—and without backup.

<u>The AM Watch Sleeper</u>. I am youthful in appearance and the youngest sergeant on LAPD. Other sergeants warn me to beware of Policeman Robert Danckwerth who can be found in the rear of the roll call room.

I call roll and Danckwerth (no one calls him Robert or Bob) immediately raises his hand. I acknowledge him and he states, "Sergeant, you're new here and need to know the rules. I sleep after 3:00 a.m., and you need to assign my calls to another unit or handle them yourself."

No laughter. If this is taking place, the others surely resent him for not carrying his weight and most officers are not shy. "Danckwerth," I reply. "A few words of advice for you: I am going to find you. Fail to answer your calls and I will have you by the balls!" This brings smiles from the others and a scowl from Danckwerth.

Danckwerth, twice that morning, requests my presence when I am farthest away from the requested location. Shortly before I arrive, he cancels the call. After 0300, I call him twice, requesting his presence in the south end for some trivial discussion. No more nuisance calls from him.

Dankwerth is probably sleeping but always answers his calls. In the quiet hours, I search for him. He likely hides in an abandoned garage or spot outside the division. Or maybe in the riverbed tunnels beneath the Hollywood Freeway, then under construction.

One night I drive into a drainage tunnel beneath the freeway, round a corner, and the siren and roof antenna begin scraping. The poured concrete roof has slumped. The channel is too narrow to open the doors or crawl out the windows. Rebar in the concrete makes the radio useless.

I start backing up, only to discover there are no backup lights (optional equipment adding to cost). It is pitch-black. My interior spotlight plugs into the cigarette lighter. Shining it through the rear window creates considerable glare, but I can see the side walls. It takes me about forty-five minutes to inch out. Should I become stuck, it is necessary to kick out the rear window and walk to a phone booth—a humiliating story that will still be told.

NOTE: The intersection of the Hollywood and Ventura freeways forms an isolated parklike area surrounded by heavy traffic. A flock of chickens roams here for years after a poultry truck overturns. A motorist spots a skeleton swinging from a tree. It is a suicide victim unnoticed for several years by millions of passing motorists.

Years later, I chance to come across Dankwerth completing his retirement paperwork in Parker Center. "Looks like you won, Dankwerth," I kid. "Now that you are retired and beyond my grasp, why not tell me where you hid out?"

He smiles and says, "Screw you, Lieutenant!" and walks away.

Liquor Store Robbery. Valley Services dispatcher "Blackie" Sawyer broadcasts, *"Armed 211 Suspects Inside Ted's Liquor Store, 7202 Lankershim at Sherman Way."* It is 0210 hours on 25 September 1966.

I am three blocks away. Blackie says, *"Max, there is no back door to Ted's. Window displays may block your view."* [Liquor stores are known for such displays, which make it difficult to look in or out. They keep Vice and Patrol from spotting underage transactions]. Blackie then adds, *"No North Hollywood, Foothill, or Van Nuys units clear for backup."*

Lights out, I glide into Ted's parking lot. Two men stand near the cash register, but the clerk is not visible. (He is on the floor.) I pull my car opposite the front door and await the two, shotgun across the hood.

The bandits soon head out, hands full of cash and liquor bottles. Upon seeing me, they run deeper into the store, apparently looking for another exit. A North Hollywood unit, hearing the broadcast, soon arrives. The suspects are armed with a .38 special revolver and a .32 auto. One has a New York PD shield, apparently stolen.

Sworn and experienced police dispatchers who know their divisions are a thing of the past. The civilians who replace them save the city a little money, but often fail to ask the right questions of those callers in need of help.

Barber Shop Massacre. *"Dead bodies in the barber shop, 6759 Lankershim,"* announces Blackie. *"P/R (person reporting) says the shooter is still inside."* It is 0230 hours on 29 July 1966.

The front door is ajar and the lights out. Fresh blood is pooling from the doorway of an interior room. No one responds to our shouts. Four bodies are inside. The shooter, .38 revolver in hand, is present but barely alive from a self-inflicted gunshot. He is apparently the P/R. One victim is the former wife of an LAPD officer. All are lured into an ambush by the shooter in a love triangle (quadrangle?).

North Hollywood is busy for one of LAPD's "slowest" divisions.

Nudie. We all know "Nudie" Cohn (Nuta Kotlyarenko from Kiev), the flamboyant "Rodeo Tailor" on Lankershim. Nudie outfits Western stars such as Roy Rogers, Gene Autry, John Wayne, Ronald Reagan, and even Elvis Presley. He claims friendship with "Pretty Boy" Floyd and other Prohibition Era gangsters.

Nudie is short and chubby. He wears rhinestone-studded suits with chain-stitch embroidery and a ten-gallon hat. His boots are mismatched in remembrance of the years he could not afford matching shoes. He drives a series of Pontiac Bonneville convertibles with steer horns on the grill, pistol door handles, and silver-dollar-studded dashboards.

Nudie dies in 1984 and his grandchildren adopt the last name of "Nudie." A fine tribute to a colorful Valley character.

End of an Era

Chief William H. Parker dies on 16 July 1966. I am in charge of his burial detail of ten officers at the San Fernando Valley Mission on 20 July. I am not alone in shedding a tear for a giant of a man.

The Chief's funeral procession is seven miles long—flashing red lights unlike anything I've seen since the funeral of Ian Campbell. Thousands attend. The American Legion Police Post 381 Band plays "Hail to the Chief" as he is lowered to rest. Taps is sounded and a rifle salute fired. We all sense the sadness of an era now lost.

Van Nuys

Captains Norman H. Judd followed by Jesse A. Brewer are two of the finest LAPD captains I have worked for. I am their AM watch commander in the early 1970s in Van Nuys Division.

Air raid sirens are tested at 1000 hours the last Friday of the month. "Satan's Slaves" are the Valley's "Hell's Angels." (The two merge in 1978.) Helms Bakery Divco trucks deliver their goods before supermarkets kill their business. Adohr Dairy trucks trail puddles of melted ice for miles. (Their name is derived from the wife of the owner—spelled backwards.) Busch Gardens (Anheuser-Busch Brewery) gives free beer for an admission price of $1.75. Flocks of escaped parrots and parakeets from their bird sanctuary are still a nuisance.

Wednesday evening on Van Nuys Boulevard is "Cruise Night," a traffic nightmare. Three miles of gawkers (spectators who stare without intelligent awareness) and exhaust fumes are to plague Van Nuys officers for almost fifty years.

The Night Jumper. An acrobatic young man is perched on the fourteenth floor ledge of the Valley Hilton Hotel on Ventura Boulevard and threatens to jump. The Fire Department arrives first. The jumper gathers a number of carbon dioxide fire extinguishers from the hotel and discharges them at anyone approaching. Sergeant Glen H. Kailey and I arrive and set up a small command post. Several firemen, irritated by the frozen blasts, are busy hooking up a hose to the roof water supply. They intend to give him one last chance to surrender before washing him off the ledge. It is too high to deploy nets.

Glen and I approach often enough to exhaust the kid's CO_2 supply. He then jumps over the edge, hanging above the pavement by his fingertips.[41] We eventually distract and grab him. His family commits him to a mental institution.

---

[41] "Police Prevent Leap From Roof of 14-Story Hotel," *The Van Nuys News and Green Sheet*, 26 January 1973, pp. 1 and 20.

Max K. Hurlbut

San Fernando/Sylmar Earthquake

My alarm clock rings at 0600 hours on my day off, 9 February 1971. Moments later an earthquake hits, rocking my Van Nuys home for over forty seconds. I go outside to note my 20,000-gallon swimming pool is half empty. Sympathetic waves slosh tons of water over my six-foot high concrete wall into the neighbor's yard.

As a former geology major, I know the area has dry, arid soil, limiting ground failure and soil liquefaction. I have only minor damage. My cat, Murphy, runs off but returns a week later, as fat as ever.

Electricity and telephone service are out. I shut off my gas and water, don my uniform, and (although now assigned to Hollywood Division) report to Van Nuys Station.

The earthquake is centered in Iron Canyon and ruptures a twelve-mile surface area with horizontal and vertical displacement as much as six feet. Two freeway interchanges and twelve overpass bridges have collapsed.

Two Sylmar hospitals are destroyed and sixty-five are dead. Ruptured gas mains are ablaze, and sewage runs in the streets.

Worst of all, the upper and lower Van Norman reservoirs, with an earthen bulwark dam, are badly damaged. If breached, the resulting wave has the potential to kill around 80,000. I serve as the command post personnel officer[42] at the Knollwood Country Club for several days before returning to the field.

The Army Corps of Engineers drains the water while we evacuate the area below and patrol for looters. Many tourists pass through for a photo op: Chief Edward M. Davis, Mayor Samuel W. Yorty, Governor Ronald W. Reagan, and Vice President Spiro T. Agnew.

---

[42] *A History of the Los Angeles Earthquake*, LAPD Tactical Operations Group, 1971, pp. 176–77.

Chapter XI

THE WATTS RIOT

A bullet bounces off the hood of 4S30 ("S" is for Sniper), our "Brushfire-7" unit. Buildings are on fire as far as we can see. Looters, engaged in the redistribution of wealth, are breaking into buildings and tossing Molotov cocktails into them as they depart.

We don't stop as we are the closest unit to shots being fired at firemen at West Forty-Seventh Street and South Broadway. Sergeant James P. Wampler is driving like a maniac. Policeman Lawrence W. Gerken and an officer (whose name I have forgotten) are hanging on in the rear. I ride shotgun. Firelight is the only general illumination, as electricity is out.

We skid up, headlights out. I open the door and roll out into the gutter. A fireman, atop the 100-foot aerial ladder of a "triple" (pump, hose, and tank), sways back and forth as he directs a stream into a burning apartment building. His crew crouches behind their engine.

Shots are fired at the ladder man from somewhere inside the building. The shooter is apparently back in his room, as even in my scoped .30-06 I cannot spot a flash. An occasional round penetrates our car or bounces off. (We later recover a slug that appears to be a copper-jacketed .30 M1 Carbine round.) I have the only rifle in the car, but do not fire as I cannot acquire a target. We shout and beckon to the fireman to come down, but he just waves back—one hell of a fire-squirter!

I lay prone in the gutter behind the engine block and wheel, offering both cover and concealment. Warm water from the pumper flows down the gutter and over me. It feels good on this hot August night.

Jim radios for a National Guard unit. An M-151 Jeep pulls up with an M60 on a pedestal mount. They fire across the top floor windows and then the ones below. Bricks fly and glass breaks, with the occasional tracer lighting up the sky en route to Downtown L.A. No one emerges. The building burns to the ground and the rubble is eventually bulldozed.

144 Hours in August

A Chippie motor officer, Lee W. Minikus, pulls over twenty-one-year-old Marquette Frye for 502 in the County Firestone District. Frye is two blocks from home. Frye's heavy mama boils up, screaming, "Police brutality!" (This happens. On LAPD, we throw the suspect into the back of the car to complete the citation or processing elsewhere.) A hostile crowd gathers and the disturbance spreads.

NOTE: A husband-wife team of California Highway Patrol officers chase Rodney G. King and call LAPD for assistance on 3 March 1992. The CHP manages to trigger the two major L.A. riots of the late twentieth century. Triple-A with guns....

I encounter young Marquette Frye while working AI. He is bright and pleasant, but a school dropout. Following the riots, he becomes a bitter troublemaker used by militant groups. He changes his name and dies on Christmas Eve (at age forty-two) of pneumonia.

Mayor Sam Yorty and Chief Parker call on the National Guard on Friday the thirteenth. One hundred engine companies are fighting fires and LAPD commits 934 policemen to the forty-seven-square-mile riot area.[43] The next day, 13,400 guardsmen are deployed. This is seven days following Lyndon B. Johnson's signing of the Voting Rights Act of 1965.

Colonel Irving J. "Bud" Taylor, Fortieth Armored Division, California National Guard, is also a gruff, salty, motor officer. He is able to paw the ground to eight (the number of citations expected of motor officers each shift), so makes it into Traffic. Bud is now William Parker's superior, which irritates the Chief considerably. (You must know Bud to fully appreciate this.)

---

[43] "Report on Los Angeles Riot," Police, Fire, and Civil Defense Committee of the L.A. City Council. Council Files 125, 342, and 343. 24 November 1965.

The First Day

Sergeant Jerome W. Rummel [nickname: "Aba-Daba" (a 1914 song) from his tendency to stutter when excited] uses Hollywood Vice and detectives to call up off-duty policeman for riot duty.

I check off officers for the first bus load. I grab a probationer and brief him on roster duty, and then go upstairs to the locker room and don my uniform. I then order myself aboard the prisoner bus, and we are off for a disorganized and confused briefing at the Police Administration Building (PAB). Upon my return to Hollywood a week later, Rummel does not appear to remember my disappearance, or at least does not mention it.

The bus soon delivers us to the command post at the Ninety-Seventh Street School at Figueroa Street. More confusion. LAPD has few shotguns, so a teletype requests loans from other departments. We end up with a number of semi-auto 12-gauge, Model 11 Remingtons[44] from San Francisco.

The 1911 Model 11 has a bronze friction ring that must be properly positioned on the recoil spring (around the interior magazine tube) to fire our heavy buckshot loads. I grow up shooting my dad's Model 11, so am drafted to disassemble them all and show others how to load and fire them, as LAPD uses pump/slide-action models.

"Blam!" The shot comes from a group of about thirty motor officers. A "one-point" safety check (i.e., pulling the trigger to see if it is loaded). Several hundred of us turn to see who fired. Also casting about for the culprit is one of the motor officers. A long curl of smoke is rising from his sky-pointing barrel. Deputy Chief Noel McQuown and Inspectors Daryl Gates and John "Two-Gun" Powers all look at each other and decide it is time to depart.

Frank Pachmayr, fellow Safari Club member, runs a gun shop at 1220 South Grand. He hands out his entire stock of new 12-gauge shotguns to LAPD officers. Some are expensive engraved sporting models. He does not obtain officers' names or record the guns passed out. He later tells me every one of these shotguns is returned following the riots!

---

[44] Officers pointing two Model 11s can be seen on the inside of the rear cover of *Anarchy: Los Angeles*, Frank Harding (Ed.), published by Kimtex Corp., 1965. (Available in the USC Digital Library.)

Max K. Hurlbut

Night Watch Sweep

We work twelve-hour shifts. Most of us do not bother to go home. We head to south-end stations for a few hours of sleep and a shower. We drop by the CP to pick up bag lunches.

Our first assignment is to form a skirmish line ahead of Hollywood Captain Charlie Crumley and Lieutenant Norm Judd. We clear rioters on Broadway from Ninety-Second Street to Manchester. Unfortunately, they reappear from between buildings as soon as we move on. (We will still be there if it is not for the Guard soldiers who eventually man posts at almost every major intersection.)

Firearms

LAPD buys Remington Model 31 slide-action shotguns (1931–1949). (Some officers incorrectly believe they are the similar-looking Model 870s, with cheaper stamped parts.) Officers check them out of the station armory through the Change-of-Watch sergeant. (He often discourages this, as it is a nuisance, usually at the expense of his End-of-Watch.)

The Watts Riot makes it apparent that each car needs a shotgun. Chief Parker purchases the Ithaca Model 37 Featherlight "Deerslayer," with Parkerized finish, which becomes known as the "LAPD Special." It has machined parts and a rifle sight to shoot slugs. The department has since gone to Model 870s, but allows some officers to purchase their own semiautomatic Benelli Super 90s. (Soldiers and policemen are aware the issue weapons their life depends upon come from the lowest bidder.)

I check out two Model 31 shotguns from Hollywood Station for our car before leaving. Number 1 is "confiscated" by Sergeant Frank Fox and Number 13 by Sergeant Richard Takaberry. (I require them to sign my "Officer's Notebook," as I am responsible for their return.) I then drive home to obtain my scoped pre-1964 Winchester Model 70 in .30-06. Carrying personal weapons on duty is against department policy, but "anything goes" for the gun battles in Watts. (Inspector John Powers commends my taste in rifles.)

NOTE: The "no personal weapons" policy is written after a detective on stakeout in a liquor store causes hundreds of dollars damage by firing his 20-gauge Ithaca Auto & Burglar double-barrel at bandits.

Those of us with military training and hunting experience are assigned to "Sniper/Brushfire" units to engage shooters beyond shotgun range. We are encouraged to remain off-the-air rather than to make arrests. We are not assigned calls. We are free to roam where the action is.

The volume of hot calls is incredible, often with no units on the air to handle them. We never see a single officer retreat from taking on swarms of rioters, as happens in future rioting on 29 April 1992 following the Rodney King verdict. Few uniformed officers realize a handful of us are actively picking-off shooters who seek the high-ground so as to kill policemen apprehending rioters in the streets below....

"Shootin' and Lootin'"

We respond to a shooting at Eighty-fourth Street and Vermont. A dead body is in the rear seat of a parked car. Too late to help and no ID on the victim. We advise Communications and move on. We pass a small market ablaze. The front windows are smashed. Two bodies are on the floor, but the fire discourages entry. What appears to be buckshot holes in the wall behind them indicate they are probably shot from the street, possibly from a passing (police?) car. We work twenty-one hours this first day.

LAPD jails 3,952 during the riots. The old Main (Lincoln Heights) Jail at 401 North Avenue 19 is closed on 4 July 1965. It reopens 11–17 August just for us. Bodies wash up in the harbor for weeks, following a bumpy journey down the storm drains and L.A. River. Old scores are settled. Informants tell us of bodies buried in backyards.[45] The thirty-four "official" deaths include a fireman, LASO deputy, and Long Beach policeman.

Some store windows are posted "Black Owned" or its equivalent. Most of these, but not all, escape destruction. (Donut shops, being associated with

---

[45] "The death toll from the fires of August 1965 was actually much higher than reported since bodies were turned to ashes or what remained of them was buried in massive rubble." Gerald Horne, "Death in the Afternoon," *Fire This Time* (1995), p. 77.

police nutrition, are not saved by this ploy.) *Jet* magazine carries an entire sixty-four-page issue on the riots:

> "The rioters' wrath was aimed at the white man....(The rioters') challenge to law and authority was complete...armed with bricks, bottles, concrete, bits of metal, knives, machetes, and guns (they) fought pitched battles with police and National Guardsmen."[46]

The above is an accurate observation.

We spot a badly injured cat at Forty-Eighth Street and San Pedro, a little after midnight, and stop to end its suffering. A bullet passes between me and Larry Gerkin and strikes the building behind us. We cannot determine from where it is fired. We suspect the poor cat is intentionally injured as a decoy.

We leave the car and prowl alleys and burned-out buildings, watching and listening for gunshots or the movement of shooters into position. The few rounds we fire are at gunfire flashes or at those who are clearly targeting and ambushing officers on the streets.

Fire Discipline

We stop to chat with guardsmen around a fire in a fifty-five-gallon drum that serves as a barricade. (There is still no electricity for streetlights.)

An old dark Buick with lights out accelerates towards the post. It rams the blazing barrel and skids into a parked car. Guardsmen circle the car and empty their M1 Garands into it. The shooting suddenly stops as clips ping out and the realization sets in that bullets are holing the car body and endangering soldiers on the opposite side.

The silence is broken by giggling from inside the car. Two highly intoxicated black men, both now (strangely) on the backseat floor, are uninjured. Their Buick is full of holes.

---

[46] "Life Inside a Riot Zone," *Jet*, 2 September 1965 (Vol. 28, No. 21), p. 4.

The Watts Riot Brick

We round the northeast corner of 103rd Street and Avalon (known as "Charcoal Alley") the evening of 15 August. A group awaits and showers us with rocks and construction debris. A brick strikes our hood, and Wampler unexpectedly hits the brakes rather than the gas. I open the door and shout, "Halt!" to the crowd. They are astonished into inaction as I reach over and pluck the brick off the hood.

A Seventy-Seventh Street black-and-white, unbeknownst to us, makes the same turn behind us and is forced to brake. We are blocking the lane, and debris in the road prevents them from going around. As we speed off, the rioters spring to life and pummel the stopped car.

I feel badly about this. (Ha, ha.) The officers escape injury, but their car experiences right-side-window failure and multiple body dings. I still have that blackened and scarred brick in a glass case, with a little brass plate describing its origins.

"Muhammad Speaks"

Shots are fired at passing officers from the roof of Muhammad's Mosque No. 27 (Western National HQ of the "Nation of Islam"), 5610 South Broadway, the night of 17 August. Responding officers shoot out the windows in a pitched battle and arrest the occupants. I am there.

Additional gunfire can be heard down the street at the United Veteran's Club at 5774 Broadway. Some of us split off and run the distance.

A new black Lincoln pimpmobile parked in front is full of bullet holes. Building occupants have escaped, apparently, into a storm drain, which is accessed through a hole in the floor.

The Detroit Riots

A dozen of us on an A-Team lay prone in the grass next to a gully at first light on 19 July 1967. A low, heavy ground fog is all that conceals us. Clanking noises reveal the approach of armor down the draw. M48-A2 medium tanks of the 146th Reconnaissance Squadron, 46th Infantry Division, Michigan National Guard, are grinding closer.

The command and driver's hatches are open, as the driver cannot see through the low-hanging fog in the gully. As each tank passes, one of us leaps aboard, and, with .45 auto, overpowers the surprised commander and crew of three. This is the only time we are to have our own Patton tanks, with 90 mm rifle, to play with.

Two years following the Watts Riot, my reserve unit [Company A, Twelfth Special Forces Group (Airborne)], jumps into the Upper Peninsula of Michigan in exercises against the Forty-Sixth Infantry Division. We play the part of Soviets invading over the North Pole in Operation Wolverine I.

Exercises are interrupted by the Detroit Riots of 23–27 July 1967. This same armor, with rubber "parade" track pads, is trucked south. (Most of the reported "tanks" in Detroit are armored personnel carriers with a .50-caliber machine gun.) We observers note the similarity with Watts: miles of buildings afire, forty-three killed, gunfights, and looting. One Guard sergeant, Larry L. Post, is shot to death. The Eighty-Second Airborne is called out—a large number of their personnel are black. Watts largely recovers but Detroit remains destroyed to this day.

Chief Parker acknowledges he makes a mistake in cordoning off the riot area to allow so-called "community leaders" to quell the rioters. These "leaders" have little influence over those defecating in their own nests. Most arrestees are middle-class blacks who have frustrated expectations and simply see an opportunity to acquire their neighbor's goods.

The McCone Commission Report[47] blames the problems on lack of jobs, insufficient schooling, and resentment of the police and authority. They recommend massive social spending in Negro communities. (A 1964 Urban League report ranks "Los Angeles *first* among the 68 cities examined" for

---

[47] "The Crisis—an Overview." Violence in the City: An End or a Beginning? Governor's Commission on the Los Angeles Riots. 2 December 1965. 101 pp.

ten factors important to blacks[48].) Ignored is the festive nature of much of the rioting and looting.

Some good riot photographs can be seen in the 1966 Annual Press Photographers publication, but their two-page written-story revolves around *their* experiences rather than on-scene reports.[49] My copy of the McCone Commission Report also contains eight pages of photos.

The Death of America

The Black Power Movement is to result in riots and incidents involving killing and destruction for years to come. President Lyndon B. Johnson signs Senator Edward M. "Ted" Kennedy's "Immigration and Nationality Act of 1965," which severely restricts Western and Northern European immigration.[50] They assure us it will result in only a "few thousand" from Africa, Asia, and Latin America, and that our demographic mix will remain unchanged. These "estimates" prove to be wildly inaccurate as hordes of immigrants from other cultures overwhelm our country and social systems.

---

[48] *The State of Black Los Angeles*, Urban League, July 2005, p. 13.

[49] "Assignment: Watts," *Just One More!* 1966 Annual, Los Angeles Press Photographers' Association, pp. 34–45.

[50] Kennedy's killing of Mary Jo Kopechne in the "Chappaquiddick Incident" of 18 July 1969 should result in his conviction for homicide-with-a-vehicle and removal from office.

Chapter XII

OLD SWAT

The origin of the Special Weapons and Tactics (SWAT) teams begins on LAPD following the Watts Riot. One man, Sergeant John G. Nelson, is responsible.[51] The LAPD Official Website ("History of S.W.A.T") and Metropolitan Division sites acknowledge this.

Policeman John Nelson is one of our instructors at the academy in 1960. He is the "psycho" I am delighted to choke-out during practical exercises on "mentally disturbed suspects." We correspond until his death from multiple sclerosis. "Once in a while," he writes on 18 October 2000, "I feel a little rankled that some people choose to take credit for what they didn't do, but I was born with an aversion to publicity and too much attention."

Attacks upon police by urban guerrilla militant groups in the 1960s make it clear the conventionally armed and trained blue-suited policeman is inadequate to confront the threat. Twenty-four of us attend a pre-Watts "Special Weapons School" on 7 January 1964[52] as part of this planning.

"We Have Met the Enemy, and He Is Us"[53]

Deputy Chief George N. Beck (father of the current LAPD chief) writes a SWAT article for the *FBI Bulletin*, which has nationwide (free)

---

[51] "Sgt. John Nelson, retired, an original member of the SWAT team, recounted how (Inspector) John Powers approached him after the 1965 riots and asked what the Department could do to improve their response to an emergency situation. Nelson was a sergeant assigned to the academy at that time and recalled his experience as a marine sniper in Korea. He wrote a 27-page report on his ideas and presented them to Commander Powers and SWAT was born." Meeting of 5 August 1998, quoted in: *L.A. Retired Fire and Police Association Newsletter*, Fall 1998, p. 11.

[52] Mimeographed Personnel and Training Bureau "Training Order" of 30 December 1964.

[53] "Pogo Possum" (Walt Kelly), Post-Hall Syndicate, 22 April 1971.

distribution.[54] His first sentence reads, "In early *1968* the Los Angeles Police Department formed a 60-man unit comprised of 15 four-man Special Weapons and Tactics (SWAT) teams." This misinformation triggers claims by other police agencies that they are first. I answer a NYPD "Emergency Services Unit" officer's mistaken claim made as late as June 2003 in the National Rifle Association's magazine.[55]

A writer asserts, "Although I didn't invent that (SWAT) concept I did coin the term some 20 years ago...."[56] "SWAT" is first used in late 1967. There is no officer by this name in the old SWAT rosters I have or in the Fire and Police Association membership rosters. The original SWAT title is "Special Weapons Marksmen and Tactical Teams."[57]

Rik A. Violano writes *SWAT Pioneers* (2006). Rik, unfortunately, neglects to consult with us original members. (He joins LAPD in 1965 following Watts and joins SWAT in '68.) Rik makes a number of serious errors, which I cover in a five-page letter to him. I also send him early photographs and directives for use in a revised edition. He tells me he relies largely upon the word of a lieutenant who also does not arrive in SWAT until late 1968.

Rik is not aware I write the first major work on SWAT[58] and that two copies are in the LAPD Library (then on the fifth floor of Parker Center).

---

[54] G.N. Beck, "SWAT—The Los Angeles Police Special Weapons and Tactics Teams," *FBI Law Enforcement Bulletin*, April 1972 (Vol. 41, No. 4), p. 8.

[55] Hurlbut, "The Debate Continues," *The American Rifleman*, August 2003 (Vol. 151, No. 8), p. 8.

[56] Gary Paul Johnston, "SWAT on Patrol," *American Rifleman* (Special Law Enforcement Issue), May 2001 (Vol. 149, No. 5), p. 50.

[57] See *SWMATT Bulletin* for "Rules" (July 1967) and Administrative Services Bureau Training Order of 1 August 1967, "SWMTT Program—Tactical Teams School." The Admin. Services Training Order of 29 February 1968 is the first titled, "SWAT Team Advanced Training School."

[58] Hurlbut, "The Special Weapons And Tactics (SWAT) Team Concept," Thesis for Master of Science degree, Department of Police Administration and Public Safety, Michigan State University, 1969, 220 pp. Announced in "L.A.P.D. in Print," *Police Administration in Review*, Municipal Reference Department, L.A. Public Library, December 1970 (Vol. 25, No 6).

Max K. Hurlbut

I am invited to teach SWAT tactics at the "Law Enforcement Program Enhancement Project" at McNeese State University, Lake Charles, Louisiana, in 1976. Colonel "Chargin' Charlie" Beckwith, CO of Operation Eagle Claw—the failed Iranian rescue mission—borrows me from the JFK Special Warfare Center to instruct on SWAT tactics and lessons learned to his new Delta Force at Fort Bragg. I also instruct the Royal Thai Border Patrol Police.

SWAT Origin

Nelson requests copies of the "Critique—Civil Disorder" reports completed by officers serving in the Watts Riot. He then invites some of us to an initial evening meeting at the academy to discuss organization and judge interest. Prior military experience is required. Considerable opposition exists on the command staff because of criticism over continuing unrest in the south end.

Operations

We organize into four-man teams in each patrol division and several detective units. As "station defense," we are more palatable and easier to justify. Team leaders are sergeants. I lead SWAT Team 8 out of Wilshire (LAPD Division 7). The team leader is also the "observer" who selects tactics and targets. My "marksman" is Angelo M. Scotillo; "scout" is Warren B. Carlson; and, shotgun man/"rear guard" is Benjamin J. Rendahl.

Nelson has me obtain maps of the storm drain system in the city. [They are not sewers, which require breathing apparatus to enter. Sewers lack oxygen, have an explosive atmosphere, and their manholes are often lined with cockroaches.] We discover some of the drains are wide enough to drive two large trucks through, side-by-side. Some drains run beneath police stations, as with Wilshire Division.

Once inside the storm drains, we find the rebar prevents compass readings and radio use. We discover someone before us codes the maze of tunnels with numbers and letters. We later confirm that black militant groups in the south end are using these tunnels as escape routes from their buildings when under siege.

SWAT Study

I fly back from Michigan State University to meet with Chief Thomas J. Reddin regarding my SWAT thesis. Black groups, including the National Association for the Advancement of Colored People (NAACP), learn of SWAT and assert we are "assassins targeting the black community."

I present Chief Reddin with a dilemma. I propose to do an analysis of authoritarianism in SWAT, which can come back to bite him. Are these the violent men of Hans Toch?[59] Are SWAT members, "Those who volunteer for elite killer units...and engage in assassinations or sabotage (and) prize assignments as snipers or scouts?"[60]

Are we heroes or psychopaths? Either way, I am obligated to publish my findings.

Reddin looks me in the eye and says, "Okay, Sergeant, let's do it! Tell me what you need." (Would recent LAPD chiefs risk this?)

I test all fifty SWAT members with a comparison of randomly selected non-SWAT officers (not a perfect control group, but the best available). I use a four-measure instrument of validated attitude scales, including the authoritarianism scales of Theodor W. Adorno, a German Jew who favors leftist authoritarians over those he considers anti-Semitic (i.e., Nazis). To temper this, I insert a dogmatism scale. (Dogmatism is positiveness of insufficiently examined ideas—an arrogant rejection of the ideas of others without considering the evidence.) I also introduce a conservatism scale and attach a statistical means to validate all. (I hope to weed out responses that are less than frank.)

I send out lengthy nine-page questionnaires to police departments in all 159 cities in the U.S. with over 100,000 population. I try to identify those with SWAT-type programs, their selection process, training, etc. I promise to share the results and place them in touch with others, if they

---

[59] Hans Toch, *Violent Men* (1969), pp. 135–136.
[60] John Hersey, *The War Lover* (1960); cited by Toch, *ibid.*, p. 213.

wish. This proves to be a big job, but I receive an excellent response of 43 percent. Chiefs in almost all cities have concerns they are attracting violent or dangerous personalities.

The Results

Test subjects are told they are taking an "opinion survey" to assist in the future recruitment of SWAT members. It is anonymous and has no affect on current members or team participation. There are no "right" or "wrong" answers and quick responses are encouraged. Examinations of groups are scheduled one after another so as to minimize the effects of history and maturation. (Some incident could affect attitudes.) The random selection process includes officers on all watches to preclude the possibility of different personalities seeking specific shifts. I administer exams in Parker Center and different divisional roll call rooms and detective offices.

Authoritarianism. SWAT members prove no more conservative or authoritarian than their patrol peers. They are slightly less dogmatic. SWAT members have more education. I conclude this makes them more receptive to the views of others (i.e., their instructors).

The SWAT guys are older (and should therefore be more authoritarian). Their younger peers—more of them currently in patrol—offset this by the nature of their jobs requiring displays of authority. The older officers have their military experiences in WWII and Korea; the newer ones more recently in Vietnam. This, too, offsets expected age and educational differences.

SWAT members do, in fact, volunteer for more hazardous military jobs. They show a preference for rough outdoor living. This appears a valid consideration in SWAT selection.

Chief Reddin is pleased with the results, which give him ammo before the mayor, Police Commission, and community groups. The "assassination of Negroes" charges are largely defused. I am sent to Panama by the Army, and, by the time I return to L.A., Reddin is a newscaster for KTLA and KMPC—an hour of arresting news.

Routine transfers and promotions of officers make it difficult to call out teams back to their old divisions in emergencies. A central command is needed and "D-Platoon" of Metropolitan Division provides it. Old SWAT and Metro SWAT coexist for several years. I eventually make lieutenant which automatically promotes me out.

We members of "Old SWAT" are recognized with plaques at the "First Annual SWAT Dinner" at the academy on 13 September 1976. Mine correctly notes my dates of SWAT assignment from September 1965 to September 1969. Thank you academy classmate, Ronald M. McCarthy, LAPD's "Mister SWAT."

The perfect SWAT operation is like a unicorn. Everyone knows what it looks like, but no one has ever seen it. A SWAT response to an active shooter is basic and quickly resolved in most cases. Old SWAT cannot call on hostage negotiators or crisis intervention officers, as they do not yet exist. Mental illness combined with substance abuse ("co-occurring disorder") is the cause of some deadly call-outs. In my day, the drug was often PCP (phencyclidine); now it is meth (methamphetamine).

Suspects can be crafty and dangerous, aside from the fact they may not be legally responsible for their acts. Less-than-lethal means of apprehending them are desirable, but often not possible. Traumatic brain injuries (TBI) found in some returning veterans of our Middle East wars are especially troubling. Their delusions and "command hallucinations" ("God orders me to kill") appear real to them.

Old SWAT has Harrington & Richardson .45-caliber Reising submachine guns, sporting rifles, and pump shotguns. We also have access to one member's semi-auto 20 mm Solothurn, a WWII Swiss antitank rifle carried in a wood suitcase. (It is purple-blue, with a silky action reminding one of a fine watch.) The Marine Corps trains us and provides access to M72 Light Antitank Weapons (LAW)—a one-shot 66 mm unguided rocket. It works well against armored doors, but its minimum arming range is ten meters. Do not stand behind one being fired!

A troubling aspect of modern SWAT is its military weaponization. The military cracks open the door and lobs in a grenade. Or bombs an entire apartment house to kill one sniper. Their mistakes are "classified" to thwart investigations and their victims labeled "collateral damage" or "terrorists."

If a civilian SWAT team goes berserk because of return fire and begins slaughtering non-combatants, there will be consequences.

Federal grants allow small departments of fewer than ten to acquire armored vehicles and heavy weaponry. Weaponization is taking place in unmanned drones now finding their way into civilian police agencies. Montgomery County, Texas, obtains the first police drone for $300,000. They quickly crash it into their SWAT "Bear Cat" armored vehicle.

Single-Officer Entry

The tactical first-responder is taught to await backup or call for SWAT rather than risk his safety in an active-shooter situation. This can take considerable time, while the toll of casualties escalates. Getting there sooner with less is sometimes required.

Killers are often well-armed but are not usually formidable opponents. They strike stunned and defenseless victims, usually by surprise. Many commit suicide or fold quickly when confronted.[61] They often do not take hostages and will not negotiate. Speed, surprise, and violent action will usually prevail. Not all gunshot wounds are fatal and an officer's mind-set should prepare him for this eventuality without deterring his aggressiveness.

---

[61] "Ohio Trainer Makes the Case for Single-Officer Entry" (Ronald Borsch, South East Area Law Enforcement Academy, Bedford, OH), *Force Science News*, No. 97, 9 May 2008.

Chapter XIII

THE EXPERIMENTAL DIVISION

Captain Stewart A. "Pete" Nelson asks me to be his adjutant and personnel investigator at Wilshire Division, 4526 West Pico Boulevard. Wilshire is designated the "Experimental Division." As early as 1966, I am loaned to assist with field exercises for Patrol Bureau Order 42, "Tactics To Be Employed in Unusual Occurrences."

We field-test things, such as nonlethal weapons and the new "pepper spray." (It is not effective on everyone, especially heavy drinkers and animals without tear ducts.) Our largest project is to develop an "unusual occurrence" procedure to handle command post deployment during major incidents such as fires, floods, earthquakes, and riots.

When some major incident develops, units respond. They become involved and go off the air. Manpower disappears into this maw with no one knowing what is happening or how many officers are involved.

Officers Elmer A. "J. R." Schiller and Jimmy J. Thompson and I plan and conduct exercises to test ideas and procedures. We write LAPD's first *Unusual Occurrence Manual* in 1967.

The first two officers arriving must remain on the air and locate a command post and staging area—an unpopular task as officers want in on the action. The senior officer becomes the field commander (until relieved by someone of greater rank able to assume command). His partner is the communications-journal officer who operates the radio and starts a log.

A staging officer is required where new arrivals can receive orders and equipment and form into teams. Eventually, there must be a personnel, logistics, and intelligence officer. An operations officer and his staff must present completed staff work—a plan of action the commander can accept or reject. Traffic control is important, or no one can respond. A flood of incoming messages can quickly clog the system. Delegation is important as some supervisors try to do everything themselves.

The best of plans go amiss on first contact. An emergency—like a gunman shooting people, a train or airplane crash, building explosion, a riot or demonstration, etc.—requires immediate attention. It can quickly escalate into a situation involving hundreds from different agencies. Strong supervision and trained personnel are essential.

We equip a "station wagon command post" with forms and radios. This expands into a larger "mobile command post." A temporary "field command post division" is eventually implemented and staffed by a "field command post cadre" that regularly trains. I remain a part of this cadre until I retire almost twenty years later—as do a number of other officers.

The Field Command Post in Action

We train (and are instructors) at the California Specialized Training Institute at Camp San Luis Obispo and with other police departments. Our "Recommendations Based on an Analysis of Command Post Exercise, 'Operation Tremor'" (20 April 1967) is widely distributed. I am the field commander/controller at various incidents and executive officer in citywide exercise, "Shaker III," as late as 11 June 1982.

I report to Colonel Douglas M. Craver at the United States Military Academy at West Point regarding field operations. I am in charge of Security for the command post on the fund-raising visit of President Lyndon B. Johnson to the Century Plaza Hotel on 23 June 1967. This one does not go according to plan.

Century City is to be LBJ's last public appearance. An unexpected crowd of ten thousand[62] gathers. The ones in the front are pushed by agitators to the rear into our lines at the front of the hotel. What is not generally known is that the Secret Service has an informant stating they will storm the hotel and "arrest" and assassinate the President. Machine guns are set up around the meeting room in preparation for stacking-up bodies should they reach this area.

Our dispersal order is ignored and fifty-one demonstrators are "thumped" and jailed by the LAPD "Thin Blue Line." None reach the hotel lobby.

---

[62] Kenneth Reich, "The Bloody March That Shook L.A.," *Los Angeles Times*, 23 June 1997, and "10,000 in Melee," front page of *L.A. Times*, "Final Edition," 24 June 1967.

Personnel Investigations

The duties of adjutant are varied. As team leader of the Divisional SWAT Team, I write the station defense plan. We use aerial photos taken at the Officer Keith G. Dupuis shooting at West Pico and San Vicente Boulevard of 16 October 1966 by two robbery suspects.

Keith, a friend, is in the 1960 class following mine. He and his partner stop two motorists because their otherwise clean car has a dirty Ohio plate. The driver jumps out and holds Keith's partner at gunpoint. Keith draws his revolver. The suspect whirls and fires his .32-caliber, striking Keith in the mouth. Keith returns fire, wounding the shooter in the arm and back. Keith dies several days later. (*L.A. Herald-Examiner* of 17 and 27 October 1966.) This is yet another incident similar to the Ian Campbell shooting.

A civilian orderly at Wilshire is stopped by a traffic officer and runs berserk. He is fired for threatening to kill officers. A theft suspect complains that two officers arrest him for stealing a hamburger and fries. Not wishing to bother with freezing or photographing the evidence, the officers eat it in front of their arrestee. Four days off without pay—an expensive burger!

I find that the Personnel Investigator portion of my job is not a popularity contest....

Chapter XIV

THE SOUTH END

I work Newton and Seventy-Seventh Street divisions in Accident Investigation and later Seventy-Seventh Detectives. Social conflict is beyond our duties and control, other than the enforcement of criminal activity. LAPD is not white, red, black, brown, or yellow; it is blue. An old but valid saying.

University Division

The old University Station (1909) at 809 West Jefferson Boulevard is my first "south end" assignment in 1961. It is surrounded by the University of Southern California. The cramped locker area downstairs in the boiler room is hot even in winter. The place still has the scent, especially in summer, of the horses they stable here at the east end.

The division moves to 1546 West Santa Barbara Avenue in 1962 and the old station is sold to USC. Santa Barbara is renamed for Martin Luther King and "University" changes to the "Southwest Community Police Station" in the pablum of a "kinder and gentler" LAPD.

Mayor Tom Bradley is fond of saying, "You could not work (as a black officer on LAPD) with a white officer, and that continued until 1964."[63] This is probably a surprise to black partners of mine in 1961 and 1962— Charlie A. Battles, Robert H. Hannibal, George Raines, and Lee O. Triggs. (Hannibal introduces me to Archie Moore, light heavyweight boxing champion and part-time actor—a personable fellow.)

A large percentage of the black community supports police officers. These folks are victimized by the criminal elements amongst them. Blacks vote for police pay raises and benefits; the Valley and West Side rarely do.

---

[63] Thomas J. Bradley (1917–1998) quoted in Albert Greenstein biography, Historical Society of Southern California, 1999, and Jean Merl and Bill Boyarsky, "Mayor Who Reshaped L.A. Dies," *Los Angeles Times*, 30 September 1998.

The latter pressure Chief Parker to deploy officers heavily in their areas as they pay the most taxes. The chief responds that he deploys us to where the crime problem is greatest.

Black leaders insist that black officers work only with fellow black officers and in black areas only. These so-called leaders then complain black policemen are tougher on their own people than are white officers. "The proposal to use only Negro officers ran counter to the policy of the Police Department, adopted over a period of time at the urging of Negro leaders, to deploy Negro officers throughout the city and not concentrate them in the Negro Area." [64]

Patrol officers are loaned on stakeouts and undercover vice operations. We are paid ten cents a mile for the use of our personal vehicles. We arrest 229 prostitutes around Western Avenue between 20 and 30 December 1961.

South End School Dropouts

Blacks and Hispanics commit a disproportionate amount of violent crime. Crime is too complicated to be reduced to mere race, but it cannot be ignored. The subject is beyond the scope of this discussion, but it is documented and undeniable. ["Blacks (in 2009) committed 80 percent of shootings and 66 percent of all violent crime in NY....Non-Hispanic whites committed five percent of violent crimes and 1.4 percent of all shootings...." (Heather MacDonald, 'New York Times,' 25 June 2010)].

Many south-end problems originate with school dropouts unqualified for jobs, except for dope-dealing and other crime. They join gangs, which considerably reduces their life expectancy. Our unphonetic spelling system erects barriers to those who fail to master it. Most employers believe poor grammar and spelling reflect stupidity.

The school system is unable to keep track of truants. Kids correctly understand they can "disappear" without consequences. Missing a week or two of classes puts them hopelessly behind, so they never return. A young black excluded from school complains it is not because he is lazy, disruptive,

---

[64] Ibid. (and) "McCone Commission Report," p. 14.

or stupid, but it's because the educational system is against him and fails to compensate for his "disadvantaged" existence.

The dropout does not watch the news. He cannot locate England, Africa, or even the U.S. on a map. He cannot identify the century of our Civil War, but knows blacks are kidnapped and enslaved by whites.

He blames whites for his inadequacies. He speaks a language distant from standard speech and wonders why he cannot find a job. There is little demand in the job market for the illiterate with a bad attitude who is barely house-trained. An overdeveloped sense of grievance and entitlement compound the problem.

The dropout riots and loots when he thinks he can get away with it. No shopping centers are looted and loose valuables are turned in to the police when a tsunami devastates Japan on 11 March 2011. The difference appears to be that we have a large "diverse" population that no longer shares the values of our society.

Intellectuals and academics who have little understanding of this underclass believe welfare and self-esteem will bring prosperity and remedy the problem. This is what a half century of state handouts has achieved. It is a sociological problem. All the police can do is attempt to enforce the laws fairly and equally.

Off-Duty University Duties

Students at USC streak naked and play practical jokes. The Coliseum and Sports Arena hire us as security when the Globe Trotters play or during prize fights. (The rate of pay is $4.60 an hour.) Ringling Brothers and Barnum & Bailey have a combined circus. Willet C. Morrell and I escort the elephants up Flower and down Figueroa streets to the delight of all.

Seventy-Seventh Street Detectives

Lieutenant Thomas P. McTighe welcomes me to Seventy-Seventh Street Detectives. I am honored to work for legendary detective Archie E. Gorgon at his burglary table. Arch is a prince of a man. (We have no desks; everyone has a spot on a long table piled high with reports.) I handle Watts burglaries, both residential and commercial—alone. My unit designation is "12W83." [The "W" does not designate Watts.[65] It is the LAPD service identification letter for "divisional detectives"].

Watts burglaries proves to be the most frustrating assignment of my career. I return from a weekend off to find five-to-ten adult felons in jail awaiting arraignment downtown with a forty-eight-hour limit. As many juveniles may be detained—all requiring petitions. My in-box has a dozen 459 reports with named suspects or ones easy to develop. My message spike is an inch or more thick with telephone calls to be returned.

Our work-week is five twelve-hour days. Our compensatory overtime piles up until the department slashes it back to the ten-day maximum. Some lose close to a hundred days; I lose over forty. Today's LAPD "donning and doffing" Federal lawsuit is won—requiring taxpayers to shell out for the few minutes it takes today's Affirmative Action Warriors to put on their uniforms. (Are civilians paid to "don and doff" their suits for work?)

I wander the "Projects" [Nickerson Gardens (the largest public housing development west of the Mississippi), Imperial Courts, and Jordan Downs—all run by the L.A. Housing Authority] alone and without problems. They are microcosms of the ills of society and dependency of individuals upon the welfare state. When I make an arrest, I call one or two black-and-whites for uniform presence and backup.

Commercial burglary losses are usually the greatest and the owners possess political clout the individual lacks. Translation: the poor folks who lose their television set or only suit of clothes go to the back of the long investigative line. Older residents never leave their homes without a few dollars in their pockets. Local punks terrorize neighborhoods and demand money. A beating results If they do not have a few dollars. Report it and much worse can be expected. A sad situation.

I make presentations at the Grape Street School and others, but there appears to be a "conspiracy of silence" or fear that prevents truly open discussion. The gangs remain long after we go home.

---

[65] "Mud Town" is renamed Watts in 1900 for Pasadena Real Estate developer C.H. Watts.

I work with forty-year Second District County supervisor Kenneth Hahn and his staff while assigned to the Police Commission. His senior deputy, Marcine B. Shaw, invites me and my bride to a combination revival/community meeting in Compton. Hueih-Hueih is Chinese and a little apprehensive—we are among only half-a-dozen non-black attendees. Marcine seats us on the stage and graciously introduces us. The music is lively and spiritual, with considerable audience participation.

Actor and comedian Mario Van Peebles stands to explain that centuries before, all people originate in Africa and are black. Someone discovers a pool of water that causes bathers to bleach white. By the time his ancestor arrives, all the water is gone except for a damp spot sufficient only to wet his palms. Peebles holds up his hands to show this part of him is white. HH laughs and has a good time.

Marcine is elected to the Compton City Council. She dies in January 2006 following decades of community service with gangs. She is not a physically attractive woman, but personable, honest, dyamic, sweet, and loyal. Being at opposite ends of the political spectrum never affects our friendship. No one can ask for a better friend. Farewell, Dear Marcine....

Michigan State

I arrive at Seventy-Seventh Street following a morning of court appearances. In the rotator folder is a sheet from the Office of Law Enforcement Assistance offering fellowships in a master's program of police administration and science to three universities: John Jay in New York City (Law), the University of California at Berkeley (Criminology), and Michigan State University (Police Administration/Criminal Justice). Two candidates will be selected from LAPD. The deadline for applying is the following day.

I type my application and fire it off. Lieutenants and above in "important" administrative assignments in Parker Center, I am told, will be selected. A sergeant in Seventy-Seventh Street Detectives is an unlikely candidate.

Several weeks pass and the chief's office phones Lieutenant McTighe. Lieutenant Carl J. Calkins (chief's office) and I receive fellowships.[66] Carl is selected for Berkeley and I for Michigan State University.

Michigan State in East Lansing is the first degree-granting police school. It is a tough year of study made more difficult by army deployments to the Northern Warfare School at Fort Greely, Alaska, and the Jungle Operations School at Fort Sherman, Canal Zone (Panama), in preparation for Vietnam. Antiwar demonstrators on campus try to disrupt the university's program to aid South Vietnam's police system. Life is otherwise good—Grandmother's Pub has all-you-can-eat "Hot Dog Nite" on Tuesdays for 25 cents.

A New York PD captain, William P. Kelly of the Fifth Division, is an OLEA fellow. Ceylon Police Senior Deputy Inspector General Edward S. Gunawardena joins us. James Conlisk, a student, invites us to his home in Chicago on weekends. His father, of the same name, is the superintendent of police for Mayor Richard J. Daley, the "Last of the Big-City Bosses." We receive an education far beyond the academic.

IBM 360. My thesis, the first SWAT study, is mentioned in Chapter XII, "Old SWAT." My analysis of authoritarianism, conservatism, and dogmatism scales is performed on the school's IBM 360 mainframe computer, one of the most successful of all computers. Most 360s are eventually scrapped for the gold and other precious metals in their circuits. They are simply too huge to store and maintain.

A brief description of the 360 may be of interest as you peck away on your latest laptop. The 360 uses punch-card program decks. The cards come in trays holding about 2,000 3×8×15-inch cards—the limit to a program size. Refrigerator-sized magnetic tape drives set next to the computer. The room is incredibly noisy and everything shuts down if the temperature climbs above 80 degrees F.

You keep track of your cards by drawing a diagonal line across the top edges of the stacked cards using a black felt-tip pen. Out-of-sequence

---

[66] Marjorie Harned to Chief Thomas Reddin, Police Commission letter of authorization, 1 August 1968. "Graduate Fellowships Won by Police Officers," *Van Nuys News and Valley Green Sheet*, 28 June 1968.

cards can be spotted by noting the position of the black mark at the top of the card. Every punch produces a "chad," a tiny rectangle of cardboard, which goes into a "bit bucket" to be discarded. (Yes, "hanging chads" are a problem.)

A "selectric" typewriter (with its golf ball-like type element) controls a keypunch machine which produces a stack of fan-folded computer printout paper. Misplace a single period and you get an error message requiring a card to be re-punched.

There is no television-like display terminal and no typing of instructions. (These are to change the world of we Luddites.) The punch cards are soon replaced with magnetic tape, magnetic disk cartridges, huge floppy disks, and the present versions. It is a brief transition period that is to alter the world.

Hoodie Terror

The south end is a busy place. "Shootin' Newton," University, and Seventy-Seventh Street lead the city in violent crimes and officer-involved shootings. These are primarily black in my day, but a trickle of Central American and Asian war refugees becomes an invasion and then an occupation.

Lawns become dirt auto junkyards and some areas look like Tijuana shanty towns complete with greasy yellow taco wrappers littering the streets. Multiple families occupy single rooms. Surly and aggressive residents resent law enforcement and control their neighborhoods through intimidation—an unhappy place for the law-abiding and police officers. One officer calls it, "The world's largest open-air asylum."[67]

The late Commander John W. "Two Gun" Powers writes me (20 August 1999) that when he came on the job in 1940, "There were no black gangs. They started when narcotics became plentiful and their turf was where they sold drugs and they killed to protect their market place."

---

[67] William C. Dunn, *Boot* (1996), p. 235.

NOTE: I retire Powers in 1971 and we correspond until his death on 15 November 2002. I proofread his memoirs, written in the language a field policeman understands: "Never surrender and take a hit if necessary—all wounds are not fatal." John earns his nickname upon being shot by a fifteen-year-old robber in 1941. He kills the shooter with his second revolver.

A month in the south-end is the equivalent of twenty years almost anywhere else. Most U.S. police officers never fire their weapons anywhere but the range, but it is unusual for a veteran LAPD officer not to be involved in shooting incidents. [Policeman Gary W. Murakami is shot to death in University Division on just his second day out of the academy (9 October 1968).]

Chapter XV

THE POLICE COMMISSION

The Police Commission is the civilian head of LAPD. It has city charter authority for the control, regulation, and management of the department. The chief of police is the general manager.

I am the Enforcement/Investigations Section leader of Commission Investigation Division for a dozen years. "CID regulates sixty-two businesses traditionally associated with organized crime: massage parlors, dance halls, tow services, arcades, etc."[68] We also conduct "special investigations" at the direction of the Board.

The *Commemorative Book* notes, "The Enforcement Section works closely with Vice, Operations, and Intelligence. Accomplishments include enforcement actions that eliminated 300 Oriental massage parlors from the City. This broke the back of an organized crime takeover of independent massage-prostitution operations. Millions of dollars from these functions were funneled into narcotics before being laundered and used for the attempted corruption of public officials. A seven-year legal and enforcement battle was won against dirty-picture arcade operations of an eastern city-based crime group."[69]

Prostitutes, driven from the massage parlors (by denial of permits for prior arrests), end up working the streets where they are more visible.

"Here Come de Judge"[70]

The mayor appoints the five-member Board of Police Commissioners to serve two five-year terms. They set department policy and meet every

---

[68] "Commission Investigation Division," *Los Angeles Police Department Commemorative Book: 1869–1984*, L.A. Police Revolver and Athletic Club, 1984, p. 261.

[69] Ibid.

[70] Clerow "Flip" Wilson's comedy sketch introduction on *Rowan and Martin's Laugh-In* (1968–1973) of an unfortunate defendant dragged before the court.

Tuesday. "Diversity" is the goal of Mayor Tom Bradley who selects commissioners who will act out his social and political fantasies.

Bradley favors "civil rights" activists as Stephen R. Reinhardt (birth name Shapiro) who is destined to become the most-reversed judge on the Ninth Circuit Court of Appeals. His ideas on "social justice" can best be described as radical. His open disrespect for his staff and for the chief of police do not endear him to many of us.

Reinhardt and his wife, Ramona Ripston (executive director of the American Civil Liberties Union), sue and disband the Public Disorder Intelligence Division, which is successful in infiltrating terrorist groups bombing and assassinating police officers. [Ironically, it is PDID's intelligence-gathering data that clears Reinhardt's name during his Ninth Circuit confirmation hearings when it shows he never actually commits a crime].[71]

Reinhardt enacts lower police standards in hiring women and minorities. He demands the active recruitment of homosexuals and collection of data on the ethnicity of every person contacted by police officers (a paper nightmare intended to reduce proactive policing). I remember him as dynamic, but cold, devious, and political.

<u>Education of the Commissioners</u>. We on the staff encourage ride-alongs and give personal explanations as to why policemen do some of the things we do. Many of the commissioners under Bradley are flaming liberals not open to viewpoints other than their own. An exception is Salvador "Sal" Montenegro, the board's token Mexican. Sal, a commissioner for seven years, begins police ride-alongs and is genuinely concerned about police-citizen contacts.

Sal soon begins speaking up in Police Commission meetings to inform his peers of what they do not see—as they never take to the field. This advice is not well received. Sal is forced to resign after he is ridiculed by other members and rebuked by Bradley over support for officers in the Eula Mae Love shooting in 1979 of an aggressive, heavy black woman with a long knife.

---

[71] Candi Cushman and Stephen Adams, "Judge Gone Wild," *Citizen Magazine*, February 2006.

The commissioners forever speculate as to why officers do not shoot the guns out of the hands of criminals or disarm machete-wielding gang members with judo tricks. They fail to realize there is no "nice" way to arrest a dangerous and combative suspect. Police work can be violent and unpleasant to view…and many now possess cameras. Officers become more concerned about getting burned and labeled as a rogue than being proactive and confronting suspects.

A community that fails to support its police in reasonable and proper enforcement efforts soon demoralizes its force. Officers respond by ceasing proactive enforcement. Doing nothing or devoting inordinate attention to minor incidents and thus being unavailable to handle more serious matters has few consequences. The pay remains the same.

The Bird Watchers

Chief Justice Rose E. Bird (1977–1986) becomes the first woman on the California Supreme Court despite having no prior judicial experience. (No problem, she's a staunch feminist.) She vacates all sixty-one capital cases to come before her. She invents an "intent to kill" requirement in felony murder cases in her search for reversible error where none exists. (Juries are never instructed on this "requirement" as it does not exist in statute.)

Bird argues, with a straight face, that a Brink's guard is shot five times in the chest at close range not to *kill* him but to cause him to *drop a money bag!*[72] A "Bird Watcher's Society" leads to her removal by the voters—not because she is a woman, but, as with many liberals, her social vision excludes the victims of heinous crimes.

The Mole Surfaces

Antipathy exists between the Commission Services Coordinator, a police commander, and Chief Daryl Gates.[73] The Commander is close, however, to

---

[72] *People v. Fuentes* (1985), 40 Cal. 3d 269.

[73] "(Jack B.) White was perceived by many in the department as being outside the mainstream of the top management surrounding Gates," Andy Furillo, "Deputy Chief Is Named Police Commission Aide," *Los Angeles Times*, 2 March 1985 (and) "White was

the mayor and to Reinhardt. I become aware, upon occasion, of a trap being set for the chief at a Tuesday meeting. I call an aide or ride the elevator with Gates so he knows what to anticipate. I am suspected of being "The Mole," but survive the scrutiny.

Politics Prevails

Voters approve a ballot initiative in 1992 altering the city charter and stripping the chief of civil service protections. Gates becomes the last chief to be insulated from political influence.

Politicizing the delivery of police services gives equity and justice a backseat to political infighting. The chief no longer serves the citizens but the mayor. Los Angeles now slides towards the corruption and politics of the pre-Parker era.

The Alphabet Bomber

Cell Block 8, Cell 115, Pelican Bay—A tall, blond, blue-eyed prisoner whiles away his time mailing death threats. Muharem Kurbegovich, Yugoslav engineer, is a most undesirable immigrant. He acquires, in the summer of 1974, the components needed for sarin nerve agent and stores twenty-five pounds of potassium cyanide and nitric acid to kill the president.[74]

An anarchist calling himself "Isak Rasim" sets off a bomb at LAX ("A," as in Airport) which kills four and injures thirty-five. A second bomb ("L," as in Locker on Los Angeles Street) fails to explode. The bombs spell out the name of Rasim's organization—Aliens of America.

Rasim taunts that bomb "I" is set to explode in a crowded area in seventeen hours. I quickly assemble a task force to examine thousands of records over five years of Police Commission minutes, as Rasim comments on a plan to firebomb and assassinate two former Police Commissioners.

---

perceived as...antagonistic toward the Chief's office." David Freed, "'Team Player' Appointed Police Department Liaison," *L.A. Times*, 18 July 1985.

[74] Nicholas E. Ashton, "LAX and the Alphabet Bomber," Security Bulletin No. 65, 14 July 2002.

(He is a lonely man who favors taxi dancers and appears to have been denied a permit for a business.) We identify several suspects with grievances. In coordination with the Criminal Conspiracy Section of Investigative Support Division, the suspects are placed under surveillance.

Kurbegovich is arrested after planting another tape in a Carl's Jr. restaurant. He is convicted of twenty-five felonies, including burning the homes of Police Commission board members Marguerite "Mama J." Justice and Emmet C. McGaughey in 1973.[75]

Discipline

LAPD is a harsh disciplinarian even for off-duty incidents. A Department of Water and Power worker, drunk on duty, electrocutes a coworker. He receives a ten-day suspension. An LAPD officer drives through a red light so as to get to roll call on time. He is fired.[76]

The commission has the authority to decide whether an officer's use of deadly force is justified, but disciplining officers resides with the chief through a Board of Rights. The chief and the commission sometimes disagree.

Chief Charlie Beck is castigated for not disciplining a detective who blasts some bandits in a car: "The detective repeatedly fired a shotgun into cars carrying armed-robbery suspects." The commission finds the officer is justified in firing the first few volleys, but that subsequent rounds are excessive because the officers are no longer under threat.[77]

The Pumpkin Field

The board appears amused at some of the difficulties in which officers find themselves. One in particular comes to mind.

---

[75] Police Commission president Samuel L. Williams to Lieutenant II Max K. Hurlbut. "Commendation on Search for the 'Alphabet Bomber'," 22 August 1974.

[76] Joel Rubin, "Rift Appears Between Beck and Police Commission Over Discipline," *Los Angeles Times*, 15 April 2012.

[77] Gary Fullerton, "United We Stand," *Thin Blue Line*, February 1995 (Vol. 50, No. 2), p. 4.

Vagabond Policeman

Two detectives work late and decide to stop in a bar before heading home out of the north Valley. It's close to Halloween, so the passenger asks his partner to pull over in a pumpkin field to select one for his kid. Their unmarked police car becomes stuck. The driver decides to hitchhike home and return with his pickup to pull the car out. They have a radio, but realize they will have some explaining to do if they call for tow service outside of the city.

The intoxicated driver is chagrined that the occasional auto does not stop. He flags down a motorcyclist and commandeers a ride home, at gunpoint, on the back of the bike. The passenger, meanwhile, becomes bored. Visibility is good with a full moon so he shoots a few pumpkins with his pistol. After reloading, he lies down between rows to await his partner. He is soon asleep.

The farmer hears shots fired and believes local kids are again raiding his pumpkin crop. He heads out and finds the unattended vehicle. It has a radio and antenna—clearly a police vehicle—and the engine is warm. Spotting empty cartridge cases, he is alarmed this may be another "Onion Field" incident. He runs home to call the police.

The wife of the driver is worried. His office says he left for home hours ago. She hears a noise in the driveway and looks out to see a motorcycle leaving. Their pickup, pushed out into the street, starts up and drives off. (Her husband does not want to awaken her.) She calls the police to report their vehicle has just been stolen.

LAPD quickly determines the plate number supplied by the farmer is theirs. The on-duty commander and a force of officers are dispatched. The commotion of their arrival awakens the sleeping passenger. The detective in his pickup also arrives at this time. The two decide to quietly retire….

Skeleton in the Wall

A downtown skid road hotel is torn down. Inside the wall of a room is the skeleton of a man apparently stabbed to death. An old newspaper found with the bones provides a possible date of over seventy years before. The hotel register still exists and shows two male occupants. One name matches the ID found on the dead man.

Detectives run the name of the roommate as a matter of routine. The over-ninety suspect is not only alive but in jail just two floors below in Parker Center. He confesses that he kills his roommate following a drunken argument. He seals his victim into the wall with plaster from a nearby hallway under repair. Other than numerous drunk arrests, he is not known to commit other criminal acts. A judge convicts and releases him.

The Badge

Chief Edward M. "Crazy Ed" Davis is my annual guest at the Beverly Hills Hilton.[78] I am president of the Southern California Safari Club. Our annual banquet and awards dinner features an "ice mountain" replenished with lobster, crab, oysters, and other seafood. Ed's enemy, Otis Chandler of the *L.A. Times*, also enjoys the table. Ed delights in hanging around chatting with his friends as he knows his presence keeps Otis away.

Chief Davis presents me with Lieutenant's Badge No. 1 in 1969. He later observes Beverly Hills PD is wearing a new badge almost like ours. Our 1940 Series-6 badge enters the public domain as the city attorney fails to renew our twenty-eight year copyright. The oval badge is the pride of LAPD as it presents a new image following scandals of the 1930s.

I become the LAPD retirement counselor for a short time in the early 1970s. Retiring officers are presented with a Series-5 "Flying Eagle" badge. (About 7,000 are sold/presented to civilians in the 1930s.)[79] Retirees now receive a small pot metal badge with a money clip on the reverse. It resembles a "Cracker Jack" prize.

---

[78] Chief Edward M. Davis to Mayor Tom Bradley, "Safari Club," official activities, "Police Department Report No. 309 for the period ending July 3, 1975." 3 July 1975. Item 2 on page 1 discusses Hurlbut's installation as president and Davis's presence at the banquet of 21 June.

[79] Letter of 8 July 1940, signed by Chief Arthur C. Hohmann, asking citizens to return these badges. (Collection of the author). Enough are recovered to supply retirees for the next thirty years.

I write the first memo requesting that retirees receive a flat full-size badge. One chief[80] (who comes up through LAPD ranks) says, "I have 9,000 cops abusing the badge—why should I add retirees to this?"

"Personnel—That's for Assholes."[81] Personnel and Training Bureau Memo of 18 October 1984 ("Retention of the Police Officer's Badge") finally authorizes retirees to keep their badges and "badge numbers shall not be reissued." Your actual badge is imbedded in bronze (later Lucite). A Protective League "Memorandum of Understanding" of 2006 with the department also allows sworn officers to buy their own flat badges.

The Personnel Division retirement counselor says retirees can order their flat badges after sworn active officers. A year passes and they "discover" that 52.27.1(b)(1) L.A. Municipal Code is amended to exclude retirees before 1993. (It says no such thing; only that retiree badges shall have a banner saying "RETIRED" so as to distinguish them from active badges following this date). We point out that this is a moot point, as 538(d)(1) of the California Penal Code authorizes a chief to issue retiree badges to all honorably retired officers. (The Penal Code trumps the Municipal Code.) This is a policy, not a legal issue. The chief can simply order it so. Personnel feels they are too "overworked" to take on additional duties, and those above cannot be bothered with it.

The years pass and excuses are given as "the amendment to the LAMC section is before the City Council" (it is not), and "the City Attorney says it is a liability issue if retirees have badges." (Then why are current retirees still allowed to purchase them?) Plenty of laws exist to cover misuse of the badge.

I write and call the Police Commission, the chief's office, the City Council Public Safety Committee, the Police Protective League, the Retired Fire and Police Association, and the city attorney. All agree it is an unfair situation that creates two classes of retirees and animosity between them.

---

[80] Hurlbut, "Your badge: A History of Conflict," *Thin Blue Line*, May 2011 (Vol. 66, No. 5), p. 28.

[81] "Dirty Harry" Callahan (Clint Eastwood) when advised of his pending transfer from Homicide. *The Enforcer* (1976).

The issue continues to languish. One retirement counselor tells me, "Time will resolve the problem." (It does for several generations of older retirees). Chief William J. Bratton sends a proposal to the Police Commission authorizing the retiree badges, which is approved by the board. It is allowed to lapse by the city attorney. New chief Charlie Beck says he will rescue it "soon," but does not.

Carmen Trutanich becomes the city attorney and his new managing assistant, Carlos de la Guerra, realizes the "liability issues" are bogus and a class action suit against the city cannot be defended. He presents an amendment to the LAMC before the city council. It quickly and unanimously passes.

Twenty-six years and four months after retiring, I receive my flat Lieutenant's Badge No. 1. Just over 200 of us survive to obtain the symbol of our long years of faithful and dedicated service. The Retirement Counselor's Section contracts the work out to the Police Revolver Club at the academy—with funding they have had all along!

The belated recognition[82] is fine, but why must so many retirees pass on with the sad realization that the "I-got-mine" generation—whom they trained—does not give a fig for their welfare, concerns, or traditions?

This is a small issue, but of importance to older retirees. Such an injustice would never occur in an earlier LAPD. Too many of today's officers—the Affirmative Action Wonders—look upon police work as a job and not a calling. Their concerns center around their pay and benefits.

The camaraderie of earlier generations no longer exists. The AAWs apparently do not realize that—if they are fortunate—they will spend more years in retirement than in harness. How will those who follow respond to *their* retirement concerns?

---

[82] George V. Aliano, "Pension Commission News," (and) Joe Sandoval, "Sacramento Area Blue Line Association," *Thin Blue Line*, August 2011 (Vol. 66, No. 8), pp. 56 and 57.

Chief R. Lee Heath

Sergeant Arthur W. Sjoquist and I discover Chief of Police R. Lee Heath (1924–1926), in his nineties, living on "The Rock" in Pacoima. We present him with a Series-6 Chief's badge on 16 June 1972.

Rookie Makes Chief on His First Day. Heath joins LAPD in 1904. He retains a phenomenal memory into old age and recalls dates, times, and names of incidents from the turn of the century. Heath tells us of his first night on the job:

Beat Patrolman Heath hears screams from a cheap hotel in Downtown L.A. He finds a prominent local political figure severely beating a prostitute. He spends most of the night transporting the lady to a hospital and "cleaning up the problem." He neglects to make his call-box ring-ins and the entire department is out searching for him.

Despite the passage of seventy years, Heath will not reveal the name of this individual. Mayor George E. Cryer instructs the chief to promote another officer (who has already paid-off the mayor) to sergeant, but Heath's supporter stands behind him to ensure it is Heath who is elevated. Heath makes captain and then chief.

I am reading John Buntin's *L.A. Noir* (2009) when an entry on page 26 resolves the conundrum: "Captain Heath acted as (Kent Kane) Parrot's proxy, transferring personnel without the chief's permission and shaking down tour operators to raise funds for the Parrot-Cryer machine....So Chief (Louis D.) Oaks decided to dismiss Captain Heath. Parrot responded by having Oaks fired instead. He then made Heath chief."

Orders from the Chief. Mary McQuown (sister of Deputy Chief Noel A. McQuown) is in charge of Personnel Records for many years. There are no packages on any officers before the 1950s. She explains that Personnel, then in city hall, is running out of storage space. Chief Parker instructs one of his sergeants to go through the packages to weed out extraneous paperwork. The only thing this sergeant believes is important are home addresses for mailing out retirement checks. Parker wasn't a perfect administrator... especially in the area of command guidance.

Motorcycle Drill Team

The late lieutenant John D. Bradley, Wilshire Division, mails me a postcard from Big Pine on 20 July 1971: "Stay away from those motorcycles—they have made more one-legged men than the Civil War. When you climb on a cycle you are just a high-speed pedestrian."

I am elected Commander of American Legion Police Post 381 for 1982–1983. As my commander's project, I propose to resurrect the disbanded Los Angeles Police Motorcycle Drill Team. Austerity budgets dissolve the Drill Team in the previous decade.

The Motorcycle Drill Team descends from two machines purchased in 1905. World War I veterans of Police Post 381 take charge of the squad in 1931. They open the Golden Gate Bridge on 27 May 1937 and are escorts for the 1932 Summer Olympics.

Chief Daryl F. Gates presents a letter to the Police Commission on 4 April 1983 (G. F. #83-094) proposing, "The reestablishment of the Department's Police Motorcycle Drill Team," as I outline. It will consist of twenty-one motor officers, one riding lieutenant, and two volunteer equipment mechanics.

Motor School. The board approves and I am off to the Motorcycle Riding School at Reeves Field in Harbor Division. I flunk out as I am unable to master slow riding despite eight years of riding the streets of L.A. on Triumph and Honda bikes. (I have picked up some bad habits.)

Two members of the Drill Team (one of them the master mechanic) make me practice, practice, practice. One day, I mount the old horse and the brake, clutch, and throttle merge. I can stop, lock the handle bars right and left, and inch through a complex cone pattern. I am reassigned to the next class in the new Griffith Park School and pass.

Team Captain. We practice in the Dodger Stadium parking lot and other places. Team sergeant Herbert C. "Pinky" Meredith is on the old team and knows the drills. Our drill master, George J. Hoffstetter, soon has us "splitting the rail" and other drills.

We perform in community parades: Hollywood Christmas Parade, Chinese New Year, Easter, Fourth of July, Cinco de Mayo, Nisei, Watts Community Beautiful, and others. We receive many commendations for promoting a favorable public image of the department. I owe much to many, especially John "J.J." Leonard and Senior Mechanic Frank M. Ortiz.

I am warned by my team, members of the four traffic divisions, that a riding lieutenant considers me a threat to his position. Despite my assurances that this is not the case, and that I am eighteen months away from retirement, I later learn he has enlisted the support of a commander friend for a little surprise....

1984 Summer Olympics

Chief Gates and head of the Olympic Games Planning Group, Commander William M. Rathburn, authorize the Drill Team to escort the torchbearer into the Coliseum as we did in 1932.[83] (The torch relay is an "ancient tradition" that is started to honor the Fuhrer in 1936.)

The Drill Team is in position on Exposition Boulevard west of Vermont, Saturday morning, 28 July, awaiting the approach of the torchbearer. A group of motor officers and their lieutenant pull in behind us, led by a police commander in his car. The commander informs me of a "change in plans." He and his team are to lead the torchbearer.

I inform the commander that Chief Gates and Commander Rathburn have personally authorized our participation, and I will stand down only for them. He then orders me to remove my team.

I beckon a nearby camera-man over and dismount. The commander asks why and I explain I wish to record the fight about to occur between us. He sputters he will have me fired for insubordination. "Do your best," I reply. (It does not help that some on my team cheer as the interlopers depart.) This is not my finest hour...or maybe it is! One must give the commander credit for audaciousness, arrogance, and boldness. "Chutzpah" is, perhaps, the perfect word.

We lead the torchbearer into the coliseum. A proud moment for us all. We are portrayed on our Kawasaki KZP1000 bikes on the cover of the fifty-

---

[83] "Motorcycle Drill Team," *LAPD Commemorative Book: 1869–1984*, p. 358 (and) "Motorcycle Drill Team Escort Duty For Summer Olympic Games," Commander's Order for Participation, Police Post 381, 26 July 1984 (and) Sgt. Roy Langheld, "The Los Angeles Police Precision Motorcycle Drill Team," *Thin Blue Line*, June 1994 (Vol. 49, No. 6), p. 39.

fifth annual edition (1984) of *The Siren* of the Municipal Motor Officers of California. (I hold member belt buckle serial 50). The *Blue Line* lists all Drill Team members participating in the escort for opening ceremonies of Olympiad XXIII.[84]

I never work with a finer and more dedicated group of officers than those on the Drill Team. As to the dispute on escorting the torchbearer—I never hear another thing about it, officially. But many know of it, including Commander Rathburn who grins and says, "No explanation needed. Well done!" We present Rathburn with the Drill Team's highest award, the first Star of Honor—a solid silver star badge. He "retires" to become the chief of police of Dallas, Texas, and director of security for the 1996 Atlanta Olympic Games.

I retire the following year and the Drill Team presents me with a suitably engraved old B. & M. (Bayless and Miles) motorcycle siren dating back to the company's founding in Los Angeles in 1913. It attaches to the front fender. You reach down and pivot a spindle against the rotating front tire—being careful to not stick your fingers into the stator ports. Thanks, guys!

> "It's been neat,
> With aching seat.
> To ride the beat,
> On L.A. Street...."

Halcyon Days[85]

Commission coordinator Homer F. Broome, Jr., presents me with the CID Eat-a-Thon champ trophy (a small gilded pig) on 16 July 1977. Carl N. Karcher signs an award certificate for my downing of a dozen Carl's Jr. superstar burgers. (I know I have my opponent when he keeps

---

[84] "Official Escort Detail of the Summer Games," *Thin Blue Line*, September 1984 (Vol. 38, No. 9), p. 18.

[85] In the myth of Alcyone, the seven days in winter when storms never occur. This sounds better than, "How I made a pig of myself."

chewing, but not swallowing.) My victory in a multidivisional burrito-eating contest at El Tepeyac in East L.A. on 28 June allows me to proceed to the finals.

My disgraced opponents train by starving themselves. My trainer, Sergeant Ron Kiser, has me eat a large spaghetti dinner the previous night so as to stretch my stomach. Alas, I resemble the race horse who wins his owner millions while receiving a sugar cube. I eat free burritos and hamburgers, but the big bettors in the detective divisions wager hundreds of dollars against me.

Detective Lieutenant (D-III) Nathan D. Johnson, an academy classmate, and I dive 110 feet onto the *Valiant*, sunk in 1930 outside the Avalon Harbor entrance to Catalina Island. It is part of our certification as PADI advanced open water and deep divers. Our instructors are David K. Weller and Arleigh E. McCree. (Arleigh and Officer Ronald L. Ball are killed attempting to defuse a pipe bomb in 1986.)

I meet with former South Vietnam air marshal and prime minister, General Ky Cao Nguyen, in Westminster on 17 May and 11 August 1980. Ky, a liquor store owner, is accompanied in exile by many on his staff. Known as the "Parachutists," "Frogmen," etc., they become involved in criminal enterprises and extortion against Vietnamese businesses.[86] Ky is personable, but supplies little useful information.

International Police Association

I join the Kenya section of the International Police Association in Nairobi in 1969 (EAK #640). I especially enjoy their tradition of retiring to their old English pub-style clubhouse on Gulzaar Street after duty to have a few beers following a shift under the hot East African sun.

I am chairman of IPA Region 6, U.S. Section (then all of the U.S. west of the Mississippi, including Alaska and Hawaii), 1978–1980. Vice Chairman Nate Johnson and I travel south to investigate bringing Mexico, Columbia, and Venezuela into the IPA.

---

[86] "Witness Claims Ky Bosses Viet Crime Ring in U.S.," *Lewiston* (Washington) *Daily* (and others), 26 October 1984.

Mexican Coronel

Arturo Durazo "El Negro" Moreno is chief of police of Mexico City (and outranks the Federal police) under his childhood friend, President Jose Lopez Portillo. He is a gracious host, and we fly to various installations in his Bell Jet Ranger. We land to assist a bomb truck crew disabled on the *via ducto* with a flat tire. They are carrying a bomb from a bank 211.

I parachute with the *Commandos Paracaidista de la Brigada de Granaderos* (the Commando Parachute Riot Police) for my Federal wings. (Acting Chief Robert F. Rock authorizes their LAPD uniform wear on 4 October 1978.)

I deliver a short speech at Chapultepec Palace in English and Spanish on 26 September 1978. It is televised on Channel 2. General Durazo then speaks and (unexpectedly) commissions me coronel/colonel of the Parachute Brigade and presents me with ID and two silver badges.

Nate and I inspect a formation of my new "command." Officers stand at attention beside the open trunks of their vehicles. One trunk contains a 60mm mortar tube and base plate. Several have M-60 machine guns with ammo. One features a flamethrower.

Lieutenant Colonel Fulvio Jimenez Turegano, the general's aide and translator, accompanies us. "Please convey my gratitude to the general for honorary command of his battalion," I say.

"It is not 'honorary,' Coronel," he says. You are their true coronel—although in your absence we will see it is properly led."

"In that case," I say with a smile, "when do I pick up my paycheck?"

"Oh, no, Senior," Jimenez replies in all seriousness, "the general—he gets the pay!"

Plata o Plomo? ("Silver or lead?"). Durazo is a traffic inspector until the late 1960s when he joins the infamous *Brigada Blanca* (White Brigade). They are known for assassinations of Communist students and putting down village uprisings against the PRI *(Partido Revolucionario Institucional)*. Under his six-year reign, the streets of Mexico City are safe.

Durazo's salary is less than mine, but he owns palatial homes and wealth in the hundreds of millions (dollars, not pesos). Every policeman kicks back bribes to him. Things begin unraveling in 1982 when the tortured bodies of twelve bank-robbing Columbians are found in the Tula River, Hidalgo. His *"Dipos"* (DIPD detectives) do it.

Durazo flees when Miguel de la Madrid becomes president. He is arrested in Puerto Rico, extradited, and sentenced to twenty-five years.

He is paroled in 1992, but dies eight years later at age eighty. The last I hear of Colonel Turegano is the following: "The Attorney General's Office of Mexico on Friday (signs a warrant) for the arrest of Fulvio Turegano Jimenez, Head of the Police Federal Judgmental Co., accused of protecting Guadalajara cartel leader Emilio Quintero Payan, shot dead on 26 April...."[87] They tell me my *comandante amigo* now sells fish in Tampico, Tamaulipas.

Nate and I travel on to Venezuela and Columbia to tour various bases and academies. We meet with generals, attorney generals, and other officials. We have various aircraft at our disposal. I jump from an old C-123 with *Los Dragones* at Maracay, Edo. Aragua, Venezuela, to complete a personal first—parachute qualification in at least one army on all continents. I continue into Argentina to the Infantry and Parachute School at Cordoba for additional jumps, and then to Peru to visit Machu Picchu.

Paladin International

I obtain California Private Investigator's License AA 9999 and form Paladin International Investigations. My sole client is a wealthy Armenian gentleman, but this is another story.

Hans-Joachim Langer and I implement security for Trans World Airlines at LAX following the D.B. Cooper hijacking in 1971. (Hans is a Luftwaffe Ace and flies 109s and the new jets and rocket plane.) We get the job done without treating you like a passenger on Con Air. We find college students make better agents than the frustrated police wannabes,

---

[87] "Mexico: Police Guard," *Wall Street Journal Europe* (Madrid), Sunday, 30 May 1993, p. 81.

pedophiles, and petty thieves now attracted to Homeland Security. The feds have yet to discover that concentrating on something that rarely happens leads to pointless activity and distracts from more frequent and dangerous threats.

An Epiphany

One Tuesday afternoon in a Police Commission meeting—listening to Steve Reinhardt drone on about police use of force and Chief Daryl Gates' lack of success in pointing out the obvious—I am struck by a simple yet intuitive grasp of what distinguishes Conservatives from Liberals. It is their differing definitions of *responsibility*.

Conservatives believe the individual has personal responsibility for his life and acts. Liberals believe society is responsible. As simple as this.

Poverty and discrimination, the Liberal says, cause an individual to turn to crime. The Conservative points out poor men who rise in industry and the millions who become comfortable with handouts who lose all ambition and taste for risk. The Conservative notes self-defense is a natural right and the possession of firearms is second in importance only to freedom of religion and freedom of expression from government interference. The Liberal blames inanimate objects for crime and wants them banned. He wants government protection. The Conservative notes that, when seconds count, the police are just minutes away.

I am happy with my job and never take the captain's exam. There is more out of life than the next highest civil service position.

Retirement

I retire from LAPD (and CID) on 8-5-85 after twenty-five years. I plan a quiet departure and buy breakfast for my enforcement team at El Tepeyac. The gracious owner, Manual Rojas, known to generations of LAPD officers, hosts a private party for us with all we can eat. My friends also organize a "surprise" steak fry at the academy and present some fine and most appreciated gifts.

Councilwoman Peggy Stevenson of the Thirteenth District (from my old Hollywood Division days) presents me with a council resolution that is an illuminated work of art; Kenny Hahn, with a calligraphy-master's county resolution from the Board of Supervisors; and, my friend, Chief Ed Davis, has a state senate resolution. The Police Revolver and Athletic Club, the Protective League, the Motorcycle Drill Team, and others are generous with their personal mementos.

Most prized of all is my Detective's Gold Card for fourteen years in the investigative field. It's certificate, with an embossed and gilded city seal and detective's badge, is signed by the very commander from the torchbearer incident of the previous year. I suspect he is pleased to see me depart, but I hold no grievances on this occasion of joy and sadness. It is tough to leave behind the friends and partners of so many years, but all things must pass.

Chapter XVI

NORTH TO ALASKA

"Where men are men, women are scarce, and sled dogs are lying little tramps."

— Anonymous

The "Spirit of Alaska" is epitomized by the sign above the bar at Chilkoot Charlie's—locally known as "Koots"—on West Fireweed in Spenard (the red-light district of Anchorage): "We cheat the other guy and pass the savings on to you."[88]

You are there to give them money. Expect the bartenders to be rude and treat you like a criminal. Drunks and fights abound with deafening "entertainment" by "Fat Guy's Freakshow" and "Homicidal (all male) Supermodels." Men greatly outnumber the women, but the ladies complain, "The odds are good, but the goods are odd."

Kodiak

I am hired as chief of police of Kodiak by one of the finest men I have known, city manager Samuel C. Gesko, Jr. After twenty-five years in the Big City, I decide to troubleshoot small "problem" departments. I vow to never again work in a town with a stop light.

Kodiak is the second largest island in the U.S. (first is the Big Island in Hawai'i). It is rugged and incredibly beautiful. It is the oldest Russian settlement in America (1792) and the first capital of Alaska. I have fifteen sworn officers and fifteen communications and corrections officers. My employee number is 333. I am the ninth chief in seven years.[89] There is

---

[88] Coined by piano player "Mr. Whitekeys," who goes on to found the Fly-By-Night Club (whose cuisine consists of Spam dishes).

[89] Roger Page, "Mirror Reflections," *Kodiak Daily Mirror*, 14 July 1986, p. 3, and others.

dissention in the department and turmoil between those who want the law enforced and political figures who do not.

One of my female officers hates her sergeant and refuses to obey his directions. I fire a couple of civilian jail employees using narcotics on duty. ("Doesn't everyone snort a little coke to get through the watch?," one exclaims.) Two women complain one of my officers stops them for DUI and releases them for sexual favors. [They refuse to testify, but I sustain the complaint. He resigns in lieu of disciplinary action.] We make 1,500 arrests in my first year and average 142 calls a day.

Northern Narcotics

Gesko, whose father is a retired Detroit policeman, wants something done about the narcotics problem. In my first week, I go to the Kodiak Electric Association and obtain the addresses of all homes with electric bills over $1,000 who are not complaining. I then have my detectives place the locations under surveillance to record the traffic of known narcotics users. We obtain warrants and put half-a-dozen marijuana farms out of business (in a population of 6,000).

The body of a local boy is dumped on the steps of the hospital, a spike still in his arm. This is the first black tar heroin identified in Alaska. Another is a suicide leaving a note blaming cocaine. Five families are known to control island dope traffic. We arrange for youthful officers to arrive as Coast Guard dependents and attempt to make buys and infiltrate the families. They are unsuccessful, as the dealers refuse to accept anyone they have not known for years.

The son of a doper family is a friend of one of the dead boys. For a ticket out and some cash, he provides us with evidence of transactions that puts one group out of business through multiple arrests and drug/money seizures. Two councilmen are involved, but there is little proof.

The high school asks my advice on controlling school drug sales. One of my recommendations is to bring "Igor," our dope-sniffing K-9, on unannounced passes down the locker hallway and conduct random locker searches. (Dealers must keep their dope secure.) Although city and school attorneys say this is legal, as the lockers are owned by the school, some are outraged at this intrusion on "student privacy." The board, under pressure, turns down my recommendations.[90]

SWAT Champs

Four of my officers form a SWAT team, as approaching armed suspects on fishing boats is dangerous. Officers also bungle a man-with-a-gun call on my arrival, one of seventy in my first year. One policeman, Gordon B. Bartel, is shot to death while issuing a citation. (He is a police chief from Michigan and attends MSU, my alma mater.)

I send the team leader, Sergeant John W. Palmer, to train with LAPD SWAT. In Kodiak SWAT's first year of operation, they capture all "five marbles," representing stages of crisis scenarios at a competition at Luke Air Force Base, Arizona.[91] They win a first place award against LAPD, SEALs, King County (Seattle), and other top teams. The city will not buy protective vests, so we ask the American Legion to chip in. The city manager is pleased, but some on the city council are unhappy with the media attention even though it is favorable.

Home on the Bay

Kodiak has limited level land, but we manage to buy a house on Cliffside Road overlooking Mill Bay. Salmon spawn, whales scrape off barnacles, and 400-pound halibut come close to our cliff. Kodiak brown bears wander down from the hills. My folks visit and we camp on Karluk Lake. They are amazed to see bears fishing and salmon so thick you cannot walk across streams without stepping on them. Each cast hooks a fish. They do not feed after leaving salt water, but irritatingly snap at lures or become snagged. (I become all "salmoned-out.")

---

[90] Cecil Ranney, "The Chief's Overview of Kodiak," *Kodiak Daily Mirror*, 22 September 1986 (Vol. 46, No. 185), pp. 1 and 4.

[91] Frank Byrt, "SWAT Team Proves Finest Among Competitors from U.S.," *Kodiak Daily Mirror*, 11 June 1987 (Vol. 47, No. 114), p. 1.

Pillar Mountain Run

Physical fitness is especially important in Alaska. I out-perform officers half my age on our semiannual PT exam with two-mile runs (at 5½ minute miles) followed by seventy-five push-ups and sit-ups in two minutes.[92]

Several of my officers, in revenge, surreptitiously enter me in the annual Crab Festival "Pillar Mountain Run." It is 9.6 miles of torture: up a steep volcanic mountain and down scree and boulder-strewn slopes. No runners escape bad cuts and the occasional broken bone. All know the donut-fueled Big City policeman will find an excuse to bow out.

I become a little lost on the run as there are no trails, but come in second in the over-forty class. Those looking forward to a cast-signing party are disappointed...although I am dinged from falls and walk with a limp for a week.

I attend the Alaska Department of Public Safety (State Trooper) Academy in Sitka in early 1987. Kodiak PD adopts an oval badge with the head of a Kodiak bear. We are nine officers short by International Association of Chiefs of Police criteria, with arrests and other activities up considerably, but morale remains high. We convict several murder suspects as well as bar 211s. [Where are they going to run on an island? They always head for a fishing boat or the airport.]

One evening I run a couple of miles up Pillar and stop to rest. An Aleut fellow I know as head of the local alcohol council is there and reaches out to shake my hand. "You are not an Aleut," I say without thinking, "but an East L.A. Mexican!" His hands contain purple gang signs, and a close look near his eyes reveals crudely removed teardrop tattoos.

He is stunned but soon admits that, as a youth in ELA, he commits two gang murders. He is released at age twenty-one and comes north to pick up a few words of Aleut. He makes his way to Kodiak and eventually is offered his job. He does well and helps many drinkers. (His favorite ELA restaurant is El Tepeyac.) I do not expose his past

---

[92] Nell Waage, "Chief is the Champ," *Kodiak Daily Mirror*, 14 January 1988 (Vol. 48, No. 9), p. 1 (and) "The Constable's Corner," *Alaska Police Standards Council*, Winter 1993 (Vol. 1, No. 1), p. 3.

and hear he continues in his position for a number of years. Good luck, Chato, wherever you are.

Shuyak Island

Hueih-Hueih ("Way-Way"), my Chinese wife, is sworn in as a U.S. citizen. An Aleut girlfriend of hers at Fort Abercrombie—a WWII coastal defense installation near our home—asks her to become their cook for a wilderness cabin-building crew on Shuyak Island. She has never been away from home long, whether in Taiwan or with me, but reluctantly agrees.

The owner of a cannery gives us a tour some days earlier. A twenty-five-pound halibut falls off the line. "Pick it up, Max, and it's yours." On the way home I explain to HH, "My job is to obtain the fish; yours is to clean and cook it." She filets it with her cleaver and cooks it in beer batter.

Three weeks later HH returns from Shuyak on their first break. No baths or electricity. Her first words are, "I met Elaine and Lisa. They say your job is to catch *and* clean the fish. I must only cook it." (She has been advised of her "rights" by her American sisters, the downfall of many Oriental ladies.)

"Things aren't working out well," I say. "I better call your dad and have him send over one of your *younger* sisters." (Silence. She is not sure of this one, as the colonel is concerned about finding them husbands.) "You may be bigger, but you must sleep sometime," becomes her favorite saying. Chinese ladies are tough....

Each week the Coast Guard drops off supplies to the cabin-building crew in Sikorsky "Pelican" helicopter 1473. I visit HH while supplies are unloaded. On one mission (2 November 1986) 1473 goes out in nasty weather on a rescue and crashes against a cliff on Ugak Island. All aboard perish.

Colt Python

The Colt Custom Shop in Hartford advertises a 150th Anniversary "Sampler" with four old styles of engraving. I order a .357 Magnum Python in rust-resistant nickel finish, with a lanyard ring on the grip. [This keeps it from slipping overboard when shooting halibut. You do not want a live 350-plus-pounder in the boat with you.] Sea lions in the harbor are occasionally cut by propellers when following fishing boats and must be dispatched.

Colt employees go on strike in 1986, and no Pythons are made. Al DeJohn, the custom shop manager, obtains parts and assembles it himself: serial KPD-1. My factory letter notes it is the only one made.

The Ghost Ship

The *Saint Patrick* is a 158-foot Florida scalloper making its way to Kodiak. A williwaw hits.[93] The inexperienced captain orders "abandon ship," despite having only a few survival suits. Ten die. It continues abandoned but under power to a little island off the north end of Kodiak where it runs out of fuel. It floats in Dog Bay for years. All refer to it as the "Ghost Ship."

George Johnson, skipper of the "Shelikof Strait," is known as "Turkey George" for answering his radio calls with a "gobble" instead of a call sign. We delight in the fresh king crab. They grow to a width of six feet and weigh close to twenty-five pounds. Their blood is white.

Sea lice are maggot-size shrimp-like critters that can strip a body to a skeleton like tiny piranha. And skeletons do not float. I hunt bison (on horseback with my old .45-70) for winter meat, and a Kodiak brown bear (with my Westley-Richards .318 take-down rebored to .338).

---

[93] A katabatic wind descending down the slope of a volcano, carrying high-density air (often from ice fields) under the force of gravity. Williwaws can reach hurricane force and be intensely cold.

Bayside Fire Department

I train as the tenth volunteer (serial 111) for the new Bayside Fire Department under Chief Earl A. Smith, Jr. I squirt fires and drive Engine 12, a 1984 Ford Western States 3,500-gallon pumper. "Hut fires" in winter are deadly and boat fires difficult to extinguish.

A message comes over the fire radio at a freon (CFC) leak call: *"The gas doesn't seem to be poisonous, Chief. We have our gas masks off and we are okay."* I have two brothers who are firemen in the Lower 48. I call them "The Evidence Eradication Team."

Al-A-Ga-Zam!

"Al-a-ga-zam" is the traditional carny greeting. The Ford Brothers Circus and Carnival arrives in trucks aboard the sea-going ferry, *Tustumena*. They feature an elephant, a lion, the usual bearded-lady, and other attractions.

The city manager and I meet with the circus manager to set ground rules. We realize most games are rigged, as they cannot earn a living if they give away too many stuffed animals. (Some games bring in over $1,000 a day.) Their cheap prizes are known as "slum."

Underinflated balloons, blunt darts, heavy bottles at the bottom of the bottle-toss pyramid, claw games too weak to grasp prizes, etc., are known to us. The few who win are usually shills. If we catch them, they are gone from the island.

We notice the ticket seller sits on a high stool. (Someone higher and louder is in command.) His actual job is to peer into the wallets of those buying tickets. A mark with money is then "accidentally" brushed by someone in the crowd who marks his back with a little swipe of chalk dust. His soon empty wallet is replaced, so any responding officer will believe the mark simply blew his cash.

Too many complaining of lost money or fishermen rolled by the trapeze ladies after-hours will result in immediate shutdown. We have few problems, but the circus departs early.

Ford Brothers have an accident in Sitka, and the lion escapes and eats one of their ponies. In Anchorage, the manager runs off with their money and they are forced to close.

> "From Ouzinkie to Akhiok, Always on the Go;
> Sun Shining Down on Kod-i-ak Joe"
> (Bar song sung to the tune of "Mexican Joe")

I have an interest in the education of Native kids, and I am invited by KANA (Kodiak Area Native Association) to speak at all of Kodiak Island's villages: Akhiok, Karluk, Larsen Bay, Old Harbor, Ouzinkie, and Port Lions. Their populations range from fewer than fifty (Akhiok) to about three hundred (Old Harbor).

The Native Claims Settlement Act of 1971 establishes corporations rather than reservations. Most villages have two distinctive structures: a Russian Orthodox Church, usually with a blue onion dome, and a modern school (courtesy of the Native Claims Act).

Akhiok, the southernmost and most remote village, consists of around twenty small shacks. In the mid-1980s there are about ten students in a huge school with blue metal roof that can house scores. A hardwood floor basketball court with lighted scoreboard seems bizarre in such an isolated fishing village. A separate plant supplies heat and electricity.

Teachers are (usually) a husband-and-wife team on one-year contract. I donate our used police vehicles and equipment to KANA. Many of the kids I speak with are sharp, but television has given them impossible dreams. They wish to escape their harsh subsistence fishing life and live the good life in Hollywood or New York. Most have no idea of how to book an airplane reservation or order from a restaurant menu. Their social skills are minimal.

Tribal elders are appreciative their children can speak to someone who can describe actual life in the Lower 48 Big Cities and its dangers. It is clear that many are not discouraged and will probably never return home to take over the family fishing boat and hut. I pass out my home telephone number and tell them to ask a policeman to call me if they ever find themselves in trouble. Several call, usually destitute and living on the streets of Anchorage or Seattle. I arrange for local officers to return them, but suspect it is just a temporary patch....

Sacred Whale Hunt

Natives pay no taxes and many are incredibly rich from oil and fisheries on their lands. Their All-Terrain Vehicle (ATV) breaks down and they simply abandon it and buy another. They claim, for example, rich salmon runs— but are initially turned down. No natives live in the area in ancient times; it is 1920s Norwegian fishermen who clear the rivers and establish the runs.

The natives counter they use this area to hunt special brown bears for their stomach and intestinal linings to use as waterproof covers for their sea-going baidarkas. With no salmon to eat, these bears do not puncture holes in their guts making them useless as waterproof covers.....

The Fish & Wildlife Service patiently explains to the Native Claims Settlement Act Commissioners that this is absurd. Bears regularly digest salmon bones without puncturing their guts. And without salmon there is nothing to attract bears to this area. They cave and still another valuable public resource is handed over to the Indians.

If you walk the beaches of the Chukchi Sea near Barrow, North Slope Borough, you will come across the remains of many whales. They do not die natural deaths. Inupiat Eskimos spot bowheads and others using sophisticated satellite images supplied by the Canadian and U.S. governments. They head out in modern high-powered boats armed with explosive-head harpoons. Wearing their Carhartt foul-weather gear they use their Caterpillar D7H and forklift to drag their catch ashore. "Aarigaa!" (Inupiaq, "Very good!"), they shout.

They often run-off us outsiders with our cameras, just as the natives on St. George do not allow photos of their fur-seal clubbing. Bowheads are endangered but our government and the International Whaling Commission permit it as a "subsistence tradition." Many of us say, "Then let the hunt be fair-chase, as in traditional times. Use umiaq (skin boats), traditional stone-and-bone weapons, and no white-man's power-gear."

Some natives used to jump on the backs of large whales to stab with a handheld harpoon.

Few, using traditional hunting techniques, will return to shore. Their families will be forced to eat at "Arctic Pizza" and Mexican cusine at "Pepe's North of the Border."

Natives are allowed to kill (and sell) polar bears, otters, fur seals, and other endangered species. My cultural and family traditions—no more ancient than theirs—allow the killing of Indians and confiscation of their lands and goods. Why are their traditions more important than mine? Indians are still scalping the white man....Time to make everyone obey the same rules.

Northern Holidays

The City of Kodiak hires a professional fireworks company to shoot off rockets with starbursts on the Fourth of July. A low cloud cover hovers about forty feet off the ground. Shells enter the cloud ceiling and a brief glow of light is seen followed by the blast of the explosion. No one, however, leaves early.

The city decorates Sitka spruce trees near the Russian Orthodox Church with Christmas tree lights. A citizen reports them missing. We find several bar patrons cozy and asleep beneath the trees despite the subzero cold and snow. Wrapped around them, beneath their coats, are the lights—still plugged in and warmly glowing.

Resignations

I serve for the term of the city manager who is told to resign or be fired in four days by the new mayor, citing his "managerial style." We all know that our largest-ever narcotics and cash seizure and subsequent investigation threaten some "important people," including two on the council and the mayor. (Kodiak, we discover, is the distribution center for the Aleutian Chain). Sam Gesko, my boss, does not back down.

Two months later, I, too, resign rather than eventually running afoul of the acting manager. Department heads are "at-will" employees with no contracts. I receive a generous settlement and glowing commendations, but leave a job undone. We have good memories and few regrets, and a better understanding of politics in the North.

The next chief is observed raiding someone else's crab pots—a big "No, No"—and departs. Another resigns after he chokes-out one of his officers during an argument in his office.[94] (I, too, have experienced this temptation.)

---

[94] "Officer Sues Kodiak," *Anchorage Daily News* ("State News"), 28 July 1991.

Chapter XVII

THE ALEUTIAN CHAIN

"Son, I used to be a Los Angeles cop, and I can shoot anyone I damn well please." [95]

The Thousand-Mile War

Air Officer Masatake Okumiya, on the bridge of the carrier *Ryujo*, stares into an Aleutian storm and heavy running seas with mountainous waves. Burning towards them out of the storm at wave height and full speed is a Martin B-26 Marauder medium bomber, both engines spewing flames as they ingest water.

Three things alarm the Japanese officer: (1) the bomber has an enormous torpedo strapped to its underside, (2) it has found them in this storm even though their pending attack on Dutch Harbor is a secret, and (3) its landing gear spacing and fixed wing indicate it is land-based (when they believe there are no airfields within a thousand miles).

Just as Captain George W. Thornbrough releases his torpedo, the *Ryujo* pitches into a wave trough. The torpedo bounces across the deck, exploding harmlessly in the waves beyond.[96] Captain Thornbrough returns to Cold Bay, a stationary aircraft carrier disguised as a salmon cannery, and loads up with 500-pound bombs. He again flies off into the storm to find the *Ryujo*, never to return.

---

[95] Daniel Depp, *Babylon Heights* (2010), p. 51.

[96] Story told by Kodiak Aleut historian Hank Eaton (who is there during the War) and Bryan Garfield, *The Thousand-Mile War* (1969), Bantam Book edition, p. 38.

King Cove

I land at Thornbrough Field, Cold Bay (*"Udaamagax"* in Aleut). It has a 10,415-foot runway now serving for emergency landings of great circle flights between the U.S. and Asia.

Chief Gary K. Eilers of King Cove is desperate to find someone crazy enough to fly here as his seasonal officer. His want ads produce no results. He is my roommate at the academy in Sitka, so I volunteer. (I end up spending a year here, and later return for a second tour.)

Japanese Internment

The roundup and internment of West Coast Japanese (Executive Order 9066), aided by the Census Bureau, eventually results in the disbursement of over $1.6 billion in reparations. Largely unrecognized today, it results in the immediate loss of intelligence for scores of Japanese radio operators and spy "fishing boats" searching the Aleutian islands for our secret airbases.[97]

Japanese concerns are not paranoia; they stem from the realization that Lieutenant General James H. Doolittle (of "raid on Tokyo" fame) is from Nome. Marshal-General Isoroku Yamamoto's blunder at splitting his forces before the Battle of Midway may have cost him the war. The split is a result of this sudden black-out of intelligence.

I know Brigadier (then Colonel) Benjamin B. Talley who builds the Saxon Fish Company cannery at Cold Bay (and other camouflaged air bases). His "Consolidated Packing Company" is more accurately known as the Alaskan Defense Command.

---

[97] Thousands of Japanese-Americans flee to become enemy soldiers. Some 6,000 "renunciants" interned at Tule Lake, California, greet the rising sun with calls of "Banzai," celebrate Pearl Harbor Day, and demand expatriation to Japan. The DOD release of MAGIC files in 1977 reveals that *hundreds* of Japanese are spies. [See Prof. Roger D. McGrath (a friend of many years), "Intern(ment) Scandal," *American Conservative*, 15 March 2004 (Vol. 3, No. 5), pp. 22–23]. The "Five-Number Codes," solved by "Madam-X" (Agnes May Driscoll) and her team that remain classified to this day, also reveal Japanese deceit.

I trod upon the Marsden Matting (PSP—pierced steel plank) on Kodiak and Umnak Islands [where Lieutenant Colonel John "Jack" Chennault (son of the American Volunteer Group in China leader) flies his P-40 War Hawks called the Aleutian Tigers]. Attacks are launched from here into the Kuril Islands and tie up many Japanese aircraft unavailable to stop our Pacific advance.

"Even by Alaska standards, King Cove is dangerously isolated. Many residents have their groceries shipped in twice a year." [98] The pay is good, however, and housing/utilities free.

An Alaska State Trooper amphibious Grumman G-21 "Goose" (made in 1941) delivers me from Cold Bay to King Cove. It can land off the beach or on the tiny dirt strip.

My police vehicle is a 1989 Isuzu Trooper. I am Badge No. 2 with Post Office Box 2. Chief Eilers works the twelve-hour day shift, and I work nights. His instructions: "I don't do night call-outs." The upwelling of the Kuroshio (Black Tide or Japan) Current, in contact with the frigid Bering Sea, makes this apparent desert one of the richest areas for seafood on the planet.

King Cove, in the Aleutian Islands recording district, is founded in 1911 by Pacific American Fisheries. It is a mixed Aleut village of about 700 non-Native and Unangan (Agdaagux Tribe—not established until 1998) natives. Five hundred more seasonal employees work for the Peter Pan Seafoods cannery (real name, Nichiro Corporation, Tokyo—and you thought *we* won the war?). The cannery and much of the town are on a sandspit and lagoon between two steep volcanic ridges.

The Aleuts are badly treated by early Russian fur traders who hold their families ransom in exchange for hunting sea otters. They are not, however, the noble peace-loving fisherfolk overrun by savage and diseased Russians. They are war-like cannibals constantly raiding the Koniag Eskimos of Kodiak and other Aleuts. Cracked, scraped, and blackened human bones are evident in their middens (refuse heaps). They raid and they hunt whales in forty-man boats.

---

[98] "Isolated Residents Want Road in Refuge," The Associated Press [*Bellingham* (WA) *Herald*], 5 September 1998, p. A-8.

Mount Dutton stratovolcano is nine miles north of King Cove. Swarms of 200 earthquakes a day are not unusual and monitored by the Alaska Volcano Observatory. We live in a trailer staked down by cables.

Huieh-Hueih works in the town's only store, the Gould Store, across the road. Winds are so severe it is not uncommon for her to crawl to work. Customers also crawl up and down the dirt roads, as it can be impossible to stand. Vehicles are sometimes blown off the roads.

A WWII joke has a sailor stationed in the Aleutians saying there is "a woman behind every tree." There are a few stunted trees in sheltered locations, but they are rare. Wood boardwalks allow reasonably dry walking. An old boarded-up shack houses the Frog Pond Theatre, seating about two dozen. It is closed for over a half century. The owner allows me inside.

Two old dust-covered Simplex Victory Model Projection Arc Lamps—exactly as I ran in San Clemente as a kid—are present. Still in the can is their last film: *Raffles* (1930), starring Ronald Colman. I run through the loading procedure and fire up two National carbon-arc rods. The picture begins, but the brittle film soon breaks.

The scenery is spectacular. Numerous aircraft wrecks are scattered across the ridges. I walk the beaches and hills on my occasional days off. I find stone spear and harpoon points, weights for seaweed nets, and other artifacts. An ancient wood ship is eroding out of a cliff near Bold Cape and may be Russian of three or four hundred years ago.

Sunken spots on nearby Deer Island are old sod huts called *barabaras*. They are pits with roofs and framework of driftwood or whale rib. A notched log serves as a ladder to a square entrance cut into the roof. Several families live inside and burn seal oil in stone lamps. (Soot, no doubt, coats their lungs.) Graves are sometimes dug into the walls. They travel vast distances in their *baidarkas* (sea kayaks) in pursuit of sea otters, seals, and whales, and on raiding expeditions. They venture out in two- or three-hatch sealskin boats as far as Fort Ross in Northern California—over 1,800 miles across open seas.

The Stick

Police work in the North is a century removed from the professional product experienced in the Southland. Rodney King will be a sissy in Alaska. "Use of force" distinctions tend to lose their significance in the North, as it's a violent world. Back-up is 600 nautical miles away in Anchorage, assuming the weather permits travel. If you go down in a bar fight, you are in trouble—no doctors or hospitals.

"Rick's Place" and "The Last Hook-Off" are the only two bars. Rick's has few problems as it is small and owner Richard R. Koso has a large electric "Hot-Shot" cattle prod—and is not reluctant to use it. The Hook-Off is better known as the "Corporation Bar," as layering hides its true ownership. [The Native Corporation sends many locals to Anchorage each year to an alcoholism program, yet sells them their liquor. I once ask the mayor about this, and he replies, "If we don't sell them their drinks, someone else will."]

A fishing boat can earn a million dollars—or nothing—in a forty-eight-hour opening for king crab or halibut. Boats from the Lower '48, Japan, Russia, and the local Aleuts cut each other's lines and nets, ram their competition, and even pepper each other with shotgun blasts. Each boat claims its own table in the Corporation Bar and they begin drinking and exchanging insults.

The wind is howling and blowing the rain horizontally, shaking our sheet-metal police station. The phone rings around midnight. "Max, come quick! I need help!" shouts Pete, the Aleut bartender. In the background is the sound of breaking glass and furniture.

"I'm on my way, Pete. Stay under the counter," I reply as I make myself another cup of coffee. I then ignore the ringing telephone.

I bundle up and walk the two blocks to the ocean-front side of the bar. The windows are painted black, but there is a crack in the edge of one that permits me to see much of the interior. When most combatants are exhausted or down, I pull on my sap gloves and make my entrance. Straight-stick drawn, I whack the shins or forearms of those few trying to fight me. I occasionally backhand someone with the gloves or poke a gut with the stick, which usually puts them down. Two rules: *don't go down* and *always win*. [Fighting "fair" isn't part of the program. A preemptive strike usually wins the battle.] No former policemen has wielded a baton here, and the fishermen take to calling me "The Stick from L.A." or "The Stick."

The local fishermen often join me in rounding up the others and fighting at my side. [This earns them the right to go home without consequences. No questions asked—unless they instigate the brawl.] No one breaks bottles to use as weapons or pulls knives. Bush villages are known to bury, usually at sea, the few who foolishly do so.

I have tucked a long coil of clothesline into my Sam Browne. I line-up those who can still walk and have them grasp the line, and then march them ahead of me to the station. We have a large jail where I patch up the wounded. (There is an on-call physician's assistant, Veronica Gehrman, who stitches and gives shots.)

Before sunup, captains realize their crews have not returned. They grab rolls of hundred dollar bills and head for the jail. Pete calls me and says, "Damages are $7,621" (a figure I know he fabricates). I divide that amount by the number of arrestees and write receipts to the captains who "bail out" their crews. (If they remain in jail or go to court, the loss of a working crew is catastrophic.) I turn the money over to Pete, and he hands me a receipt. No court; no records. A business expense the captain deducts from the crew's bonus. All is well in King Cove.

Bear-anoia

Brown bears have large territories and congregate only during salmon runs. Aleuts have a deathly fear of them, although living around them for centuries. People killed by bears are rare occurrences and usually involve a sow with cubs. We often find young bears shot. Not one has attacked anyone in King Cove since it was founded in 1911—until six-year-old Anton Bear is killed in July 1992 when he runs from a sow and two cubs feeding at the town dump. He triggers the pursuit instinct of the yearling.

I am patrolling the King Cove dump on foot about midnight in summer to discourage foraging bears. (It is still light.) A huge boar comes around a bush and rears up. We are only a few meters apart, and he is considerably taller. I draw my Glock .40 and train it on his head (the skull bone is thin) to await his decision. I finally fire a round in the air. He "whuffs," turns around, and ambles off.

I am soon to become chief in tiny Whittier, Alaska, where black bears are a nuisance. State law allows killing a bear in self-defense, but there are usually no wits. I put out written notice that to claim self-defense, you better have claw and bite marks on you or you will be prosecuted and your weapon confiscated. The "self-defense" shootings come to a halt.

Aleut Justice

Aleut families hate each other over unremembered feuds going back, perhaps, a thousand years. They cannot trust each other to fairly police themselves, so they hire us outsiders. If something goes amiss, they can fire us without embarrassment to themselves.

Aleuts resolve conflicts the old-fashioned way. In the olden days, a troublemaker is ostracised (a death sentence, as a banished individual rarely survives) or is executed by a blow to the head. We might hear that Nik-Nik molests his nephews and has not been seen recently. Relatives tell us he "disappears" while fishing or hunting. Any investigation is met with silence and shrugs.

I find a large, live, king crab sprawled across the hood of my Trooper outside our trailer from time to time. My wife finally spots Rudy P. Dushkin, a man I have arrested for drinking offenses and escorted to jail in Anchorage, leaving another crab. Rudy can be "obnoxicated" and is a fighting drunk. I must make him "do the chicken" (choke him out) to control him. He says he leaves me crabs to eat because I am the only one who does not punish him after he gets to the jail. I am a little surprised he can remember such details, but take it as a compliment in using only reasonable force. I tell all that such things are not personal, but few probably believe it.

Max K. Hurlbut

The "Dark Crazies"

Many Alaska natives (and my Chinese wife) lack the enzyme that metabolizes alcohol. This drug devastates communities. Native love for alcohol has them counting their birthdays in dog years.

Bush communities in the North are dark most of winter. Natives cannot venture out in storms or onto the ice to hunt. The "Dark Crazies" can claim them. Confined to their huts for months, they drink and fight and form close personal relationships with their families and sled dogs. They occasionally murder entire households.

I pull quills from the faces of local dogs and fishhooks from the faces of kids. We book relatively few offenders, as the nearest courts are in Sand Point (the Shumagin Islands) or Unalaska (Dutch Harbor on Amaknak Island).

Peter Pan reports a $25,000 Hyster forklift is stolen and driven off a gangway into the water during a storm. A month of questioning identifies the culprits—twin-brother outside fishermen.

My first question is usually, "You know why I'm here, don't you, Inar?" (The response can be enlightening.) Older Natives rarely lie. The younger ones often do, but are usually betrayed by little tells. I take advantage of the fear of many jailed Lower 48 fishermen to become stranded here and be forced to eat *tepa* (Yup'ik: "stinky heads") and *muktuk* for years. [The food *is* different. We pay a fee and eat at Peter Pan with the slime-liners.]

The suspects' fishing boat eventually returns and I change their names to "Defendant." They confess. It appears to be a drunken prank gone amiss but is still a felony "criminal mischief" offense. We meet with their skipper who turns over $25,000 cash for a receipt. I give the money to Peter Pan and obtain a receipt. The amount is subtracted from the offender's crew share. The fishermen have a good story to tell their grandchildren. Balance is again restored.

Some serious crimes, we suspect, go unnoticed. A man overboard from an ice-encrusted fishing boat may slip—or have a dispute with another crewman. He is gone before the boat can turn around. Sea critters reduce a fresh body to a non-buoyant skeleton in hours.

The Mayor's Challenge

Mayor Harvey D. Mack, thirty-four, sees me running almost every day along Airport Road. He challenges us to an Independence Day race—the "Big Hill Marathon." (A race he always wins.) Eilers is younger than I, but conceals a heart condition that is to kill him. Big Hill looks to be about a mile-and-a-half run up and down East Volcanic Ridge, but so steep one must scramble on hands and knees in places.

I maintain a constant pace, allowing Mack to lead. I intend to overtake him in a final burst of speed. Alas, Mack (unintentionally, I believe) dislodges little rock slides, forcing me farther behind. He wins by a good margin.[99] Our competitors—fishermen who train at the local bars—are not a threat. My second-place prize is a surprise (and generous) bonus check. Thank you, Harvey.

Lack of medical facilities is a problem. I break a tooth and cannot get out for more than a painful week because of nasty weather. It costs me $1,500 to get to a dentist in Anchorage. Some die from injuries and illnesses that are not a problem elsewhere.

I borrow our Remington 870 shotgun with eighteen-inch barrel and buy some 6-shot at the Gould Store. I discover seasonally camouflaged Willow and Rock Ptarmigan on the brush-covered slopes of Mount Dutton. (The Rocks are found higher on the more barren faces.) They are tough but delicious when HH cooks them in a stew.

I return from a hunt on the volcano's slope one day to find a note on my Trooper windshield, in the handwriting of Chief Gary, humorously accusing an "unknown officer" of stealing the company shotgun and leaving town.

Gary finds a note on his windshield explaining that this officer was, no doubt, kidnapped by a band of sex-crazed cannery girls and barely escaped with his life and honor. The details, however, are so disgusting they must

---

[99] "Aleutian Style King Cove Celebration," *Aleutians East Borough Advocate*, 26 July 1991, pp. 13 and 22.

remain unknown to the sensibilities of the bachelor chief as they might trigger a seizure—resulting in said officer's promotion to the newly opened job as chief of police....

"How did you know of my heart condition?" asks Gary. "I didn't, until now," I reply. He is dead just four years after retiring from King Cove.

Chapter XVIII

THE PRIBILOFS AND PRINCE WILLIAM SOUND

Over the years we've gone back and forth,
Up to the still white frozen North.
Where mountains of ice and fire rise,
In sudden swoops to the startled skies.

Where dark cloud monsters puff their cheeks,
And scrape their bellies across the peaks.
Where a weary day is a long half year,
And out of the icebergs dead men peer….

(Apologies to Don Blanding, poet laureate
of Hawai'i and my vagabond hero.)

Tunnel Town

Whittier is often described as the weirdest town in Alaska—a remote fogbound dogpatch where almost the entire population of 248 lives in a single fourteen-story concrete monolith out of a Soviet Five-Year Plan. Floors are waxed to a hospital shine and there is the faint scent of humans who need to get out more.

Eccentricity is the accepted norm. T-shirts say "P.O.W" (Prisoner of Whittier). Before road access in 2000, Whittiots[100] can only escape by driving onto a train flatcar for a twelve-mile ride to the Seward Highway through two tunnels. The Whittier (Anton Anderson) Tunnel through the Chugach Mountains is 2.6 miles long. (*Runaway Train* is filmed here in 1985.)

---

[100] Prince William Sound residents of Cordova are called "Cordavers" and Valdez people are known as Valdiseases. Those in Homer are "Homeroids." A little "Alaska humor."

Robert "Cowboy" Wardlow never leaves Begich Towers (also known as BTI) in eight years. In death he remains. His ashes rest in a container on the shelf of the first-floor "country store."[101]

Vagabonds Head North

Hueih-Hueih and I (again) drive up the gravel Stewart-Cassiar Highway and through Whitehorse on the fiftieth anniversary of the Alaska Highway. (Once a wilderness highway, it is now a highway through the wilderness.) We cross the Arctic Circle (latitude 66 degrees, 33 minutes, 44 seconds North) on the Dempster Highway into Inuvik using gasoline in jerrycans provided by the gracious Dawson City Mounties, as the only gas station is closed on Sunday. (Visiting policemen are celebrated in the Yukon.)

We rent a small plane and fly to Aklavik near the shores of the Arctic Ocean to see the gravesite of Albert Johnson, the "Mad Trapper of Rat River." He leads Mounties on a 48-day, 150-mile foot chase before his final shootout in February 1932.

We ferry across the Yukon River at Dawson City on a motorized raft and pass all three shacks in Chicken, Alaska (prospectors could not spell "Ptarmigan").

We detour to the isolated settlement of Eagle. Sourdough and former chief of police Erwin A. "Nimrod" Robertson has an excruciating toothache, which leads him to pull several teeth—with a pair of rusty pliers—until he gets the right one. His greatest personal fear is of being devoured by wolves.

Nimrod, eighty-four, out of food and caught in a blizzard in December 1940, realizes he cannot make it home and that his time has come. He locates a creek about to be frozen over and lays down in its waters. Townsmen find his body encased in ice—but undisturbed by wolves—and bury him in Eagle.

We bounce across the gravelled Taylor Highway into Tok and down through Anchorage.

---

[101] Doug Ward, "Isolation Attracts Loners, Eccentrics," *Vancouver* (B.C.) *Sun*, 8 January 2001, p. A5.

The Bird House

A giant goofy-looking blue, red, and yellow papier-mache bird protrudes from a one-room log shack in Bird Creek off Milepost 100 of the Seward Highway next to Turnagain Arm. Inside the sloping bar and floor are walls covered with business cards, women's underwear, and signed bank notes. (They are drink-insurance for prospectors who may be broke on their next visit.) The tavern burns in 1996.

We drive onto a rail flatcar at Portage for the twelve-mile run into Whittier. Whittier, at the head of a fjord (Passage Canal), is built by the army in fear of a Japanese invasion. It is named for the glacier perched above the town (which is named for the poet). It is an old Indian and Russian portage site used by the gold "stampeders" of 1898 to reach the Interior. Tugs now tow barges from Seattle with stacked intermodal (shipping) containers. Trains run 24/7 to take them out.

The city council hires me in May 1992, a time of austerity, to replace four regular and two seasonal officers. The city is broke, but needs to hold on another few years until road access can bring tourists to view the magnificent scenery and wildlife. Recall petitions circulate to remove the mayor and entire council and to fire the city manager.[102] Four department heads are terminated. Those who hire me are soon gone. The head of the medical clinic, an alcoholic, is also forced out.

The winter population is low, but more than 700,000 pass through in the summer. I am police chief and director of public safety, with a small fire department, ambulance service, and search & rescue operation. The abandoned Buckner Building, once the largest in Alaska, houses hundreds of men and is a city under one roof with theatre, shooting range, hospital, and even a morgue. It now sits unoccupied, with all its windows destroyed, plumbing and wiring torn out, and ice coating the floors.

Crime is low but nuisance calls abound. Alaska attracts marginal personalities from the Lower 48. Many arriving in the Last Frontier have criminal and antisocial backgrounds. I find we harbor a Nevada fugitive

---

[102] "Recall Petitions Issued," *Whittier City News* ("An occasional Newsletter by the City of Whittier"), 15 April 1993, first and sixth pages. The Editorial notes, "Face it, Whittier has a reputation for meanness all over the State…unfortunately, well-earned."

wanted for shooting at officers with a 12-gauge sawed-off shotgun during a drug bust. (I jail him but Nevada does not extradite anyone beyond the Lower 48.) We have a male prostitute, an armed robber, several arsonists, dope dealers, and the usual burglars and sex offenders.

Winter arrives shortly after the first "termination dust," a light snow that coats the hills and terminates summer. Spring is joyously heralded by the arrival of seasonal Mexican and Filipino fish processors—Whittier's answer to the swallows returning to Capistrano.

Winter temperatures in the Interior reach more than 60 degrees F. below zero, making it difficult to survive or to even go outside. It is dark twenty-four-hours a day in winter and light around the clock in summer. Whittier, in summer, averages 197 inches of rain; winter snows average 241 inches. Foot tunnels run beneath the town, as surface movement is not always an option.

Storms and winds through Portage Pass shut down aircraft traffic and any hope for evacuation to Anchorage, about 65 miles to the northwest. Avalanches sometimes block the two tunnels and halt train traffic—the only way out—for weeks. A number of elderly people live in town (as rents are low), and industrial and fishing accidents claim victims.

My lone police officer is soon to depart to take a job in Colorado. We make a good team because we are both certified officers and firemen, Red Cross emergency medical technicians (EMTs), licensed by the Alaska Railroad to drive our 1981 Chevrolet Rail Ambulance (the last one on the continent), PADI deep and open water divers, and parachutists. We operate a thirty-two-foot Munson seagoing ambulance, go out in kayaks, rappel down glaciers (as graduates of the Army Northern Warfare School), and are former military policemen (so as to deal with the many Alaska military bases and personnel). We are also mushers but dog sleds are not an option in tiny Whittier. We soon discover most of these skills are not wasted.

City Marshal

I am appointed the first city marshal[103]——the traditional Alaska Bush title. This enables me to serve civil processes and to auction boats, bringing in a little cash for the city. I read the municipal code and discover a small ordinance change that will transfer payment for jail guards from the city to the state. I apply for grants, and we are given title to a thirty-six-foot boat from Fish & Wildlife and a forty-two-foot aluminum craft from the Coast Guard. I eventually build our volunteers to a force of forty-two.

Arresting misdemeanants requires sending an affidavit to the assistant DA in Anchorage who decides upon its merits and has the visiting magistrate sign a warrant, which we serve. Bail is then set, and we collect it for the court. I suggest we simply have the offender sign a traffic citation as a voluntary "promise to appear" then try him by the next visiting magistrate. Should he fail to appear, a warrant can be issued. This works well and saves considerable time and paper shuffling.

We make many minor arrests but only recommend prosecution for the more serious offenses. (A man torching our community outhouse receives forty days in jail and must rebuild it at his own expense.) I give offenders the choice of "community service" or an appearance before the visiting magistrate. (They soon realize she will then ask me for a recommended sentence.) The other department heads send me their wish lists. In winter '94 we supply 580 hours (72½ days) to Public Works to shovel snow and drive heavy snow-removal equipment.

I Have a Plan. A local man fills in as a deputy on my days off. One seasonal officer is hired in summer. (It takes a minimum of five officers to staff one position around the clock, according to the International Association of Chiefs of Police.) Four full-time officers and a dispatcher handle 1,454 incidents the year before. We two process 1,523 incidents my first year. My wife is the (unpaid) dispatcher, jail guard, rail ambulance driver, and EMT. The problem is to gain control of the 911 system. Drinking and bar fights generate almost all the after-hours call-outs and 85 percent

---

[103] "Agenda," Public Hearing, Whittier City Council of 7 June 1993, Item 11.B.3: Ordinance 295-93, "Providing for the Office of Marshal in the Department of Public Safety," (and) "Whittier Police Chief Now City Marshal," *Whittier City News*, 10 June 1993, fourth page.

of daytime calls. Several intoxicated Whittiots enjoy calling me about 0300 hours to chat. Police are the only department available 24/7....

Eighty-Six List

I call the Alcoholic Beverage Control Board of the State Department of Revenue to see if a plan I have will legally pass muster, as I anticipate complaints. I explain that the local bartenders are friends of their clientele, and, of course, make money off their desire for alcohol. Rather than take care of the problems that result, they call me. We have fatal traffic accidents (on about five total miles of dirt roadway), robberies, rapes, assaults, drownings, and other drinking-involved incidents. Title 4 of Alaska Statutes requires bars to close only the three hours between 0500 and 0800.

I propose an "86 List"—a list of locals who are prohibited from being served in the Anchor Inn or Sportsman's Inn because of their abuse of alcohol. I select the names and the time on the list (thirty days, first incident). Any bartender not honoring it is to be fired. This allows them to tell a customer they would like to serve him, but that ass of a marshal is to blame. A third incident in a month gets the bar's beverage license before the state board for revocation. I obtain the council and city manager's approval—and their promise not to override my decisions. ABC is interested to see if it can work in other communities.

The first on my "86 List" is city councilman Robin A. Gaboury, a tough ironworker. He "peels rubber" with his "muscle car" around and around Begich Towers at 0400 hours one morning. People shout, "Kill him!" and "Lynch him!" He boasts of his spot on the list and insists that others support the program. An interesting development is that some "friends" of the listees offer to buy them booze—but at a considerable markup!

Another councilman, owner of the "Sportsman," has his license revoked. I cite a third councilman for theft of cable television service. I jail the mayor's boy for burglary. The town sees we do not play favorites and the rules begin to be followed. Our call load drops, and I can get a night's sleep without having to break up a bar fight. The 911 calls drop from twenty to thirty a day to just *three* during the entire month of April 1994.

Air Crashes

Portage Pass lies between Maynard Mountain (the Whittier Tunnel) and Portage Glacier. It forms a natural venturi, where the tapering constriction in the middle causes an increase in the velocity of the wind. It suckers in pilots who know it as the best route into Prince William Sound from Anchorage. Planes ice up here even in summer.

I search Portage Pass in my wolf-hide parka and on snowshoes in howling winds whenever there is an overdue plane in winter. My snowshoes have metal crampons that permit climbing slopes of crusted snow. Exposed flesh freezes in moments in 85-mph winds at minus 20 degrees F. I carry my Ithaca "LAPD Special" 12-gauge on a sling beneath my jacket or a 7.62 rifle. My hands are occupied with poles.

Two aircraft go down, with fatalities, in a twenty-four-hour period.[104] Workers at the Army Tank Farm (fuel storage) hear a "whump" but cannot see anything because of bad weather. We locate the wreckage on a narrow ledge above the Whittier Tunnel. It is so steep we must remove the bodies by helicopter sling.

A Fed-Ex pilot in his private Cessna-185 scrapes his port wing on a cliff and cartwheels across the mountain. We find party favors strewn around the bodies of his wife and two kids. His license shows his birthday is the following day. He is flying to an island camp for a party and risks the poor visibility rather than turning back.

Foot Casts of Snow on Bare Ground

Our "evidence camera" is my personal Nikon N-90. My most unusual photographs are footprints made by a burglar at the Harbor Store.

There are about two inches of snow on the ground at the time of entry. The suspect compresses the snow as he walks upon the rolled pebble surface. The wind then gently blows away the loose snow surrounding the denser casts. We are left with a trail of dozens of perfect white "footprints" of compacted snow on a dark surface in the exact shape of the shoes. The

---

[104] Liz Ruskin, "Plane Crash Kills Four," *Anchorage Daily News*, 24 August 1992, pp. A-1 and A-5.

footprints are left by an older style "bunny boot," with tread worn by only one man in town—a local doper….

Starting the New Year with a Bang

In the early morning hours of the 1994 New Year, I chance to look out our eighth-floor window. A naked man is running across the snow and railroad tracks. "What now?" I ask my wife as I head out. He rapes a woman and is fleeing, as her screams alert neighbors. Another trip out by rail to the Sixth Avenue lockup in Anchorage.

With so many women using their gender disparity to their economic advantage, rapes are not as frequent as one might imagine. (Yes, ladies, I realize rape can also involve issues of control, anger, or power).

Barricaded Suspect

My relief officer is in Anchorage. His almost-eighteen boy, with a behavioral disorder, starts drinking. [Whenever there is a gun theft in town, I question Danny first. If he does it, he confesses and shows us where he hides it.] "Shots fired" calls start coming in. As I race up the stairway, my wife radios that Danny phones. He, too, hears the 911 calls regarding him on his dad's home-radio set.

"Tell Max if he comes up here, I'll stick a bullet in his head!" shouts Danny on the (recorded) 911 line. "I have a .45 auto and a Mini-14 rifle and will nail him through the door…I've got armor-piercing bullets and I'm gonna start blasting!"

I speak with Danny for about thirty minutes. The metal door makes it difficult to converse, so I ask him to open it a crack so we can hear better. He does and I kick it open. I "bear mace" him rather than shoot, as his only weapon in hand is a small kitchen knife. He falls to the floor shrieking. The Intake Unit of McLaughlin Youth Center in Anchorage takes him. He later hangs himself….

State Record Narcotics Haul from Cruise Ship

A passenger reports a brown sticky substance leaking from an overhead panel on the *Regent Star*. We seize 213 pounds of hash oil with a street-value of $4.5 million.[105] (Clue number one is its Jamaican crew.) We cannot seize the ship under the Racketeer Influenced & Corrupt Organizations Act (RICO) as the ship is under Coast Guard protections for joining a special "anti-forfeiture" inspections program (which appears to contain a few flaws). The *Star* would make a fine addition to our growing fleet.

Romance on the Rocks

A young lady of eighteen arrives on foot through the tunnels during a storm. She is soaked and has a sad tale. Her late mother tells her she is born following a one-night liaison with the chief of police of Whittier who gives his name as "John Smith." She wishes to find out more of her dad but suspects the name is phony.

I advise her that no chief has a name of Smith, but I will check the few old files in my safe. I find a note from the first chief, Gordon M. Whittier (a coincidence) that states, "Officer John M. Smith gets a girl p.g. and will not marry her....He leaves on the morning train without notice. Do not rehire." The lady departs without leaving a forwarding address but promises to call back. (She never does.)

Some months later, Trooper Corporal Patrick L. Hames, with Judicial Services, calls regarding a change of venue for a felony trial. He mentions he is the first officer hired on the Whittier PD in June 1974. I ask him about John Smith.

Whittier is fired in his first year for "local politics." "Mike" Smith and a girlfriend park on the concrete boat ramp at Smitty's Cove. They become so engrossed they fail to notice the incoming tide. Smith calls a friend to tow the police car from the water. The story comes out when the transmission burns out because of salt water immersion.

---

[105] "Hundreds of Pounds of Drugs Seized," *Anchorage Daily News*, 4 June 1992, p. B-6.

Out of Town by Sunset

Our best friends (and landlords) in Whittier are Chou "Joe" and Anne Shen. Joe, owner of the Anchor Inn, is robbed at gunpoint a few years before our arrival. In my safe is a letter from the irate district attorney who complains about the police chief. The suspect, not thinking out his getaway, fails to realize the outbound train is not running that day! He unloads his revolver and walks to the police station to surrender.

The chief escorts the suspect to the tunnel and orders him to walk out. No time-consuming and messy reports. The chief is subsequently fired, but not for this incident. He is on record for complaining of too many conflicting orders from the mayor and council.

Rail Ambulance

Hueih-Hueih and I attend the Alaska Railroad's Engineer Course to learn rules of the rail and license us to drive our 1981 Chevrolet High-Rail (highway rail) or Hy-Rail (hydraulic rail) Ambulance. It has steel hydraulic rail-wheels that lower onto the tracks. The double rear-drive wheels rest upon the rails and propel and brake the ambulance.

The rail ambulance is the only way out of town in bad weather. We try to schedule runs between freight trains, but this is not always possible. We can communicate by radio with the dispatcher in Anchorage and the local train engineers, but not when in the tunnel. Most freights are unscheduled and we can be surprised at any time.

The tracks are not well maintained. Where they widen or narrow in places, a heavy freight "squeezes" them into line. The light ambulance, however, will derail. We carry jacks, steel levers, and wedges to pry it back onto the tracks. A locomotive takes about a mile to stop. One of us must run a mile-plus down the tracks each way and crimp torpedoes (aluminum foil packets containing black powder) to the tracks which explode when run over and (hopefully) alert the crew to activate the braking sequence.

I back over a frog [106] and derail the ambulance in Portage, blocking the Noon Shuttle (a "non-preventable" incident). My new boss, the city manager, is aboard and scowling down from a flatcar. [I, of course, point to my wife who is furiously shaking her head. (Ha, ha)]

Donald W. Jubb, our instructor, later presents me with the coveted Alaska Railroad Safety Award, an engraved letterman's tool (largely for my efforts in preventing cruise-ship crews from crossing the tracks in town). One of the shuttle engineers allows me to operate his locomotive through the tunnels to Portage on occasion (with him also in the cab).

Tourists sometimes report "tunnel fires." Diesel locomotives fill the tunnel with smoke, which persists for long periods. Inside the tunnel all is dark. Headlights do not penetrate the smoke, and the headlamp of an oncoming locomotive cannot be seen until it is upon us. We watch the speedometer closely while in motion but do not touch the steering wheel. Our ambulance can outrun locomotives, even in reverse. We have some close calls but no serious collisions.

Iron doors at each end of the tunnel keep out stray moose, but unequal pressure on both sides of Maynard Mountain can create a rush of air that blows off the opposite door to the one opened. Ice must sometimes be chipped from the doors and rails—backbreaking labor in subzero weather.

Hueih-Hueih and I take out a fisherman who has his thumb torn off by a boat winch. It takes us over five hours to shovel snow and chip ice in Bear Valley, just before Portage. Each run enriches the city by $300. Opening the tunnel roadway, which straddles the tracks with a smooth concrete surface, is the death knell for the rail ambulance. It is the last one on the North American continent.

Deadly Glacier

Ash from an eruption of Mount Spurr darkens the August sky,[107] turning day into night, and coating the twenty-six glaciers in the area like chocolate

---

[106] A steel device to guide train wheels over the intersection of two tracks. The "frog" resembles the frog of a horse's hoof.

[107] "Mt. Spurr Erupts," *Anchorage Daily News*, 19 August 1992, p. A1.

sundaes. I commend my fire chief for, on his own, using our pumper to wash the corrosive ash off parked cars.

Blackstone Glacier is on the opposite side of the ridge behind Whittier, a little over a mile to the south. It is popular with kayakers. Hueih-Hueih and I sometimes patrol Blackstone in a tandem kayak.

A kayaker ventures up to the face, just as a section above calves. The kayak is sliced in half and the man killed.[108] His girlfriend, in a second craft a short distance behind, says he paddles through the brash (small floating chunks of ice) close to the face to fill his canteen with melted water. I tell her that the water to almost a mile out is fresh from melting runoff and is safe to drink. The North can be deadly for cheechakos.

Babes as Shields

A city worker, noted for his drinking, doping, and fighting, gets into an argument with his wife as she drinks up his beer supply. He beats her and kicks her out into the cold. She calls us.

Terry Bridge and I respond to find their apartment destroyed. Larry Roberts, intoxicated, is irritated by our lack of action against his wife. He grabs his twenty-month old daughter and holds her as a shield while breaking a heavy glass pitcher against a cabinet. This leaves a handle with two projections of broken glass with which he threatens to gut us.

Larry is in a narrow hallway where we cannot effectively grab him or use our batons. Going away is not an option for the safety of their child. Waiting him out is not working. We are reluctant to squirt our chemical mace—the earlier strong CN—as the child is so young.

I go in first, in a feint, to distract Larry. Terry is to concentrate on the child; to go in low and catch her if she falls. Larry slashes out, cutting the top of my left hand, but I jerk him off balance and am quickly behind him with my arm around his neck. Terry dives for the little girl as Larry "does the chicken." We have only seconds to 'cuff him and bind his legs. He regains consciousness and becomes a wild man, kicking and flailing.

---

[108] Pamela Doto, "Calving Glacier Crushes Man Kayaking in Sound," *Anchorage Daily News* (Metro Section), 19 June 1993, p. B1.

Larry is to tell his bar buddies that I zap him with a super stun gun. (They behave better without knowing the truth.) Larry checks into the gray bar hotel. Terry writes a good arrest report (93-112 of 31 January 1993; Assault-II on a police officer), which I use to request Larry's termination from city employment. No one else is as good with heavy snow-removal equipment, so he remains.

A dozen years later we visit Whittier unannounced. I spot Larry working on one of the docks with his back to me. I walk up and announce, "You are under arrest, Larry!" He stiffens and without turning around says, "I'm being good, Max."

I am commissioned by the State Troopers to enforce regulations beyond our city limits. We have other adventures, but the call load is down to almost nothing. I have an unheard of solve rate of 100 percent of all crimes known to me—both misdemeanor and felony. (I have a captive audience and many informants.) I am bored. Locals now call me "Whispering Max," as the nerves die in one vocal cord, and three operations do not help. It is time to retire, although we are asked to remain.

The city council throws a big farewell party for us on the "Triangle." The barbecuing is done by Robin Gaboury, with sisters Barbara "Babs" Reynolds and Brenda Tolman—our good friends and town characters—and the Shens. Most of the town turns out. Former Mayor Kelly Carlisle and Ben Butler (the current mayor) present me with a council resolution and appoint me "marshal emeritus." It is most touching.

The Pribilofs

The city manager of Saint George, the Pribilof Islands, asks me to implement a VPSO (Village Public Safety Officer—native police) program. "Other husbands take their wives to Hawai'i, " says Hueih-Hueih. "You take me to the Bering Sea in the middle of the winter storm season!"

Hueih-Hueih and I—with our tabby Manx, Poopie (don't ask), "Cat of the North"—fly out of King Salmon across the pack ice. St. George is about thirty-five frozen and wind-swept square miles of rock. The Great Martyr Russian Orthodox Church is the dominant building. VPSOs are natives who learn enough about "white man's law" to call in the Troopers when a serious crime is committed or an arrest is necessary. We emphasize that they are community "first responders"—problem solvers who must be fair, impartial, and the voice of reason.

I apprehend two Aleut kids attempting to burn down "House No. 25" next door, but soon discover native crime is not the problem. The village has 178 residents, but there are 700-plus young people working in two beached crab processor ships: the "Northern Alaska" and "SnoPac" at Zapadni (Russian: "West") Bay. I meet with the ship managers and they agree to immediately fly out any of their people who cause trouble on the island. The conflict grinds down to a mild roar.

VPSO duties include repairing buildings, pumping gas for islanders, and anything else the council wishes. The harbor master is about to depart for Australia. He teaches me his most critical task: guiding fishing boats in by radio as they make two right-angle turns into Zapadni Bay. The bay is shallow, and the boats can only proceed when a wave reaches a certain height on one particular rock. The tide tables must be closely coordinated. A boat grounding on sand and rocks will be at the mercy of subsequent waves and easily wrecked.

I must sit in my big red 1990 Chevrolet Scottsdale Suburban for several hours a day, lining up fishing boats and giving them the "go" signal. I don't lose one (because I set the imaginary wave marker a foot higher than recommended).

I discover some papers on General Harrison Gray Otis when he is "special treasury agent" for the Seal Islands (Pribilofs) in 1879–1881. I forward copies to his great-grandson, Otis Chandler, final member of the family to hold the title as publisher of the *Los Angeles Times*. Otis is most appreciative. The statue of the Civil War soldier (pointing his right arm) in MacArthur Park, Los Angeles, is of General Otis.

Arctic foxes are everywhere. They gather outside the window, where Poopie sits, rolling in the snow and trying to entice her outside to play. (I see no other cats on the island and can imagine why.)

Last Train to Nowhere

Travel during our decade in the Land of the Midnight Sun is not easy.

I visit Dutch Harbor and hunt moose in Nome with my friend, Chief Robert L. Kauer. (We are not successful.) Wyatt Earp runs the Dexter Saloon in Nome from 1899 to 1901. One of the strangest sights in Alaska is seen off Mile 31 of the Council Road.

Three rusting 1880s 0-4-4 Forney-type steam locomotives (the last in existence) of the Council City and Solomon River Railroad are stranded and sinking into the tundra next to the Bering Sea. Enormous gold dredges, some with the operator's tools still lying about, litter the landscape. Miners transport horses north to move their goods—but are forced to kill and eat them at the end of summer. Local grasses are not sufficiently nutritious to feed them over the winter.

We rent dogs and sleds from Howling Dog Farm in Willow (Mile 66, George Parks Highway). Farther north on the Parks, between Nenana and Fairbanks, is "Skinny Dick's Halfway Inn." Dick is dead, but his roadhouse—featuring tacky and inappropriate merchandise—lives on.

We cross the Arctic Circle [109] on the Dalton Highway (aka: the North Slope Haul Road or Alaska 11) and set foot in the Arctic Ocean at Deadhorse and Prudhoe Bay to visit our oil. We bounce across 16 miles of tundra and beach south of Barrow on an all-terrain vehicle to the memorials at the 1935 crash site of Will Rogers and Wiley Post. Natives vandalize both.

We hand-pull a cable tram over the river in McCarthy to hike to the abandoned Kennicott Mine (misspelling of Kennecott Copper Corporation). Sitka, Skagway,[110] Soldotna, Indian, North Pole, and Coldfoot—all hold memories for the vagabond.

---

[109] The line north of which there is a continuous twenty-four hours (at least once a year) when the sun does not rise above the horizon, and there is one entire day the sun does not set.

[110] Frontier mining towns in the States are lucky to have an officer or two. Dawson City has 30 mounties and 203 soldiers of the Yukon Field Force assigned to keep the peace during the Klondike Gold Rush. (They also collect a 20-percent gold royalty and withhold

Max K. Hurlbut

Alaska's Picturesque Speech

"Speaking American" does not always translate into "speaking English." Mainstream English is not spoken in either Watts or East L.A., nor is it in Alaska.

"Herring chokers" are women employed in herring reduction plants. We all know "hooch." It is a derivative of *"kootznahoo,"* an obscure Tlingit name for a distilled native rum (or) *"hootchinoo,"* the name of a tribe that distills a local liquor.

An "Alaska divorce," in the world of crime, is to murder one's spouse. Crazed Whittier criminals rarely plead "not guilty by reason of insanity"— juries don't notice anything odd and convict them. Prostitution is considered a time-share business as the property in question is occupied for such a short period.

Many words exist for ice and cold. Most know "breakup" is when winter ice on rivers melts enough to break and flow. (The very definition of "sourdough" is a "cheechako" who has remained long enough to experience a breakup.) Hundreds of thousands of dollars are won by those guessing the date and time, to the minute, of the Tanana River breakup in the Athabascan village of Nenana.

Winter weather is the toughest part of the North. It's not always 60 degrees below zero; sometimes it is only 40 degrees below. We tell tourists it is so cold that spring visitors are startled when winter curses thaw with sudden bursts of profanity. (Did I mention that, once a sourdough, you begin to exaggerate to cheechakos?) It is true, however, that the state bird is the mosquito!

---

alternate claims for the government.) Two Maxim guns are positioned atop the White and Chilkoot Passes. The major Canadian concern is that Americans will annex the Yukon and join with nearby Alaska.

Duct and Cover—A Tacky Heritage

Homeland Security sends out a ripple of code-orange panic a few years ago when they urge everyone to stock up on duct tape.[111] Duct tape is a cultural symbol in the Far North. Anchorage holds an annual Duct Tape Ball. Performers at the "Fly-By-Night-Club" play rolls of duct tape as musical instruments. Dog mushers stick it on their faces to prevent frostbite. It holds together aircraft wings in the Bush.

Duct tape is also a tool of the criminal element. The corpse of Joseph E. Vogler, leader of the state's secessionist Independence Party, is found bound with duct tape in 1994. (He is buried in Dawson City, the Yukon, per his wish to not be buried under the American flag.) Fishermen patch bullet holes in their boats (and themselves) with it.

A cardboard box wrapped with duct tape is an "Alaska Samsonite." Broken headlights or windshield shot out? A little Visqueen and duct tape solve all. And why use a razor when you can stick-and-rip? The only thing you cannot do with duct tape is to eat it. For this we have Spam.

Native Cuisine

Not all officers are willing or able to work under the harsh conditions of bush life: limited electricity, no running water or flush toilets, and no stores—even for groceries. You sometimes eat *tepa* (sockeye salmon heads fermented by burial), berries in hooligan (candlefish) or seal oil, and oogruk (bearded seal) flipper fermented in blubber, intestine soup, etc.

The cold can be deadly. Getting lost or injured and starving to death happen a lot. Into the Wild (1996) describes the slow starvation of a California man, known for his lack of preparation in "living off the land." He calls himself "Super-Tramp." He manages to kill a moose with his .22 rimfire rifle, but tries to smoke it rather than cut thin slices to air-

---

[111] They recommend (10 February 2003) creating a safe area within homes by sealing rooms with plastic sheeting and duct tape. [*Snopes* reports three Israeli Arabs suffocate after doing so. ("Smother of Invention," updated 8 March 2008).]

dry it. It spoils. Marginal personalities can go nutso, as at McCarthy in March 1983. A former computer programmer murders six of twenty-two residents.

Chapter XIX

"THE TOWN TOO TOUGH TO DIE" [112]

Trouble in Tombstone

"This Court cannot possibly be oblivious to the state of anarchy that is present in the City of Tombstone."[113]

"Tombstone is to the point of armed insurgency and believe me, it is well armed."[114]

"Fourth Tombstone Marshal Appointed This Year!"[115]

Crisis leading to the gunfight behind the O. K. Corral of 26 October 1881? No, just business as usual in the "Town Too Tough to Die."

Salmon to Scorpions

Tombstone Magistrate Alfred J. Pickett calls. He is a military judge and a fellow legal instructor at the Army Intelligence Center at Fort Huachuca, Sierra Vista, Arizona.

"The new Reform Mayor, Delmas E. "Gene" Harper (aka: "Dirty Delmas" to his opposition), has a problem," says Al.

Gene Harper comes on the line and states, *"My six-deputy Marshal's Office is running amok. They've generated $12 million in lawsuits and claims in the last 18 months for false arrests, excessive force, and other*

---

[112] Slogan coined by *Tombstone Epitaph* editor Walter H. Cole on the front page of the 26 February 1931 edition.

[113] Statement of Tombstone City Attorney P. Randall Bays in Superior Court, Bisbee, Cochise County. Quoted in: Pat Koester, "Judge Stops City/Protects Marshal/Then Quits," *Tombstone Tumbleweed*, 26 June 1997 (Vol. X, No. 44), p. 3.

[114] "On Your Mind," *Sierra Vista Herald-Bisbee Daily Review*. Author's file. Undated in week following Monday, 9 June 1997.

[115] Headline, front page, *The Tombstone News*, 16 December 2005, (Vol. 1, Issue 18).

misconduct. How soon can you travel?"[116] (I am in Alaska.) Could Richard Boone, as Paladin in "Have Gun—Will Travel" (1957-63), turn down such a summons?

Deputy Criminals

The hiring of felons and misfits is an old Cochise County custom since Deputy Albert "Burt" Avord, Tombstone tough and train robber, rides for Sheriff John H. Slaughter over a century ago. Word at Fort Huachuca is, as a civilian, you can become a crook or a *cop*. Or join the Cochise County Sheriff's Office and become both!

Modern Tombstone city marshals last as long as eleven years[117] in office and as short as ten hours.[118] Job tenure, I am advised, relates to how much "dirt" the marshal has on the mayor and common council members. The situation that unfolds is worse than I anticipate. Five of the six deputies have backgrounds that disqualify them for service in any professional police organization.

I terminate one deputy who has an indictment for vehicular homicide, arrest for rape of a fifteen-year-old, writes NSF checks, is dishonorably discharged from the navy for drug use, and lies on several police applications.[119] I attempt to have him decertified by Arizona POST for violations of their rules. They tell me (despite no statute of limitations on

---

[116] Bob Candland, "Harper Appoints Professional Police Manager as Marshal," *Tombstone Tumbleweed*, 17 July 1997, front page. Steve Schmidt, "New Marshal Tames the 'Town Too Tough to Die'," (Lake Havasu, AZ) *News-Herald*, 22 November 1998, p. 10A (and) "Marshal's Law," *San Diego Union-Tribune*, 26 October 1998 (Vol. 7, No. 299), pp. A-1 and A-15.

[117] Gordon W. Fischler (1971–1982), "Gordon Fischler," *Tombstone Epitaph*, 3–17 December 1982. The last elected Marshal. Dismissed for unknown reasons.

[118] Debra K. Mackey (16 November 1982), Ellen Walp, "Policewoman: First Female Marshal Appointed; Serves Only One Night," *Epitaph*, 3–17 December 1982. Resigns because of a "lack of experience" after a night on the streets.

[119] Bob Candland, "Tombstone Senior Deputy Indicted for Homicide in '87," *Tombstone Tumbleweed*, 5 September 1996 (Vol. X, No. 2), pp. 1, 3, 5.

their rules) that the charges are "too old." I reply, "And his two victims are still dead!"

NOTE: My copy of the DPS report (87-72598), one of the most thorough I have seen, interviews fifty-three civilian witnesses to driving, intoxication, and the violations that are the proximate cause of death. Nine police (from three departments) and medical personnel testify concerning Daniel O. Romero's intoxication.

A grand jury issues a true bill on 14 August 1987 charging vehicular homicide, three counts of felony assault, and reckless driving. Interestingly, the crimes are committed in Willcox where Romero's uncle, Guillermo "Bill" Morales, is the chief of police. (Morales soon dies at age forty-eight.)

The late Alan K. Polley, Cochise County District Attorney, dismisses the case for "insufficient factual and legal basis." (His most notorious quotation is, perhaps, "No more plea bargains."[120])

Romero supposedly is hired in Parker as an "undercover high-school officer" despite no prior police experience. Parker Chief of Police Robert S. Caples, another former Hollywood Division roommate, knows that Romero is hired by their previous chief, but never actually appears for work. He is a "phantom employee." The chief who "employs" him is the former lieutenant of Romero's uncle in Willcox....

Marshal Edward E. Schnautz, who hires Romero in Tombstone, drops into my office to tell me he is ordered to sign on Romero or lose his job. Ed, an acquaintance of many years, dies at age forty-nine.

Another deputy is arrested (before becoming a police officer) for CCW. He is caught with a .357 Magnum, an Ingram Mac 11 machine pistol, a ski mask, and a bogus "Military Intelligence" badge.[121] After I get rid of him, he goes to another Arizona agency and lasts less than a year.

---

[120] Paul Rubin, "Smuggler's Paradise," *Phoenix New Times*, 28 June 1989.

[121] Bob Candland, "Deputy Convicted in 1993 Weapons Charge," *Tombstone Tumbleweed*, 12 September 1996 (Vol. X, No. 3), p. 1.

The mayor fires the previous marshal, Robert D. Gerencser, for insubordination and failing to properly manage the department. Unruly and defiant crowds shout, "Seig Heil!" and assault a reporter in council meetings.[122] Two councilmen are rabid supporters of the marshal and the corrupt faction he represents.

Cochise County Corruption

The Tombstone Common Council of the 1880s is split in their support of local factions, as now. I hire honest and experienced deputies—retired from other Arizona law enforcement agencies—who have good judgment and common sense. The Council, which previously employs misfits and criminals, refuses to hire them.[123] [The dismissed officers, however, are quickly hired, as deputies, by their buddy, the Cochise County sheriff, as soon as I am rid of them.[124]]

West Coast police officers (and other professionals) will read some of this chapter in disbelief. A sheriff or chief hiring officers known for their brutality, drug use, and serious felonies—with their crimes openly documented in the local newspaper—will get them fired or recalled in most jurisdictions. The liability exposure is horrendous for the local taxpayers. Complain about the iron grip of local l.e., and bad things will happen to you. The "investigation" will invariably show the cause as some terrible "accident" or violence attributed to an unidentified Mexican drug cartel.

The Feds may have crushed the Jim Crow America of Macon County, but have little interest in the thugs of Southeastern Arizona. "At the present

---

[122] Pat Koester, "Marshal Ordered to Turn in His Badge," *Tombstone Tumbleweed*, 19 June 1997 (Vol. X, No. 43), front page (and) Bob Candland, "Batters Reporter—City Marshal and Deputies Do Nothing But Laugh," *Tombstone Tumbleweed*, 19 September 1996 (Vol. X, No. 4), front page.

[123] Pat Koester, "Council Slashes Marshal's Department," *Tumbleweed*, 19 February 1998 (Vol. XI, No. 26), front page.

[124] (Sheriff) Dever said he was not concerned about the deputies' past history." Pat Koester, "Sheriff Dever Hires Gerencser, Romero, Houston," *Tumbleweed*, 15 January 1998 (Vol XI, No. 21), pp. 1 and 7.

time it is an accepted fact among Federal Law Enforcement agencies and the U.S. Attorney's Office (Tucson) that law enforcement corruption in the border communities of Arizona has reached a crisis state. It is the opinion of the SAC/IA Tucson that attacking only the Customs corruption is like putting a bandaid on cancer."[125]

Francisco D. "Frank" Hidalgo (the only former deputy I retain) and I work twelve-hour watches, seven days a week. The publisher of the *Tumbleweed*, Robert I. Candland, is a former San Diego police officer. He is aghast at what is going on. He writes editorials telling the town of council attempts to get us so exhausted and discouraged that we quit. Our slots are finally restored after local seniors become alarmed.

Anonymous flyers then appear all over town accusing Candland of being a serial killer of prostitutes.[126] They fire shots at his home, make threats to lynch him, and destroy his newspapers and racks.

Twenty Miles From Water & Two Feet From Hell

Starting pay for Tombstone deputies is $21,486 a year ($24,876 after ten years). Arizona is short 1,200 certified officers. Competition for qualified bodies is intense. Half a dozen former LAPD partners who retire to become Arizona officers advise me against taking the job. Many Arizona officers resent West Coast policemen because of our inflexible stance on corruption and professionalism (i.e., we cannot be bought). Honesty is considered a character defect.

Arizona Highway Patrol Audit (or) "I Smell a Rat"

The former marshal, realizing he is in trouble, requests an audit of his operation from the State Department of Public Safety's "Inspections and Control Unit" to counter charges of incompetence.

---

[125] Opening statement in "United States Government Memorandum" to the Regional Director (Internal Affairs, Department of Treasury) Southwest Region, from John W. Juhasz, Special Agent in Charge, Tucson, 29 January 1990, 4 pp. File SSEC-1-IA: TU.

[126] Leo W. Banks, "Paper Tiger," *Tucson Weekly*, 14–20 August 1997, pp. 14–16.

The "Operational Inspection of the Tombstone Marshal's Department," #5-95, states (Executive Summary): "The internal problems revealed in this audit are fairly minor and easily correctable....Property and evidence operations at the Tombstone Marshal's Department overall function well" (page 34).

DPS detectives ignore the criminal backgrounds of deputies, complaints of false arrests and beatings, civil suits, and firings from other Arizona police departments. Personnel complaints supposedly result in "appropriate conclusions and reasonable dispositions" (page 21).

I request the presence of *Tumbleweed* editor Bob Candland and other witnesses for the opening of the 8×12-foot evidence room. Its steel door is locked and the key "lost." The Public Works director torches it open.

Bales of decomposing marijuana—thousands of pounds—are stacked deep and to the ceiling. There are few evidence reports to identify the guns and dope on the shelves. An opened package contains thirteen pounds (not ounces) of cocaine, with a total of around forty missing pounds (or kilos—both units are mentioned in separate notations). The Sheriff's Department (it is a joint-arrest) later indicates they have an old seizure of forty-nine pounds that may or may not be related to this case but find it, too, is missing or destroyed.

Lies, Damned Lies, and Statistics

How is it possible a DPS audit team fails to notice and comment upon the bales of marijuana, preventing entrance to the TMO evidence room? The lack of paperwork, missing dope and firearms, and other discrepancies are obvious and alarming.

I ask Candland to print: "Max says either DPS enters the Evidence Room and LIES about what they see; or, they do not enter the room and LIE about what they do not see!"[127] A friendly DPS trooper stops by the station and advises me to be careful, as some on his department intend to "get me."

---

[127] Bob Candland, "Lost: 40 Pounds of Cocaine. Found: 49 Pounds of Cocaine," *Tombstone Tumbleweed*, 18 September 1997 (Vol. XI, No. 4), pp. 1 and 7.

I tell him, "No they won't, because I have the goods on them!" I never hear anything more regarding this.

NOTE: A retired LAPD commander is a friend of retired deputy chief Vernon L. Hoy, who becomes the director of AZ-DPS (1976–1980). He visits Hoy who implores him to stay on as his bodyguard. "(Hoy) had a difficult time (at AZ-DPS) due to a strong organized crime influence with law enforcement….since a bomb had been recently found beneath his police car." [Quoted in a report, "Remembrance of Chief Vern Hoy," 20 November 2007, in "The Rotator," a confidential L.A. Police Officers' site.] Hoy believes the bomb is rigged by a DPS officer!

Devious Dever's Dope Disposal

I request Sheriff Larry A. Dever to pick up and destroy my remaining cocaine, as they do for other police agencies in the county. They supposedly transport it to an incinerator at an old mine in New Mexico.

Two plainclothes deputies arrive in a rental van. The senior deputy is in the Arizona National Guard and one of my old students from Fort Huachuca. Call him Bob. I have scales and a test kit available. Bob refuses to weigh or test the product (to be sure another substance has not been substituted) or to issue a receipt. This is basic to our business.

Sheriff D. explains this is his policy: "We seize so much dope, Max, that it is cumbersome to weigh it and issue receipts." I request that a (classified) unit on Fort Huachuca destroy my narcotics—they issue receipts. (I am beginning to understand the sheriff's nickname of "Larry Devious.") The sheriff has some good policies, such as his anti-illegal immigration stance, but others that are "peculiar." It is peculiar he does not end up in his own jail.

I tell Larry I know Bob. Bob's boy, a suspected dope dealer, is recently found hanged in his Sierra Vista furniture store. (Another "Cochise County Suicide.") I suggest that, as honest as Bob may be, his collecting narcotics and not issuing receipts may be misinterpreted or a conflict of interest. Larry laughs and hangs up.

Deputy Hidalgo documents this incident, and I advise the mayor, city clerk (a former San Bernardino County deputy), and city attorney. They request a meeting with the sheriff, who instead sends his undersheriff to reiterate their narcotics policies. The "person of interest" is the former marshal who originally seizes the missing dope five years before and writes the conflicting memos as to kilos or pounds. (He is interviewed but refuses to discuss the incident.)

A responsible citizen soon comes into my office to say he is gassing his auto when the undersheriff drives up to speak with the former marshal. This individual, not knowing of our confidential meeting, overhears the two discussing what went on concerning the missing narcotics.

Holding the BAG

Tombstone is one of seven departments in the county that provide an officer to the Border Alliance Group. (Sierra Vista, the largest city, refuses to participate at this time). BAG is capable of conducting narcotics operations in towns with insufficient officers to combat local problems. BAG shares costs and assets. A sound idea. BAG is renamed NET (Narcotics Enforcement Team) in 2012.

Cochise County prosecuting attorney Alan K. Polley (the same one dismissing the Romero homicide indictment) discovers (October 1997) their office of five attorneys "misplaces" $250,000 in BAG grant monies. They quietly try to cover the loss by removing RICO funds from participating cities. They get caught, and apologize. Polley conveniently dies. They have no auditing program and it is never explained what happens to the cash….

Badges with a Green Glint of Corruption

Sheriff Dever objects—in the BAG meeting of 20 October 1998—to a (confidential) report I write to the Tombstone Council critical of his administration of BAG operations. I ask to see his copy of the report, which he is holding. (Plagued with leaks, I start coding my reports to individual councilmen.) As suspected, it is from one of the two who support the fired corrupt officers.

I stand in the presence of county police chiefs and federal agents and tell them of my concerns with BAG and the sheriff's improper handling of narcotics. You can hear a pin drop. The sheriff and undersheriff are ashen-faced. One chief later tells me everyone in the room has similar experiences but must live here, so I should not object. What is disturbing to me, the outsider, appears "normal" to locals. Local feds (including Drug Enforcement) tell me they do not pursue corruption in Cochise County as the cases just become "lost or forgotten." I am to learn there are sound reasons to keep quiet.

Devious does not allow public access to his public jail records. They are known to be inaccurate.[128] The money collected for phantom bodies is rumored to go into his pocket.

Restraining Order

I soon receive a "Restraining Order and Injunction Against Harassment" (CV 980314-HA) from Cochise County Deputy Danny Romero saying he is now "afraid" of me, and I must stay out of Bisbee. A tad peculiar as I have not seen or spoken with him since I terminate him fourteen months earlier. He also cannot describe the (legally required) instances where I supposedly threaten him.

Romero is now a resident and deputy in the Douglas area, about twenty-seven miles southeast of Bisbee. Douglas is almost fifty road miles from Tombstone and is not mentioned as "off-limits" in the order.

The purpose of the restraining order, of course, is to keep me out of any more BAG meetings held in the sheriff's office in Bisbee. I am subpoenaed to testify on a felony case in superior court—in Bisbee. I tell the deputy working courthouse security (a friend and Tombstone resident) he should

---

[128] David M. Morgan, "Phantom Inmates in Cochise County Jails? The Official List Isn't Right, But Why?" Cochise County Record, 29 April 2013.

call his boss and tell him I am here should he wish to *attempt* to serve his restraining order on me *personally*. He says with a smile, "It's a little boring around here; I think I will."

Larry D. never shows up. I am told the story is a source of amusement around the courthouse as no one taunts the sheriff in his fiefdom. Such a restraining order is legally indefensible and is soon quashed by City Attorney Randy Bays, much to the irritation of the sheriff.

The Only Honest Man

I leave the courthouse and drive through the Mule Mountains on Highway 80 back to Tombstone. I am told that John Pintek (1914–2010), former Cochise County Attorney, has a 160-acre ranch off the highway. Pintek's father is loaded on a train and dropped in the New Mexico desert in the Bisbee Deportation of striking copper miners in 1917.

Pintek, sometimes described as "the only honest man in Cochise County," is a rabid Democrat. I tell him I am an unrepentant Conservative but wish to know what is going on in the sheriff's office as I am under siege. We hit it off, and I call in to my office and wife to tell them I will not make it back until evening.

John spends a career fighting corruption in Cochise County. He has stories concerning the "endemic perversion of justice" by individuals as four-term Sheriff Jimmy V. Judd, a late relative of Sheriff Dever. [John F. Pintek, the old man's son, defeats Judd and is the sheriff between the two. Sheriff John and I remain friends to this day.]

An organized campaign of "dirty tricks" is used against Sheriff Pintek. They actually obtain a restraining order to keep him out of his own office![129] (Restraining orders in Cochise County appear to be a *Devious* tactic.) Meanwhile, the gruesome chronicle of beheadings, torture,

---

[129] A female Dever supporter (hired by Judd) in the office of the sheriff claims Pintek uses a computer for political purposes. She tries to keep the sheriff out of his own office as she fears "retaliation." The employee appears to be the actual violator and withdraws her order once the situation becomes public. "Judd ran law enforcement down there as his private fiefdom for years." "The Skinny: Hardball in the Hinterlands," *Tucson Weekly*, 24–30 October 1996.

kidnappings, and extortion—regular features of life a few miles to the south—are ignored.

The O.K. Corral

A few words regarding the conflict of the 1880s may clarify what makes southeast Arizona of today a bastion of corruption.

A loose confederation of Texas cowboys,[130] under N.H. "Old Man"[131] Clanton, raids across the border and massacres Mexican ranchers in the early 1880s. He is likely present at the Skeleton Canyon Massacre of Mexican smugglers along with Johnny Ringo, "Curley Bill" Brocius, and Frank and Tom McLaury. Clanton is later killed in the nearby Guadalupe Canyon Massacre—almost certainly by Rurales (*Guardia Rural*) taking their revenge upon the cowboys.[132]

Tombstone is founded in March 1879 by Ed Schieffelin, who is told by soldiers at nearby Fort Huachuca that, courtesy of the Apaches, all he will find is his tombstone. The town grows quickly and two factions emerge: *Democrats*, who are Confederate sympathizers and small ranch owners; and, *Republicans,* the capitalists, miners, gamblers, and lawyers. The cowboys, impatient with the time and effort necessary to raise cattle the traditional way, rustle cows in Sonora and sell them to local butchers to feed a rapidly growing population (of between ten and fifteen thousand).

Flooding of the silver mines and burning of the Cornish pump engine in the Grand Central Mine of May 1886 lead to abandonment of the mines and depopulation of the town. The few who remain are the small ranch owners—whose descendants still hate the Earps and any law enforcement officers they cannot control. They rustle cows in the 1880s but now send

---

[130] The term "cowboy" then means rascal, ruffian, and robber.

[131] Clanton's nickname is probably a play on his first name of *Newman*. He is about sixty-five at the time of his death in 1881.

[132] Terry "Ike" Clanton (clan cousin) and five of us relocate the original ruins of the Clanton Ranch off the San Pedro River near the ghost town of Charleston on 20 November 1998. (See photos on Net under, "5th Annual Clanton Days Rendezvous"). Ike locates the grave of the original Ike Clanton and petitions the Tombstone Common Council to rebury him in Boothill. They turn him down.

autos, guns, and money south and white powder and illegal aliens north. Family ties long ago replace political parties as antagonists.

Vengeance Ride

Wyatt B. S. Earp fires a shotgun blast into Frank Stillwell in the Tucson train yard and turns from lawman to avenger. With two sheriff's posses (Johnny Behan and the Charleston Cowboys) in pursuit—but not anxious to catch up—Wyatt and companions track down and kill "Indian Charlie" Cruz and "Curly Bill" Brocius.

Wyatt Earp is the lawman all of us fear we may one day become. He is never a town marshal or a county sheriff. He serves fewer than five years as a peace officer. (He is a gambler, prospector, and saloon owner.) He is known for his honesty and minimal use of force. (A drunk he jails in Wichita awakens to find his $500 roll intact.[133])

Frontier towns demand tough marshals. Cowtown fathers do not want their best customers, the Texas cattlemen, killed. They want them alive, having a good time, and spending their money.

A Matter of Justice

Books are written analyzing Earp's vendetta. The answer, however, is simple and relates to today's problem: "Can a nation of laws survive when the laws fail to work?"

Tombstone Chief of Police Virgil Earp is shot from ambush and his arm shattered. Morgan Earp is shot through a window of Campbell and Hatch's Saloon and Billiard Parlor. The shooters are known. Cowboys are seen fleeing these shootings and other evidence ties them in. Ike Clanton and cohorts are brought to trial. A dozen fellow cowboys "testi-lie" they are playing cards with them in Charleston at the time.

---

[133] Casey O. Tefertiller, *Wyatt Earp—The Life Behind the Legend* (1997), Deluxe Edition No. 100 of 150, p.13. One of the most unbiased and meticulously researched Earp books. I attend Casey's party at the *Tumbleweed* office on 18 October 1997 following his release of this book at *Helldorado*. It is nominated for a Pulitzer Prize.

Vagabond Policeman

The courts prove impotent and it is impossible to obtain convictions. The town turns against the Earps. False rumors are spread of their involvement in crimes. Wyatt and his young brother, Warren, are the only ones to remain. They, too, will likely be murdered and their killers unpunished. This issue of justice versus the law is what has kept alive the thirty-second gunfight and the vengeance ride for so many years.

Wyatt Earp is long gone, dying in his Los Angeles bed in 1929 just short of his eighty-first birthday. Every time you see John Wayne in *Stagecoach*, *True Grit*, or *The Shootist*, you are seeing Wyatt Earp. Hugh O'Brian plays Earp in the 1955–1961 television series *The Life and Legend of Wyatt Earp*. [Stuart N. Lake, Earp's biographer and author of *Frontier Marshal* (1931), is the advisor]. John Wayne tells O'Brian his image of the West is forever shaped by chance meetings with the old lawman on studio back lots. [For a charming fictional account of this relationship, see the movie *Sunset* (1988).]

Vigilance Committees

Chief Clancy Wiggums enters Springfield Police Station at 1000. The phone shows a backlog of seventy-five 911 calls. Wiggums deletes them all, saying, "Can't you people take the law into your own hands?"[134]

Taking the law into our own hands is an old American tradition. We Americans are fond of violent solutions to social problems. Mob rule may even be the purest form of democracy. Tory wit and Warden of All Souls, John H. A. Sparrow, tells the story of two castaways who reach an island where their first sight is a gallows from which a corpse dangles. "Thank God," says one, "it's a civilized country."

---

[134] Hank Azaria, "The Secret War of Lisa Simpson," *The Simpsons*, Season 8 (1997), Episode 25.

Citizens of Los Angeles lynch[135] twenty-two or more Chinese in 1871 (the Chinese Massacre).[136] L.A. Mayor Stephen C. Foster temporarily resigns office in 1855 to lead a lynch mob.

The popular Western view of lynch law is of cowboys who get stray horses and cows tangled in their loops or who make clerical errors with a branding iron. Angry mobs break them from jail to hang them.

The Bisbee Massacre

John Heath is the leader of a gang that shoots to death four in a botched Bisbee robbery. He leads the posse astray, but all six are captured and jailed in Tombstone. Heath, tried separately, receives a life sentence. His companions are sentenced to hang. Locals consider this inadequate punishment and break Heath (but not the others) from jail and hang him from a telegraph pole at First and Toughnut on 22 February 1884.

Vigilance committees are rarely in conflict with local law enforcement despite Western movie portrayals. Most lynchings are of *convicted* criminals where mobs fear that technical appeals will free the guilty. Vigilance committees are organized, not because there are no established institutions of law enforcement and justice, but because they cannot be relied upon to punish the guilty.

The American criminal justice system places enforcement of the laws within the domain of the ordinary citizen, not the state. Citizens, with but minor differences, have the same powers of arrest as do police officers. The people claim the right to dispense with the formal administration of law when justice is not served. Vigilante action is, thus, not so much in opposition to established law as a supplement to it. When the government is the greatest lawbreaker, how can we rely upon it to give us justice?

---

[135] The common definition of lynch is "an extrajudicial execution carried out by a vigilante mob to punish a transgressor or to intimidate a population." California law enforcement officers know lynching as, "Taking, by means of a riot, a person from the lawful custody of a peace officer" (405a PC).

[136] "Day That L.A. Doesn't Care to Remember," *Los Angeles Herald-Examiner* (United Press International), 25 October 1971 (and) Hurlbut, "The Chinese Massacre," *The Link* (Police Historical Society), March 1997 (Vol. 4, No. 1), pp. 2–5.

"Kiss My Six-Shooter"

"A well-tied tie is the first serious step in life."
— Oscar Wilde

"Folks around here get nervous with anything around their necks."
— Author

Hooded diarist George Parsons administers the vigilante oath of the Tombstone "Committee of 100" to applicants: "Kiss my six-shooter." [137] Parsons and his vigilantes side with the Earps.

Marshal Benjamin Sippy (15 November 1880 to 28 June 1881) holds off a mob with his shotgun while protecting gambler and murderer Michael "Johnny-Behind-The-Deuce" O'Rourke. "Sippy was... cool as an iceberg (as) he held the crowd in check."[138] This incident is sometimes credited to Wyatt Earp, but contemporary accounts say he is not present. It becomes the grist for numerous Western movie plots.

O'Rourke is jailed in Tucson, but escapes and is never tried. He is "mysteriously" shot and killed in 1882 in the Sulphur Spring Valley after he is again caught cheating in a card game.

Boot Hill

"Here Lies Lester Moore;
Four Shots from a .44.
No Les'
No More."

Lester Moore is the Wells Fargo agent in the border town of Naco. Cowboy Hank Dunstan appears daily for an overdue package. It finally arrives, beat to hell. The furious Hank perforates Lester, but not before Les

---

[137] Earl Chafin (Ed.), *The Private Journal of George Whitwell Parsons* (1879–1887), Vol. II, p. 14.

[138] *Tombstone Epitaph*, 27 January 1881, front page.

finishes off his killer with a single shot. (An early example of the customer "going postal.")

Concrete-like soil encourages shallow slit trenches for graves. (You are buried sideways, with no coffin.) Rocks piled on top discourage coyotes. "Proper" residents are buried in the "new" (late 1884) Tombstone cemetery on West Allen Street.

Boot Hill closes in 1884 but is restored after the popularity of Stuart Lake's *Frontier Marshal* in 1931. Some burial records exist but are later destroyed in a church arson. Newspaper articles and courthouse records reveal the names of a few. The original headboards are wood.

Ranch hands cannot afford hotel rooms on riding to town, so they camp at the outskirts. [Tombstone is in the Sonoran Desert at 4,540 feet. It sometimes snows in winter.] Guess what they burn for firewood? Time and souvenir hunters pick off the rest.

A rancher friend, Frank Shelby Bennett (1931–2005), says he is hired, as a kid, to arbitrarily place the current markers, as no one knows who is buried where.[139]

Historian and retired Tucson PD detective Stanley G. Benjamin and I spend days researching his book on *Tombstone Lawmen* (1999). I am the fortieth city marshal/chief of police (not counting a few absentee and unpaid "acting" stints of less than a month by the sheriff between appointments).[140]

My photograph is taken with the Boot Hill marker of the town's first marshal, Fred White (page 3). Fred is shot to death by "Curley Bill" Brocius, who is then "buffaloed" by Wyatt Earp. Stan notes that 118 years separate us. The second marshal (30 October to 15 November 1880) and fourth (28 June to 29 October 1881) is Virgil Earp.

---

[139] Carlos Arias, "Heritage Buried in Unmarked Grave," *Tombstone Epitaph*, 19 December 1997 (Vol. CXVII, No. 9), pp. 1 and 2.

[140] Stanley G. Benjamin, *Tombstone Lawmen: 1880–1999*, "Book 1 of 500" (1999). See pages 1, 3, 39, 42–43, and 49 for Marshal Max.

Rotten Row[141]

Tombstone is a marvelous historical area mixed with kitsch and tourist traps. Gunfight reenactors from opposing businesses get into fistfights while aggressively rounding up tourists. Phony memorabilia and overpriced artifacts are for sale. Two competing stagecoach lines constantly squabble over who can park where and how aggressively they can solicit customers. One stage owner eventually becomes mayor and forces out the other.

"Boot Hill," at 408 North Highway 80 (Fremont Street), is leased to a local woman in 1993 for $4,254 a year, plus four percent of gift sales. She refuses to release profit records, although it is known that greater than 600,000 visitors each year stuff bills into the donation box. City Attorney Randy Bays attempts not to renew the lease as it is illegal for an individual to profit from a city-owned historical property. Mayor Harper loses the next election and the city attorney and I are not reappointed at the end of our terms. The cemetery lease is still an issue years later.[142] Another profit-making scheme at the expense of the taxpayers.

Fires in June 1881 and May 1882 destroy much of the town. (As with George Washington's hatchet, despite two new heads and three handles—it's still the "original.") Schieffelin Hall (1881), the Birdcage Theatre (Christmas, 1881), the County Courthouse (1882), and a few others still stand.

The (estimated) 7.6 Sonora earthquake of May 1887 destroys Charleston and lowers the Cochise County water table. Before the drought of 1891–1892, summer "monsoon" rains produce sheet flooding that

---

[141] Fourth Street between Toughnut and Allen Streets. "The reason was that all the lawyers had their offices on it....It first attracted the learned and the eloquent because it was only two jumps from the courthouse and less than that from the nearest saloon." C. L. Sonnichsen (Ed.), Billy King, *Tombstone* (1942), p. 161.

[142] Laurie Laine, "Battle for Boothill," *Tombstone Epitaph* 25 March 2005 (Vol. CXXII, No. 18).

spurs the growth of grass and wildflowers. Gama, sacaton, and bunch grasses grow to a man's knees in the Sulphur Spring Valley east of town. Overgrazing and lack of water soon destroy the large ranches and cattle industry. Surviving ranchers subsist largely on smuggling. Tombstone dwindles to about 150 residents.

Drunk Driving—Horse

The Tombstone Marshal's Office (TMO) and Tombstone Jail are in a small building behind city hall at 315 East Fremont Street. (My office is a remodeled jail cell). It is next to the vacant lot behind the O.K. Corral,[143] actual site of the famous gunfight.

I drive slowly up Allen Street (to keep from running over inattentive tourists) when I spot a local cowboy and stage driver, David E. Drerup, atop his Palomino "Almond Joy." He suddenly spurs A.J. and charges full speed towards a tourist stagecoach belonging to the competing livery.

Almond Joy bounces off the team and begins jumping, prancing, and turning in circles, clearly out of control. I run up and pull Drerup off. I am hit by the odor of drinks from the Crystal Palace, his favorite watering hole.

I handcuff Drerup as Almond Joy makes his escape by running westbound on Allen towards his stable. A bunch of German tourists—followers of Karl May—surround us and begin clapping. They believe it is another street performance.

Drerup, normally easy-going and sober, blows a 0.195 blood alcohol. He pleads "guilty" and is jailed for twenty-four-hours with a $500 fine. The *Tumbleweed* picks the story off our log and it becomes international news.[144] Tom Brokaw of *NBC Nightly News* broadcasts it and a friend, Dr.

---

[143] The origins of "okay" are not clear. Most trace "O.K." to Martin Van Buren's (failed) 1839 presidential reelection campaign ("Vote for 'Old Kinderhook'") or to the Pennsylvania Dutch expression "Oll Korrect." The abbreviation O.K. is a newspaperman's joke, in that neither the "O" nor the "K" is correct for "all correct." Some old livery tack is stamped "O.K.," so it may also be a brand name.

[144] Pat Koester, "Man on Horse Arrested for Drunk Driving," *Tombstone Tumbleweed*, 19 March 1998 (Vol. XI, No. 25), pp. 1 and 12 (and) Aaron DeLashmutt, "Town Goes

Sven Wahlroos, fellow member of the Adventurers' and Explorers Clubs, hears it on the Coconut Radio while he is sailing on an HMS *Bounty* replica between New Caledonia and New Zealand. Hugh O'Brian, star of *The Life and Legend of Wyatt Earp*, sends an autographed 8×10 glossy. My ephemeral "fifteen minutes of fame...."

This, unfortunately, is not the end of the story. Drerup is stabbed to death exactly a year later by the very woman who bails him out.

POST Certification

I challenge the Arizona Peace Officer Standards and Training process through passing seven written exams, day/night firearms qualification and computerized "when-to-shoot" scenarios, a pursuit/defense driving course, PT exams (not adjusted for age—I am fifty-eight), and a background investigation. A POST compliance specialist inspects the marshal's office and finds "no deficiencies."[145]

The certification issue has become a "big deal" as the two bent councilmen comment upon my "lack of Arizona qualifications" at every meeting.

One councilman, a former one-year Tombstone deputy, cannot read or write and has a fellow officer complete his few reports. He never attends an academy and is never "certified." His favorite story, as a WWII soldier, is being placed in charge of a group of a dozen German prisoners. He executes them and reports them as "escaped."

The Common Council has difficulty conceiving certification as a minimum requirement with little relationship to competency and performance. Arizona law requires an officer to be hired *before* he can be certified. "Basic" is their only level of certification.

International with Arrest," *Tombstone Epitaph* (Local Edition), 10 April 1998 (Vol. CXVII, No. 15), p. 2.

[145] AZ-POST "Certification Letter" of 22 December 1997 (and) Bob Candland, "Tombstone's Marshal Hurlbut Receives State Certification," *Tumbleweed*, 1 January 1998 (Vol. XI, No. 19), pp. 1 and 5.

Waste of Finite

Arizona Revised Statutes differ from those in other states. One traffic offense that comes to mind is "waste of finite" (ARS 28-702.01). This "waste of a finite resource in short supply" (gasoline) is the civil offense of driving between 56 and 65 mph when the maximum speed is posted as 55. I have seen it written for two or three miles over 55. The fine is small and cannot result in suspension or revocation of a driver's license. (I stop local enforcement of this silly regulation, often used to harass outsiders and to seize their cars.)

Speed Trap and No Tickets for Locals

I tell deputies no more "speed trap" citations at the bottom of the Highway 80 hill at the northwest end of town, where there is an abrupt change of speed limits.

The long-standing policy is to cite only tourists and outsiders for traffic offenses.[146] I am told, "You cannot write tickets and get votes." I change this policy with the support of Mayor Harper, explaining: "How do you feel about becoming someone else's 'outsider' as soon as you leave city limits? A citation is to gain compliance with the rules, not just to confiscate your money."

> "Never Send to Know for Whom the Bell Tolls;
> It Tolls for Thee."
> — John Donne

The "don't-cite-locals" policy is brought home by a sweet elderly lady with poor eyesight. I see locals pull over and stop when they see her approaching in her battered old car. The previous marshal and I both confiscate her license, as her last accident is a head-on while driving on the

---

[146] One Marshal, Roy McNeely, is fired for writing tickets to locals: "I came here and people would run stop signs right in front of me," Storer Rowley, "Modern Sheriff Upsets Tombstone," *Chicago Tribune*, 31 December 1985 (and) William B. Farley, "Marshal McNeely Ousted," *Epitaph*, 10 October 1986, front page.

wrong side of the road. DMV twice reinstates it over our well-documented protests.

I cite her but am not successful in stopping her from driving, even though several volunteer to take her shopping and on errands. (She makes an effort to drive only at times I am not around.) I am castigated for my "meanness" by her friends—until, cresting a hill on the wrong side of the Charleston Road at excessive speed, she finds another car in front of her. She swerves off the road, overturns, and is ejected.

I am returning from a three-day medico-legal death investigations class at Sierra Vista PD. I see a cloud of dust ahead near Milepost 12. I am the one who finds her with a broken neck. I make the death notification and stop by to tell the former marshal. Bobby G. has his good side and is saddened, but not surprised, by this news.

Auto Boot Hill

Several locals point out a ravine outside of town off Middlemarch Road leading to the Dragoon Mountains containing the remains of numerous cannibalized automobiles. I discover TMO is in the business of impounding the autos of Mexican tourists for minor violations, such as "license plate light out" and "no turn signal." (These are not all illegal immigrants, unlicensed drivers, or those with improper registrations.)

Required notifications are not made and the vehicles are sold at auction. Those who complain are given the "Cochise County shuffle" and eventually referred to DPS—a dead end. Some are unhappy at this sudden loss of revenue when I put a stop to this "organized theft ring."

Mormon Mafia

Much of Cochise County (and Arizona) is run by what locals call the "Mormon Mafia." Sheriff Devious is one of the Saints.

Brigham Young sends his Church of Jesus Christ of Latter-day Saints into the "Mormon Corridor" in the mid to late nineteenth century. Colorado City and Saint David (about 15 miles northwest of Tombstone on Highway 80) are Mormon bastions. The former is known for its notorious polygamists.

(A woman's way to Mormon heaven is to seal with a "chosen saint.") Large colonies of Mormons exist south of the border. There is considerable cross-border traffic between them.

A chilling behind-the-scenes view of Mormon beliefs is found in Scott Anderson's *The Four O'Clock Murders* (1993). It details a series of murders—at 4:00 p.m. on the 144th anniversary of the assassination of Mormon founder Joseph Smith—by the followers of Ervil LeBaron. Authorities identify the one giving the execution orders: a man buried in a Texas grave twelve years before.

Multiple Mormon Gods have their own universes. A *saint* can become a *god* if he attains the highest level of heaven.

Blood Atonement

Utah bans their firing squad in 2004 but shoots Ronnie Lee Gardner on 18 June 2010. He requests this method of execution because of his Mormon heritage.

"Blood atonement" is the literal spilling of blood. It is the only way a Gentile (non-Mormon) can be assured of passage to heaven, provided he is "atoned" by *true believers*.[147] It is not considered murder and is a "blessing" to us non-believers who are otherwise doomed to perdition. (This goes a long way to explaining how the Saints justify their annihilation of the men, women, and children in the Baker-Fancher wagon train at Mountain Meadows, Utah Territory, in September 1857.) Claiming undeserved welfare and fraud against others is not a sin in the eyes of the Lord.[148] Neither, apparently, is selling dope.

"Cocaine Borane"

I take my firearms training simulator (FATS) qualification in Douglas on the border with Agua Prieta, Sonora. The police station is the old El Paso and Southwestern Railroad Depot (1913).

---

[147] Anderson, p. 16.
[148] Ibid., p. 92.

Douglas Police Chief, Judge Ronald J. "Joe" Borane, also known as "Cocaine Borane," accumulates "unexplained affluence" and is the largest landowner in Cochise County (over 200 homes and ranches). He is worth millions. (His police salary is about $40,000 a year.)

Borane crashes his car in 1986, killing his passenger. Despite a blood alcohol of 0.17, he is never charged. (The county attorney is, again, Alan Polley.) One of Borane's properties is sold to a Mexican cartel head and is discovered to house a cross-border tunnel used to smuggle tons of cocaine into Cochise County.[149]

Borane is arrested in 1999 for drug running and money laundering. (Polley is now dead.) He is found guilty of "fixing traffic tickets" and serves ninety days in jail. Crime does pay in Cochise County!

Tombstone Silver Badges

Applicants for city marshal list their qualifications as: "I can kill a rattlesnake with my bare hands; I have no experience in law enforcement other than getting parking tickets; and, I could do very well in a fast-draw situation."[150]

Richard T. Brubaker, son of a previous marshal, is appointed. He wears his father's badge and carries a revolver with diamonds and rubies inlaid into antler grips. He "resigns" on 15 October, two weeks after his appointment. More on this shortly.

My first badge, made by Southern Jewelry, Houston (who makes them for the Texas Rangers), is cut from a Mexican silver cinco-peso coin.

Eddy L. "Big Ed" Douglas of San Pedro Saddlery carves a handmade circle-star badge from a chunk of Tombstone silver. He also crafts beautiful

---

[149] Sam Dillon, "Small-Town Arizona Judge Amasses Fortune, and Indictment," *New York Times*, 30 January 2000 (and) Bill Conroy, "Firestorm: U.S. Border Corruption" (Chapter 9), *The Narco News Bulletin*, 13 April 2004. The Dillon article comments on many crimes concerning Borane and his long "disregard of the law" in Cochise County. Action is, not surprisingly, never taken against him by the sheriff....

[150] City marshal appointment of 11 September 1987. (Taken from "Minutes" of the Common Council: Stan Benjamin, *Tombstone Lawmen* (1999), p. 36.

leather belts for deputies.[151] A packet of silver badges, one for each deputy, arrives from Lawman Badge Company of Peculiar, Missouri. They are hand-engraved on the face and the reverse. These are of no cost to us. The previous marshal agrees to accept them if we certify that a limited edition sold to collectors is the same issue. No one profits except the maker. (The mayor, council, and city attorney authorize this in a time of austerity budgets.)[152]

Weapons

The Colt Custom Shop crafts a nickel-plated engraved "Peacemaker" in .45 Long Colt, serial TMO-1, which I wear for ceremonial purposes. My duty weapon is a Glock Model 22 in .40 S. & W. In my trunk, I carry my 12-gauge Ithaca LAPD Special pump shotgun and a scoped Ruger Mini-14 in .223.

Tombstone has a bank, a credit union, and numerous shops. Many retirees and reenactors relive the "West-that-never-was" and go about armed. (As a life-benefactor member of the NRA, I note this is not negative—it keeps crime low.) We are not sure, however, which side some will enter into should something go down, but many await the opportunity!

I advise the banks and businessmen, should they be held up, to not resist. No shootings in town, if possible. We will attempt to remain unseen and follow the suspects out of town. We will not (immediately) enter their businesses. If we believe the suspects are present, we will phone and ask the owner/clerks to step outside. If they do not, we assume it is a hostage situation and go to Plan B.

The nearest town is Saint David (15 miles). Fort Huachuca and Sierra Vista are 17 miles. A dirt road leads to Gleeson (16 miles). We will alert the Cochise County Sheriff, DPS, and Sierra Vista PD to set up roadblocks. We will follow and engage the suspects in the desert. We all carry rifles in

---

[151] Ashley Adams, "Marshal Gets Handmade Belt," *Tombstone Epitraph* (Local Edition), 26 September 1997 (Vol. CXVII, No. 3), p. 2.

[152] "New Badges," *Tombstone Marshal's Log*, 1 July 1998, pp. 1 and 2.

the trunk. (No sane officer goes into a gunfight with just a pistol if he is otherwise armed.)

Tombstone Underground

An underground complex exists beneath Tombstone. A hole in Toughnut Street near Fourth grows from an inch to several yards across in three days. Sections of the street and nearby walls soon collapse. We enter the old Goodenough Mine shaft and find tools and a recent mining operation. (Silver and calcite crystals remain.) "The plan?" says Mayor Harper. "We'll just sit back and let it fall in…"[153] The Nebraska mine-owner is cited. Timbers with dry rot are shored up until the next event.

An estimated 380 miles of tunnels run beneath Tombstone. Large stopes (stepped and inclined caverns where lenses of ore are removed) are everywhere. School kids distribute hard red and yellow candy reminiscent of the old carbohydrate rations stored in five-gallon tins for the Civil Defense Program of the 1950s.

We follow old ore cart rails to the 500-foot level, where a sealed tunnel is broken open. The remains of the candy, crackers, and other containers are scattered about. Calcite crystals glisten from the ceilings of huge caverns. Kids throughout the years disappear in here, forever. If your light source fails you are doomed in the maze of passages.

We soon reach the water table laced with cyanide and mercury from mining operations. (Everyone in town drinks bottled water.) Many homes do not have sewer hookup or septic tanks. Holes for toilets are drilled through the ceilings of some caverns. One or two old giant Cornish pumps are supposed to be submerged by rising waters when the miners go on strike. They reportedly pump five million gallons each every twenty-four-hours.

---

[153] Rhonda Bodfield, "Parts of Tombstone Sinking," *Tucson Citizen Morgue* (Part 2: 1993–2009), 25 July 1997.

Special Investigations Team

We have two shooting deaths, which normally the county or DPS detectives investigate. Both departments fail to appear. Sheriff Devious tells me they will be "too busy on other assignments"—in the future!—to respond.

I form our own "Special Investigations Team" (SIT) of retired officers who will respond for ten dollars an hour. They include a polygraph operator and former Tucson detective; a homicide investigator and PhD in criminal psychology who specializes in interviewing; a fingerprint and forensics expert who testifies all over the state; a forensic photographer and former police officer; the editor of the *Tumbleweed* who is a PI, ex-San Diego officer, and instructor at Arizona academies; and, a retired DPS officer and drug enforcement chief.[154] Over 200 years of law enforcement experience are thus added to TMO.

Our photo expert enhances a worn videotape at the Circle-K and identifies two theft suspects. A small thing, but few agencies in the state are capable of this. We can lift latent prints from bodies (new for the time—heated fixed photo-paper transfer) and other innovative techniques.

We soon are called upon by other agencies for assistance. The sheriff complains to POST we are "uncertified vigilantes." POST realizes what is happening and that several are too old to pass PT exams for certification. SIT is not making arrests as peace officers (I handle this), so it is determined to not be a problem.

My ace-in-the-hole for assistance is the Sierra Vista PD under Chief Arthur J. Montgomery. They are one of the most professional and efficient police operations I have seen in any state. Their command staff is superb. Once they realize what we are attempting to accomplish in Tombstone, they offer every assistance. One of their detectives conducts my POST background investigation (D.R. 97-33594). My deputies and I attend many of their

---

[154] "Marshal Forms Special Investigative Team," *Tumbleweed*, 30 July 1998 (Vol. XI, No. 49), pp. 1 and 14.

training classes and exercises. We exchange intel, something the sheriff's office refuses to do.

Tombstone Turmoil

Two of my four deputies are shot to death in their cars following my departure. Fifty percent of my department become Cochise County suicides!

Reform mayor "Dirty Delmas" Harper is defeated in a close election (with a number of irregularities which he chooses to not contest). City Attorney Randy "Randi" (as in Hindi for "prostitute") Bays—we all have local nick-names—and "Mad Max" Hurlbut are not reappointed. I am flattered that over 200 sign a petition to retain me, and a number of locals take out full-page ads and write of this "latest outrage where professionals fighting corruption are removed in favor of those with shady backgrounds."

The marshal appointed to follow me is a former Tombstone deputy who is forced to resign—after several months on the job—following an investigation of shotgun blasts fired into the Birdcage Theatre.[155] His partner, Bobby Gerencser, is "cleared," so the new kid, Paul J. Kostellic, takes the fall. Their new marshal of ten days, Richard T. Brubaker, is supposedly fired for conducting a poor investigation and not being "certified." Brubaker tells me he is actually fired "for doing *too good* of an investigation."

Kostellic is hired by Yuma County sheriffs. He becomes a sergeant and resigns two weeks after becoming a watch commander for reasons he and the department will not disclose.

The new marshal quickly disbands my team of professionals on the special investigations team and substitutes a band of teenage "cadets" who cause problems and are liability concerns. They dismiss my most competent deputy, Dennis J. Wahlen (a Mormon and retired Mesa PD officer),

---

[155] Lisa Ishikawa, "Deputy Cleared in Report," *Tombstone Epitaph* (Local Edition), 15 January 1988 (Vol. CVII, No. 13), front page.

who objects to the new illegal traffic stops and unprofessional nature of operations. Dennis writes:

> "I find it difficult to believe that the citizens of Tombstone continue to allow themselves to be treated like idiots by the current Mayor and Marshal....The only conclusion I can draw from what I've seen and heard is that the people who live in Tombstone just don't care; ethics, honesty, and integrity are not prerequisites for elected and appointed officials."[156]

They reinstitute the old speed trap and again exempt locals from traffic citations (unless they speak out against the new administration). They once more seize the autos of passing Mexicans, and, along with Bisbee, hold monthly car auctions.

I start receiving phone calls and notes complaining of various excesses by the new marshal's office:

> "I did not complain when the new Mayor failed to reappoint me and selected a crony of many years with no managerial experience and questionable and unexplored background. An executive should be able to select his own staff."[157]

The editor requests a series of articles exposing their latest moneymaking schemes and other shortcomings. I comply.

Automobile Seizures

Marshal Kostellic admits he is profiling Mexicans to seize their autos for sale and tells a reporter: "They are coming through here in droves and

---

[156] Wahlen, "Former Deputy Speaks Out," Letters to the Editor, *Tombstone Tumbleweed*, 28 October 1999 (Vol. XIII, No. 10), p. 5.

[157] Hurlbut, "Popularity Contest vs. Crime Fighting," Letters, *Tumbleweed*, 23 March 2000 (Vol. XIII, No. 31), p. 11.

it would be crazy not to take advantage of it."[158] Some are illegal aliens but most are not. I detail the wrongness and illegality of this and the exposure of the city to liability. I point out that despite the seizure and sale of hundreds of cars, no narcotics runners are being profiled—a legal technique. Not an ounce of narcotics is found on one of the hottest drug routes along the border.[159]

The *Tumbleweed* editor gives Kostellic and the mayor an opportunity to respond, but they never do so. Car seizures and auctions, joined by Bisbee, increase. The auctions bring in hundreds of thousands of dollars and are a big chunk of city budgets. Tombstone hires two more deputies to process them and lists their car stops as "calls for service" to justify the additional personnel.

Auctioning the transportation means of others is an old Tombstone tradition. Marshal James Porter McDonald tries a horse in the Fairbank Court (*Territory of Arizona vs. One Brown Horse*). The horse, with no one to speak for him, is found guilty of "straying on the public domain" and sentenced to be sold at public auction on 17 July 1906.

I write to the Arizona Municipal Risk Retention Pool (AMRRP), which insures seventy-four cities. I include documentation of the auto-seizure scam and suggest they may wish to send an investigator to Tombstone and Bisbee. AMRRP orders both towns to immediately cease this activity or lose *all* insurance coverage. The Tombstone mayor announces (*Tumbleweed*, 18 January 2001) they must stop as the Risk Pool will no longer insure their huge auto storage lot in Bisbee. Ha, ha. (No, Mayor Escapule—that is NOT what they tell you.)

The towns still manage to seize and process forfeiture paperwork on thousands of vehicles. Over 75 percent of owners are not charged with violations.[160] Most cannot afford the $5,000 or more necessary to hire an attorney to fight the seizure, so they lose their autos.

---

[158] Jennifer Bass, "Marshal Snatching Cars to Increase Revenues," *Tombstone Epitaph*, Local Edition, 26 February 1999 (Vol. CXVIII, No. 11), front page.

[159] Hurlbut, "Racial Profiling, Tombstone Style," *Tumbleweed*, 16 March 2000 (Vol. XIII, No. 30), p. 11.

[160] Tim Vanderpool, "Car Country, USA," *Tucson Weekly*, 7 October 2004.

Death of Hidalgo

Frank Hidalgo is a personable and hardworking officer. I write several glowing commendations and discipline him for poor judgment in two off-duty incidents, but he shows promise. He is the only deputy I retain from the original gang.

Marshal Paul Kostellic and Hidalgo have a "heated argument" almost leading to blows."[161] The marshal finds him a job in the nearby Patagonia Marshal's Office. Should things not work out, Frank is promised he can return. Kostellic soon sends Frank a letter stating he is terminated and cannot come back. Frank is also experiencing problems with his girlfriend, the member of BAG from Tombstone.

A psychologist calls me from a Tucson mental hospital saying Frank admits himself and has a "hit list," which includes me, Candland, Mayor Harper, the city clerk, and others having a role in terminating his fellow Tombstone deputies (but not the current marshal who tricks him out of his job). I call Kostellic who verifies this and says he discovers Frank has a "behavioral problem" and "passes him along"[162]

Frank is found shot to death in his car just outside Patagonia. Santa Cruz detectives list it as a suicide. In support of this is an unreleased note leaving his goods to his BAG girlfriend (who has a restraining order against him).

NOTE: Frank applies for a "psycho" pension. In Arizona, this falls entirely upon the jurisdiction currently employing him. Frank works Tombstone for eight years and Patagonia for just eight weeks. The Patagonia marshal tells me he finds out he is lied to regarding Frank's mental state and qualifications for the job. Patagonia intends to sue Tombstone—until his death makes the issue moot. Thunder should be booming down the Tombstone City Hall and into the Marshal's Office. As usual, there is silence.

---

[161] Log. Telephone call to Kostellic, 9 August 1999, 1010 hours.

[162] Ibid. (and) Hurlbut, "Hidalgo's Equivocal Death," *Tumbleweed*, 30 March 2000 (Vol. XIII, No. 32), p. 4.

Disturbing elements point to homicide:

1. Frank tells his roommate (a Patagonia deputy) he fears being killed because he knows of a murder committed by "a (unnamed) Tombstone official." [Some of us suspect the homicide is of a Huachuca City lieutenant accused of "nocturnal visits to the evidence room" and found shot in the forehead with a .22-caliber rifle. It is classified as a "Cochise County suicide," but his chief, Dennis L. Grey, insists it is murder.][163]

NOTE: This is not an unusual event. A BAG deputy, Jack Ray Hudson, Jr., is caught stealing cash, drugs, and guns out of the evidence room on 4 July 1995. He shoots to death Lieutenant Danny P. Elkins, Yuma PD, and Sergeant Michael L. Crowe of DPS. This is around the time Marshal Kostellic is the watch commander.

Why would Frank, fearing a death threat, bother to kill himself? Is it possible the one making the threat carries it out?

2. Two death reports are written: Patagonia (#990970) and Santa Cruz (#990926009).

The Patagonia report is basic. Frank is found in the driver's seat with a hole in his forehead. A Glock 22 in .40-caliber is in his hand. The car is closed up, except for the driver's side window being down a half inch. The cartridge case is missing.

Patagonia Marshal Jerry C. Morgan asks to meet with the investigator, as he believes Frank's death is a homicide. All his department is there—except one—whom the others believe is involved in the shooting. (The reports do not explain why.) Frank's roommate tells of his fear of being killed but knows little more. (One would think this might pique his curiosity.)

---

[163] Lt. Thomas Self is found shot to death in his home on 29 August 1996. Margie Cady, "Police Chief: Death was Murder," Sierra Vista Herald, 17 September 1997.

NOTE: This is apparently a lively discussion as the sheriff's detective lieutenant orders them to "not take matters into their own hands." One gets the impression the investigator is mentioning these things in his report "to cover his ass" should the information come under later review.

3. Later in the afternoon a "shots-fired" call is received from a resident near the death scene. A county deputy responds to find the Patagonia marshal and his department (sans the suspect deputy) test-firing a Glock to see where the casing ends up. Their search of the death car and surrounding area proves negative.

The next morning, the county lieutenant arrives and tells the marshal and his deputies that if they continue their investigation, they will be arrested and booked for "interfering"!

The following day, the investigator asks the marshal to provide him with social security numbers and other personal data on himself and his deputies at the scene "for identification purposes." The marshal refuses and obtains legal counsel.

Another day passes and the sheriff searches Frank's car for the missing casing. It is never recovered.

4. The sheriff prevents the Patagonia deputies from investigating but does little of his own. Routine forensic procedures are not followed:

   * Frank's hands and head are not bagged. (Does he fire the pistol?) The "investigation" does not mention any powder residue, tattooing, imprinting, etc., to indicate contact or a close shot.

   * The weapon is not test-fired to see if it matches the bullet in Frank's head (no exit wound). Why is there no comment on such obvious and basic concerns?

   * Center forehead, where Frank allegedly shoots himself, is an unusual spot for a weapons expert. This might result in a lobotomy and years as a living vegetable. Officers most often "eat their gun" to sever

the medulla, which instantly disrupts involuntary functions such as breathing and heart beat.

* The death car is not printed. Is it possible someone is with him?

* The first officer on the scene says the window is cracked about half an inch. (He does not mention if the air conditioner, ignition, and engine are running). Is it possible Frank is shot from outside the car? The cartridge casing could have escaped, from inside, through the half-inch opening and then been stepped on. Why isn't a metal detector brought in or the soil scraped and sifted? Why are not the dash and interior dismantled to find that casing? Its location (to determine from where the gun is fired) may reveal if it is murder or suicide.

* The autopsy report is not available. Does the blood chemistry reveal anything of interest? The body is quickly cremated.

* Blood spatter is mentioned, but its location and pattern are not described.

* No canvassing for witnesses takes place. Does anyone see anything? Locals report the noise of test-firing. Does anyone hear a shot in the time frame of death?

No discussion takes place regarding the danger Frank believes himself in. This is a major concern. The routine forensics procedures described above are performed, even in Arizona, for any such death. A threatened police officer dying in such a manner normally receives considerable attention, especially since his fellow officers believe he is murdered. The "investigator" instead threatens the officers who are trying to find answers. The "suspect-deputy" is not questioned.

I pass the reports on to my SIT forensics expert and twenty-year San Diego homicide investigator, Dr. Thomas Streed. He believes it is a homicide being covered up. LAPD Robbery-Homicide Lieutenant Donald J. Foster is in agreement.

Frank's Tombstone memorial is not attended by a single Tombstone officer, although Patagonia is well represented. I write a note of condolence and call Frank's parents. They tell me I am the only one who calls or writes.

Death of Hudson

Duane Raymont Hudson is a lieutenant on the Huachuca Police Department. He comes to Tombstone on a Community Oriented Policing Services (COPS) grant. Ray goes nutso for a waitress in a local café. The two live in a trailer in the almost-ghost-town of Gleeson, down a dirt road about 16 miles east of Tombstone.

Deborah A. Hudson is found shot to death on 19 September 2001. Ray is the obvious suspect as he and his pickup disappear. A deputy calls me to say Ray will be found murdered—shot to death in his vehicle in Mexico. Ray is found shot to death in his Ford pickup near Caballo Lake in *New Mexico*...

Sheriff Larry Dever does not issue a want, warrant, or a BOLO (Be On Look-Out) for Ray. Devious states there is no evidence that Ray (a friend of his) commits a crime....The only news coverage of Ray's death is apparently a brief item ["Man Sought in Wife's Slaying is Dead," Arizona Daily Star (Tucson), 13 December 2001].

Debbie's son, Justin St.Germain, is a wild kid who resents authority and is involved in petty mischief in Tombstone. He believes Ray murders his mother. Justin has read Ray's and Debbies' death reports and spoken with County investigating officers. (Tombstone deputies are brusque and uncooperative with him).

Debbie is shot multiple times, in the head, with a .25 mouse gun that is never recovered. Ray is shot with a small 1941 Browning F.N. .32—in the LEFT temple. Unknown what becomes of Ray's duty weapon. Justin states ["Son of a Gun" (2013), p. 215], "The medical investigators... located an entry wound in the left temple and an exit wound in the right."

I remember Ray as right-handed, as does my surviving deputy, Dennis Wahlen, himself a lefty. In our group photograph in front of the Marshal's

Office (see page 419), Ray is wearing a right-side holster that can be assessed only with his right hand. Pepper spray is on his left (weak) side. He wears his watch on his left wrist. As with Deputy Frank Hidalgo, it seems unlikely he would shoot himself with a mouse gun and risk lobotomizing himself. Another minor but peculiar thing is that Ray leaves behind, in his trailer, his beloved dog, "Chance." He also abandons at least two of his long guns.

Deputy Wahlen, myself, and others suspect Frank, Ray, and Debbie (and possibly Lt. Tom Self, who also works with Hudson in Huachuca City), are all murdered by the same third party who is probably in local law enforcement....

Marshal Kostellic is dismissed and hired by Sheriff Larry Dever.

Border Woes

Two employees of the "Spangenberg Gun Shop" on Fourth Street tell me the owner, James R. "Diamond Jim" Marshall, is illegally smuggling guns into Mexico. A third man, a former employee, signs an affidavit that Diamond Jim is converting semiautomatic weapons into full-auto. A fourth, a former employee, says he quits rather than continue filling out false gun sales paperwork to forward to ATF.[164]

My informant in the gun shop, on two occasions, tells me of gun shipments about to go to Mexico. I call the Tucson Field Office of the Bureau of Alcohol, Tobacco, Firearms, and Explosives and request a "license inspection"—and advise exactly where to "inspect." They promise to send out a team on both occasions, but fail to do so. They later claim that "unexpected business" takes them elsewhere.

My informant presents me with a note in the handwriting of Diamond, instructing him on points to make in a false complaint to ATF detailing my "harassment" of D.J. that the informant (falsely) chances to overhear. Diamond names two ATF agents he says are "in my pocket."

---

[164] Hurlbut, "Illegal Manufacture and Possession of Automatic Weapons and Improper Reporting of Gun Sales." Letter to Tucson ATF of 16 April 1998.

Two ATF agents show up in my office one morning and read me a Miranda warning, but deny it is a custodial interrogation.

"You don't mind if we record this, do you?"

"Of course not," I reply. "I am already recording this myself. Before you begin, let me guess why you are here? You have a complaint from Jim Marshall that I am harassing him. I have three affidavits in my desk. One of them says Diamond Jim boasts he has two ATF agents 'in his pocket.' Coincidentally, their names are the same as yours. You have the right to remain silent; anything you say can...."

The two look at each other, stand, and depart without a word.

My written complaint is ignored by ATF. These small-time gunrunners are called "hormigas"—ants. Hormiga Diamond Jim, fifty-four, is dead a few months later. The gun shop is sold. Just another Cochise County coincidence.

Or has ATF, unbeknownst to us, been using "Diamond Jim" to smuggle guns into Mexico in "Project Gunrunner?" Why would rich and powerful cartels engage in nickel-and-dime purchases of semi-automatic arms when they can buy fully automatic weapons by the shipload from foreign sellers at far lower prices?

"Fast and Furious"

"Project Gunrunner," out of Tucson ATF, leads to "Fast and Furious" in Phoenix. These ATF/FBI pseudo-stings involve the sale of thousands of guns to the Sinoloa Drug Cartel—considered the most powerful on the planet. They end up in the murders of hundreds of Mexicans and at least one U.S. Border Patrol agent, Brian A. Terry.

The probable motive is that ATF states, "More than 90 percent of guns recovered in Mexico come from the United States."[165] (Most of Mexico's guns, cheap "war surplus," come from Russia, China, and Israel.) ATF wants to generate some "proof"—even if they must

---

[165] Julian Aguilar, "Do Texas Guns Fuel Drug Violence in Mexico?," *The Texas Tribune*, 8 April 2010. President Barak Obama parrots this "90 percent" figure many times.

supply the weapons themselves—so as to enact even stronger U.S. gun-control laws.

Security Theater

No one can deny the FBI's expertise in thwarting its own terrorist plots. They plan a terrorist attack, infiltrate Muslim communities to find recruits, and supply them with the money, weapons, and expertise—then jump in at the last moment to save a grateful nation.

FBI Bombs World Trade Center

The World Trade Center bombing of 26 February 1993—second only to nine-eleven—results in FBI self-glorification for quickly capturing the suspect who supposedly insists on a return of his $400 deposit for the rental bomb truck.

Emad Ali Salem, a former Egyptian army officer, is offered a million dollars by the FBI to set up the World Trade Center bombing sting. He does not trust the FBI so tapes over 100 hours of their conversations. "On the tapes, Salem recalls that the FBI had planned on building the bomb with a phony powder and grabbing the people who were involved in it."[166] No substitution occurs. Six die and over 1,000 are injured. No one is held responsible and it is not explained why the FBI supplies real explosives.

American Kristalnacht

"If it's a 'Civil Rights' violation to subdue a resisting Rodney King, then what is it to burn to death a religious nut and 85 innocent men, women, and children at Waco?"[167] The Seventh–Day Adventists' collective crime is that

---

[166] Ralph Blumenthal, "FBI Allowed WTC Bombing," *Los Angeles Times*, 28 October 1993 (and) *New York Times*, 28 Oct 1993, p. A1.

[167] Hurlbut, "A Law Enforcement Double Standard," *American Handgunner*, Sep/Oct 1995 (Vol. 19, No. 118), pp. 119–120.

their leader fails to purchase a $200 tax permit to convert a semi-automatic rifle to full-auto.

A California state court absolves the officers in the Rodney King case because the entire videotape shows he is struck only when disobeying commands to stop resisting. The feds, however, see this as an opportunity to discredit a municipal police organization by making it into a racial issue.

FBI/ATF agents are driving those tanks at Waco and asphyxiating those kids with CS gas in confined spaces. No agents are prosecuted or disciplined. Texas Ranger Captain David Byrnes, Waco Task Force commander, accuses the FBI of removing the bullet-riddled front door from evidence and destroying it. They also destroy the cars parked outside, with bullet holes that support the Branch Davidian version of the shootings following the fifty-one-day siege.

The feds are adversaries rather than partners of local law enforcement. "The FBI is not your friend and will do what it can to put you in federal prison."[168] The Phoenix office refuses to look into Frank Hidalgo's death, saying, "It's a local matter."

Farewell to Tombstone

The green glint of corruption returns to Tombstone badges. A deputy is terminated for issuing a traffic citation to the mayor's wife (*Tombstone News*, 13 January 2006).

"Marshal Lance Crosthwait (alleges) that the entire Marshal's Office was corrupt and the deputies are taking bribes, doing drugs, drinking on the job, and asking sexual favors in return for (not) issuing citations. Crosthwait also says that $40,000 is missing from his RICO funds."[169]

George Parson's Tombstone *Journal* entry of 30 May 1882 notes: "Bad state of things. People don't care here. Never saw such apathy. Am glad to leave the cursed place."

---

[168] Sgt. Paul M. Weber, "Defense Rep Corner: LAPD and FBI," *Thin Blue Line*, September 1995 (Vol. 50, No. 9), p. 24.

[169] Larry Noyes, "Mayor Tells Citizens 'They Don't Matter,'" *The Tombstone News*, 3 February 2006 (Vol. 1, Issue 25), front page.

Marshal Virgil Earp says, "All in all, the situation (in Tombstone) is a grim and lonely one for a lawman. An officer doing his duty must rely almost entirely upon his own conscience for encouragement."[170]

Return to Tombstone

Fourteen years later, in the Arizona Centennial, I return to Tombstone to see my ailing ninety-plus-year-old boss, Delmas Harper. I stop in to say "hello" to the latest city marshal, Billy Cloud, and others. "Tell Sheriff Devious I am back in town should he wish to serve that old restraining order....!"

Dearly Departed Devious. That very afternoon of 18 September 2012 the sheriff drives off the road in his 2008 County-owned pickup and dies in the resulting roll-over. No other vehicles are involved. He is conspicuous that day by his absence from the dedication of the Brian A. Terry Border Patrol Station at Naco. He never misses an opportunity for publicity....

The Coroner (of another county) reports that Dever, supposedly a non-drinker (according to the next sheriff), has a .29 percent blood alcohol. His most serious injury is a dislocated shoulder. Cause of death: "Accidental, from multiple contusions." One observer wryly notes, "One does not expire from multiple bruises, nor from a dislocated shoulder."[171]

"Rumors will spread," says 'Dirty Delmas,' "that 'Mad Max' somehow has a part in his demise." Just another Cochise County conundrum.

"Whistle me up a mem-ory,
Whistle me back where I want to be.
Whistle a tune that will carry me,
To Tombstone Terr-i-tory."

---

[170] *San Francisco Daily Examiner*, 27 May 1882. Quoted in Donald Chaput, *Virgil Earp— Western Peace Officer* (1994), p. 239.

[171] Dave Gibson. "Sheriff Larry Dever's Autopsy Results in More Questions Than Answers," Examiner.com, 10 October 2012.

Max K. Hurlbut

[Theme song for "Tombstone Territory," sung by William M. Backer. Wednesday night 93-episode ABC Western series (1957-1960).]

Chapter XX

THE ARMY

> Sometimes the only way to know whether the stove is hot is to touch it."
>
> — Anonymous

I start army life as an MP. It seems the thing to do. The military policeman's job can be the toughest in law enforcement. You deal with men in their prime who are trained in weapons and the violent arts. MPs handle misdemeanor investigations, and the felonies go to Criminal Investigation (CID).

Basic Combat Training

The third day of six in the reception center at Fort Ord, California, the first sergeant asks for college graduates or anyone with "proven leadership abilities" to step forward. Everyone has learned this is a trap to snag bodies for unpleasant work details. "I'm your man, Top!," I shout. (The first sergeant is the ranking enlisted man and actual company leader, despite what the captain believes.) "What are your qualifications, Maggot?" "I lead by example *and* persuasion, First Sergeant!"

Apparently impressed that I am the only one of his enlisted swine (this is what he calls us) to recognize his rank, I am assigned to lead two fire teams of twelve men in Company B, the Ninth Battle Group, Third Brigade. [I know ahead of time that squad and platoon leaders do not get KP ("kitchen police")]. This is also before they stop taking stubborn troops behind the barracks for lessons in obedience.

My pay, as a private (E-1), is $78 a month, but with excellent (although not always well-cooked) meals. The posted mess hall motto is: "Take all you want, but eat all you take." You stuff dry and hard things into your pockets and eat the wet stuff in line, as your next call-out is always moments away.

We enjoy long winter hikes and firing our M-1 Garand rifles in an early version of "train fire" (pop-up targets out to 1000 meters). I trade my C-ration cigarettes for candy bars. I still carry a P-38 can opener on my key chain. (It requires about thirty-eight punctures to open a can of C-rats). It never breaks, rusts, or needs sharpening or polishing. It cleans boots, fingernails, and is a great little screwdriver.

NOTE: I am later attached to the Australian airborne who use a similar but larger tool called a FRED (Field Ration Eating Device). The troops call it the "Fucking Ridiculous Eating Device."

Conscription

The Selective Service System ("the Draft") is far from perfect, so many of us volunteer. One in my squad loves the army, but is legally blind. We stand behind and point him down-range on the firing line. He rarely hits anything, but can strip and assemble his weapon faster than anyone. His discharge comes through in week four.

"Fire in the Hole!"

We are trained by World War II and Korean War infantry veterans. One of them saves my life (and his). We fire recoilless rifles, the Browning Automatic Rifle (BAR), mortars, and other weapons of the era. On the close combat course we throw MK-2 defensive (fragmentation/"pineapple") grenades.

I am standing inside one of two small circular concrete structures on grenade qualification day. The rest of the class is nearby behind a concrete wall, observing through periscopes. On the command of "pull," I remove the pin and am in the cocked-arm position awaiting, "throw."

"Fire in the hole!" shouts a sergeant from the other enclosure. My instructor suddenly clamps my grenade hand with both of his, and we fall to the floor. [A safety handle ("spoon") on the grenade, when thrown, pops off and releases the spring-loaded hammer, which detonates a five (sometimes four) second fuse.]

A deafening explosion stuns us. With quivering fingers I slowly replace the pin through the holes in the lever of my grenade, rendering it safe.

Private Bobby Sorkin, a butterball of a draftee, is never able to strip his rifle. He bounces along behind the rest of us as he cannot keep step. He is in the next grenade position. Not awaiting commands, he lobs his grenade up and to the right—into our enclosure. My instructor sees it coming and kicks it into the sump—a hole in the floor for this very purpose. The grenade fragments shoot straight up. We are deafened for several days, but otherwise unhurt.

Sorkin is frog-marched away, never to be seen again by us.

Military Police

Advanced Individual Training (AIT) for MPs is at the Provost Marshal General's School at Fort Gordon, Georgia, in the heat of the summer.

James G. Caldwell is a Huntington Beach, California, police officer. Upon graduation from the Basic MP Course, we have several weeks before the Advance Course begins. We expect to be assigned town patrol with the nearby Augusta Police. [Erskin Caldwell's *Tobacco Road* (1932) still exists, and we can almost see poor Jeeter Lester walking along with his sack of turnips.] The author and my MP friend are not related.

Jim and I are assigned guard duty at the post gate—eight on and eight off. We require fresh khaki uniforms—at our own expense—with spit-shined boots and belts every few hours. We get little sleep and see no end to this duty. The regular post MPs work one shift a day with two days off each week.

Jim and I notice something odd. Cooks going off-duty drop off pies, cooked meat dishes, and other nice things for us. We begin inspecting the autos of departing white-dressed cooks. We find cases of canned goods and even sides of beef and pork being stolen. Two days of capturing a number of the fort's culinary personnel and our names are mysteriously removed from the duty roster. We must remain on post, but have no duties to perform until classes begin.

MP weapons are the Colt .45 auto, .30 M1 carbine, and M3A1 .45-caliber submachine gun called the "Grease Gun." It is a simple, cheap, stamped-sheet steel weapon. It can be fired single-shot by tapping the trigger. It's only shortcoming is having a single rather than double-stacked thirty-round magazine. The magazines are hard to load and susceptible to feed malfunctions.

Cuban Crisis

My unit, the 387th MP Battalion, is not called up for the Cuban crisis. On returning to LAPD, I join an army reserve unit, the 316th Military Police Detachment (CID), as their clerk. I eventually serve on Active Duty Training as a CID Agent at Fort Meade, Maryland, and at the Presidio of San Francisco.

One of the lesser-known plans of this era is "Operation Northwoods."[172] It's a CIA false-flag plot authorized by the Joint Chiefs of Staff. Acts of terrorism are to be committed in American cities and blamed upon Fidel Castro. Americans are to be shot down in the streets. A false hijacking of a plane by "Cuban pilots" is to be reported crashed with all aboard killed. (There are apparently to be no actual victims.) President John F. Kennedy puts a halt to it.

"De Oppresso Liber" (To Free the Oppressed)

A motor officer friend, Edward A. "Bud" Harper, convinces me to take the Special Forces Assessment tests in 1966: Situational Reaction Under Stress, PT, Language Aptitude, and Intelligence/Personality. Then off to Benning School for Boys in Georgia for the Airborne Course and Fort Bragg, North Carolina, for SF. I am a staff sergeant with an MOS (Military Occupational

---

[172] Gen. Lyman L. Lemnitzer, "Justification for US Military Intervention in Cuba," Memorandum from Joint Chiefs to Secretary of Defense, 13 March 1962 (and) James Bamford, *Body of Secrets* (2001), p. 82.

Specialty) of Operations/Intelligence in Company A, Twelfth Special Forces Group (Airborne).

We "Green Berets" are instructors in guerrilla warfare rather than snake-eaters. Our basic job is to jump behind lines and organize/train resistance groups in unconventional warfare. We practice by taking over small outposts and working our "pupils" up to conducting conventional infantry operations. One of my important jobs is vetting our recruits so we do not become infiltrated and terminally surprised.

"No Obstacle Too Difficult"

While attending Michigan State University I am assigned to Detachment B-3 of Company B, the Twelfth Group, out of Livonia, Michigan. Vietnam is on fire, and we are on twenty-four hour mobilization alert. Orders send us to the Northern Warfare School at Fort Greely, Alaska. (Climbing in and out of crevasses in Gulkana Glacier is similar to conditions in the limestone gullies where we are headed in Southeastern Asia.) Then to the Jungle Operations School at Fort Sherman, the Canal Zone.

The Japanese defeat of the British by attacking Singapore through the Malaysian jungles in 1942 prompts the U.S. Army to train in tough jungle terrain. The French experience in Indochina further suggests we get our act together.

Green Hell

We exit our C-130 at night, at 800 feet, engines spitting fire, over Gatun Drop Zone. It's an equipment jump, with over 100 pounds of ruck. The full moon shines through my canopy and we land in warm, waist-deep water off the DZ—softest and easiest jump ever. Hard to believe they pay us for such a vacation. Fun, travel, and adventure—FTA!

The second lieutenant in charge of my team kicks a downed black palm tree in the everlasting gloom of triple-canopy jungle. The spines penetrate his boot and he is taken out with a massive infection.

I am now in charge of guiding my A-team across the Isthmus. We are given a shotgun with six rounds to bag survival game. We eat insects, caiman, sloths, and snakes (while avoiding the nocturnal bushmaster and fer-de-lance varieties). We cross water obstacles on brush-stuffed poncho rafts. I supplement our rations by doling out a small supply of smuggled chocolate bars. (Hey, we are "unconventional.")

We are on noise and light discipline. Dry land is unusual, so we sleep in net hammocks. One night, we hear a "thump," and one of the men screams. I flick on a small light to reveal that a three-toed sloth has fallen out of a tree. It climbs another only to encounter a hammock. It makes its way upside down on this "branch," puncturing the hide of the soldier unable to get out of his hammock. (His nickname, forever, is "Sloth.") The sloths are green (from algae in their fur), slow, and bad-smelling. Perfect little soldiers. This one makes a fine breakfast. Fierce red ants also climb the trees and rain down on anyone disturbing the vegetation. A nasty place.

We are constantly in water, so cut holes in our (expensive) Corcoran elk-hide jump boots to let fresh water in and out. (This is before fabric "jungle boots.") Those who do not end up evacuated for warm-water immersion foot. The bad odor is your flesh decaying.

One day we emerge from the jungle and see a ship moving across the green grass horizon with no water in sight. We are at Gatun Locks near the Atlantic entrance to the Panama Canal. All on my team are awarded the coveted "Jungle Expert" patch and certificate.

Back at Fort Sherman, we find Cokes are a nickel and the local rum is about 35 cents a gallon. I still drink the stuff with enthusiasm. (My Chinese wife calls it "cockroach juice.") This is the first place I see "Agent Orange." It is in fifty-five gallon olive-drab barrels with an orange stripe painted around the middle. I'm told it beats whacking weeds.

The Mustang

I receive a direct commission to first lieutenant in the Military Intelligence Corps. (I branch-transfer from MI to Special Forces when we receive our own Branch in June 1987). One thousand "Yarborough" knives (named for

General William P. Yarborough, the "Father of SF") are made for us graduates of the "Q" (SF Qualification) Course and SF Tab holders. My Yarborough is number 150.

I am assigned to the 297th MI Detachment (Special Forces). We train constantly but never receive orders to Vietnam, although we have submitted the paperwork. A major disappointment.

I volunteer for the MOB DES (Mobilization Designee) Program. I report to a regular army unit for thirty to ninety days of active duty a year. (The California Military and Veterans Code generously requires LAPD to give thirty days of paid military leave a year plus unlimited time without pay.)

I am assigned to the Institute for Military Assistance (later renamed the John F. Kennedy Special Warfare Center) and the First Special Operations Command (SOCOM) at Fort Bragg on Smoke Bomb Hill. We deploy rangers, SF, the Rapid Deployment Force (Eighty-Second Airborne), psychological operations, civil affairs, and others worldwide. Much is "compartmentalized" so as to deny covert missions.

Incident at Bragg

My slot is Chief of Counterintelligence, later renamed the Security Division. (See the first page of the "Tar Baby" chapter).

Vietnam is over. Special Forces-qualified officers tend to stay in place and do not get their "tickets punched" (acquire varied experience in other units). Our "unconventional" approach (few formations, "borrowing" of supplies and equipment from other units, informal uniform wear and weapons, etc.) alienate officers who now get promoted over their "less qualified" SF peers.[173] The most innocuous comment in your Officer Efficiency Report can get you "passed over" for promotion. If passed over twice, you are discharged, even if within weeks of retirement. It becomes a backstabbing world to retain your career.

---

[173] "The American military promotion system washes out the combat leaders, who tend to have rough edges, in favor of bureaucrats and managers." William S. Lind, "Droning On," *American Conservative*, September 2009 (Vol. 8, No. 12), p. 18.

Special Forces is almost eliminated. I am in a shortage branch; MI rather than infantry. My situation is also complicated by reporting to two commands—the unit I am assigned to and MOB DES program managers in Saint Louis.

"Loose Lips Sink Ships"[174] The colonel (later general) assembles his staff because word of deployments is leaking out. The foreign press, with lights and television cameras—and our opposition—greet us on the beaches and drop zones. The Rapid Deployment Force and SF go into "isolation" before deployment. We report to a secluded and guarded area—sometimes for weeks—to train. No communications, even with families, is allowed.

The colonel tasks his staff for our individual assessments. The others write lengthy reports on SIGINT (Signal Intelligence—Soviet satellites and listening devices) and stress the need for more secure communications equipment. My report makes but two brief points:

1. Fort Bragg is an open post (informally manned gates allowing civilian access) and should be better secured.
2. Third-world countries usually cannot afford sophisticated commo and electronics gear—but can deploy cute young girls to work in the post exchange and mess halls to date our enlisted personnel.

The colonel convenes his staff. "We have, newly assigned to us, the most qualified Counterintelligence Officer in this man's Army." He then calls me up to polite applause. I know I am dead as I look out on the faces of the others. I am the only one of them not infantry and not active duty for the duration.

My future deployments tend to be to remote areas doing things others avoid: testing Soviet equipment in the Sudanese desert, critiquing troop movements to the Congo, advising unpopular allied units in contact with insurgents and mercenaries, etc. (I am to learn that the difference between

---

[174] "Beware of unguarded talk." WWII propaganda phrase of the War Advertising Council.

Vagabond Policeman

an unemployed mercenary and a highwayman is mostly one of timing.) Some of my more interesting assignments follow.

The Technology Trap

We occasionally outfox ourselves, especially when attacking countries that lack our technology.

The USAF dispatches two squadrons of F-15E Strike Eagles to Iraq in the First Gulf War. Iraqi Scud missiles are chewing up Israel despite our claims of their inaccuracy (to mislead the Iraqis as to their effectiveness). The missiles are launched at night from flatbed tractor trailers on main highways.

LANTIRN (Low Altitude Navigation & Targeting Infrared for Night) pods take high-resolution views of a 4.5-mile swath below the plane. Pilots await the flash of a Scud launch and follow the main highway to the target.

Desert Storm commanders are elated at the over 100 kills and have the pictures (from a $5-million camera) to prove it. Nellis Air Force Base (Las Vegas, NV) displays planes that are "Scud Aces."

A team is sent to Iraq to determine the effectiveness of Desert Storm air campaigns. They report the numbers of Scud missile-launchers destroyed as—ZERO!

The Iraqis realize a truck on the highway near a missile launch is dead meat. The Scud crews erect a plywood/junk parts truck/missile cutout near culverts. They then launch their missiles and quickly drive off the roadway under the highway and turn off their engines. As soon as we blast the decoy, it's back on the highway to pick up another missile.

Pulling the Pin

My seven-plus years of enlisted time place me behind my peers on the promotion curve. My thirty-first and final year brings me to a time when SF is being gutted. (I am an 18A—Special Operations Officer). I am kicked out—passed over twice. Making 0-6 (colonel) will give me another six years, but it is not to be.

I see injustices over the years: a private who loses his rifle suffers greater consequences than a general who loses a war. Most security classification is to cover up embarrassments or fiascos, not because something is important to national security. Such is modern army life.

My boss at Fort Bragg, Lieutenant General J. T. Scott, sends me a "Star Note" thanking me for my "31 years of demanding 'Service in the Shadows,' 25 of them with Special Forces." A Meritorious Service Medal from my command in Saint Louis mentions attachments to the Chinese Army Special Warfare Command and Royal Thai Army and Border Patrol Police.

Chapter XXI

ROYAL THAI BORDER PATROL POLICE

They come at midnight. Vietnamese infantry cross a shallow and slow-moving stream by the faint light of a cloud-guttered moon. The pop of my star-parachute flare triggers them to hit the deck, when they should be running towards us, out of the kill zone. An inexperienced patrol, and we punish them with a hailstorm of fire.

We jump from twin-engine DHC-4A Caribou STOL (short take-off and landing) aircraft, courtesy of Air America, and are in place thirty hours before the patrol arrives. We know they are coming, just not when.

Thai Village Scouts ("Or Sor," abbreviation for "Kong Asa Raksa Dindaen"—Volunteer Defense Corps) and "Thahan Phran" ("hunter soldiers" or rangers), a volunteer militia, keep good watch on Vietnamese troop movements in Cambodia. The Vietnamese are chasing the Khmer Rouge into Thai refugee camps and shelling them. They cannot readily distinguish between the Cambodian invaders and the displaced Thai and Cambodian villagers.

Cambodians are alienated by the Vietnamese presence. They are traditional enemies. Two Vietnamese infantry divisions (about 10,000 officers and men) are strung out along the border extending to the Gulf of Thailand. The Royal Thai Border Patrol Police are more flexible than the army and have more tactically located outposts. We sting the Vietnamese long after American troops depart.

The thirty-two man platoon I advise jumps at 350 feet with tattered T-10 parachutes. (We bury them upon landing—locals then dig them up when we leave as the fabric is prized.) Opening shock of the 'chute is followed by immediately hitting the deck. We don't bother with reserve parachutes as it is not possible to deploy them in time. My little Thai shits jump with close to 200 pounds of claymores, ammo, and the occasional mortar base plate and tube. The T-10 supports about 360 pounds.

Thumper

I pack a French MAT-49 submachine gun, converted to Soviet 7.62×25mm Tokarev in a Griswold bag. It takes a thirty-five-round magazine. I rarely fire it. It is a souvenir plucked from a dead Vietnamese and probably originates with a French soldier. I prefer the M-14 rifle or its European equivalent in 7.62×51mm. Most of our operations are close contact with restricted visibility, so the heavy rifle gets left behind.

My weapon-of-choice is "Thumper," a 40mm M79 grenade-launcher. I carry an assortment of rounds in claymore bags (which hold two dozen "airburst" or high-explosive cartridges each). I am my platoon's "mini artillery." Thumper sends out a giant, slow-moving bullet that requires about 30 meters of travel to arm. It is effective out to around 150 meters. Being within five meters/sixteen feet of touchdown is guaranteed to ruin your day. I carry four shotgun/buckshot rounds in case of closer trouble.

I favor the Colt .45 auto, but the weight of it and extra magazines is a trade-off. My fatigue uniform and gear carry no identifying marks, for obvious reasons. It is not usually possible to bring back the dead and wounded. (No helicopter "dust-offs" as in 'Nam). We do not sacrifice live bodies for dead ones.

Some Vietnamese units have been fighting, constantly, since before WWII. They are excellent infantrymen. It is not unusual for them to employ additional following or flanking units. We obviously prefer to place our light machine guns in enfilade to rake the longest line. They counter by spreading out and moving in areas of natural cover. If we smell a rat, the unit is larger than anticipated, or our exit plan is compromised, we let them pass. We occasionally split our force for a secondary ambush as a little surprise. Nothing too elaborate or complicated.

We pummel the Vietnamese hard for about a minute. I carry my old LAPD brass whistle to sound break-off. One long blast on it and we move out. (They have excellent light field artillery.) We plant a few claymores along our departure route to discourage rapid pursuit. We must sometimes move or hide for a day or more before breathing easily.

American infantry retreats to fortified camps and depends upon firepower superiority. We are light infantry—we protect ourselves like cats, not turtles. We use stealth, rapid movement, and careful selection of our targets. As Sun Tzu advises, we charge downhill, not uphill. A secondary mission is to locate units for conventional forces. Our "trail-watchers" in support of border control are occasionally misused as infantry, as with U.S. MIKE (Mobile Guerilla) Forces earlier in 'Nam.

The Cause of Conflict

Cambodia and Laos come under Communist control in the early 1970s. Norodom Sihanouk, last of the god-kings, fears the Vietnamese but considers the U.S. and South Vietnam as his real enemies. (Most GIs are unaware Saigon is once known as Prey Nokor and part of the kingdom of Cambodia.) He declares "neutrality" but allows the Communist build-up and invasion of the south. We then bomb eastern Cambodia.

Sihanouk is deposed and flees to Beijing to set up a government-in-exile known as the Khmer Rouge. Cambodian General Lon Nol gives the Vietnamese Communists one week to leave—a declaration of war (as the soldiers do not wish to return home to face us Americans).

Brother Number One in Year Zero

The U.S. and South Vietnam invade Cambodia on 30 April 1970. Civil war breaks out and Communist/teacher Saloth Sar, aka Pol Pot ("Brother No. 1"), marches into Phnom Phen in Year Zero (1975). He brings to Cambodia the thirty-two Hindu hells presided over by eighteen-armed Yama, judge of the dead. He executes close to a quarter of all Cambodians in his three-year Maoist "agrarian reform," many for just being able to read. He eliminates all machinery, schools, and money.

Anyone wishing to observe the difference between a labor camp and an extermination camp needs to visit S-21 (Tuol Sleng) Prison and Cheong

Ek, a dozen miles southwest of Phnom Phen, better known as the "killing fields." Piles of skulls remain on display.

NOTE: I employ an agent (Pierre Ong-Vien, aka Sok Ngi) who owns a single tramp freighter that plies the South China Sea. He reports taking a shipment of tractors up the Mekong ("Mother of Water")—the first solid evidence of the Khmer Rouge departure. Ong-Vien now owns a restaurant in Paris and sends the occasional card.

The Vietnamese army defeats the U.S. in 1973 and invades Cambodia on Christmas 1978. (That famous photo of a helicopter evacuating the "U.S. Embassy" in Saigon is actually the evacuation of the CIA station by Air America.) Pol Pot flees into the jungle on the Thai border, where, for a decade, he launches attacks on the Vietnamese and Cambodian government.

The Chinese (allies of the Khmer Rouge) invade North Vietnam in early 1979 to buy their Cambodian friends some time. The Vietnamese army thrashes the Chinese in just seventeen days in the Third Indo-China War.

The Vietnamese army overruns all rebel camps in Cambodia, forcing the Khmer Rouge into Thailand where they mix with refugees. The intact Rouge army of about 35,000 is shipped weapons by both China and the U.S. with the assistance of the Thais.

The Rouge plant thousands of mines (as taught by their British SAS friends in Malaysia), which still kill and maim hundreds of Cambodians every year. The Rouge force Thai refugees to carry their supplies back into Cambodia through heavily mined fields. [The Vietnamese, in turn, plant the largest minefield in the world, known as K-5 (the "Bamboo Curtain"), from the Gulf of Thailand to the Lao border.]

The Vietnam War economy is in shambles by the late 1980s, and they withdraw from Cambodia. The U.S. and Britain insure the murderous Khmer Rouge are allowed to retain their seat at the U.N. General Assembly until 1991, preventing war crimes trials against them for genocide! (We appear to be against genocide only when a certain group in the Middle East pretends to be its only victims.)

The U.N. "disarmament program" takes weapons away from the rural Cambodian militias who provide the provincial defense against the Khmer Rouge. The Rouge begin kidnapping and executing tourists. Brother No. 3, Leng Sary, denounces Pol Pot for corruption and leads a defection of troops from the Pailin area—rich in gems and timber. Lacking a financial base to pay us for supplies, the Rouge are routed. They execute and cremate Brother No. 1 on a pile of old tires.

Police Aerial Reinforcement Unit

PARU of the Border Patrol Police—not the Army—is the special warfare unit with an "ambush and patrol" platoon. We work out of Camp Naresuan, Hua Hin District, Prachuap Khiri Khan Province, southwest of Bangkok on the Gulf of Thailand. (King Naresuan of Siam kills the invading Burmese Prince in personal combat atop elephants in AD 1593.) King Bhumibol Adulyadej has his summer palace here and is provided executive protection.

Duel

We set up an ambush in an area of ravines and thorn bush—nasty country similar to that of East Africa—inside Cambodia. The patrol we are expecting arrives early, before darkness. Instead of the usual flare, I send an airburst round from Thumper towards the radioman and (I presume) their officer near him. They go down. We often get just quick glimpses of the enemy and try to keep out of his view as well.

Following our fusillade and some ineffective return fire, I see a Thumper round arc out of the distant brush headed towards ME! I am the one eating dirt as it passes high, exploding on ground contact. I thump two rounds back, only to spot another headed my way.

The firing stops on both sides as I and my opponent dart from place to place. I try to put one round where I think he is and the next where he is headed. I get one quick look at him. He's tall, dressed in faded black (not the usual camouflage) similar to the old peasant Viet Cong garb and a floppy tan cap. I get the impression he is Oriental but never clearly see a face. He has dropped his ruck and appears to be wearing a grenade vest (for Thumper rounds) and carrying several tan bandoleers of M79 ammo. Much neater than my M18 claymore bags with straps, but a hot and heavy outfit to wear.

Caught up in our exchange, I realize it is past time to move out. Our little personal game may be giving them time to set up a counter-ambush or to outflank us. Both sides, it appears, just hunker down to enjoy the respite and show.

On debriefing, I ask if the others get a good look at my opponent. Several say he is a Caucasian! A French mercenary, Soviet advisor, or American deserter? A little mystery that, on occasion, still creeps into my thoughts. I also wonder if he ever wonders.

The King and I

A U.S. Air Force colonel and I meet King Bhumibol (Rama IX) at the Grand Palace in Bangkok. His Majesty decorates us as "Knights Commander of the Most Exalted Order of the White Elephant," a lesser order, but still appreciated.

I carry, for years, an Adventurers' Club flag. I ask the king if he will sign it. I hand it directly to him, which I quickly realize is a faux pas. (Thailand has the world's strictest lese-majeste laws; even casual comments and actions can result in arrest.)

The king waves off his aides and signs it. (It also carries the signatures of the presidents of the Republics of China and Korea and military figures around the world I have met.) The king speaks English, and we are both born a few miles apart in Massachusetts. I find we both play alto sax and are firearms enthusiasts. A small world. He is worth about $30 billion, however, and is worshipped. Thai elephants rough me up and roll me into the dirt. I still display the flag in my library.

"Lucy's Tiger Den"

Lucy's Tiger Den is where we members of American Legion China Post 1 (in exile) gather in Bangkok. Alban J. "Gus-the-Tiger" Rydberg runs his thirteen-stool bar at 38/40 Thanon Surawong, near the infamous Patpong Street. He serves "hobo beans," onions, and beef stew—free—to his Air America and military patrons. Tiger passes in the Philippines in 1990. Farewell, Amigo.

An American in Thailand and Cambodia

An American farang's biggest mistake in Thailand can be stepping off the curb and looking left. The next is dating a bar girl who can turn out to be a beautiful *katoey* ("ladyboy" or "woman of the second kind"). Never take a *tuk-tuk* ride without first bargaining. The bars charge you for "lady drinks" which are not drinks at all, but expensive blocks of time of thirty to forty-five minutes. Ping-pong shows are not about table tennis.

I teach public administration on a state department contract for the Bangkok Campus of Kensington University. My bride accompanies me on one of our three honeymoons. We travel with Chancellor Matt (Norvel) Young of Pepperdine University (I am a Pepperdine Associate) and Dr. George V. Chilingar of USC, instructors and administrators.

"Bridge Over the River Kwai"

My wife, Hueih-Hueih, likes the fictional 1957 movie of the construction of the Burma Railway in 1942–1943. It is filmed in Ceylon, but the original bridge in Thailand still exists. (It is destroyed by allied bombing but repaired.) The river's actual name is the *"Khwae Noi."* Its round truss spars are original.

The Japanese second-in-command, Sergeant Major Risaburo Saito ("Colonel Saito" in the movie) is respected by the prisoners for his fairness, although conditions are brutal. Lieutenant Colonel Philip Toosey, POW leader, later defends him in his trial after the war.

The lyrics of the tune—the "Colonel Bogey March"—are whistled rather than sung. This is because many of us—with the British military—remember the somewhat vulgar lyrics of the original song: "Hitler Has Only Got One Ball." The variant I am most familiar with begins:

"Hit-ler has only got one ball,
Goring has two but ve-ry small.
Himmler is somewhat sim'lar,
But poor Goebbels has no balls at all."

The Elephant Never Forgets

We have business in Chiang-Mai and visit nearby Mae-sa Elephant Camp. We climb a hill and see a female chained to a tree. Her baby, of about 400 pounds, sees me and affectionately rubs me, pushes me down, and rolls over me in the dirt. He ignores the others and pursues me until mahouts restrain him.

Two years later, I must visit the area on an army assignment. I climb the same hill and observe mama chained to the same tree. Junior is now half-grown, probably close to 5,000 pounds. He turns towards me and begins to run down the hill. Alarmed, I head to a nearby tree in hopes of escaping him.

The elephant charges past me without a glance. He zeroes in on an elderly lady tourist grasping a small bunch of bananas. He mugs her, grabs her bananas with his trunk, and runs back up the hill. Although relieved, I am a little disappointed.

Vendors selling brass knuckles along with Buddha images perhaps best illustrate Thailand's mix of violence and veneration. The Thais are true peace-loving people—to a certain extent. Buddhist males over twenty must practice monkhood for at least three months. Thailand is one of the eleven Axis powers. They have been at war with Burma and Cambodia/Laos for several thousand years.

"Born to the Naga"

Naga (*"neah"* in Khmer) translates as king cobra or a reptilian race of beings. Seven-headed stone nagas are everywhere in Cambodia. (They represent seven societies and an association with the seven colors of the rainbow). Odd-headed nagas are male and even numbers are female.

"Tiger" Rydberg has a photograph on his wall of "Queen of the Nagas—Killed by the American Army." Funny to us, but not to Thais and Cambodians. It is not exactly a hoax, but an oarfish found by SEAL trainees near Coronado, California.

Bamboo Train to Battambang

"The problem with taking the easy way out is that the enemy has mined it."
— U.S. Army Infantry School, Fort Benning, Georgia

Cambodia is hammered back almost to the stone age. Several surviving locomotives crawl on dilapidated one-meter tracks. The armored locomotive pushes a couple of flatcars. Passage is free on the first car and half-price on the second. Sort of a rolling mine detector. Maimed and blinded people are everywhere.

I enjoy a "bamboo train" ride on a norry into Battambang. It is a bamboo platform resting on two bogie axles with small rail wheels. A six-horsepower engine and fan belt propel you to around 25 mph. When you encounter a "train" headed in the opposite direction, the one with the fewest passengers must disassemble to let the other pass. No gasoline stations exist. Petrol is peddled by the roadside in old beer and soda bottles.

Stepping off the roads anywhere in Cambodia is one of the more dangerous moves on the planet.

Max K. Hurlbut

Execution by Elephant

Elephants are revered and symbols of royal authority in Cambodia and Thailand. They are used as instruments of state power. Elephantry—war elephants—are used by the Greeks and Romans as well as in India, China, and other Asian countries.

Elephants, unlike horses, will intentionally step upon and crush people and other animals. Males are used as females will run from a bull. Its thick hide protects it from arrows and slashing weapons. The high position of the rider gives good visibility but is a target for ranged weapons. The advent of cannon ends the widespread use of war elephants, but they are employed in battle as late as the 1890s.

Crushing by elephant can be slow or quick. He plucks off limbs and skillfully uses blades and chains attached to his trunk or tusks as weapons. Victims are deserters, captured enemy soldiers, criminals, and tax evaders—or those who simply irritate the monarch.

Death by elephant remains common but accidental or when they go into musth (spiking testosterone levels in bulls). Both domestic and wild elephants are extremely dangerous to humans at this time.

A "white elephant" is a burdensome possession, which cannot be disposed of by its owner and whose cost is out of proportion to its usefulness. Thai kings give them to obnoxious courtiers in order to ruin them. Such a fine gift cannot be refused…or you may meet the *other* elephant.

Jungle Meet

Our platoon is moving through some border villages when we spot a few Caucasians in the middle of nowhere. They are a Canadian World Health Organization group of volunteer well-diggers. Their leader introduces himself as Dr. Donald S. Sharp. "That's interesting," I say. "I have a cousin in Massachusetts of the same name."

"I have a cousin in California with the same name as yours," he replies.

Don is working for the Canadian Health Sciences Division out of Ottawa. We have not seen each other or corresponded since we were kids in New England. We now keep in touch.

Chapter XXII

TAMING THE TIGER

My Room 404 of the Grand Hotel in Taipei is not popular with locals. The Chinese pronunciation of the numbers translates as: "death—spirit—death." (Most hotels in China lack a fourth floor, just as American ones eschew a thirteenth).

I leave L.A. on Northwest Orient 21 to connect in Tokyo. A crash at Haneda Airport forces our flight to sit in Honolulu. Two other travelers, CIA officers, and I decide to wander into the garden section of the airport. We return thirty minutes later to see our aircraft lifting off without us. A Japan Airlines plane makes an unscheduled stop to pick us up (my friends' luggage contains important gear), and we intercept our original flight just touching down in Tokyo.

So begins my Chinese adventure—which continues through today.

I board a coal-fired WWII Japanese steam engine to Ping-Tung in the south. The right-of-way is determined by the engineer snagging a large brass token in a loop pouch from the station master—a leftover from the WWII Japanese Rail Administration. It prevents train wrecks.

I am on orders (published entirely in Chinese) by the Republic of China—a most unusual procedure—requesting my attachment as an advisor to their Special Warfare Command. A little surprise from my buddies at Fort Bragg who have contacts with General Leslie R. Forney, Jr., of the Military Assistance Advisory Group. [U.S. orders are later cut for me to "Act as intel officer in Chinese Airborne Forces exercises while assigned to MAAG China" (T-03-38420 of 14 March 1977).]

Lieutenant Colonel Chen Hua-Min, who speaks and writes excellent English, is assigned to me. The heat and humidity are terrific, and I change into fatigues. An airborne recruit class is departing "on their first jump" and asks if the newly arrived captain will honor them as their "wind dummy"?

Wind Dummy

Lieutenant Colonel Chen excuses himself while I 'chute up. A wind dummy is usually a 150-pound pack, tethered to a parachute, thrown out of a transport plane on its first pass over a drop zone. It can also be an experienced jumper. The pilot and jumpmaster watch it descend and judge where the winds will carry their troops on the next pass, as their T-10 'chutes are not maneuverable and recruits are inexperienced with wires, trees, water, and other obstacles. The best jumper will break bones on rocks.

The class breaks into song. I stand in the door of the Kaiser (not Fairchild) C-119 Flying Boxcar. It is one of the few planes that will not fly on one engine. President Chiang Kai-shek wants C-130s, but we are concerned these superior-range planes will be used to invade the mainland. The 119 has not been made since 1955 and I am around long enough to know how to rig it for jumping.

The green light comes on and I receive a tap from the jumpmaster. I look up to watch the canopy deploy (better than counting and awaiting the opening shock). I am out at 1,250 feet but cannot spot smoke on the drop zone (which gives you wind direction). I pass over dry sweet potato fields and am descending into a giant rice paddy with earthen berms. About 150 feet to go, and I can smell the odor of the local fertilizer rising on a hot day.

I climb my risers to "pop" them in an attempt for a stand-up landing in eighteen inches of water to avoid the safer PLF (parachute landing fall), which requires a roll with full-body contact. I still end up splashed with— why be polite—human sewage! A lieutenant, struggling to suppress a smile, is standing on the berm with two privates carrying buckets of fresh water, which they pour over me. The C-119 passes over much lower, but no one else is exiting. I wave. If this is an "accidental" drop, how do they know where to send the bucket brigade?

This is the strangest initiation I have experienced and take it in good humor. Chen asks me not to spread it around back home as they enjoy welcoming us airborne "round eyes." My Bragg buddies are to ask, forever, how I enjoy my "paddy jump."

I make eighteen jumps and qualify for their "Three Plum-Flower" (Master) Wing and "Rough Terrain" Wing (number 502)—jumps into forest, mountains, and water (with the Army Frogmen unit). Lieutenant General Lu Shao-Hsich holds a farewell party for me with his staff. He presents me with ROC Advisor's Badge No. 8646 and many little gifts. I am overwhelmed by their courtesy and generosity.

Matsu and Quemoy

I return to Taiwan often. (Sometimes the only passenger on chartered 747s bringing Vietnamese orphans to the U.S.) We travel to Kinmen (Quemoy) and Matsu Islands on the ten-hour night crossing of the troopship *Taima* out of Keelung Harbor to Fuao Port on Nangan Island.

The People's Liberation Army attacks Kinmen at high tide on 25 October 1949 (before my time, of course). Beach obstacles (still there) and a receding tide strand their amphibious vehicles. Their "human wave" attacks are chewed-up by the Kuomintang (Nationalist) "Bears of Kinmen"—old M5A1 light Stuart tanks. After exhausting their ammo, they roll over the enemy trapped on the beach. The Chicoms lose their entire force. (The survivors join the KMT rather than return in disgrace.)

The Commies start shelling the Islands in 1958, with over one-half million shells in forty-four days. For twenty years,[175] they bombard the islands on Tuesday, Thursday, and Saturday. The Nationalists fire back on Mondays, Wednesdays, and Fridays. (Sunday is a holiday.) So much shrapnel is deposited that mining remains a productive business. I have two brass and steel Maestro Wu knives made from shells by famous blacksmith Wu Chao-Hsi.

The islands are honeycombed with tunnels and artillery positions. Fort Ti-Han (the "Iron Hamburger") and a huge artillery shell (Baersan Battle Monument) in Huxia Village on Lieyu ("Little Kinmen") are things few tourists visit.

---

[175] The Director General of the "Economic and Cultural Office" in Seattle (belatedly, on 20 November 2001) awards me the "823 Campaign Badge of Honor" and "U.S./ROC Mutual Defense Commemorative Badge (1955–1979)."

We arrive on Matsu[176] (named for Mazu, goddess of the sea and protector of sailors[177]) in Magang Village. Foul weather and horizontal rain find us in Cin-bi Village, Baigan—built of stone and largely abandoned.

We discover the "Middle of the Sea Bar" in Building 54—a great place to weather the storm. Small stone frogs are everywhere. (A Chinese general once wins a victory by turning local frogs into soldiers.)

We arrive in the Penghu Islands in the Pescadores by ferry. Near Si-Yu lighthouse and radar installation is an enormous 240 mm twin rifle—a decoy made entirely of concrete. In Magong, one can buy, for ten U.S. dollars, fossilized coral or agate chops[178] with your name in Chinese characters. I buy one for my brother-in-law, a Korean War vet. Unbeknownst to him (until now) it reads, *"Wua-shih tong-shing lian."* (I am a homosexual.)

The Colonel's Daughter

I marry Su Hueih-Hueih—the name of an orchid. She is a school teacher and classical dancer—and the colonel's daughter. She is born a tiger on the Chinese zodiac; I am a poor rabbit. (The twelve signs correspond to birth years, not to our Western months.)

Hueih-Hueih is one of a handful selected by her government to dance at the exposition in Osaka, Japan, and in Hong Kong. The Consulate has her training others and performing in San Francisco and Anchorage. Our

---

[176] Females are considered unlucky on ships or in tunnels. The "lady" identifier is removed from the ideogram, making it masculine but retaining the pronunciation. Mazu, thus, becomes Ma-tsu.

[177] Mazu is a real person; a fifteen-year-old swimmer born in March 960. She stands on the shore, wearing red clothes, to guide fishing boats home in bad weather. She has a vision of her family perishing during a typhoon. She reaches out to save her father who slips from her grasp. Her tomb is on the island, guarded by two general-demons, Thousand Miles Eye and With the Wind Ear. She is worshipped throughout much of Asia, with over 1,500 temples dedicated to her in twenty-six countries.

[178] Chops are legal signatures and must be registered by your bank. They are hand-carved and as different as signatures. Every time you cash a check, they verify your chop with the original registry. Lose it and it is difficult to re-register another one.

wedding is in the Grand Hotel and our witness (official) is Su Nan-Cheng, Mayor of Tainan. She does not speak English nor I Chinese. (But she is smarter than I and quickly learns English.)

Colonel Su Yuan Jihng, HH's father, is a cavalry officer who comes over with Chiang Kai-shek in 1949. His General Grant tank eats Japanese Type 95 Ha-Go and Type 97 Chi-Ha armor. He goes into battle with the heads of Japanese soldiers festooning his tank. "It flushes the Jap infantry from their holes," he explains. (Should they capture him, it will not go well.) The colonel dies of colon cancer. He refuses all treatment, including pain medication, and dies hard. A tough old bird!

Chinese Food

Yes, the Chinese eat dog, snake, and almost everything that walks, crawls, swims, or flies. The most unusual thing I find is a Cantonese dish called San Chi-ow Tsai ("three squeak mouse").[179]

HH visits her mother every year. A few years ago she takes me to a new restaurant chain, the "Modern Toilet." They feature a marton (toilet) menu with such delights as stews and curries served in miniature toilets followed by dessert of "Poo-Poo" ice cream. Seats are toilet stools. The noodle and peking duck establishments of an earlier era have been replaced with American fast food establishments.

We pay respects to Colonel Su in his niche in Dasi (Big Creek), Tao-Yuan County. Chiang Kai-shek's tomb is at nearby Sze-Hu ("Love Lake"). We watch the Changing of the Guard ceremony, no longer as precise as it once was. The surrounding Cihu Park contains statues of Chiang salvaged throughout Taiwan during recent political turmoil. Many are badly damaged during the administration of Chen Shui-Bian. America is not the only country to sever its roots.

VACRS (Vocational Assistance Commission for Retired Servicemen) awards me its Medal of Honor (number 2301) in December 1980.

---

[179] "Squeak number one" comes when you grasp the live hairless young mouse with your chopsticks; "squeak number two" is dipping him into the hot sauce; and, "squeak number three" is when you pop him into your mouth.

Speaker Lin Ting-Sheng gives me their Friend of the Taipei City Council plaque. I have keys to the cities of Taipei, Tainan, and Kaohsiung. I am a life member of VFW Flying Tigers Post 9957 (Taipei) and life member of the Taiwan Veterans "Badge of Honor" Association. Hueih-Hueih and I fly both the ROC and U.S. (Betsy Ross) flags.

Crazy Dog Wave

Hueih-Hueih and I stand, with our backs to the ocean, on a stone shelf about thirty-five feet above the water at Ye-Lio. A mushroom-shaped rock about fifteen feet high separates us. HH's classmate is taking a photo.

Our photographer's mouth opens and her eyes get wide. She turns and runs. I immediately grab hold of the rock stem while HH, out-of-reach, stands on the other side with her umbrella open. A fong-go-lan ("crazy dog wave") rises about forty feet above us and crashes down. I am able to hang on to the rock but see HH swept away into a trough, heading for the edge. She is grasping her umbrella and half of it is visible above the water. I run and am able to pull her out before she is swept over the cliff. A group of school kids on a nearby rise politely applaud.

We return to HH's home in Nei-Li Village and she tells the story of the rogue wave appearing out of nowhere. The following day, her mother, knowing I like to take pictures, invites me to her Buddhist temple to photograph a ceremony. (A clue should be the colonel, standing in the background, shaking his head and frowning.)

The priest and his son, dressed in traditional costumes, begin dancing around me and throwing down half-moon shaped pieces of wood to the floor. Mother and priest get down on hands and knees to examine the characters written on them. This is repeated many times.

Back home, I ask HH about the ceremony called "Chiu-Shea." She looks it up in her Chinese-English dictionary. The one-word definition: "exorcism"! Guess which of us is possessed by the devil and needs a lot of work? Mom scowls at me and dad rolls his eyes. Suspicions confirmed about the *gwai-lo* (Cantonese: "ghost man"). (An Asian who thinks and behaves like a white is called a "twinkie" or a "banana"—white inside but with a yellow exterior.)

"Uncle Chicken"

Few cities are as beautiful at night as Hong Kong. Neon lights dance off the dark waters of Victoria Harbour towards TST (Tsim Sha Tsui—"Pointed Sandy Mouth") East waterfront. Here, in Kowloon, is the office building of my dear friend, Alex K.K. Lam and his sons, Wilson and Winston. The Peninsula Hotel, the Hong Kong China Ferry Terminal, and some of the finest restaurants on the planet are here.

Alex is "Uncle Chicken" to most of Hong Kong. (He signs his name with a little chicken caricature.) He makes his first fortune with chicken farms in the New Territories and is a champion jockey in his youth. We are both Pepperdine Associates and he attends President Ronald Reagan's first inauguration with several of us.

I meet British police officers in the Hong Kong Riots of 1967. Peoples' Republic of China Red Guards, during the Great Proletarian Cultural Revolution, clash with the police. More than fifty people die. I have a souvenir of the conflict—a black rattan police shield. The rioters throw spears of sharpened steel pipe against the police, which penetrate their rattan shields. They quickly order new ones made of fiberglass.

Uncle Chicken introduces me to many Hong Kong *Chinese* police officers who do most of the dirty work on the streets. It is a real education.

Triads

Chinese Triads (three points on a circle: heaven, earth, and man) start as resistance forces opposing Manchu rule during the corrupt Ch'ing Dynasty (1644–1911). Their emblem is a triangle.

The Heaven and Earth Society evolves from a political movement into a criminal organization. Crackdowns by the Chicoms force them to migrate to Hong Kong, a British colony. They divide Hong Kong into nine regions. [Nine is the element of gold in the *I-Ching* (classical "Book of Changes") trigram.]

Triads produce much of the counterfeit goods sold in the U.S. They smuggle aliens, manipulate stocks, extort businesses, and commit identity theft. They murder and are big in gambling and prostitution.

Numbers are of considerable importance to the Chinese. [I tell HH I select our phone number (734-4444) to discourage her sisters from calling. Four is pronounced the same as "death."] She protects her car with a license plate number of 888 for good luck and "booming" fortune.

The Triads use numeric codes as ranks. The *I-Ching* contains a divination system similar to Western geomancy. The leader is "489," a reference to the "mountain" or "dragon master." The number "426" is a military commander or "red pole" (enforcer). Old Charlie Chan films refer to "25," which is a spy or undercover officer. (It has come to mean "traitor" or "informer.") The "49'ers" are ordinary members ("dog soldiers"), and "blue lanterns" (with no number) are uninitiated members.

Triads are not to be confused with tongs, which are more recent and labor-union oriented. Triads are supposedly outlawed in Hong Kong in 1949 with the Societies Ordinance. They are in every major U.S. city and number as many as three million worldwide. They are largely ignored by U.S. police and military, as we do not understand their structure, language, and scope of operations.

Hong Kong Handover

Prime Minister Margaret ("Attila-the-Hen") Thatcher later expresses regrets over the loss of Hong Kong under her watch on 1 July 1997. Is a language misunderstanding involved?

The Second Convention of Peking in 1898 gives Britain an additional ninety-nine years of rule. Why not 100 years, a number of significance to the Chinese? The number "99" also means "eternity" or "forever." There is evidence the treaty is intended to be renewed in perpetuity. To the Brits, however, the number "99" is simply the one preceding "100." This should suggest some understanding of other cultures by those dealing with them. Ignorance can prove to be expensive!

As a little aside, banning firecrackers in Los Angeles some years ago allows evil spirits to creep back into Chinatown. Not significant to us other than a minor safety issue, but of importance to those who believe.

Alex slips me a small, flat, tissue-wrapped item a little larger than a Zippo lighter on my promotion to army captain. It is an old amulet of brown-yellow jade and contains the carving of a Han Dynasty (206 BC–AD 220) soldier. (I trust he is not one of the palace eunuchs who cause the Han downfall.) Inscribed are the words, "One Hundred Battles; One Hundred Victories."

It is an ancient soldier's good-luck piece, probably from a tomb. I rarely wear jewelry, but I sometimes jump into Cambodia with it beneath my fatigue shirt. One never knows. It might make a good souvenir for some Vietnamese soldier better with his Thumper than I.

The DMZ

I cross the Thirty-Eighth Parallel in Korea with Pepperdine Chancellor Norvel Young and several others. It is the most heavily militarized zone in the world. The film in our cameras is mysteriously fogged, we think, near the Freedom Bridge over the Imjin River—a vehicle X-ray technology not supposedly available for another dozen years.

In Panmunjom, we visit the remains of the poplar tree near Observation Post 5 where two U.S. officers are murdered with axes in 1976. (We do nothing to retaliate, which affects morale and opinions in all of Asia on the lack of U.S. temerity—we appear to them a "Paper Tiger.")

We meet with President Chun Doo-Hwan in the Blue House, Seoul, on 8 November 1984. He is a gracious host and presents us each with pierced ceramic vases engraved with his name in gold. He guides us through the Hyundai INI Steel Factory in Seoul. Chun is later sentenced to death for treason and bribery, but his sentence is commuted.

Chapter XXIII

UP ABOVE AND DOWN UNDER

It is not true the only reason anyone lives in Canada is because Lord Cornwallis loses at Yorktown.

The first of thirteen foreign parachute wings I earn are Canadian. In October 1973, my Twelfth Special Forces Detachment trains the Canadian Airborne Regiment in desert warfare at Fort Irwin in the Mojave Desert before their deployment to Egypt as the UN Peacekeeping Force. They are splendid light infantry and Canada's finest military unit. [The regiment is disbanded in 1995 after the "Somalia Affair," where a captive is tortured and killed. Rather than punish the perpetrators, Canadian politicians destroy the unit and demoralize their entire military.]

Canadian Army North Pole Expedition

Bad weather forces us to hold over at Resolute Bay, a small Inuit hamlet on Cornwallis Island. I befriend the resident mountie, Corporal Wilson A. MacLennan, who patrols about a million square miles of the Northwest Territories. When out in the bitter cold, he favors Cree Indian dress. The RCMP vehicles are kept running twenty-four-hours a day so as to not freeze up. They are shut off only for short periods for servicing.

We fly in a Canadian Forces C-47 to Lake Hazen Base Camp, Ellesmere Island—and the northernmost Canadian village of Grise Fiord. Vikings from the Greenland colonies reach here in the late AD 900s. Igloos are cut from the snow by our Inuit guides and we rest upon reindeer hides with dense undercoat and hollow air-filled hairs. A small lamp flame warms the interior.

We travel about by dogsled. Eskimo sleds differ from the Indian. The Indian sled runs dogs in columns, so they can pass between trees. Inuit dogs run in a fan, each with its own tether to the sled. Their diet of oily fish requires them to defecate frequently. This is done quickly, with one eye on the approaching sled.

Geographic Pole

We load a Twin Otter with barrels of extra fuel for our 492-nautical-mile run to the North Pole. (We hand pump it into the fuel tanks in flight.) Landing conditions must be perfect. We must land on a lead—a crack in the ice forming over a channel of open water, which quickly freezes to provide a smooth path. The pilot judges its thickness by its color of blue. Too thin and we break through with no hope of rescue. Sun is required so as to cast shadows of otherwise invisible "ice sharks" and other projections.

We touch down at latitude 90 degrees north on 9 April 1979, 1734 hours Greenwich Mean Time. We have an Omega Global 500 Navigation system tied in to seven stations. It is accurate to within +/-30 meters. We rotate the plane while the pilot remains in place, never shutting down the engines. We quickly take measurements of ice thickness, temperature, and other conditions. It is relatively warm at -40 degrees Celsius (and a corresponding -40 Fahrenheit).

The Pole, of course, has no length or width. It's a mathematical point where the imaginary line of the earth's axis intersects the surface, depending upon wobble. The USS *Nautilis* determines sea depth here at 13,410 feet in 1958.

USAF Lieutenant Colonel Gale J. Raymond is an international courier (and fellow member of American Legion China Post 1). He sets up a temporary post office and creates some unique postal covers for us.

Magnetic Pole

We take readings near the center of the North Magnetic Pole, then at latitude 76 degrees, 38 minutes North, and longitude 99 degrees, 18 minutes West—Allard Island, mouth of Young Inlet off the north coast of Bathurst Island, NWT.

The pole moves in an ellipse. Compass needles point here, it's believed for centuries, because of iron ore deposits. We now know it is simply the point where the earth's magnetic field points vertically downwards.

Border Guards Abandon Posts

Canadians have no bill of rights and are paranoid about firearms. Word spreads that an American murder suspect on a motorcycle may be en route up Interstate 5 from California. Sixty Canadian border guards flee four crossings here on the British Columbia/Whatcom County border, leaving them unguarded and stranding thousands of motorists.[180] The Canadian Border Services Agency defends them because "they have the legal right to refuse to work if they believe they are in imminent danger." This happens several times.

Considerable "gun violence" occurs in Canada, whose firearms laws disarm the public, so criminals can go about their business without fear of harm from their victims. Four RCMP officers are shot to death in Alberta in the Mayerthorpe Tragedy. They are raiding a marijuana farm. The suspect then shoots himself.

Robert "Willy-The-Pig-Farmer" Pickton, just above us at Port Coquitlam, B.C., is suspected of possessing a firearm. They find the remains of girls he shoots and feeds to his pigs. Pickton admits to killing forty-nine and regrets not having the opportunity of making it an even fifty.[181] He will eventually be out as the maximum sentence for murder is "life in prison," with parole at twenty-five years.

"E-Pana"

Hueih-Hueih and I make a dozen trips up and down the Alaska Highway over the years. I must ship my duty weapons ahead to Alaska, as even police officers are not allowed to transport their guns. I once have our car torn

---

[180] "Canadian Border Guards Flee After 'Dangerous' Traveler Warning," Associated Press (Fox News.com), 25 September 2006.

[181] Tom Leonard, "Pig Farmer 'Killed 49 Women But Wanted 50'," *The Telegraph* (U.K.), 23 January 2007.

apart at a border crossing when I mention being a U.S. police officer. (When they ask, I now reply, "Retired civil servant.") Once across the border, you are usually okay with real officers.

We sometimes take the Canadian ferry through the Inland Passage to Prince Rupert and drive east to Prince George on the "Yellowhead" (Highway 16), a distance of about 450 miles. This isolated forest road is locally called the "Highway of Tears." Over forty girls disappear and are murdered here, apparently by more than one serial killer. "E-Pana" is the name given to the investigation by the RCMP.[182]

Down Under

I make five jumps at the Australian Parachute Training School at RAAF Base Williamtown in New South Wales. Three are on Salt Ash DZ and two are into Shoal Bay and Nelson Bay.

The Australians have a unique view of jumping. We (U.S.) go through a week of physical torture, followed by two weeks of training on various jump towers and apparatus. Our first jump comes in week four (now week three). Australians jump their trainees on the first day—into water. This gives students a realistic feeling for their future training, without the broken legs and ankles of inexperienced jumpers. Most enjoy it and become enthusiastic paratroopers.

We jump from the tail gates of Caribous, just as in Thailand. Great white sharks are visible in the bay below, which accounts for an assault boat pickup for each jumper.

One jumper shuffles down the ramp, looks below, and screams. He turns, scrambles back up (not an easy thing to do), and clutches a seat. His refusal to jump is not a disgrace as not all are suited for the duty.

---

[182] "E" is the RCMP designation for all things British Columbian. "Pana" is the Inuit god who oversees souls in their frozen underworld.

Chapter XXIV

TEST-JUMPING FOR THE RAF

The British experience a fifty-percent malfunction rate on a parachute (the PX1-Mark V) with the first anti-inversion net.[183] I am invited to find out what is wrong by my Fort Bragg friends.

To learn British jump techniques, I attend the Depot the Parachute Regiment and Airborne Force at Aldershot, Hampshire, about 37 miles southwest of London. We jump from WWII barrage balloons anchored 700 feet above Queen's Park drop zone. No reserve is used as the jump altitude is too low for it to take a breath.

The Aeroplane and Armament Experimental Establishment at Bascombe Down, Wiltshire, is next. I jump from a Hercules C-130 at 4,000 feet. A T-6 Harvard photo-plane pulls up to the left door just before I jump. As I exit, it falls with me, filming the descent.[184]

Using British jump techniques, the malfunction rate remains high. I pinch the Capewell cutaway releases and fall free, deploying my reserve 'chute. Using American jump techniques, the Mark V works fine.

Problem Solved

The Brits lack paratrooper transport planes in WWII, so they convert bombers by removing the lower gun turrets. Jumpers hop out the bottom in a weak exit. Americans make a vigorous exit to get away from the side of the plane (except in jets, where you want to avoid the engine exhaust).

---

[183] The anti-inversion net is an eighteen-inch nylon mesh running around the skirt of the parachute. It prevents inversion malfunctions—cigarette roll, "Mae West" (looks like a giant brassiere)—where the parachute tries to turn inside out. Such malfunctions increase the rate of descent and make deployment of the reserve problematic, as it may not "catch air." Inversion malfunctions injure and kill many jumpers.

[184] I later request a photograph or two and receive a letter from flight lieutenant J.A. Johnston [AEN/02/106(P) of 20 October 1976] stating, "Unfortunately, only cine cameras were operating…so there is no record in 'stills' of your descents."

The British reserve handle is on top and requires an upward pull. Hands fold over this handle on exiting, which causes elbows to protrude. The elbows (like wings of a miniature airplane) create lift and turbulence. The U.S. reserve handle is on the right. On exiting, we hold the right hand over it, with elbows tucked tightly against the body. Our legs are together.

A vigorous exit, combined with a tight body position, result in a smooth opening. A weak, sloppy exit encourages twists or entanglement in deploying shroud lines—a recipe for disaster.

The Brits cease jumping from balloons, and, in early 1993, close Aldershot to jump training. The rest of the world quickly adopts the simple but effective anti-inversion net. Hundreds of inversion malfunctions no longer take place, and future paratroopers are saved injury and death.

Recognition. My Letter Orders of 5 June 1976 are amended (T-07-15310 of 26 July 1977): "To attend British Army Parachute School and to Test-Jump PX1-Mark V Parachute." This is it for U.S. records.

Twenty-nine years later (21 October 2005), the Russian Academy of Natural Sciences, U.S. Section, awards me their gold Crown and Eagle Medal of Honor. Scientists Without Borders presents me with their gold George V. Chillingar Medal of Honor. It's nice to be remembered.

Lili Marlene

James Warner Bellah (*She Wore A Yellow Ribbon*, *Fort Apache*, *The Man Who Shot Liberty Valance*), good friend and fellow member of the British United Services Club (officers serving with the British army), introduces me to Austro-Hungarian movie producer Andre de Toth. We become friends and he later attends my wedding reception.

Eyepatch and rugged good looks make Andre a favorite with the ladies. [One of his seven wives—and he has nineteen children—is Veronica Lake, known for her peekaboo hairstyle.] His best-known film is the 1953 *House of Wax* starring Vincent Price—the first 3-D film I project at the San Clemente Theatre. Andre is the director whose one eye places him in the odd position of being unable to see the results.

Andre shoots the greatest opening (and perhaps the most ironic ending) of any war movie in *Play Dirty* (1969) with Michael Caine. It is to be his last film. The credits roll on a dusty Jeep bouncing across the North African desert, a dead man in the passenger seat.

The driver is listening to "Lili Marlene," sung by Lale Andersen. He soon switches caps and tunes his shortwave to "Lili Marlene," sung by Marlene Dietrich.

This symbolic crossing from German to British lines is considered too subtle for U.S. audiences, and he changes the second song to, "You Are My Sunshine." The film is a masterpiece that remains powerful.

Colonel Bellah, soaked in castor oil from the rotary engine—where the entire motor rotates around a stationary crankshaft—masters flying the unstable WWI "Sopwith Camel" and fighting its gyroscopic precession on turns. "Much more deadly than the Red Baron," he says.

The Colonel is in the WWII Burma Campaign on the staff of Admiral of the Fleet and last Viceroy of India, Louis Mountbatten. His boy, John Bellah, is a career University of California detective and prize-winning technical author on emergency vehicle testing. Son James, the black sheep, is best remembered for an incident in high school, when smoke and tear-gas grenades clear the classroom. James is quickly apprehended—as he is the only student at his desk wearing a gas mask….

Chapter XXV

FLUNKING FRENCH

Commandant Colonel Jean-Charles Ziegler kisses me on both cheeks, and I am forever and proudly a para-frog: *Le Brevet No. 413968, ETAP Stage 6610 du 26 May 1978.* I am attached to the Second Foreign Parachute Regiment (*2^e Regiment Etranger de Parachutistes* or *2^e REP*—the Legion's Corsican Regiment).

Completing the Airborne School at Pau (*L'Ecole des Troupes Aeroportees*) is tough. We jump from Nord 2501 Nor-Atlas planes with double booms that resemble our C-119s. Their TAP 661-12 chute has a twenty-eight-foot canopy, not much larger than our twenty-four-foot reserve. You come in hard and fast. Their P.T. is not just tough but brutal. (But they eat well.)

I am intel officer for Operation Colibri ("Hummingbird") XIV with the Legion and the German airborne out of Fliegerhorst, Allgau, Bavaria, in June 1976. The Germans jump us in gusting thirty-knot winds, so as to complete our required five jumps out of C-160 Transalls. I snap a quick photo showing three malfunctions in our single drop. We are blown off course, and I end up doing my PLF (parachute landing fall) in a concrete irrigation ditch. Dents in my helmet and some scraped hide, but no broken bones. Others are not so fortunate, but no one complains.

Battle of Kolwezi

Kolwezi is a copper, cobalt, and uranium mining center in Katanga Province, the Congo (Zaire). I monitor the 2^e REP movement to Kinshasa in May 1978 after rebels (including Fidel Castro's Second Cuban Division) invade from Angola and begin killing whites. The French stage in Kinshasa and jump into Kolwezi. Around 250 European hostages are executed, but the legionnaires surprise and do a number on invaders.

The Two "Surrender Monkeys"

French intelligence accurately reports no "Weapons of Mass Destruction" in Iraq, and no links to 9-11. President George W. Bush and Vice President Richard ("I-had-better-things-to-do") Cheney, who obtains five draft deferments, need to divert attention away from their fabrications and pending war crimes—the illegal invasion of Iraq.

An outbreak of American buffoonery never seems far from the surface. Bush and Cheney begin referring to the French as "surrender monkeys" and encourage such juvenile and transitory antics as renaming French fries as "Freedom fries" in congressional cafeterias. They are also unsuccessful in boycotting French wine.

This annoys many of us veterans, especially those who serve in France. [Although French waiters delight in being rude to Americans, they are even more insulting to German and English tourists.] And how many Americans remember that the Statue of Liberty is a gift from the people of France?

"We Are Here, Lafayette."

A mutual dislike arises between the Anglophile FDR and General Charles de Gaulle. FDR instructs our commanders to not inform the Free French of operations on their soil. Many Frenchmen see us as ingrates. De Gaulle feels marginalized and pulls out of NATO following the Suez Crisis of 1956. He deploys nuclear weapons aimed at the Soviets (the *Force de Frappe*) and tells them, "If you assemble at the Fulda Gap and Hessian Corridor (traditional invasion routes), I will kill 80 million Russians." The Soviets know we will not commit suicide but are not sure of de Gaulle. He possibly prevents WWIII.

Without the French, we will be singing "God Save the Queen" and eating lousy British food. The French give us 40 of their 109 regiments of infantry and 75,000 sailors during our Revolutionary War. They also drag Spain in on our side. Comte de Rochambau's 5,500 soldiers join Washington's Continental army to press the Brits at Yorktown. (He loses more men than does Washington.)

A quarter of the French navy, under Admiral de Grasse, blocks the British from escaping while Admiral Barrass transports siege guns that will chew up Cornwallis's army. He surrenders. The horrendous expense bankrupts France and triggers the Revolution and Reign of Terror. King Louis XVI (literally) gives his head for us.

General John J. "Black Jack" Pershing lands in France in June 1917. He kisses the sword of Napoleon Bonaparte, and, at the grave of the Marquis de Lafayette, pledges unalterable friendship: *"Nous voila, Lafayette!"* Words that stir true Americans.

Surrender monkeys? Take a moment to read G.J. Meyer's comments in *A World Undone* (2006). French casualties for the first month of WWI are 265,000. More than ten percent of their officers are dead. France loses as many men *every day* of August 1914 as we lose in three and one-half years. On one day (22 August 1914—Battle of Mons) the French lose twenty times our total losses in Iraq and Afghanistan. The French, in a country 57,000 square miles smaller than Texas, lose 1.3 million in this one war. Twice as many French troops as Americans die in Vietnam. The French sometimes adopt "attentisme," a wait-and-see strategy, but cowards they are not!

La Golondrina

My favorite song as a vagabond policeman is *"La Golondrina"* (the "wandering swallow"), especially as sung by Brendan O'Dowda. It is a poignant Mexican "song of farewell" many know from Sam Peckinpah's film, *The Wild Bunch* (1969). [It is written by Dr. Narciso Serradel Sevilla (1843–1910), who fights against the emperor, Ferdinand Maximilian I. He is captured and deported to France.]

Cinco de Mayo

The Mexicans defeat the French at Pueblo in the glory that is Cinco de Mayo. Capitaine Jean Danjou, a quartermaster with sixty-two legionnaires and two officers, is attacked by 2,000 revolutionaries on 30 April 1863. He makes his stand in Hacienda Camaron, a nearby inn, and is soon killed.

Five surviving legionnaires, out of ammunition, refuse to surrender and make a bayonet charge. They are subdued and allowed to return to France. Danjou's wooden hand can still be seen at Aubagne in the south of France.

"March or Die"

Tricolor flags wave in the breeze. In the Place de la Concorde (where Louis XVI loses his head) are stands for the Bastille Day (14 July) Review. Elite units march down Champs-Elysees (Elysian Fields—"Place of the blessed dead") to *"La Marseillaise,"* possibly the most stirring of national anthems. [Compare Mireille Mathieu's rendition with Roseanne Barr's disgraceful screeching of "The Star Spangled Banner" in July 1990. Both can be found on YouTube.]

The slow march of the legion (88 steps per minute instead of 120) is led by pioneers (*"sapeurs"*), huge bearded men in leather aprons with axes over their shoulders. They hold the position of honor ahead of the infantry. In battle, they precede the infantry, so as to clear mines and cut away enemy defenses. Their short life span allows them privileges, such as the wearing of beards. The legion eighty-eight-step "crawl" usually has them as the last unit in a parade. (This is the authentic marching pace of American units during our Revolutionary War).

The para marching song is *"La Legion Marche Vers le Front,"* lifted from the Waffen SS, *"SS Marschiert."* (Where do you think those unemployed German soldiers go following the war?)

The mandating of open borders—insisted upon for NATO countries by the U.S.—is the single most disastrous development for France (and all of Europe) in recent times. No nation (including America) can maintain its sovereignty without border controls.

Those denigrating France insult our heritage and are not worthy of licking the dirt from a French private's boots. The long-term consequences of American arrogance and rude attacks upon the French are readily apparent in our hypocritical foreign policy and series of defeats in the Middle East. Things our friends, the French, try to alert us to and prevent.

Chapter XXVI

SPRINGTIME IN GERMANY

Detachment B-3 of the Twelfth Special Forces hosts a number of foreign enlisted men. (SF is the American Legion.) One is captured in North Africa and sent to a U.S. POW camp. He wears his original *heer* (army) first-pattern *fallschirmschutzenabzeichen* (falling-umbrella-shooter's-badge). None of us object. The war is long over.

Bundeswehr paratroopers, following the war, are not allowed to wear anything resembling Wehrmacht insignia (our "de-Nazification" program). The Luftwaffe diving-eagle-grasping-a-swastika becomes an allied style wing-with-a-wreath—bronze, silver, or gold, designating the class—around a center parachute. Look closely at their beret insignia: it is the old swooping eagle minus the swastika!

Oberstleutnant (Lieutenant Colonel), then Major, Heinz Henn and I are the only foreigners attending the British Airborne School at Aldershot. We become good friends. Heinz is the GLO (ground liaison officer) for *Jagdbombergeschwader* (Fighter-Bomber-Attack-Group) 32 (aka: "JaboG 32"), of the First Air Division out of Lechfeld Airbase, Augsburg, Bavaria.

Heinz and I work as the U.S./German team in field exercises in the 1970s and 1980s. We both shoot up extra ammo at various bases. One time, during a formal match, I shoot a perfect score with pistol, rifle, and machine gun, and qualify for the gold *schützenschnur* ("shooting cord"), worn looped on the right shoulder.[185] I am awarded a gold "Expert Infantry"/Efficiency badge. Through Heinz, I attend the German Airborne School at Altenstadt, a WWII antiaircraft center.

I attend Oktoberfest and see Franzl Lang, der Jodlerkonig, perform, as well as Angela Wiedl. [The "echo" in her marvelous song "Leo"—across

---

[185] The *schützenschnur* has interesting origins back to the Eighty Years' War (1568–1648). Spanish troops are ordered to hang any Dutchman carrying a musket. Spanish musketeers begin carrying ropes slung over one shoulder.

the Danube in Regensburg—is her father, famous child soprano Wilhelm Wiedl.]

Through YouTube, one can now hear performers available only with great difficulty in my time. For a unique generational experience, click on "Heintje—'Mama'" (German Version, 1967). Little Hein ("tje" is a Dutch diminutive suffix) Simons also sings an English version. *Das lied ist schoen.* Truly the golden voice of an angel.

Chapter XXVII

SUMMER IN THE SUDAN

Democratic Peoples' Republic of the Sudan

We roll into trenches as the drone of twin-engine, slow-moving, Soviet Antonov An-26's (NATO: "Curl") aircraft are heard approaching from the north. The air crews expect little resistance as the nomadic villagers, in mud and brush huts, rarely have operable firearms.

We see the Russian crews kicking and rolling bombs made from welded oil drums out the ramp. They contain Semtex which is red-orange with no odor. [Until, following the bombing of Pan Am 103, metallic detection taggants and a vapor signature (odor) are added]. Clever pilots, however, sometimes shut down their engines and glide in….

I punch holes in at least one engine with my .458 Winchester Magnum—apparently with little effect. (Shooting at the pilots and air crews is discouraged). They make several more passes, this time from a higher altitude. I would like to say I downed a Soviet plane during the 'Cold War,' but it is not to be.

I fly to Khartoum on five days' notice. We give the Sudanese two C-130 Hercules cargo planes in exchange for examining their Soviet gear. Of interest is a tether attached to a cargo parachute, which fires a retrorocket, allowing soft landings for heavy loads. We use multiple parachutes and drop vehicles on sleds at low altitudes, frequently with disastrous results. The Soviets use a small 'chute to stabilize a fast descent, allowing better accuracy. A rocket slows the load a moment before contact—a superior system they have perfected after some twenty-five years of experimentation.

I meet Colonel Ahmed Mursi, commander of First Para. and acting chief of staff. I make eight jumps from an ME-8 Soviet copter (NATO calls it the "Hip") on Merkiat DZ, with a grade of "Very Good."

I head south to Juba in February 1978 to link up with professional hunter David G. Ommanney (out of Nairobi) at Bambouka Camp. Although finding no big elephant, we cover considerable country.

The People's Republic of the Sudan is Islamic fundamentalist and engaged in a civil war with the South: Arabs vs. animists and Christian Nilotes (the Dinka and Nuer—tall, slender peoples noted for their long-distance running abilities). The Arabic language is imposed upon them, along with Islamic religious beliefs. Starvation and disease are everywhere. (An estimated two million die in several years.)

It appears the area between the Eighth and Tenth parallels is "neutral" ground. The dreaded Janjaweed (formed from the Arabic words for "man," "gun," and "horse")—gunmen of the Arab tribes—are still a decade away, but are already starting to make their presence known over grazing disputes and cross-border raids.

Human intel and satellite photos show isolated camps and structures we cannot identify. Most are mining operations for gold, copper, and uranium. I was a former geology/mining engineering major and current big game hunter. During an Army physical, the doctor noticed I have exceptional color vision and am able to distinguish between subtle variations. This minor talent has little practical application, except I can spot camouflage others cannot readily see.

The only white European-appearing people with an excuse to be in this part of the world are Soviet or East German advisors and Western big game hunters....The Chinese are now here in big numbers, but not this early. We wander into camps to buy supplies and to recruit local trackers and bearers. I glance around at the machinery or earth-moving operations and pocket a few ore samples.

The Pitfall

Our scout is a Katanga soldier named Hapana (Swahili for, "It does not matter") Fikiri. Fikiri spots a "bee tree," a hollow log placed in a bush to attract bees for a hive and honey, off the trail. While he's at one end smoking the bees, I pull on a plug of brush at the other.

Hundreds of angry African bees pour out, and we both run. For some reason, the bees ignore me and go after Fikiri. I jump into the truck with our hunter and we follow. Fikiri resembles a Looney Toons' cartoon, leaping over logs and rocks with a swarm of bees in pursuit.

Over the camp-fire that evening, I apologize for disturbing the bees and hand him a nice gratuity to somewhat ease the pain of his many bee bumps. The camp crew can hardly suppress their mirth, as he is their unpopular and authoritarian supervisor.

Some days later, we are near Wadi Mura, dry but for a few months of the year. Dust and powdered ash from native burns cover everything. Walking is made difficult because of many termite castles—mushroom-shaped and rock-hard. Mounds of stone, ancient Zande graves, are common. Old offering pots decorate many.

Our path splits and tunnels through thornbush. Fikiri whispers, *"Tembo."* *"Bia* (beer)*?"* I whisper back. (*"Tembo"* is Bantu for "elephant," but also a popular Congolese beer from where he originates. American "humor" does not always go over well.) He shakes his head in irritation and says, *"Endopho,"* wagging his hands beside his face like large ears.

I hesitate before entering the opening as something seems amiss, but I do not know what. I see no elephant sign, but that is not unusual as the natives spot spoor not visible to us. *"Hatari"* (danger) shouts our guide. He pulls out a cigarette lighter and sets the thick carpet of leaves at my feet on fire.

The dried leaves are not from the bushes above them. The fire reveals an enormous pit, about fifteen-feet deep and covered with sticks to support the cover of vegetation. Poisoned *punji* sticks are placed where it narrows at the bottom. It is a medieval style *trou de loup* (wolf hole) in use from the time of Julius Caesar. It is a man trap, something rarely seen in native pits. Elephant pits need only be a few feet deep as they have difficulty stepping up.

Fikiri is upset. He thinks it is clever repayment for the bees for me to step into a shallow elephant trap, not realizing how deep it is. He offers to refund his "tip." (I refuse to take it back, of course.) We never determine its origin, but it is likely Azande.

Some Azande are Christian but most practice witchcraft. They poison chickens for answers and guidance to life's problems. They claim to be ongoing victims of Arab slavers. I would like to learn more, but our time is limited, and we must move on.

Escape from Khartoum

I make my way back to Khartoum by small plane and truck. I visit the tomb of Muhammad Ahmad, "the Mahadi," whose men behead General Charles "Chinese" Gordon in 1885. (Gordon is an early Christian fundamentalist who tries to convert the Mahadi).

I am told at my hotel that I am being sought by men from "the government"—not Brigadier Khalifa's Parachute Regiment—and I may be in some kind of "trouble." Can I please go elsewhere so as to avoid any unpleasantness? Ooh-oh! Good advice. This is not long after terrorists shoot up the Saudi Embassy here and execute the American ambassador and his charge d'affaires. [We don't get so excited about such matters in these pre-"Islamo-Fascist" days. It comes with the job.]

I hide until dark and head on foot to the camp of the First Battalion of Grenadier Guards on a "Desert Rat" Exercise in Omdurman, near the confluence of the White and Blue Niles. Large numbers of refugees make it easy to move about. I explain to their captain that I am being sought for "questioning," probably related to my travels in the South. It helps that I know Lieutenant Colonel R. G. Southerst, CO at Aldershot, and others.

I am carrying my ruck with one fatigue uniform and my Browning .458 Magnum with lots of ammo, plus a bunch of canteens. They loan me a British uniform and hide my rifle in their armoury. "Don't open your mouth, Yank, until after we depart."

Several days later, we board a Vickers VC-10 for the seven-hour flight to Brize-Norton (where I test jump the PX1-Mark V a couple of years before). The VC-10 has four jet engines—all on the tail. The seats are backwards (i.e., they face to the rear).

Customs at LAX is curious as to why my passport shows entry into Khartoum, followed by a stamp in Juba and exit from London-Heathrow. "LAPD," I explain, and pass through. (Most of them know me from my security work with TWA.) I am pleased to be home again.

Chapter XXVIII
MBOGO

Mbogo, the Kenya cape buffalo, is considered by many White Hunters[186] to be the most dangerous of the African "big five" (elephant, cape buffalo, lion, leopard, and rhinocerous).

The great wild ox, *Syncerus caffer*, unlike his smaller "el toro" cousin in the bull ring, charges head up so as to hook and smash in the instant before impact. He is a ton of bovine bad news. His bullet resistance is legendary. Wound him and you will most certainly get his attention. He is short-tempered and alone in his resolve to follow through on a charge once started. The late professional hunter/writer, Peter H. Capstick, sums it up with an unusual formula: $B + LS = F$ (Buffalo, plus Lousy Shot, equals Funeral). Historical precedence indicates the funeral will be yours.

The buffalo has a heavy boss of horn and bone protecting his brain. His ability to store oxygen in his brain under stress and in pain gives him endurance after suffering mortal wounds. He has no weak spots in his natural defenses of sight, hearing, and smell. He can do anything better than you in the bush, including running four times your best speed.

I am hunting in Block 57 (Masai) with Karel L. G. "Boet" Dannhauser of Ker, Downey and Selby out of Nairobi in December 1969. Boet is busy repairing his Land Cruiser, so his Masai tracker and gunbearer, Selel, and I wander off to hunt camp meat.

I carry a Rigby .470 Nitro Express double-rifle from Shaw and Hunter (aka Kenya Bunduki), the old Nairobi gunsmiths. It is charged with 500-grain Kynoch solids in case of trouble.

Selel speaks only a few words of English, and I just know a few of Swahili. He and Boet pursue Kikuyu terrorists in the Mau-Mau uprising

---

[186] "White Hunter" is a term now shaded with parody and derision by those ignorant of the African colonial period. In my time, it is a definition of adventure, courage, honor, and sportsmanship. The politically correct replacement is "professional hunter." I do not entirely disagree with this as some African hunters-for-hire are now black and competent, although the time of the traditional safari is long past.

(1952–1960). Selel always carries his long-bladed spear from his Masai moran (warrior) days, as well as an old 8mm (7.92×57mm) Mauser dating from the early 1900s.

Selel pads barefoot along a dusty narrow trail. He spots fresh spoor of a buff leading down into a ravine. Generations of animals create a tunnel through thorns so thick it is impossible to step off the trail. Selel stops long enough to fold his long earlobes, pierced and stretched by a large wooden plug, so they will not snag and tear on the thorns.

Selel stops and beckons me up. The trail starts up a hill and the big buff is standing at the top, head turned back towards us. Selel steps behind me. I quickly kneel and line up the ivory front-sight bead low and behind the animal's right shoulder. Selel later tells Boet he sees the puff of dust from my bullet strike. It is too high, but clips an artery above the heart. A fatal shot, but not one that immediately drops him.

I bring the barrels back down, expecting to see a crumpled up buffalo. Instead, the buff turns and heads downhill at us. (He may not know where the shot comes from and simply runs in the wrong direction.) I recall thinking he looks like a cartoon of a bull's head, surrounded by the dust of his charge, with only his hooves methodically reaching out.

I line up the bead on his nose and fire barrel number two. Part of his left horn explodes and flies off. I know we are doomed to be trampled as I eject the empties and ram in the two live rounds I carry between the fingers of my left hand. Too late to help.

Selel drops his spear and calmly kneels next to me. He fires his little 8mm (the equivalent of our .30-06 round), and we are enveloped by the dust cloud. The bull is down but so close I can reach out and touch him with my rifle. Selel, realizing the futility of a kill shot, knee-caps him. The bull is glaring at us and pulling himself towards us. I end the struggles of this magnificent beast with a shot to the base of his skull.

The buff's skull and horns, expertly repaired by Zimmerman Ltd. on the plains of Kamiti (near the notorious maximum prison), are above the entrance to my library. I greet them every day with a smile. Next to them is a Masai shield and two crossed spears with Boet's framed statement that he uses them to kill a leopard and lion raiding his livestock after his rifles are confiscated by officials disarming white settlers.

Boet stays with me during a visit to Los Angeles the following year. He later writes me, on 4 November 1970, of being gored by a buff who hooks him and holes one of his lungs. Boet loses his rifle but is able to reach his .357 Magnum revolver. I smuggle him a box of pointed, armor-piercing tungsten carbide .357 rounds, which he credits with saving his life. He fires a single shot under the buff's chin into its brain.[187]

Boet recovers from the goring, only to die in a light airplane crash in South Africa at age forty.

Those who experience Africa from a zebra-striped minibus in a game preserve tell me they have photographed hundreds of cow-like buffalo without incident. No doubt true. Those of us fortunate (or foolish) enough to track Mbogo into thick thornbush, the sweat pouring off and the flies buzzing in the unnatural silence, have different memories.

Jailed in Egypt

I visit Cairo in 1969 and wander up the Nile to Luxor and other ancient places. The Israelis are bombing and launching raids along the Suez Canal. Egypt responds with its War of Attrition. Few tourists, other than Soviet advisors, are around. (They do not tip so are not popular with locals.)

I head into the Sinai, a land bridge between Africa and Asia. The dilapidated train stops at a small station in the middle of the desert. I walk a short distance to where a dirt path crosses the rails. I take a photo of a two-wheeled ox cart crossing the tracks. Two scruffy men carrying .45 autos grab me. They are local policemen who take me to their small jail—a shack—and roughly toss me inside. No one speaks English. My train leaves.

---

[187] This incident and my experience with the double-rifle convince me to buy a .458 Magnum bolt-action rifle containing more than two rounds. Jacques P. "Jack" Lott, technical editor of *Guns and Ammo*, builds a .458 for me from a 1935 Browning, with which I take elephants in the Congo and other dangerous game. Jack, too, is gored and nearly killed by a buffalo. Jack also credits me, indirectly, with "saving" Boet in the February 1991 edition of Petersen's *Handguns* magazine, page 34.

Another comes along in a few hours, and I am taken in handcuffs to a larger settlement.

The commandant at the military post speaks English. I am surprised to learn I am apprehended for being an "Israeli spy" taking photographs of "military installations." The "installation," he explains, "is the railroad track."

"I am an Eisenhower-American," I tell him. "The ones who kick the invading Israeli army out of your Sinai a dozen years before. Besides, the Israelis are not stupid. They certainly are aware of these rails across the desert." He smiles and agrees—but still confiscates my roll of film. My arresting officers are disappointed to see their "spy" released, as I wave farewell from the train back to Cairo. Foiled again!

Chapter XXIX

BONGO IN THE CONGO

Astronauts Lieutenant Colonel Stuart A. Roosa (Apollo 14), Captain James A. Lovell, Jr. (Apollo 8 and 13), hunter/outfitter Bert Klineburger, and I enjoy a Fourth of July (1973) dinner at the new Kinshasa (Leopoldville) Intercontinental. The others are returning from an unsuccessful hunt for bongo and elephant but are already planning for the next. I am about to start my foot safari, only the second season the Congo (Zaire) is open to hunting. I am to be the last.[188]

We are clean shaven but vow to grow mustaches and keep them until we down our big elephant. I have kept this silly vow forty years even though my hunt is successful.

Christopher J. Matchett, my professional hunter out of Mannheim, West Germany, and I load our rifles for our drive to the airport. Bandits and rebels frequently shoot up cars along this route as it is traveled by those with assets.

A short flight to Kisangani (Stanleyville) in a Fokker 27 and on to Isiro by truck. We enter the Ituri Forest and when the track runs out, proceed on foot into a great swamp known as the Aka. We hire local natives as guides and porters. Money is of little use in the bush. Payment is in Egyptian cigarettes—three a day—cigarettes, not packs. They also get a portion of the meat we shoot. A (mandatory) government official who accompanies us (at my expense) discourages greater payment so as to not disrupt the local economy.

Our quarry is the western bongo and forest elephant. The bongo, elusive but not endangered, is Africa's number one trophy.

The Democratic Republic of the Congo (the old Belgian Congo and Zaire) has vast triple-canopy rainforests inhabited by hunter-gatherers. Tribal

---

[188] President Mobutu Sese Seko orders nationalization ("Zairianization"—seizure of all foreign businesses) in November 1973. Estimates of his personal wealth range from $4 to $15 billion. He adopts a national motto of "Debrouillez-Vous" ("Figure It Out for Yourself"). The collapse of the copper market the following year destroys the economy of his already impoverished country. He is anti-Soviet and enjoys the support of the U.S.

warfare and massacres by invading bands drive tribes deep into the forest. It is not unusual to come across butchered human remains. Cannibalism, a Congo tradition, returns as a means of survival.

The people are incredibly poor. Probably 80 percent of those we encounter own almost nothing and have no food for their next meal. They live in lean-to sheds of cardboard (if they are lucky) and grass. No welfare exists. Diseases kill them by the thousands. (Ebola is of unknown origin, incurable, and kills most of those infected.)

Murder for Meat

I meet Belgian ethnologist, Jean-Pierre Hallet, who lives among the Efe pygmies. The Congo tribes, he notes, are all cannibals. Their motivation is not religious or beliefs in the magical virtues of human flesh, but of hunger. In prehistoric times, corn, bananas, and pineapples do not exist in Africa. Only a handful of edible roots and fruits are to be found. The few animals are too wary or formidable to easily capture. The only thing they can readily catch is each other!

Hallet's books, *Pygmy Kitabu* (1973)—"kitabu" is Swahili for "book"—and *Congo Kitabu*,[189] describe the dining habits of various tribes.

The province of Maniema, south of Kisangani, is about the size of New York State. It's very name means "man-eaters." Explorer David Livingston, viewing incredible scenes, exclaims, "I am overcome, nauseated by all this human blood."

"The natives devoured diseased corpses as well as those freshly murdered, macerating the bodies in water until the flesh was nearly putrefied, and then eating it raw."[190] The Bapoto sell living men piece-by-piece. They mark each area of the captive's body with colored clay as buyers select their favorite cuts. When all the parts are sold, the living jigsaw puzzle is carved up and distributed. The intestines are favored because of their fat.

---

[189] Hallet, *Congo Kitabu*, (No. 296 of 450, Special Edition, dedicated 24 May 1972), Chapter 4 ("Land of the Man-Eaters"), pp. 57–80.

[190] Ibid., p. 58.

The Bangala prefer riper meat, requiring the Belgians to post guards at the cemetery in Leopoldville.

Leopard Men

The 1943 movie *The Leopard Man* is about a serial killer. Edgar Rice Burroughs's *Tarzan and the Leopard Men* (1931) is not popular as—back in the early '30s—audiences prefer to see the African as a "noble savage."

Leopard men (Anyoto) exist in the Congo as a secret society. They don bark-cloth tunics with black spots and a genuine leopard tail attached to a belt. They wear an iron bracelet with dangling blades, so when making a fist, they jut out between clenched fingers—like a leopard's claws.

Leopard men attack from behind in a fury of slashes. They favor women, children, and the weak. By day, they are peaceful farmers. Hallet says they appear to lack a conscience and believe that a "leopard" within them, not a real man, is guilty. The Belgians hang many in this cult, but few report them for fear of retribution.

The Whip and Iron Collar

Arab slavers resolve the immediate problem of Livingston's "rivers of blood." It becomes more profitable to sell prisoners than to eat them. Most slaves are captured by their black neighbors for sale to the Evil White Man.[191]

The purchase price of a healthy native in a Congolese village is about 40 cents. The slave's market value is about $1,800 during our Civil War. (How does this compare with your investment rate of return?) With "independence" and foreign invasions, cannibalism returns to the Congo as a necessity. Anyone who doubts it is taking place today has only to

---

[191] *Roots*, the award-winning 1977 television miniseries, accurately depicts Kunta Kinte as being captured by members of his own tribe and sold to slavers. Researchers, checking Alex Haley's supposed source, discover Kinte exists but dies before leaving Africa. Haley copies his story from a book, *The African* (1967) by Harold Courlander. Judge Robert J. Ward rules, "Alex Haley perpetrated a hoax on the public."

visit numerous sites on the web,[192] or, better, visit Ituri Province (currently administered as a district of Orientale).

Dispatches from the Bush

Most natives wear ficus bark clothing and carry short slack-string bows. Long-bladed (up to six inches) arrows are for game. They leave a blood trail and weaken the animal. Barbed points are for humans. If pulled out, the head remains embedded and must be pushed through. Small triangular metal points—wrapped in strips of rawhide and treated with care—are poisoned. (An alkaloid called "strophanthus" is boiled from the sap, seeds, and pods of a flowering vine.)

I trade small knives and camp items for bows covered with monkey fur, large-bladed spears, and unusual edged weapons such as wrist knives. A flat iron throwing knife resembles a swastika with extra blades. It is thrown horizontally to sever limbs. (It is believed to disappear a century before.)

Two for One

The bongo is a large reddish-brown antelope with white stripes and lyre-shaped horns. At the time of my hunt, it is never photographed in the wild. Snap a twig and it is gone. One hunts them with solid bullets from an "elephant gun" as they are heavy-bodied and trees are usually in the way. One fellow member of the Southern California Safari Club (Emerson Hall) goes on seventeen bongo safaris and never sees one....

An explosion of red and white bursts through a thicket after fifteen tedious days of tracking. My snapshot strikes the bongo's neck, killing it instantly. Zakuoanda, our Azande tracker, moves beyond the bongo and lets out a whoop. A second and unseen bongo is down about twenty meters away after being hit by the same bullet. It is a welcome addition to the larder of the protein-starved natives. (They are most impressed by Bwana's magic rifle.)

---

[192] "UN Condemns D.R. Congo Cannibalism," *BBC News* (World Edition), 15 January 2003. More than 350 witnesses describe killing and eating people around just the town of Beni.

Astounded PH Chris Matchett formally documents the incident on 20 July 1973 in the Bas-Uele District (currently overrun by the "Lords Resistance Army"): "This was an authentic case of that oft-repeated story of two animals with a single shot. In this instance it happened on what is considered to be Africa's rarest trophy."[193]

Track of the Elephant

The small-bodied and short-tempered forest elephant is known for his imaginative and aggressive sorting out and annihilation of careless native and bwana intruders. He raids crops at night and holes up in the deep forest by day. He is so at ease terrorizing natives that in coming for a white hunter, he is known to veer off to instead pursue a native. Rumors spread of a man-eating bull elephant in the vicinity. He is probably seen carrying around a native's arm or leg, as they are wont to do upon occasion.

The client hunts alone, without the usual back up of the PH. One must present evidence, for granting of a permit, of shooting at least one elephant and other dangerous game. "Buck fever" can have adverse consequences in elephant hunting.

Triple-canopy jungle is dark with little light penetrating. Leafy vegetation does not grow without light. Few animals are present as there is little to eat. Wind and breezes cannot penetrate. All is quiet. Fresh elephant sign is easy to follow. An elephant becoming aware of a pursuit will usually crouch down and wait in ambush. Elephants are fast and can run silently through a thicket, with their trunk clearing the way.

We walk from village-to-village until one is found where crops are raided the night before.

Natives know individual bulls and are anxious to be rid of them. There is little contact with the outside and no welfare. If your crop is destroyed, your family starves. Only in America do you see overweight "welfare queens" living a life of leisure and plenty at public expense.

---

[193] Kent Cannon, "Bongo in the Congo," *Petersen's Hunting*, March 1976 (Vol. 3, No. 3), pp. 50–53.

Forest elephants, unlike their savannah cousins, have small feet. Their pads form around twigs to keep from snapping them. They come fast. They are known to curl their trunks and whip them out. A bone-breaker of a punch. They do not have "digger" tusks (one that is favored to uproot trees) that become worn or broken. Their ivory is, thus, symmetrical, unlike those of East Africa.

I catch up to my elephant pulling down vines in a copse. A close approach makes shot placement easy but is complicated by his senses, intelligence, and destructive power. The ground is soft and wet. I am able to mask my steps with his and the vines he tugs on. I am about fifteen meters away and still cannot see him, other than a vague shape. His borborygmus (stomach rumblings) are especially loud.

A large ear suddenly unfolds and his trunk goes to it. I believe the ear traps scent, and he has gotten a whiff of me. This movement exposes his ear hole and eye—alignment for the perfect brain shot. (The brain is about the size of a gallon milk jug encased in a couple of feet of bone.)

I fire without thinking of squeezing the trigger. I do not recall hearing the sound of my hand-loaded cartridge or noticing the heavy recoil. He disappears from view. I move closer and find he has simply slumped on his front knees without falling over. He appears dead, but I fire an insurance round and sit down, back against him, to await the others. I hold out my arm and it is trembling. The energy is drained out of me.

Tom-toms announce the kill. Over and over, they replicate words in Lingala, the local Bantu language. Scores of cooking fires are lit around my elephant. Natives pour in—laughing, shouting, and all chattering at once. My PH takes over, organizing the hacking out of the tusks and removing the ears (for fine leather) before allowing the locals their meat.

I find a small knoll from where to watch the show by firelight well into the night. Natives slit the abdomen and crawl inside to strip the fat from the intestines—eaten raw like candy. Others outside are chopping at the ribs with axes and razor-sharp machetes. An occasional scream or curse indicates someone outside has cut someone inside. But the merriment overshadows all.

Smoke from the fires goes straight up to spread out at the first canopy supported by centuries-old enormous teak and mahogany trees. This is a memory that will be with me until the end.

Nothing is wasted. Bones are split and the marrow eaten. By morning, all that remains is a large stain surrounded by sapling stumps and campfire ashes. It brings to mind the old joke:

"How do you eat an elephant?" Answer: "One bite at a time."

Home Again

It is easier to enter Africa than to depart. Chris drops me off in Kisangani. French is the only European language anyone admits to speaking. Hotel personnel suggest it is unwise to venture out until it is time to leave for the airport. In my week here, I see no other whites. Many blacks are openly hostile, possibly in memory of an earlier visit by the 2ᵉ REP. (Ha, ha.)

The airport is chaos. Scores of locals are waving handfuls of money at the lone clerk for the daily flight to Kinshasa (about 760 miles). Like them, I have an open ticket. I am down to my last ten dollars in U.S. currency. The Zaire is (officially) fifteen to one U.S. dollar.[194]

The clerk looks at me—I am taller than anyone else and the only white face in a sea of black—and shakes his head. I know he wants my dollars as he cannot keep his eyes off them. The plane leaves without me, as it is to do for the next four days.

I resolve to try one last time before making my way to the waterfront to hire space on a raft. It is a week-long trip on the swift and dangerous Congo River. As I must sleep, it is a possibility I will be robbed or worse. I stand to the rear of the day's crowd with my arm just half raised, and the clerk beckons me forward and accepts my bills.

The seven-foot tusks weigh 85 pounds each. They make up a glass-and-brass table, where I type this in our cedar-log home. The bongo wins First

---

[194] The Zaire is worthless. It is replaced in 1993 by three million New Zaires to one Old Zaire. They, too, are not worth anything.

Place Awards (Africa) in both the Southern California Safari Club (1973) at the Beverly Hills Hotel and the Los Angeles Chapter of the Safari Club International (1974–1975) at the Beverly Wilshire. The SCI also presents me with a special Flock Shooter Award—a metal sculpture of a nineteenth century African hunter with a three-barreled rifle. (A flock shooter is one who shoots into a flock to bring down more than one bird.)

The Last Safari

I go on five (hunting) safaris: Kenya, Uganda, the Congo, the Sudan, and Rhodesia (where I obtain a magnificent giant sable)—and visit friends in the Rhodesian Light Infantry. I combine some of my hunts, as you have surmised, with military assignments. A good cover.

I am the only non-millionaire in the 100-man Southern California Safari Club. We meet in Walter and Peter O'Malley's clubhouse at Dodger Stadium. I am elected their president in 1975–1976, probably to make decisions as some are reluctant to cooperate with their business rivals.

Otis Chandler, publisher of the *Los Angeles Times*, may be the best example of a club enigma. He is liberal and an outstanding athlete who leads an adventurous life. Otis downs an irritated elephant in Mozambique, saving several in his safari. He is stomped by a musk ox in the Northwest Territories of Canada. We build water holes for desert bighorn sheep and contribute to various wildlife efforts. Otis allots me prime space in the *Times* for occasional articles criticizing the government and powerful groups, such as ranchers gaining public lands for grazing—who then kill off the wildlife.

I no longer hunt, but am irritated by the antigun and "animal rights" people who hire others to do their dirty work and have no idea where their hamburger or shoe leather come from. These are the same people, who, in their affluent ignorance, successfully lobby to stop hunting in Africa and other places.

Natives poach much of the game. African politicians are elected on promises to turn parkland over to their burgeoning populations, who then slaughter the poor animals which have no place to go. Hunters usually kill humanely, giving the animal a far less painful death than it experiences from the teeth and claws of a predator or bone-breaking trap of the poacher. Hunters seek the older trophy animal, usually past his prime. Poachers are not so considerate.

A large portion of the fees for big game hunting go to the tribes where the animal is taken and to hire game wardens. When they stop the hunting, no money is allocated for antipoaching. Gangs move in and slaughter the animals by the thousands in the most despicable ways.

It is ironic that hunters are the ones who love and protect the game. Their absence dooms the magnificent wild animals, which, only several decades ago, roam the savannahs, swamps, and forests in great abundance.

Chapter XXX

THE TAR BABY[195]

I am modest to a fault, but the commentary in this chapter necessitates some qualification. My Officer Efficiency Reports (OERs) from the First Special Operations Command (Airborne) at Fort Bragg, North Carolina, contain the following extracts:

* 10 September 1982 — Assigned as: Chief of Counterintelligence, JFK Center for Military Assistance: "Major Hurlbut is the most qualified unconventional warfare counterintelligence officer in the Army today."

* 14 February 1986 — Chief of Security Division, First SOCOM: "Major Hurlbut assumed management of the Division in the absence of its normal Chief...Knows the counterintelligence business and the Army—Gets things done....Promote ahead of contemporaries."

* 20 Jan 1989 — Special Projects Officer, First SOCOM: "LTC Hurlbut's contributions to SOF over the years are legion. Past assignments to the Republic of China Special Warfare Command, Thailand, the Sudan, Australia, Argentina, Germany, France, Great Britain, and others have given him an understanding of Special Operations Forces that is unique. Promotion to Colonel a must."

* 6 Sep 1979 — Legal Instructor, U.S. Army Intelligence Center and School, Fort Huachuca, Arizona: "During the last year CPT Hurlbut test-jumped using Soviet equipment in the Sudan, completed

---

[195] Br'er Rabbit punches and kicks the tar baby (a trap), becoming increasingly stuck and unable to extricate himself. "Song of the South" (1946). Walt Disney and RKO Radio Pictures from story by Joel Harris.

the French Army Parachute School and observed their airborne movement to Zaire."

This does not make me an authority but gives me some familiarity with the subject. The following is what I observe over three decades:

The Scam Begins

The Secretary of State, General Colin L. Powell, stands before the United Nations on 5 February 2003 and makes a speech that leads to war. He shows photographs and schematics of Iraqi "mobile biological laboratories of mass destruction." I am aghast. They are clearly U.S. hydrogen gas generator vans used by an artillery division to inflate weather balloons to gather atmospheric firing data. Any second lieutenant of artillery, infantry, or MI will recognize them.

Powell, on 8 June 2003, admits that "some suggest" the vans are for weather balloons, but he sticks with his original assessment.[196] More than two years later, he admits this and other "reasons for war" are false.[197]

The Flawed Generation

As baby boomers (born 1946–1964) prepare to exit stage left, the rest of us evaluate their destruction of the Republic.

Boomers' parents, toughened by the Depression, indulge their self-absorbed brats who duck the challenge of Vietnam and turn to sex, drugs, and rock and roll. Neo-con draft-dodgers like Vice President Dick Cheney, classified 1-A, receive *five* draft deferments[198] because, "I had other priorities." Exceptional and truly patriotic kids emerge to make us proud. But most are programmed to avoid all forms of risk, harassment, adventure,

---

[196] Heidi Collins, Transcript of press briefing by Colin Powell, 8 June 2003, 0910 ET. CNN.com Transcripts.

[197] "Powell Regrets UN Speech on Iraq WMDs." Calls it a "blot on his record." ABC News Online, 9 September 2005.

[198] Katharine Q. Seelye, "Cheney's Five Draft Deferments During the Vietnam Era Emerge as a Campaign Issue," *New York Times*, 1 May 2004.

and unfairness. They remain no less annoying as they age—the "me" generation.

My generation vanquishes Communism. Boomers spread like kudzu and produce whiners and incompetents as presidents Clinton, Bush-the-Lesser, and Obama. Under them, both political parties become wings of the same bird. Boomers' sense of entitlement, devotion to spending and welfare, addiction to debt, and endless warfare against weak third world nations, bankrupt us and give us reputations as war criminals, bullies, and hypocrites. They weaken us through feminism and increase crime through permissiveness and diversity. For their generation, no one exists but themselves.

"Blowback"

9-11: My wife's birthday. The serial number on her Glock .40. The destruction of the Twin Towers. The only surprise to many of us is that it is so delayed. We invade Iraq and kill 567,000 children (under five years old)[199] in a decade of bombings and sanctions. We enable Israel's theft of 90 percent of Palestine and the slaughter of its inhabitants. Islam is a religion of warriors and vengeance. What do we expect will happen? "Bring it on!" shouts an insolent Bush. And we whine when they do.

Intel Ignored. "Bin Laden Determined to Strike U.S.,"[200] and "Terrorists Rotating Through Florida Flight School" are two of forty "President's Daily Briefings," before 11 September 2001, mentioning al-Qaeda and the probable use of hijacked aircraft against New York City. Osama Bin Laden says 9-11 is collateral damage for U.S. participation in the Israeli genocide of Palestinians and the theft of their lands.[201] Also the stationing of a foreign

---

[199] Admitted by Secretary of State Madeleine Albright on *60 Minutes*, 12 May 1996, when she coldly tells the world, "We think the price is worth it." Rahul Mahajan, "We Think the Price is Worth It," *Fairness and Accuracy in Reporting*, November/December 2001.

[200] Thomas S. Blanton, "The President's Daily Brief," (excerpt from the 6 August 2001 PDB). The National Security Archive. Released 10 April 2004.

[201] If I give you a weapon and money so you can kill a neighbor and steal his home, what am I guilty of? Any police academy rookie will answer, "You are a *principal* and equally guilty of homicide and grand theft." The same concept applies in international law.

army near the holy cities of Mecca and Medina (we never leave following the Gulf War). Bush says, "They hate us for our freedoms!"[202] Whom do you believe? OBL is not known to lie. He never takes "credit" for 9-11.

American Exceptionalism[203]

Americans believe we are unique and "good people," as our democratic institutions and human rights concepts have elevated us into moral giants above all others. (To demonstrate this goodness, we send armies against those with inferior values.)

Our slogans like "War on Global Terrorism" (We even have a medal for this one—how do you conduct war against a tactic?), "Bring 'em on!,"[204] and campaigns as "Enduring Freedom" (right out of a Chinese five-year plan) are Orwellian. Keep in mind that attacks against military targets—yes, that includes in the U.S.—by definition are not "terrorism."

A brief overview of the modern Middle East may be helpful to see what is done in the name of we, the American people:

Axis of Empire (or) Roots of Terror

Various Islamic sects combat each other for centuries in the Middle East. The British and French cause additional problems by arbitrarily carving up tribal areas in the secret Sykes-Picot Agreement of 1916.

The CIA and the British engineer the overthrow of the democratically-elected government of Iran in August 1953. We depose Prime Minister

---

[202] Bush, Address to Joint Session of Congress, 20 Sep 2001. *American Rhetoric*.

[203] "American Exceptionalism" is coined by the American Communist Party in the 1920s and used by Stalin in 1929. Uri Friedman, "American Exceptionalism': A Short History," *Foreign Policy*, July/August 2012 (and) Robert Wenzel (*Economic Policy Journal*), "President Obama's Haunting Anti-Liberty Inaugural Speech," LewRockwell.com, 24 January 2013.

[204] A threat to any insurgents defending themselves against a U.S. invasion (3 July 2003). Bush is photographed smirking to the front row of the Press Corps (27 May 2006) after admitting this "tough talk" is a mistake. "'Bring 'em on!' Bush's Legacy of Death in Iraq." WhatReallyHappened.com.

Mohammed Mosaddegh and replace him with Shah Mohammad-Reza Pahlavi. President Jimmy Carter undermines the Peacock Throne and the shah is overthrown in the revolution of the ayatollahs, leading to the 444-day Iranian hostage crisis at the U.S. Embassy.

The USS *Vicennes* shoots down Iran Air 655 on 3 July 1988, killing all 290 civilians aboard. (We falsely claim the *Vicennes* is in international waters when she is illegally in Iranian waters in the Strait of Hormuz.) The captain "mistakes" a climbing A300 Airbus on its daily flight for an "attacking F-14 Tomcat." Bush-the-Elder decorates the ship's captain. [There is considerable speculation in the intelligence community that the bombing of Pan Am 103 over Lockerbie five months later—killing 270—is accomplished by a Libyan in the pay of Iran.]

We (the CIA) sucker the Soviets into invading Afghanistan in late 1979 in revenge for Vietnam. Afghan Arabs (the Mujahideen) wage war against the atheist Communists. We support a young, wealthy Saudi named Osama Bin Laden. The fundamentalist Taliban ("students" in Pashto) emerges from the madrassas (Islamic seminaries) established in Pakistan. Pakistan supports the Taliban because both oppose their "real enemy," India.

Gulf War/Kuwait

The CIA is again on the job to assist Saddam Hussein and his Ba'athist Party gain power in Iraq. Saddam emerges from the 1980–1988 war with Iran—pushed by President Carter to counter Iran's Khomeini Regime—and badly needs oil money. The Kuwaitis are slant-drilling into the Rumaila Field and stealing his Basrah light crude.

Saddam asks American ambassador April Glaspie if it is okay to invade Kuwait (recently part of Iraq). She later denies giving him the "go-ahead," but he slyly tapes their meeting.

Houston oilman George H.W. Bush, realizing most Americans never hear of Kuwait and do not care about it, employs the public relations firm of Hill and Knowlton—better known for their "tobacco has no verifiable links to cancer" campaign. They cook up a story that enrages the American public and demonizes Iraqis.

The Incubator Hoax. Volunteer nurse Nayirah, age fifteen, testifies before Congress on 10 October 1990 that Iraqi soldiers enter the al-Addan Hospital and throw out 312 babies to die so as to take the incubators back to Iraq. Months later, we learn that Nayirah is the daughter of Kuwaiti prince Saud Nasir Al-Sabah of Kuwait's ruling family and *ambassador to the U.S.*[205] Nayirah is not a nurse and is not in Kuwait during the Iraqi invasion! Several hundred thousand Iraqis must die for this lie.

The Missing Army. Our Gulf invasion is flawed. G.H.W. Bush, to a joint session of Congress (11 September 1990), claims an Iraqi army of 850 tanks is in Kuwait, poised to invade Saudi Arabia. The Soviets then release satellite photos to the world showing American armor in place, with no one opposing us.

"Washington Bureau reporter Jean Heller reported that satellite photos of the border between southern Kuwait and Saudi Arabia taken on September 11 and 13, 1990, by a 'Soviet company,' revealed 'no evidence of a massive Iraqi presence in Kuwait'....Satellite imagery expert Peter Zimmerman said, 'All of us agreed that we couldn't see anything in the way of military activity.'"[206] Why does the rest of the world know this, but not the American public?

No Quarter. Two brigades from the First Infantry Division (Mechanized—the "Big Red One") use plows mounted on tanks and earthmovers to bury alive thousands of Iraqi soldiers defending the "Saddam Line."

---

[205] Excellent documentation of this hoax can be found in John C. Stauber and Sheldon Rampton, *Toxic Sludge is Good for You!; Lies, Damn Lies and the Public Relations Industry* (1995), Chapter 10, Common Courage Press; 236 pp. See also, "'Wagging the Dog': The Great Incubator Scam of 1990," *Revolutionary Worker*, #944, 15 Feb 1998.

[206] John R. MacArthur. *Second Front: Censorship and Propaganda in the Gulf War* (1992), pp. 172–173 (and) "Our Government Has Already Been Caught Lying About Iraq," *Representative Press* (and) Jean Heller, St. Petersburg Times, Front Page, 6 January 1991.

No surrenders are accepted.[207] No Americans are killed. General Norman Schwarzkopf's staff estimates 50,000 to 75,000 Iraqis are suffocated in their trenches!

Highway of Death. Major General Barry McCaffrey, *two days after the cease fire*, orders the Twenty-Fourth Infantry Division (Mechanized) to fire on tanks loaded on trucks and headed back to Iraq. As many as 150,000 Iraqis—many of them fleeing civilians—are slaughtered.[208] No serious American casualties are reported. No surrenders are accepted, a violation of the Hague and Geneva Conventions. British pilots return to their base, refusing to bomb defenseless soldiers and civilians. A more cowardly and dishonorable act is difficult to imagine. Something to remember when the U.S. calls for "war crimes" trials against some foreign despot.

Like Father, Like Son

Bush-the-Lesser declares, soon after taking office, "Israel's enemies are America's enemies."[209] Following 9-11, the cold war is over, and we are the planet's only superpower. We have the sympathy of the world. Our economy is robust, and we have a monetary surplus.

Our second war of aggression against Iraq—a prostrate Arab nation that plays no part in 9-11 and does not threaten us—unites twenty-two Arab countries and fifty-seven Muslim ones (one-fourth of the world's population) against us. Much of the rest of the planet views us as hypocrites

---

[207] "Iraqi Death Toll." *Frontline* (PBS)—The Gulf War. See also, Patrick J. Sloyan, "Buried Alive: U.S. Tanks Used Plows to Kill Thousands in Gulf War Trenches," *Newsday*, 12 September 1991, p. 1.

[208] "This is surely one of the most heinous war crimes in contemporary history," Joyce Chediac, "Massacre of Withdrawing Soldiers on the 'Highway of Death,'" Commission of Inquiry for the International War Crimes Tribunal, 11 May 1991. President H .W. Bush violates the Hague Convention of 1907 governing Land Warfare by declaring (on 27 February 1991) that no quarter will be given to withdrawing Iraqi soldiers. See also, Seymour Hersh, "Overwhelming Force," *New Yorker*, 22 May 2000, pp. 49–82 (and) Malcom Lagauche, "Remembering the Highway of Death," Countercurrents.org. 28 February 2010.

[209] John J. Mearsheimer and Stephen M. Walt, *The Israel Lobby and U.S. Foreign Policy* (2007), p. 202.

and bullies—a dangerous rogue state controlled by a paranoid Israel to stomp on its many enemies. The attack on Iraq makes as much sense as if we had bombed New Zealand following the Japanese attack on Pearl Harbor!

* "Facing clear evidence of peril, we cannot wait for the final proof—the smoking gun—that could come in the form of a mushroom cloud."[210]

* "Who would benefit from a war of civilizations between the West and Islam? Answer: One nation, one leader, one party: Israel, Sharon, Likud."[211]

* Senator Ernest F. Hollings (D-South Carolina) acknowledges, "The U.S. invaded Iraq 'to secure Israel' and everybody knows it."[212]

* British Prime Minister Tony Blair admits Israel plays a key role in the decision to attack Iraq.[213]

It is beyond dispute that Iraq does not possess "weapons of mass destruction," has ties to al-Qaeda, attempts to obtain "yellow cake" uranium, etc. [See the "U.S. Senate Select Committee on Intelligence (2004 and 2006), 9/11 Commission Report" (2004), and the "Multinational Iraq Survey (Duelfer) Report" (2003).]

---

[210] George W. Bush, Speech in Cincinnati, 7 October 2002. Transcript: The White House, Online.

[211] Patrick J. Buchanan, "Whose War?" *Neo-Conned!* (2005), p. 142. [A play on the words, "Ein Volk, ein Reich, ein Fuhrer:" Nazi slogan on the Anschluss (annexation) of Austria in 1938].

[212] He also refers to "the cowardly reluctance of my Congressional colleagues to stand up and say what is going on." Remarks by Hollings. Congressional Record: Senate, 20 May 2004, pp. S5921-S5925.

[213] Chilcot Hearings (London). Quoted in Ray McGovern, "The Push of Conscience and Secretary Clinton" ("Tony Blair Admits Israeli Role"), *Counterpunch*, 24 February 2011.

* "The people can always be brought to the bidding of the leaders. All you have to do is to tell them they are being attacked, and denounce the pacifists for lack of patriotism and exposing the country to danger."[214]

Facts are apparently burdensome details that can safely be ignored. (Google: "935 lies"[215]). As each stated objective for the war is proven a lie, Bush finds another—for a grand total of twenty-seven documented false causes.[216] Bush delights in questioning the patriotism of those disagreeing with him. He never understands that a *patriot* is one who loves his country; it is a *nationalist* who loves his government. He refers to the heads of North Korea, Syria, and Iraq as "Hitler." (A much better example is closer at hand!)

Bush purges the CIA of those questioning cooked intel so as to chill dissent. "Defense Secretary Donald Rumsfeld and his neoconservative allies set up the 'Office of Special Plans' (OSP), a Pentagon office connected to a similar operation in Israeli intelligence…giving information of questionable reliability to the hawks."[217]

Ray McGovern prepares Bush's "Daily Intelligence Briefing." He writes, "On the eve of the invasion I and 45 other senior officers of the CIA and other intelligence agencies wrote to President George W. Bush that the 'drumbeat of war' was based not on intelligence, but lies."[218]

---

[214] Reichsmarschall Hermann Goering (founder of the Gestapo) to Intel Officer Gustave Gilbert. Nuremberg, 18 April 1946.

[215] Two nonprofit journalism organizations (Center for Public Integrity and Fund for Independence in Journalism) document 935 false statements (totaling 380,000 words) made by seven top administration officials in the two years following 11 Sep 2001 about the national security threat posed by Saddam Hussein's Iraq. Charles Lewis and Mark Reading-Smith, "False Pretenses," *The War Card*, 23 January 2008.

[216] Devon M. Largio, "Uncovering the Rationales for the War on Iraq: The Words of the Bush Administration, Congress, and the Media from September 12, 2001 to October 11, 2002." Thesis for B.A. in Political Science, University of Illinois (2004), 205 pp.

[217] Allen Dennis, "Cultural Revolutions," *Chronicles*, July 2006 (Vol. 30, No. 7), pp. 7–8.

[218] John Pilger, "Behind the Arab Revolt is a Word We Dare Not Speak," *Truthout*, 24 February 2011. McGovern, 71, Army officer and CIA analyst, stands with his back to Hillary Clinton in silent protest at her George Washington University speech on 15 February 2011. He is beaten, handcuffed, and dragged from the room by the Secret Service.

A Genuine Intel Failure

U.S. and Israeli intelligence fail to predict Arab revolts against our puppet dictators in Egypt, Libya, and other countries. [The collapse of the Soviet Union is also a surprise. How can this be?]

We have not figured out that terrorism is a consequence of abandoning the foreign policy of our Founders who warn against "going abroad in search of monsters to destroy." Bin Laden is not in a cave but retired in a comfortable estate in Pakistan, in plain view, and without bodyguards.

The most interesting commentary on Bin Laden's death comes from Jay Leno: "Shooting OBL in the head and disposing of the body in the ocean— who did this, the Navy SEALs or the Sopranos?"[219] (It's called, "Getting rid of the evidence," Jay.) OBL the martyr, not the imprisoned or legally-executed criminal. The issue to Muslims is not his death but his resistance against Western imperialism.

Why is an unarmed OBL, clearly the best of all sources, shot to death in a house without guards? Is it he or one of his 54 siblings or 600 relatives posing as a double? SEAL Team 6 is at least as capable as the average police SWAT team. It is, obviously, another White House-directed assassination. With no body supposedly left to examine.

Lieutenant General William E. Odom [Director, National Security Agency (NSA)] describes Iraq as the "worse strategic disaster in American Military History."[220] Many high-ranking officers retire to speak out[221]—or are relieved of duties because of their opposition.

There is a "near revolt of junior officers over the bogus reasons given for war in Iraq."[222] Enlisted soldiers often resist by going Absent Without Leave

---

[219] *The Tonight Show*, NBC, 3 May 2011 (Season 19, Episode 4034).

[220] Speaking at "Watson Institute for International Studies," Brown University. Reported by Molly Ivins, "General View of Iraq War; It's a Disaster," *Chicago Tribune*, 19 October 2006.

[221] Naomi Klein, "Seven Retired Top U.S. Military: Bush Screwed Up on Iraq." *The Guardian* (U.K.), 6 December 2004.

[222] Scott Horton interview of William Buppert (retired SF/MI officer). 13 December 2010. Minute 3:50. AntiWar Radio.

(AWOL) or desert: "Since 2000, about 40,000 troops from all branches of the military have deserted, according to the Pentagon."[223]

Soldiers are taught to dehumanize the enemy to believe killing him is not only okay but just. The high incidence of violence, suicide, and mental problems among returning soldiers is not surprising.

The jovial self-laudatory commentary of Apache helicopter crews gunning down civilians (two Reuters journalists and a van clearly containing kids) in Baghdad,[224] or a "kill team" of a dozen Fifth Stryker Brigade soldiers shooting civilians in Kandahar Province for sport (and collecting heads and other body-part souvenirs)[225] is nightly news in the rest of the world, but not shown in the U.S. until a foreign journalist releases the story in WikiLeaks. Soldiers and their commanders (demonstrating a lack of discipline and control) are rarely punished—only those exposing them.

Sanctions and bombings destroy Iraqi water, sewer, and power stations. Hospitals are without any medical supplies to include even aspirin and bandages. "By 1995 food was so scarce that a (rationing program) provided 1,100 calories per person per day."[226] Compare this with: "The prisoners at Auschwitz were getting at most from 1302 up to 1744 calories for 24 hours."[227] The Nazis feed Jews in their labor camps more than the amount of food the U.S. allows Iraqis!

---

[223] "Desertion," Wikipedia (and) Ana Radelat (Gannett News Service), "Thousands of Troops Say They Won't Fight, *Air Force Times*, 5 July 2006.

[224] Michael Collins, WikiLeaks Video—"Collateral Murder, Baghdad, 12 July 2007," 5 April 2010: The Army refuses to release the tapes to Reuters, stating the deaths are caused by a "firefight with insurgents." The female journalist is hit with 30mm cannon fire and run over by an armored personnel carrier. There is no "firefight." No one involved is prosecuted, but those leaking evidence of these crimes are jailed.

[225] Jason Motlagh, et. al., "Afghanistan: Victim's Families Denounce U.S. 'Kill Team,'" Time.com, 12 October 2010.

[226] Anthony Gregory, "America's Peacetime Crimes Against Iraq," LewRockwell.com, 1 April 2011.

[227] "Central Commission for the Investigation of German Crimes in Poland," *German Crimes in Poland*, Vol. I (1946), Warsaw, p. 69.

The Tenth Crusade

General George Washington, in his Farewell Address, warns us of a "passionate attachment" to foreign nations, the "mischiefs of foreign intrigue (and) to guard against the Impostures of *pretended patriotism*."[228]

President George Bush falls in with the "neo-conservatives" who believe in Big Government, massive spending, unlimited immigration, and are in thrall to the Likud Party. Bush, in addressing the media on 16 September 2001 (and at Elmendorf Air Force Base on 16 February 2002) refers to the pending Iraq war as "This Crusade."[229]

"Crusade" is a word Islamic peoples understand. Nine Crusades (1095–1272)—and the line continues through Jerusalem and on to Baghdad.

A small newspaper article notes two package bombs are sent to Chicago from Yemen.[230] One is addressed to "Reynald Krak." Al-Qaeda appears to have a sense of humor. This is a Middle Eastern nickname for George Bush! Krak was Renaud de Chatillon, French knight of the Second Crusade. He wantonly kills Muslim pilgrims and is beheaded by the famous Kurdish warrior king, Saladin. Krak is so cruel and feared he becomes the Christian bogeyman to generations of Muslims. George equals Jazzer ("Butcher") Krak.

Lieutenant General William "Jerry" Boykin declares, "We in the Army of God…have been raised for such a time as this."[231] Swell!

Bush admits ordering waterboarding and other "enhanced" interrogation techniques.[232] President Barak Obama, continuing Bush administration's war crimes, says, "I don't believe anybody is above the

---

[228] "George Washington's Farewell Address," 19 September 1796.

[229] Manuel Perez-Rivas, "Bush Vows to Rid the World of 'Evil-Doers,'" CNN.com, 16 September 2001.

[230] *Seattle Times*. 3 November 2010, p. A-2.

[231] Kelley B. Vlahos, "Doctor Chaplain and the Army of God," AntiWar.com, 19 October 2010.

[232] Bush, *Decision Points* (2010), pp. 170–171. Helen Thomas, "Bush Admits He Approved Torture," *Seattle Post-Intelligencer*, 1 May 2008.

law. On the other hand I also have a belief that we need to look forward as opposed to looking backwards."[233] I see—torturing and killing your neighbor is a serious crime—but killing and torturing thousands is just a quaint statistic.

Guess which country is forever demanding war crime trials for various petty tyrants and those who mistreat our people who become their prisoners? Looking forward, I can see future presidents believing they, too, are above the law and can commit crimes without retribution.

Americans have no idea of the intense anger in foreigners when we blithely exclaim, "The U.S. is a nation of laws." President Theodore Roosevelt writes during WWI, "To announce that there must be no criticism of the President, or that we are to stand by the President, right or wrong, is not only unpatriotic and servile, but is morally treasonable to the American public."[234]

Bush fails to appear to give a keynote address to a Jewish group in Geneva on 12 February 2011. Members of parliament demand his arrest on war crimes, causing him to overfly neutral Switzerland.[235]

Intelligence and War Crimes

"President Bush has admitted, for the first time, that his decision to go to war in Iraq was based on 'faulty intelligence.'"[236]

* "Former Joint Chiefs Chairman Gen. Hugh Shelton says Bush Administration officials…pushed to go to war…and there was absolutely no intelligence, zero, that pointed toward the Iraqis."[237]

---

[233] James Hanley, "Obama Won't Prosecute Bush for War Crimes," *Dispatches from the Culture Wars*, 13 January 2009.

[234] Roosevelt, *Kansas City Star*, 149, 7 May 1918. "In His Own Words," Theodore Roosevelt Association.

[235] Bridget Johnson, "Bush Cancels Switzerland Visit," *Fox Nation*, 6 February 2011.

[236] "Bush Admits Faulty Iraq Intel," *CBS News*, 11 Feb 2009 (and) "Bush Admits He Was 'Wrong.'" *The Village Voice News*. 13 Dec 2005.

[237] Alexander Belenky, "Gen. Hugh Shelton: Bush Officials Pushed For Iraqi War," *The Huffington Post*, 24 October 2010.

* "The Senate Intelligence Committee has finally gone on the record: The Bush Administration misused, and in some cases disregarded intelligence which led the nation into war....The Administration repeatedly presented intelligence as fact when, in reality, it was unsubstantiated, contradicted, or even non-existent."[238]

* "The Iraqi weapons fiasco, in the words of the ranking member of the House Intelligence Committee, could be the 'greatest intelligence hoax of all time.'"[239]

* "Any future Defense Secretary who advises the President to again send a big American land army into Asia or the Middle East should 'have his head examined.'"[240]

The evidence that President Bush and his Administration commit the most serious of war crimes, a war of aggression, is beyond dispute:

* The International Military Tribunal at Nuremberg holds: "To initiate a war of aggression...is not only an international crime: It is the supreme international crime."[241]

* Chief U.S. war crimes prosecutor at Nuremberg: "A prima facie case can be made that the United States is guilty of the supreme crime against humanity, that being an illegal war of aggression against a sovereign nation...."[242] Not only should Saddam Hussein be tried,

---

[238] Seth Colter Walls, "Senate Report: Bush Used Iraq Intel He Knew Was False," *Huffington Post*, 5 June 2008.

[239] Eric S. Margolis, "The WMD Farrago," *The American Conservative*, 28 July 2003 (Vol. 2, No. 15), p. 21.

[240] Thomas Shanker, quoting Secretary of Defense Robert Gates: "Gates: No More Wars Like Afghan, Iraq Ones," *The Seattle Times*, 26 February 2011, p. A-3.

[241] Bruce Broomhall, *International Justice and The International Criminal Court* (2003), Oxford University Press, p. 46.

[242] Benjamin B. Ferencz (Chief U.S. Prosecutor, Einsatzgruppen Case, Nuremberg War Crime Trials). Quoted in Jan Frel, "Could Bush Be Prosecuted for War Crimes?"

but also George W. Bush." (Ferencz, 25 August 2006). The "Good Germans"[243] are now the "Good Americans."

Torture

The U.N. Convention Against Torture, pushed through and signed by President Ronald W. Reagan, cannot be more explicit in obligating the U.S. to prosecute anyone in this country who authorizes or engages in torture. Article 2 makes it clear *there are no possible circumstances justifying its use*: "No exceptional circumstances whatsoever, whether a state of war or a threat of war, internal political instability or any other public emergency, may be invoked as a justification of torture, (3.) An order from a superior officer or a public authority may not be invoked as a justification for torture." (Adopted by the General Assembly, 9 December 1975.)

Major General Antonio Taguba leads the first investigation of the Abu Ghraib prison/torture scandal in early 2004. He gives us "a glimpse into Bush Administration policies of torture and murder."[244] Rather than commend him for upholding the honor of the army, he is forced to retire. The truth, in an empire, cannot go unpunished.

The Department of Justice (sic) solemnly decides not to prosecute those who torture and those covering it up—by brazenly destroying hundreds of tapes of "enhanced interrogations." The example of WikiLeaks is that it is okay to commit crimes and destroy evidence, but revealing such crimes and evidence will be prosecuted. A "nation of laws"?

WorldAlterNet, 10 July 2006 (and) Cesar Chelala, "Nuremberg Set a Valid Precedent for Trials of War-Crime Suspects in Iraq's Destruction," *World News Daily*, 27 May 2009.

[243] Frank Rich, "The 'Good Germans' Among Us," *New York Times*, 14 October 2007 (and) Harley Sorensen, "Fear Can Turn Us All Into 'Good Germans.' We Must Resist It," Common Dreams.org, 29 April 2002. (The latter contains interesting commentary from a self-described "recovering Jew.")

[244] Ray McGovern, "Army's Mafia Abuse of Pvt. (Bradley) Manning," Consortiumnews.com, 4 March 2011.

* "DOJ has never prosecuted a violation of the torture statute, 18 U.S.C., Sec. 2340."[245]

* "Torture does not work. Previous torture advocate, General Jean Jacques Massu, who led the French counterinsurgency campaign in Algeria in the 1960s and used torture widely, later declared that it fails to secure useful intelligence....Even the CIA Inspector General concludes that waterboarding in the 'War on Terror' failed to yield any valuable intelligence pertaining to immediate security threats."[246]

* "No good intelligence is going to come from abusive practices....the empirical evidence of the last five years, hard years, tells us that." [Lieutenant General John Kimmons, Senior G-2 (Army Intelligence Head)].[247]

General Peter Pace, chairman of the Joint Chiefs of Staff, tells the National Press Club (17 February 2006), "It is the absolute responsibility of everybody in uniform to disobey an order that is either illegal or immoral."

The Washington, D.C., Constitution Project "Task Force on Detainee Treatment" (2013) concludes that torture, by the Bush Administration, is "indisputable" and that many are tortured to death.

We use torture, not to obtain useful intelligence (as the situation has changed or "moved on"), but to try to justify the administration's reasons for war. Those who pay the consequences will be our future POWs, as *we Americans have forfeit the protections of civilized treatment!*

---

[245] "Counterterrorism Detention and Interrogation Activities, Special Review"; Office of Inspector General, Central Intelligence Agency, 7 May 2004. Section 40, page 19. (Pages 1 to 14 "Denied in Full").

[246] Ruth Blakeley, "British Troops Use Torture," *Guardian* (U.K.), 3 November 2010.

[247] Pentagon News Briefing just two hours following President Bush's public announcement that he is approving torture. "News Transcript," Department of Defense, 6 September 2006, *Federal News Service*.

Everything You Know Is Wrong

I am but a minor spear carrier in a far greater production. Many of my views on these pages once prevailed in the Army. Most disinformation, once projected against the enemy, is now directed against the American public. (This is illegal, but an amendment in the Defense Authorization Bill now "permits" it—another little thing hidden from the public).

"Full Bird" (O-6) and above are the politicians who value the scramble for the next highest rank as their mission in life. Most favor any war and the current top-heavy rank structure. Rarely do they sacrifice their careers to speak out against what is wrong. The "warrior ranks" are lieutenant colonel (O-5) and below.[248]

Military service, a civic obligation in my time, is now a matter of choice. Those choosing to serve no longer represent a cross-section of America—and they know it.[249]

Immature kid-soldiers are whipped into a fighting rage ["Hoo-ah! (Army), "Oo-rah!" (Marines—probably from the "Aaruu-ga" sound of a diving klaxon), and "Hoo-yah!" (SEALs)]. This is not heard in my day. Officers falsely tell them Iraqis plan 9-11, and those "towel-heads" opposing us are al-Qaeda terrorists soon to invade the U.S.

"Al-Qaeda is never more than 300 men in 2001" (on 9-11)."[250] "CIA Says Less Than 50 Al-Qaeda in Afghanistan."[251] Our excessively hooh-ahed 170,000 man army (and an equal number of "contractors") fight a few

---

[248] "In the politicized U.S. military, no officer can advance beyond the rank of lieutenant colonel unless he toes the political line," Paul Craig Roberts, "Following Orders is No Excuse," NewsMax.com, 12 February 2006. "As a rule of thumb, don't believe anybody above the rank of lieutenant colonel. That's the rank most warriors are forced to retire at. Most of the rest are politicians in uniform." Charley Reese, "This is the Month," LewRockwell.com, 11 September 2007.

[249] "I have given two cousins to the war, and I stand ready to sacrifice my wife's brother." Maine humorist, Artemus Ward (Charles Farrar Browne), on the Civil War.

[250] Quoting CIA Chief Leon Panetta. Eric Margolis, "Why Bin Laden's Ghost is Smiling," LewRock-well.com, 2 May 2011.

[251] Jake Tapper, "CIA Says Less Than 50 Al-Qaeda In Afghanistan" (ABC News Senior White House Correspondent), *Morrison World Media Morning Post*, 27 June 2010.

hundred local, goat-herding, part-time insurgents because we have invaded their country and slaughtered their families. They somehow resent this.

Defeat in the Middle East

We face an adaptive enemy who lives in holes and has no supply lines. His weapons are often handmade. He cancels our airpower advantage by fighting in such a way that targets are limited. He makes us swat flies with expensive sledgehammers. In close quarters, he can inflict as many casualties as he absorbs. He is not trying to win battles.

His mission is to win the allegiance of other Arabs. This is called asymmetric warfare. (We eventually form an Asymmetric Warfare Group to enhance training and close the gap created by this threat.)

Bush tells us, "Fight them over there so we don't have to fight them over here."[252] [Do any ponder how poor herders and farmers are to purchase airline tickets or (without an air force or navy) somehow arrive on our shores? How are they to resupply?]

Terrorism. Terrorism is a force-equalizer used to combat a technologically superior enemy. It works. The goal of any organized terrorist attack is to goad a vastly more powerful enemy into an excessive response. The terrorist finds a weakness and exploits it. There is no perfect defense. We concentrate on how to prevent the last attack.

Our penchant to view technology as the answer is a recipe for endless spending and disaster.

It costs us over $50 million to kill a single Taliban insurgent.[253] It takes an estimated 300,000 cartridges, of various calibers, to kill just one insurgent.[254] (It was about 15,000 rounds in World War II and 50,000 in Vietnam.) We no longer are a nation of riflemen.

---

[252] Patrick J. Buchanan. "Is Bush Misdiagnosing the Malady?" LewRockwell.com, 9 February 2005. "Before we invaded Iraq, not one American had been killed by an Iraqi in a dozen years."

[253] Matthew Nasuti, "Killing Each Taliban Soldier Costs $50 Million," *Kabul Press*, 5 November 2010.

[254] John Pike (director of Washington military research group, "Global-Security.org,") states, "The GAO's figures (show) US forces expended around six billion bullets between

The Department of Defense does not release insurgent/civilian casualty figures. (They might upset you.) Television commentators and politicians are forever using any number of Iraqi dead from 30,000 to 100,000. (They support an illegal war and are now stuck with its consequences.) Reliable figures exist to dispute these low counts: "As of July *2006* there have been *654,965* excess Iraqi deaths as a consequence of war…the most common cause being gunfire."[255] This is more deaths than during our Civil War—in a country much smaller. A British polling agency says the violent Iraqi death toll is up to 1,220,580 by August 2007.[256]

General Stanley A. McChrystal, commander of U.S. and NATO forces in Afghanistan, states, "We have shot an amazing number of people, but to my knowledge, *none* has ever proven to be a threat."[257] Locals have also learned how to use us to eliminate rival villagers.[258]

Graveyard of Empires

Lady Jane Butler's haunting Victorian painting of "The Retreat from Kabul" shows Dr. William Brydon, on a tired pony, struggling to leave a bleak landscape. He is the (supposed) lone survivor of a 16,500 man British army during the First Anglo-Afghan War of 1842. This painting should

---

2002 and 2005…it works out to around 300,000 bullets per insurgent."

[255] Gilbert Burnham, MD, et. al., "Mortality After the 2003 Invasion of Iraq," *The Lancet*. Johns Hopkins Bloomberg University School of Public Health (Baltimore) with Al-Mustansiriya University (Baghdad) and the Massachusetts Institute of Technology. Second Survey, using death certificates and household follow-ups, 11 Oct 2006. See also, Hiroaki Sato, "The Self-Inflicted Costs of a 'War of Choice,'" *The Japan Times*, 25 July 2011. This methodology is far superior to all others.

[256] Opinion Research Business survey quoted in Wikipedia, "Casualties of the Iraq War." Criticized as too high by some, but no numbers are submitted to counter these figures, so they must stand as best evidence. (Wikipedia is not always accurate or reliable).

[257] Richard A. Oppel, Jr., "Tighter Rules Fail to Stem Deaths of Innocent Afghans," *New York Times*, 27 March 2010, p. A-4 (and) Laurence M. Vance, "The Criminality of War," Lew Rockwell.com, 13 April 2011. See also, Nima Shirazi (Brooklyn), "The Invisible Dead," *Wide Asleep in America*, 9 August 2011.

[258] Jason Ditz, "Tribesmen Use US Drone Strikes to Settle Local Scores (in North Waziristan)," Anti-War.com, 23 May 2011.

hang in the Office of the President and in the Pentagon. We learn nothing from the Brits and Soviets.

Right and Wrong

Muslim culture is so bizarre and inscrutable that they seem offended when foreign armies bomb, invade, and occupy their countries. Contrast this with the furious response of Americans against people who have nothing to do with 9-11. Islam is a religion of warriors and of revenge. What does any thinking and rational person believe is about to take place?

I am asked the question in a nightly discussion period (on a voyage to remote Pitcairn Island), "Do Americans know the difference between right and wrong?" This question is more profound than it might first appear. This is the legal definition of insanity [the M'Naghten Rule; 18 USC, Sec. 17 (1984)], still a defense in most U.S. states and in former British colonies.[259] "Collective insanity" is an interesting view of Americans by foreigners (who, in this instance, are our U.K. allies).

The question remains valid and demands an answer.

An LAPD Academy classmate writes a 600-plus page book on use of force and ethics in local and federal police agencies. Yet he sees little ethical conflict with invading countries on false pretenses and the torture, slaughter, and economic sanctions (Acts of War) against their citizens. An executive above-the-law is also of little concern. He sends out e-mail literature demanding revenge against those who dare to strike back at America, but ignores the Israel theft of our defense/nuclear secrets and their sale to hostile nations. Justice and "right and wrong" were once important to him. How can this unique American myopia of otherwise intelligent and fair-minded people be explained?

---

[259] Daniel M'Naghten attempts to assassinate British prime minister Sir Robert Peel (founder of the "Bobbies") in 1843.

Generational Gap

Conservative William S. Lind is one of the first to point out that the U.S. military "just doesn't get it."[260] We still believe that wars are decided by who puts the most firepower on targets.

Second Generation Warfare: Developed by the French army in World War I. Reliance on indirect fire. Summed up by the French maxim: "Artillery conquers; infantry occupies." It inwardly focuses on rules, regulations, and drills.

Third Generation: Maneuver warfare (the German blitzkrieg). It is decentralized and depends upon speed and flexibility. It values initiative over obedience and self rather than imposed discipline.

Fourth Generation Warfare: Against entities that are not countries. The "battlefield" includes the entire enemy's society. The enemy's military becomes irrelevant. The U.S. develops stealth bombers; the insurgent's "stealth bomber" is a suicide bomber or a car with a bomb in the trunk—which looks like every other car. An indirect attack on the enemy's culture, say, through drug trafficking, is another such tactic. "Ninety-five percent of all suicide attacks are in response to foreign occupation."[261]

The U.S. military is stuck in drawn-out second generational warfare.

We favor drones and air strikes over artillery. Bin Laden calls drones his "best weapon." A single drone kills as many as eighty civilians at a tribal jirga (official meeting) in North Waziristan. Scores of other examples are known in attacking gatherings such as wedding parties.[262]

---

[260] Lind, et. al., "The Changing Face of War: Into the Fourth Generation." *Marine Corps Gazette*, October 1989.

[261] Extensive research at University of Chicago's "Project on Security and Terrorism" examines *every one* of 2,200 worldwide suicide attacks from 1990 to 2010. In 2000, for example, there are twenty such attacks and only one against the U.S. (USS *Cole*). Now, they number in the hundreds, with almost all directed at Americans. Prof. Robert A. Pape, "It's the Occupation, Stupid," *Foreign Policy*, 18 October 2010.

[262] "80 People Reportedly Killed in U.S. Drone Strike in Pakistan," Xinhua News Agency (Beijing), 17 March 2011. *Time Magazine*'s Tim McGirk reports we kill all but two women in a wedding party of 112 in an Afghan village. Tom Engelhardt, "The Wedding

Computer-gaming kids of the CIA and air force, sometimes half-a-world away, are making the decisions to fire these things against those openly carrying arms and at "military age men" (age twelve and above), or at large gatherings. (Anyone who has been to these areas knows everyone is armed against bandits and warlords.) Such drone strikes are war crimes and considered murder under U.S. and international law.

Does anyone care? What if a foreign nation, such as China, similarly targets U.S. families because of, say, our oppression of human rights and religion at Waco? We pay the drone victim's families a pittance and claim to never have killed a civilian—as those women and kids are "collaborators" as shown by their proximity to the "terrorist dead." We are again outraged and confused when our allies in these countries turn their guns on our soldiers and police advisors.

Texas Congressman Ron Paul notes the deaths of our soldiers are from those who have had their loved ones and friends killed as "collateral damage."[263] General Stanley McChrystal calls it "Insurgent math: For every innocent person you kill, you create ten new enemies."[264] Hezbollah ("Party of God") wins the first modern fourth generation war—against Israel[265]—when they drive the IDF from Lebanon after inflicting heavy casualties on their Jewish invaders. The Israelis are after their water supplies.

You fight a fourth generation war by avoiding conflict as much as possible and by responding to attacks with small, specialized units who live in the field (not in garrison), and who know the language and people. (Our current army is incapable of responding to rapidly changing conditions or engaging in sustained light infantry tactics.)

Crashers," Tom-Dispatch, a project of The Nation Institute, 13 July 2008 (and) "American Anniversaries from Hell," *Huff Post*, 29 March 2013, taken from Engelhardt's, *The United States of Fear* (2011).

[263] "Ron Paul's Texas Straight Talk" video (9 August 2010): "The Cycle and Violence in Afghanistan." Congressman, Fourteenth District.

[264] Quentin Sommerville, "Kabul to Miss Respected McChrystal," BBC News, South Asia, 23 June 2010.

[265] Lind, "Wars Without Countries," *The American Conservative*, 7 April 2003 (Vol. 2, No. 7), p. 20.

You cannot kill all members of an insurgency. You are limited to eliminating the conditions that spawn it. You must build a network of informants so expansive that attacks can be stopped before they happen. You use federal, state, and local police agencies, as much as possible—rather than soldiers (whose mission and training are different)—to track terrorists/insurgents. Diplomatic rather than military solutions are almost always more successful.

Lawrence of Arabia

Disbanding the Iraqi army and belittling it before its population is a horrendous error. Soldiers, unable to support their families, become raiders and insurgents. We ignore the lessons of King Darius and Xerxes the Great of Persia who successfully incorporate the soldiers of conquered nations in their armies. Alexander the Great and others have similar success. We forget what happens to the French in Algeria, the Brits in Palestine and Aden, the Soviets in Afghanistan, and to us in Vietnam and Somalia.

Rambo III (1988) should have been shown at West Point. Captured American Colonel Trautman lectures Soviet Colonel Zaysen about how stupid it is to invade Afghanistan: "Those poorly armed and equipped Freedom Fighters have never given up to anyone. You can't defeat people like this....You started this damn war and now you have to deal with it!" Prophetic words.

Few of our commanders read T.E. Lawrence's, *Seven Pillars of Wisdom* (1922)—required reading at Command and General Staff College in my day—discussing fifteen principles of modern desert guerrilla warfare. Lawrence marches away from the enemy into the desert to become a silent threat using raids perfected by the Bedouin tribes. He is a phantom who stings the enemy and forces them to deploy troops everywhere at their considerable expense.

The Arab Bulletin (1916–1919), edited by Lawrence, allows the reader to follow the Arab revolt week by week, ending the Ottoman domination of the Arabian Peninsula. (About 114 issues of 30 copies each are reprinted in

1986 in a four-volume set.) They are indispensable to understanding today's conflict. Osama Bin Laden appears to have used them to defeat us.

"Fire the Generals"

A long-suppressed report emerges: "Today's general officer corps is failing badly and is unfit for command."[266] American generals are known for an unwillingness to stand up and be counted; to put country before career.

Despite fighting an insurgency in Iraq, the army has no counterinsurgency experts until eighteen months into the war and "failed to halt the inhumane treatment of the population." A State Department official, "summed up the consequences of the clumsy, brutal occupation, saying, 'We underestimate our daily humiliation of Iraqis....We don't understand when someone kills a brother, it calls for a revenge killing."

The excessive use of force and the policy of treating any Arab suspected of opposing the U.S. military occupation as a "terrorist" has another unintended effect. Thousands of recruits and sympathizers join the rebellion from inside and outside the country.

"It was always the intrusive U.S. military occupation that was the fundamental problem....It remains a sad commentary on the generals that they have shown so little spine in the face of a disastrous occupation and an incompetently run war."[267]

The Longest War

The Bushes tell us we are in imminent danger of attack by a petty Middle Eastern dictator who never threatens us. Those pointing out obvious flaws in his story are attacked as unpatriotic and risking the safety of the nation. We become the drunk, looking under the streetlight for his car keys. He knows he did not drop them there, but that is where he can see best.

---

[266] Colonel Douglas Macgregor, "Fire the Generals." Special to the *Defense and National Interest* (Project on Government Oversight), preface to Second Edition, 30 April 2007.

[267] Ibid.

The best way to prevent this from happening again is education. A group of traditional Conservative patriots create a magazine before the war, *The American Conservative*, to educate people on how the country is being duped into an illegal and unjust war. Insufficient numbers read it or believe it. Investigative journalists are replaced with high school reporters who print what the government directs.

Our ignorance of American and world history, geography, finance, other cultures, and religions—and discarding the lessons of our Founding Fathers—leads us sheep to disaster. We appear unable to recognize our own hypocrisy: focus on the crimes of others; ignore our own.

A democracy depends upon its people being educated in the important questions of the day so as to influence decisions by voting for those who represent their point of view. If this is subverted by "journalists" who are cheerleaders for the current administrtion, and our representatives vote to the dictates of a foreign power, then the "Tree of Liberty must be refreshed... with the blood of Patriots and Tyrants!"[268]

A likely reason for this press disinterest is that national disasters are often bipartisan. Both Democrats and Republicans become eager to cover-up their mistakes. Governmental surveillance of journalists and politicians uncovers little secrets that are career-enders. Cooperate and vote or publish what we want and your indiscretions will remain hidden....

The American people can never be free if we cannot control our government and its policies. Allowing a rogue nation to direct our foreign policy is beyond disastrous. If we remain ignorant, all is lost. We must prosecute those who lie us into war and trash our Constitution and hard-won rules of land warfare hammered out in blood at Nuremberg.

Prosecuting foreigners and ignoring our own war criminals will cause the loss of our way of life and of the natural rights enumerated in our Bill of Rights. Our leaders gain control of our judicial system and exempt

---

[268] Thomas Jefferson to William Stephens Smith (Paris, 13 November 1787). Quoted in Anthony Martin, "The Blood of Patriots and Tyrants," *Columbia Conservative Examiner*, 4 April 2009.

themselves from the law of the land. This must be stopped. The "Patriot Act," unread by Congress, replaces our Bill of Rights.

Hypocrites in uniform complain of "cowardly" insurgents planting IEDs against military targets while praising our appropriately named "Reaper" and "Predator" drones that routinely kill scores of noncombatants.

Army sniper, Staff Sergeant James Gilliland, Third Infantry Division, receives considerable publicity for his many kills. He is quoted, "Enemy soldiers have no morality, no ethics....They have never heard of the Geneva Convention, they will never comply with its content."[269] Interesting commentary from a division invading a country that does not threaten us—and one accused of torturing its prisoners. Gilliland's home address in Alabama and details of his family are readily available on the net. Yet no "terrorists" have taken them out, largely confining their strikes to military targets present in their own countries. How can this be? Is it possible we have been lied to by our government?

States arose in the fifteenth century to provide security. Part of the reason we are now in crisis is that we cannot even protect our Pentagon in the nation's capitol, much less our national borders. An invasion of illegal immigrants becomes an occupation. We create a police state in the name of Homeland Security, yet ignore millions of aliens pouring across our borders. Both parties support "amnesty" and a "reform of immigration laws" (i.e., not enforcing them). Corruption and military spending greater than all 194 other nations combined bankrupt us.

Our so-called War on Terror evokes Xerxes's war on the waters of the Hellespont. Sending our second-generation 170,000 man army and armor to Iraq/Afghanistan is as irrelevant as sending a Macedonian phalanx. Taking on a non-state entity as al-Qaeda or the Taliban becomes irrelevant if we "win" and catastrophic if we lose.

While we fight al-Qaeda in Pakistan and Afghanistan, we supply and support (with Special Operations troops and drones) the same al-Qaeda in Libya and Syria. [We suddenly turn against the same Syrians who are our

---

[269] Major John L. Plaster, "Shooting with Today's Top Snipers," *American Rifleman*, May 2012 (Vol. 160, No. 5), p. 48.

allies in our war against Iraq. We do the same against Saddam Hussein in Iraq and Muammar al-Gaddafi in Libya.] How do other potential allies in the Middle East view our changing loyalties? *Cui bono?* To see who benefits from these betrayals and chaos, read the next chapter on "The Samson Option."

We Americans truly live in a "bizarro world."[270] As General Charles Lord Cornwallis's 8,000 troops march out to become prisoners of war at the Siege of Yorktown (1781), his band plays the tune, "The World Turned Upside Down":

> "If buttercups buzz'd after the bee,
> If boats were on land, churches on sea.
> If ponies rode men and if grass ate the cows,
> And cats should be chased into holes by the mouse.
> If summer were Spring,
> And the other way 'round,
> Then all the world would be upside down!"

Memorial Day. Memorial Day keeps coming and going with the same stories honoring veterans of a dishonorable war. The body counts and destruction continue with little interest from the public or press. The same number of troops remain in place—a curious presence after Bush declares "Mission Accomplished" over a decade before. It's reminiscent of the 1960 *Twilight Zone* episode, "The Hitch-Hiker," where Inger Stevens keeps encountering the same hitchhiker on a cross-country trip. Her continuing sense of uneasiness concludes with the realization that she died in a traffic accident and the hitchhiker she eventually picks up is Death.

Iraq Remembered

The lasting image of Iraq will be of George Bush, in a supreme moment of presidential buffoonery, prancing across that carrier deck in a flight suit

---

[270] A "DC Comics" (1958) fictional planet where everything is backwards, inverted, or similar but not quite right.

to declare "Mission Accomplished"—just as the insurgents are digging in and striking back.

The Undiscovered Country

Many countries consider our form of "democracy" to be a luxury (or lunacy) they cannot afford. Millions of welfare-seeking and poverty-stricken foreigners are clamoring to sneak across our borders. Data suggests about three million Americans go abroad each year to live.

Most do not renounce their U.S. citizenship, but several thousand do.[271] Those departing are the wealthy and talented in the twenty-five to thirty-five year range. They just disappear from the tax rolls. We are the only country (along with Nazi Germany, Soviet Russia, and apartheid South Africa) to tax citizens to expatriate. (It was free until George "No-New-Taxes" Bush imposed a $450 exit tax.)

America is now a security welfare-warfare state where we are on the doorstep of tyranny. The year 2015 marks the funeral of the Magna Carta of 800 years ago. Few Americans understand the significance of their loss—that the king is bound by the law—any more than they mourn the trashing of our Constitution by the last few Presidents and our Congress.

A Matter of Time

A wealthy individual or group will bribe an Israeli supply sergeant, a Russian scientist, or Pakistani general to acquire a nuclear device.

The container it is in will not have to pass customs—it will detonate in New York Harbor, the Potomac River, Long Beach, Seattle, or who knows where. We will then "retaliate" against an enemy selected for his lack of ability to respond in kind rather than his culpability, as directed by our foreign overlords.

---

[271] Robert E. Bauman, "Escape from America Continues," LewRockwell.com, 18 March 2011.

Chapter XXXI

THE SAMSON OPTION

One of the first things an army counterintelligence (CI) officer learns is to assess the threats and risks posed by those seeking our military and technological secrets. We aggressively counter espionage and terrorist threats in coordination with other U.S. and foreign assets. My special area of study and concern is the Middle East.

Ask almost any CI officer which country is the most aggressive in spying against us. It is our "friend and ally"—Israel![272] All countries seek intelligence on each other. Israel, thus, cannot be faulted for doing what is in her best interests. A line exists, however, that friendly nations do not cross. Rarely are the Germans, Brits, French, or even Arabs caught spying upon us. If caught, they are punished and sanctions taken against their countries. Israeli spies, however, can expect deportation followed by a U.S. cover-up at the highest levels.

The Israeli threat involves the theft of most of our conventional and nuclear weapons systems and their sale to the Chinese and Russians. One instance is so serious as to be an Act of War that may end our very existence. What seems especially suicidal is that the U.S. is Israel's lone defender and supporter. Without our financial, military, and diplomatic aid, Israel will cease to exist. Why do they feel compelled to attack and to alienate us? Sun Tzu said, "Know your enemy." This chapter shines a light on what drives him.

Criticism of Israel brings cries of "anti-Semitism." Anti-Semitism used to be hatred of Jews; now, it is anyone who questions what Israel does. A Jewish friend tells me it is an "in" joke. Semites are "the descendants of Shem (six-hundred-year-old son of Noah," i.e., the peoples of the ancient

---

[272] A Pew Survey found "72 percent of military leaders…believed that backing Israel seriously damages America's image around the world." John J. Mearsheimer and Stephen M. Walt, "A Dwindling Moral Case," *The Israel Lobby and U.S. Foreign Policy* (2007), p. 109.

Near East). Most Zionists are Ashkenazi, descendants of the Turkic Khazars, from Eastern Europe. They do not contain a drop of "Semitic" blood, whereas most Palestinians and Arabs are true Semites. Ask not if it is anti-Semitic. Ask, is it the truth?

* "The FBI, DIA, and the General Accounting Office (the investigative arm of Congress) regard Israel as the country most actively engaged in espionage against American targets."[273]

* "Israel...has become a major supplier of weapons and weapons technology to China....A classified Defense intelligence Agency report states that Israel was suspected of sharing restricted U.S. weapons technology with China related to a battlefield laser gun."[274]

* "Chinese fighters carry Israel's potent Python-3 heat-seeking missile developed by Israel (from) the Sidewinder missile that the U.S. sold to the Jewish state."[275]

* "The Government of Israel has been an important source of the People's Republic of China's acquisition of advanced military technology according to a recent Congressional Investigative Report on Chinese Espionage."[276]

* A "Memorandum to the Record" to Senators Orrin G. Hatch and Patrick J. Leahy, U.S. Senate Committee on the Judiciary, discusses the acquisition of our W-88 nuclear warhead, the "most advanced

---

[273] Philip Giraldi (CIA Station Chief), "Deep Background," *The American Conservative*, 27 September 2004 (Vol. 3, No. 18), p. 25 (and) J. Michael Waller, "These Spies Steal American Jobs," *Reader's Digest*, February 1998, p. 168.

[274] Bill Gertz, "U.S. Identifies Israeli Drones Targeting Taiwan from China," *The Washington Times*, 8–14 July 2002 (Vol. 9, No. 28), p. 23.

[275] Rowan Scarborough, "Chinese Arsenal Born in America, Analysts Say," *The Washington Times*, 30 April–6 May 2001, p. 17.

[276] Document reproduced in Gordon Thomas, *Seeds of Fire* (2001), Dandelion Books, Tempe, Arizona, p. 126.

nuclear warhead in the U.S. arsenal," by the Red Chinese through the Israelis.[277]

The Enemy Within

Patriot and whistle-blower Edward J. Snowden's 2009 memo reveals our National Security Agency (NSA) is not only secretly collecting America's communications, but passing all to Israel! We know that Presidents Bush and Obama—and their administrations and many in Congress—have violated their Constitutional oaths and place a foreign nation, Israel, above US interests.

Betrayal of allegiance to the U.S. during wartime is treason! It is punishable by death. Treason includes giving government security secrets to other nations, even if friendly. Misprison of treason is the concealing of such knowledge about the acts of traitors.

Why does Israel desire this mass of data about American citizens? Answer: It is to uncover little indiscretions of politicians, industrialists, and journalists. And to blackmail and recruit turn-coat agents to betray our country. [Look what happens to four-star general David Petraeus, CENTCOM Commander. NSA/Israel uncover e-mails linking him to an extramarital affair and, through the FBI, bounce him out as Director of the CIA. Petraeus' crime: He testifies, truthfully, before the Senate Armed Services Committee on 16 March 2010 that Israel is a burden and a danger to the U.S....]. How do you feel about the government of Israel, with connections to the "Jewish Mafia," having all of your financial and banking data?

Israel's m.o. is to sell, to the highest bidder (usually China), its military and industrial espionage secrets. "Enhanced PROMIS," which follows, is a prime example of such an Act of War against America.

It may take a "regime change," as envisioned by Thomas Jefferson, to give our country back to loyal Americans. We must weed the traitors out of government who favor any foreign nation over ours. A few trials and

---

[277] Ibid., dated 22 December 1999.

executions—and renditions to, say, Arab nations for interrogations—will do wonders, as the Neo-Cons did under Bush.

The Middle East must be cleared of nuclear and chemical weapons. Blockade Israel—food, medicine, machinery, power, water, & sewage facilities—as was illegally done to Iraq. Give them 30 days to surrender their WMD or level their known nuclear sites as near Dimona and Soreq. Send in weapons inspectors as was done in Iraq and Iran. If they resist, level Tel Aviv as we did in Fallujah and much of Baghdad. Use drones to target their political and military leaders and military-age males as we are currently doing in eight countries we are not at war with. Revoke the passports of dual citizenship holders and deport them, with no right of return.

We will finally have attacked a country that actually threatens and assaults us.

A PROMIS Enhanced

Remember Dr. Wen Ho Lee? He makes front-page news for months as the Taiwanese spy who steals our nuclear secrets from Los Alamos Laboratory and passes them to the Chinese Secret Intelligence Service. Lee's fifty-eight counts of espionage are quietly dropped without explanation.

District Court Judge James A. Parker publicly apologizes to Lee for "governmental misconduct which has embarrassed the entire nation." Lee is then awarded $1.645 million.[278]

Chinese nuclear weapons technology goes from the 1950s era to our latest advances traceable directly to Los Alamos. The FBI zeroes in on Dr. Lee despite the Department of Justice *[sic]* and Central Intelligence Agencies knowing what actually happens.

A Washington, D.C., couple, William A. and Nancy Hamilton, own a small software company called Inslaw. They sell an incredibly sophisticated program called "Enhanced PROMIS" (Prosecutor's Management Information Systems) to DOJ (for $9.6 million) for the U.S. attorney to keep track of his case load. DOJ sees its intelligence potential and passes it to the

---

[278] *Lee v. Dept. of Justice*, 287 F. Supp. 2d 15 (D.D.C. 2003), aff'd 413 F 3d 53 (D.C. Civ, 2005).

CIA, which gives it to Rafi Eitan, head of the Israeli Defense Ministry's scientific spy unit, the Lakam (Bureau of Scientific Liaison).

Eitan (who admits his involvement) has Lakam programmers add a trapdoor—a microchip that enables PROMIS to search the database of its host and release captured data in microbursts disguised as computer noise. They sell the program back to Los Alamos National Laboratory through British newspaper tycoon, Robert Maxwell.

The Israelis, in a joint Chinese-Israeli "fishing boat" operation off Puerto Penasco (Rocky Point), Sonora, transfer the stolen data to the Chinese.

Two Canadian mounties, Investigators Sean McDade and Randy Buffam, in Project Abbreviation, discover Maxwell sells Enhanced PROMIS to the Canadian Secret Intelligence Service and Los Alamos. They write, "The Israelis now possess all the nuclear secrets of the United States."[279]

DOJ fails to pay the Hamiltons for their software and tries to drive them into Chapter 7 bankruptcy. DOJ loses and the story becomes public. The U.S. media remain silent. Even Rupert Murdoch complains of the "Jewish-owned media" ("CNN Opinion," 28 November 2012).

Neo-con Michelle Malkin, interestingly, publishes an article complaining that the DOJ secretly turns over a copy of PROMIS to the Israeli government, and it ends up in the hands of Osama Bin Laden![280] She notes President George Bush's "9-11 Commission" ignores the role of PROMIS in facilitating 9-11 and "the wholesale sellout of our national security."

Why isn't Israeli treachery front-page news as was the innocent Dr. Lee? I am not aware of its mention by any U.S. television station or newspaper.

This is an Act of War that may result in the annihilation of America. (The U.S. "Cyber War Doctrine" defines a cyber-attack as a conventional Act of War.) Why are Americans not outraged? This is a far more destructive event than the 9-11 Twin Towers attacks.

---

[279] Thomas, *op. cit.*, p. 90. See also, Allan Thompson and Valerie Lawton, "RCMP Cast Wider Net in Software Spy Probe," *Toronto Star* (Ottawa), 4 September 2000.

[280] Malkin, "America's Spy Software Scandal," *Conservative Chronicle*, 16 July 2003 (Vol. 18, No. 29), p. 31.

Atomic Spies

Is it a surprise that Harry Gold, Klaus Fuchs, Morton Sobell, David Greenglass, Morris and Lona Cohen, Julius and Ethel Rosenberg, and other Jews steal our atomic bomb secrets for the Soviets? (Only the Rosenberg's sit in "Old Sparky" at Sing-Sing in 1953.) Klaus Fuchs also confesses to the FBI of his involvement in passing our hydrogen bomb secrets to the Soviets.

Jonathan J. Pollard passes such critical technology to Israel that neither the U.S. nor Israel will reveal all that is stolen.[281] It is traded to Russia, supposedly so they will allow more Russian Jews to emigrate to Israel.

> "Whatever happens, we have got,
> The Maxim Gun, and they have not."

[Written by Hilaire Belloc after British General Sir Herbert Kitchener slaughters the Dervishes at Omdurman (1898).] The natives now possess our Maxim gun—Thanks to Israel.

The Samson Origins

Several Israeli Defense Force (IDF) officers attending U.S. Army Command and General Staff College tell of the graduation of their paratroopers. They wind their way up the "snake path" of the horst (rock block forced upward between two faults) of Masada on the edge of the Judean Desert, by torchlight, for a mystic ceremony.

Several of us suggest this may not be the best image for an elite fighting force. Almost a thousand Zealots oppose Roman rule of Judea and harass them with raids from atop Masada. For over two years, the defenders awaken each morning to look down on the busy Roman Tenth Legion slowly building an earthen ramp closer to their walls.

Ten Zealots kill their men, women, and children, and then draw lots to see who will kill each other.

---

[281] "The greatest traitor in the history of the United States," Gordon Thomas, *Gideon's Spies* (2009 edition), p. 4.

We ask, "Why not fall in battle and put a serious dent in Flavius Silva's 'Legio X'? Your families will survive as slaves and make more little Zealots."

They reply, "It is not our way." This Masada ceremony is soon halted.

Samson/Shimshon, captured and put on display by the Philistines at Dagon's Temple in Gaza, asks God to give him strength for the last time. He then pushes apart the temple pillars, bringing down the roof upon himself and his enemies (Judges 16:30).

And herein lies the threat. Israel never signs the Nuclear Non-Proliferation Treaty (1970) embraced by 189 nations. [Non-signatory states are India, Israel, and Pakistan. North Korea is a party but withdraws in 2003.] Israel does not permit inspections but is believed to have in excess of 400 nuclear devices. David Ben-Gurion, first prime minister, calls their nuclear arsenal "Golem."[282]

Many of us intel officers consider Israel as our "crazy aunt in the attic."[283] Israel is aggressive and paranoid, but escapes punishment because of Big Uncle Sucker's protection. They promise to bring down the roof upon everyone if all else fails:

* "The frightening possibility that Israel may unleash these weapons of mass destruction is preoccupying strategic planners."[284]

* "Most European capitals are targets for our Air Force....We have the capability to take the world down with us. And I can assure you that will happen, before Israel goes under."[285]

---

[282] Michael Collins Piper, *The Golem: A World Held Hostage* (2007), 182 pp.

[283] In Jewish folklore, the Golem (a Frankenstein's monster conjured up by Talmudic rabbis to destroy their enemies) rests in the attic of the Synagogue of Prague. The Golem, which can destroy its creator, is sometimes the informal name given to the Israeli nuclear program.

[284] Ross Dunn, "In War, Israel Retains the Samson Option," *Sydney (Australia) Morning Herald*, 21 September 2002.

[285] Martin Van Creveld [Professor of History, Hebrew University of Jerusalem. He is a critic of the Iraq war and believes President Bush should be tried for his war crimes.]

* "What would serve the Jew-hating world better...(than)...a nuclear winter....Or invite all of those tut-tutting European statesmen and peace activists to join us in the ovens?....The ultimate justice."[286]

Before the start of World War II, Jewish hysteria and suicides are widespread.[287]

Master and Servant

"Israeli Prime Minister Ehud Olmert said a telephone call he made to U.S. President George W. Bush last week forced Secretary of State Condoleezza Rice to abstain in a U.N. vote on the Gaza War, leaving her 'shamed.'"[288] Olmert says he calls Bush out of a speech in Philadelphia ten minutes before the U.N. Security Council is to vote on a Gaza ceasefire resolution. Rice, who authors and introduces the resolution, becomes the only one to *not* vote for it! The IDF continues its invasion, despite the fourteen to one vote, killing 1,400 Palestinian civilians, with only half-a-dozen "friendly fire" casualties of its own. Collective punishment—just another Israeli war crime.

Is there is a more obvious example of the master/servant relationship between Israel and the U.S.?

I Love Israel Most. Republican U.S. Senator from Illinois, Mark Kirk, says his entire reason for being in Congress is to advance the cause of Israel. New York Democrat Senator Charles "Chuck" Schumer (from shomer or "guardian" in Hebrew) repeatedly states his priority is "to advance the interests of Israel." (Any clue as to why Jesse Jackson refers to New York City as "Hymie-Town" to a reporter from the "Washington Post"?) Republican Mitt Romney actually campaigns for President of the United

---

Quoted in David Hirst, *The Gun and The Olive Branch* (2003), p. 459, and "The War Game," *The Observer* (Sunday *Guardian*), 21 September 2003.

[286] David Perlmutter, "Israel: Dark thoughts and Quiet Desperation," *Los Angeles Times*, 7 April 2002, opinion page.

[287] "Suicide Wave Follows Curbs. Self-Destruction by German Jews Keeps Rabbis Busy," *Los Angeles Times*, 1 December 1938, pp. 1 and 4.

[288] "Olmert Calls Bush to Force Change in U.N. Vote," dalje.com (Jerusalem), 13 January 2009. See also (same heading): Jeffrey Heller, Reuters, 13 January 2009.

States in Israel in 2012 and promises to support their positions and wars over the interests of the U.S. He brags of regularly receiving Israeli intel briefings. This is beyond scary.

Control of U.S. Foreign Policy

* "Don't worry about American pressure on Israel. We, the Jewish people, control America, and the Americans know it!"[289]

How can less than two percent of the American population that is Jewish control our president, Congress, and foreign policy? (Wouldn't it be refreshing for our representatives to realize that the 98 percent of our population that is not Jewish also deserve representation!) A member of the Israeli Knesset (Uri Avnery) reveals:

* "The Israeli government rules Washington, D.C., more firmly than ever. The new Congress is even more loyal to Israel than the old one, if that is possible." (3 October 2001).

"US senators are nearly all Israeli senators. Ditto for US congressmen. Hardly any of them would dare to criticize the Israeli government on any issue. Criticizing Israel is political suicide....For five decades, at least, US Middle East policy has been decided in Jerusalem. Almost all American officials dealing with this area are, well, Jewish."[290]

---

[289] Prime Minister Ariel Sharon to Shimon Peres. Kol Yisrael Radio interview as reported on *Media Monitors Network* and in David Irvine's, "Action Report," *Washington Report on Middle East Affairs*, 3 October 2001 (posted 11 October).

[290] Uri Avnery, "Ship of Fools 2," *Counter Punch*, 22 December 2010. Also, *Gush Shalom*, Avnery's column, 18 December 2010. Avnery, a member of the Knesset, is a terrorist for the Irgun who fights in the 1948 war. "Welcome, Chuck," Anti-War.com, 12 Jan 2013. [See also: James Petras, "Major Jewish American Organizations Defend Israel's Humiliation of America," World News Daily Information Clearing House: "In plain English, we (of the U.S.) are a people colonized and directed by a small, extremist and militarist 'ally' which operates through domestic proxies, who, under any other circumstance, would be openly denounced as traitors."]

* Even Reuters recognizes Israeli domination of U.S. foreign policy:

"Judging from the extent to which one partner defies the will of the other, decade after decade, the world's only superpower is the weaker partner."[291]

* "Congress is Israeli-occupied territory."[292]

* "Every member of Congress lives in absolute fear of being denounced by the pro-Israel lobbies as unfriendly to Israel, which would immediately result in that member losing their seat in the next election....Congressional subservience to Israel revealed itself as so exaggerated last week that many Americans took notice—and some started to speak out."[293]

* The American Israel Public Affairs Committee (AIPAC) "is an extremely dangerous domestic enemy...founded in the 1950s with the support of the Israeli Foreign Ministry (to) lobby for sustained American financial, diplomatic, and military support of Israel, but, curiously, it has never been required to register under the Foreign Agents Registration Act (FARA) which would require full public disclosure of finances."[294]

* Tam Dalyell, British Labour Party deputy known as "Father of the House," says, "A Jewish cabal has taken over the government in the United States and formed an unholy alliance with fundamentalist Christians."[295]

---

[291] Bernd Debusmann, "Who is the Superpower, America or Israel?" Reuters, 21 February 2011.

[292] Patrick J. Buchanan, McLaughlin Group, 15 June 1990. (Sometimes noted as "Capitol Hill is Israeli-occupied territory.") Quoted in *Anti-Defamation League*, September 1999.

[293] Rami G. Khouri, "Netanyahu Was Powerful and Misguided," *The Daily Star* (Lebanon), 28 May 2011, p. 7.

[294] Philip Giraldi, "The Veto from Hell," AntiWar.com, 24 Feb 2011.

[295] Jo Dillon, "Dalyell Attacks 'Jewish Cabal,'" *The Independent* (UK), 4 May 2003.

Israeli control over the U.S. government and its policies is hardly controversial. It is simply a known fact. Several more short quotes show the range of the problem:

* "To criticize (the Israeli government) is to be immediately dubbed anti-Semitic....People are scared in this country (the U.S.) to say wrong is wrong, because the Jewish Lobby is powerful—very powerful."[296]

* Israeli Foreign Minister Ilan Baruch quits his post because "Israel's foreign policy is wrong and (is turning) Israel into a pariah state." He also says, "Claims of anti-Semitism are simplistic and artificial."[297]

* "The Israeli Prime Minister has a lot more influence over the foreign policy of the United States in the Middle East than he has in his own country."[298]

Attack on the "USS *Liberty*"

The assault on the USS *Liberty* by unmarked Israeli aircraft and torpedo boats in international waters on 8 June 1967—probably to blame Egypt or Syria—kills thirty-four seamen and marines. (Israel favors false-flag operations to trick others into fighting its enemies.) Napalm is dropped and our sailors are machine-gunned in the water. It remains, "The only maritime incident in U.S. history where (U.S.) military forces were killed that was never investigated by Congress."[299] How can this be?

---

[296] Archbishop of Capetown, Desmond Tutu. "Apartheid in the Holy Land." Speech in Boston, MA, quoted in the *Guardian* (UK), 29 April 2002. (Tutu is a strong supporter of Israel and Zionism.)

[297] *Israel News* (Ynet). 2 March 2011.

[298] Congressman Paul Findley (R-Illinois). *They Dare to Speak Out* (1985), p. 92.

[299] Charles K. Ebinger, "The Attack on the USS *Liberty*: Lesson for U.S. National Security," Brookings Institution, 8 June 2010.

Admiral Thomas H. Moorer, chief of naval operations and chairman, Joint Chiefs of Staff, states, "I've never seen a President...stand up to them (the Israelis). If the American people understood what grip these people have on our government, they would rise up in arms."[300]

The Lavon Affair. Israeli intel cells enter Egypt and bomb the American Embassy, American School, and the U.S. Consulate Library in Cairo. They leave behind "evidence" implicating Muslims as the culprits. A firebomb detonates in the pants of one Jew, but he lives to I.D. his fellow terrorists and their plot. Most members of this cell are caught and commit suicide. Two are hanged. Israel denies involvement for 51 years, saying it is an "anti-Semitic conspiracy," until deciding to honor the three survivors in 2005. Many Jews call it "Esek HaBish" (the Mishap). Pinhas Lavon, Israeli Defense Minister, calls it "Operation Susannah." (The signal to set off the explosives is the playing of this American song on the radio).

"Cognitive Dissonance"[301]

Marxist-Islamist terror organization Mujahedin-e Khalq (MEK) attempts to assassinate USAF Major General Harold Price and kills Colonel Lewis L. Hawkins, Colonel Paul Schafer, Colonel Jack Turner and other Americans. They attempt to kill President Richard Nixon and kidnap the ambassador to Iran, Douglas MacArthur II.[302]

"Obama administration officials leaked to NBC that Israel had teamed up with a violent cultish, U.S.-terror organization called the Mujahedin-e Khalq to assassinate Iranian scientists."[303]

American neo-cons in Congress, a four-star general, a former intel chief, U.S. governors, and others receive thousands of dollars from MEK

---

[300] "Betrayal Behind Israeli Attack on USS *Liberty*." Interview by Paul Findley, 24 August 1983, *They Dare to Speak Out* (1985), p. 161.

[301] Inability to accept evidence that your core beliefs are wrong.

[302] "Mujahedin-e Khalq Resource Page," quoting 31 May 1980 issue of *The Mojahid* (and) Manda Z. Ervin, "MEK Is Not Part of the Iranian Opposition," *Pajamas Media*, 20 January 2011.

[303] Trita Parsi, "Is Israel Flirting with Iranian Terrorists?" *Open Zion*, 15 May 2012.

to remove them from the U.S. terror list.[304] This is "material support for terrorist groups"—a felony. [One wonders what our Justice *[sic]* Department actually does? They clearly support terrorist groups.] The Joint Special Operations Command (JSOC) conducts training for MEK at the Department of Energy's Nevada National Security site, 65 miles northwest of Las Vegas[305] (a nuclear site which authorizes guards to shoot trespassers). The Mossad also trains MEK.

Anti-Semitic? No—ANTI-AMERICAN!

Frummer Friends

Israel is a religious and a Socialist state. As individuals, Jews can be delightful companions; as a group, they often become involved in intrigue and subversion of the states where they reside. They can be found behind the scenes whispering in the ear of the prince. Their loyalties lie with family and Halakhah, the collective body of Jewish law, not the nation that shelters them. Other people resent this. It has resulted in Jewish diaspora over the centuries.

Jerusalem is the crossroads of complicated cultures remembering slights dating back several thousand years. The easily-cheated pilgrims of three faiths will never reconcile their differences. "All men are holy here, and there is nothing more irritating than a neighbor, equally holy, of a different faith."[306]

My experience is that most Arabs do not hate Jews or Americans. They hate our government for invading their lands and killing their people. They see the U.S. enforcing U.N. resolutions that result in armed aggression against them; then see us block more than sixty U.N. resolutions directed against Israel to cease slaughtering Arab civilians and stealing their lands.

Proof exists that Islamic "terrorist groups" and plots are largely manufactured to create a security state and the destruction of American

---

[304] Scott Peterson. "Iranian Group's Big-Money Push to Get Off US Terrorist List," *Christian Science Monitor*, 8 August 2011.

[305] Seymour M. Hersh, "Our Men In Iran," *The New Yorker*, 6 April 2012.

[306] William L. Dietrich, *The Rosetta Key* (2008), p. 23.

rights: NOT A SINGLE NEO-CON OR ARCHITECT OF THE WAR AGAINST MUSLIMS is assassinated! Surely, a sophisticated terrorist group that executes a complex 9-11 attack is able to kill a few unguarded former Bush administration officials, poison our reservoirs, or car-bomb a shopping mall or airport.

Americans do not read *Haaretz* or *Al Jazeera*; they only watch the Likud/Fox News version of events. There are many good Jews and good Muslims. You will not discover this, however, from the U.S. media. (Can you trust those who label the truth as "hate speech"?)

One instructor at the Intel School at Fort Huachuca begins his lesson: "U.S. and Israeli officials—or do I repeat myself..." (Okay—It is I). Especially laughable is the television program *NCIS,* where a female Mossad agent (Ziva David), assigned to a Kidon (assassination and sabotage) unit, becomes a U.S. naval agent. (Speaking of the fox in the chicken coup.) This gives Americans a distorted view of the conflict between our criminal investigation and intelligence units and those of our adversary, Israel. And why does the U.S. not spy on Israel?

I have frummer friends. When Jews meet, they often ask, "Are you frum or frei?" "Frum" is Yiddish for being committed to observance of the 613 Mitzvot (Commandments). The Mitzvot are principles of law, ethics, and religion. (*Mitzvah* is singular; *mitzvot* plural.) Some apply just to men, to women, and a few (twenty-six) just within Israel. If you wear a *kippa* (*yarmulke*), keep *shabbos*, kosher, etc., you are probably *frum*, not *frei* ("free" from keeping the ancient Commandments). I have assisted my Jewish neighbors as a *shabbos goy* (i.e., a non-Jew performing tasks prohibited to them on the Sabbath).

Teachings of the Talmud

Both Judaism and Islam are comprehensive Semitic legal systems as much as religions. The teachings of the Talmud are the glue holding together the Jews of different origins. The *Artscroll Schottenstein Talmud Bavli* (English/Aramaic; 73 volumes, over five million words) is massive.

Some modern works are cleansed of ugly verses, but Talmudic Law "is absolutely united in its hostility to all non-Jewish peoples."[307]

Rabbi Isidore Epstein labors over fifteen years to edit the first complete English translations of the Babylonian Talmud (*Talmud Bavli*) in 1938.[308] Few Christians know it exists. For a glimpse, click on Folio 57a of Tractate (book) "Gittin (a legal document)," under the heading "Seder Nashim (Woman)." Also, see Sanhedrin (Higher Courts of Law) 79b. (Some on-line translations omit these paragraphs so as to not alarm Gentiles.)

This may be enlightening to Christian fundamentalists who believe in Armageddon or that God stands behind Israel. A Jewish God has another fate in store for Jesus and His followers.

"Joshua Fit de Battle of Jericho"

Reading the book of Joshua (probably written in the late 1300s BC) provides a clue to the current genocide of the Palestinians. "Joshua" continues the story of the Israelites after their Exodus from Egypt. It describes the conquest and destruction of the Amorite and Moabite peoples, the annihilation of Jericho, and the ethnic cleansing of the seven peoples of Canaan—the original Palestinians. Still up to their old tricks.

Israel demands the destruction of Iran. The book of Esther (*Megillat Esther*) in the Hebrew Bible tells a story of palace intrigue and genocide thwarted by the Jewish Queen of Persia. The Caliph's evil Vizier, Haman, is hanged, along with his ten sons. The Jews then slaughter the Persians. Many Persians convert to Judaism because of the "fear of the Jews" who "slew of their foes seventy and five thousand" (Esther 9:16, King James Bible). The Feast of Purim still commemorates this massacre. (The computer worm

---

[307] F. Roderich-Stoltheim, *The Riddle of the Jew's Success* (1927), pp. 221–222. [The author's real name is Theodor Fritsch (1852–1933), a German political scientist. Amazon.com and other book sellers have banned a recent "Noontide Press" reprint as it deals with the centralization of the German economy in Jewish hands before the rise of Hitler.] And you thought only those nasty Nazis burned books.

[308] Rabbi Dr. Isidore Epstein (Ed.) (president of Jews College, London). "Come and Hear," *The BabylonianTalmud* (1938). Internet version of 1431 folios. (Click on Index in Table of Contents to see into which pot of bodily fluids you will be boiled-in for eternity.)

"Stuxnet" is discovered by Iranians because the Mossad cannot resist coding in the name "Esther.")

Cyrus the Great overthrows Babylonia and allows the Jews to practice their religion and return to their homeland (537 BC). Darius the Great succeeds him and completes building the Second Temple (515 BC). What have the Jews ever done for the Persians/Iranians in appreciation for these great gifts—other than demand their destruction? Iranians have not attacked another country in the centuries since Thermopylae. How about Israel in just the last decade?

Tony Kushner, playwright, has his honorary degree from City University blocked because he criticizes Israeli treatment of the Palestinians.[309] These petty and vindictive things take place in prewar Germany until the Germans have enough of it. "Kristallnacht" erupts when illegal immigrant, Polish Jew Herschel Grynszpan, shoots Ernst Vom Rath, a German diplomat in Paris who is attempting to assist him.[310] (It does not escape the Germans that their Communist enemies: Marx, Lenin, Trotsky, Stalin, and most Soviet Commissars are Jewish.)

It never occurs to Jews they may, themselves, be the cause of their opposition over the centuries. They are always the victims; always right and never wrong. They are the "Chosen of God" and first users of the term "Master Race." (Read Rabbi Mendel Schneerson, friend of Bush, Sr., for Jews as a "superior Master Race....A non-Jewish soul comes from three satanic spheres," etc.)

When Jewish terrorists (including three future prime ministers of Israel) are blowing up British hotels and restaurants and torturing to death British police officers, these countries do not make revenge attacks against Jewish civilians. Yet when Palestinians attack Israeli military outposts, Israelis bomb and shoot hundreds of Palestinian civilians. "Collective punishment" remains a popular Israeli war crime.

---

[309] Sharon Otterman, "Protests Over Blocking Honorary Degree," *Seattle Times*, 6 May 2011, p. A-20.

[310] "Kristallnacht: A Nationwide Pogrom, November 9–10, 1938." *Holocaust Encyclopedia*. U.S. Holocaust Memorial Museum, Washington, D.C.

Palestine is surrounded by a 26-feet high, 470-mile concrete and steel wall. Israelis call it the *"Hafrada"* (separation) wall. It turns all of Palestine into a concentration camp.

Israeli Labor Camps

Israel builds "labor camps" for the "internment of undesirables."[311] Reuters (11 June 2012) and others report the rounding up of African migrants as they "threaten the Jewish character of the state." The *Telegraph* (U.K.) and others report (11 January 2013) rioting against blacks across Israel, where they are beaten and their homes and businesses burned. This is the equivalent of the U.S. demanding the round-up and deportation of blacks as they threaten our racial makeup! And not a word of this in the major U.S. media. Why?

Killing for Women's Rights[312]

As to Israeli "freedoms" compared with nearby Arab countries who demean women: "The powerful Orthodox community is compelling women to sit separately in the back of buses…and use separate sidewalks on one side of the street…women are compelled to swathe their bodies in garments that reveal nothing but faces and hands….An 8-year-old girl is spat upon in the street because her clothes are not 'modest' enough."[313]

Women cannot testify in rabbinical courts, which handle all divorces. There is no affirmative action in Israel. Yet Jewish women lead the feminist movement in the U.S.: Lillian Wald, Ernestine Rose, Maud Nathan, Bettye (Goldstein) Friedan, Gloria Steinem, Bella Abzug, and others.

---

[311] Jason Ditz, "Israeli MP Calls for Sending All Human Rights Activists to Work Camps," Anti-War.com, 31 May 2012 (and) Dana Weller-Pokak, "Israel Proposes Work Camps for Illegal Immigrants," *Haaretz*, 5 November 2009. "Blacks in Israel Under Sustained Violent Attacks," *Atlanta Black Star*, 5 June 2012 and 11 January 2013.

[312] The Pentagon and First Lady, Laura Bush, reframe the Afghanistan war from revenge to "women's rights" to justify invasion. Madeleine Bunting. "Can the Spread of Women's Rights Ever Be Accompanied by War?" *The Guardian*, 2 October 2011.

[313] Uri Avnery, "Shukran ('Thanks'), Israel," *Gush Shlom*, 31 December 2011.

Ethnic Cleansing

Zionist author and columnist Benny Morris states, "There are circumstances in history that justify ethnic cleansing."[314] (He is referring to Palestinians, not Jews.) "It was necessary to cleanse the hinterland…and the villages." Any discussion of the holocaust is incomplete without Jewish quotes as this one—and they are numerous!

Holocaust Denial

The *shoah* (Hebrew: "disaster") is a hot subject that is not allowed to be debated—and is actually criminalized. Genuine historical research on the "holocaust" is labeled "revisionism" or simply "anti-Semitic," without regard for the evidence and truth.

A number of Jews [as Norman G. Finkelstein, *The Holocaust Industry* (2000)] describe the *shoah* as a tool to extort German and Swiss banks and governments for endless reparations—money which does not get to the camp survivors or their heirs. Others point to evidence the "concentration camps" are labor camps and note that famous Nazi-hunter Simon Wiesenthal's claims to survive *thirteen death camps*[315] appear highly exaggerated. (Just how does one survive thirteen "death camps"?)

Stanislaw Ryniak, the first person imprisoned in the Nazi "death camp" at Auschwitz in 1940, dies in 2004. He is liberated in May 1945 and is eighty-eight at his death! How is he overlooked? "Arbeit Macht Frei?"

Few deny that many Jews (and other "undesirables") are murdered in Nazi Germany, but at issue are the exaggerations, scams, and Israeli/Jewish embrace of the very atrocities committed against them. Why are Jews not leading the world in human rights by example and effort? "Never again!" they shout, with their boots upon the necks of their

---

[314] Daniel Levy, "Of Herrings and Elephants: Benny Morris and 'Palestinian Rejectionism,'" *Open Zion* (The Daily Beast), 16 April 2012. Quoting Morris from a 2004 interview with *Haaretz*.

[315] Hella Pick, Simon Wiesenthal (1996) and *Seattle Times Parade Magazine*, 29 February 2004, p. 17.

neighbors. Isn't this the very conduct that has caused them difficulties through the ages?

Why would Germans bother to tattoo numbers on the arms of those they soon intend to kill? How do the thousands of survivors live long enough to become 'living skeletons'? (German civilians, not in camps, are also starving to death by the thousands.)

What do Auscshwitz camp records, once thought destroyed by invading Soviets, tell us about the numbers of inmates? Why have they not been released since the Soviets make them available to the Red Cross in 1989? "The Institute for Historical Review"—called by some a "Holocaust denial organization"—sends a team to review them in 1995. These records show rosters of sick people over extended periods—who are not executed. Hundreds of inmates are actually released. There are few shipments of the coke necessary to run crematoriums—it appears used to manufacture fuel and munitions for the military.

Documents confirming gas chamber killings or an extermination program would be long ago used by the Soviets to discredit their Nazi enemies. The "Cleveland Indy Media Center," out of Seattle, publishes "Auschwitz Death Certificates" in March 2007. Although some are missing, a total of 68,864 deceased individuals are listed; fewer than half are Jewish.

These questions and others are legitimate subjects of historical inquiry and research. Unless uncovering the truth is to be avoided at all costs.

Eisenhower's Crusade in Europe (1948), Churchill's six-volume Second World War (1948-54), and de Gaulle's three-volume Memoires de guerre (1954-59) do not mention Nazi gas chambers, a genocide of Jews, or of "six million" Jewish victims. A most curious omission, as all three are known to dislike Germans....

A discussion of these issues is beyond this work, except to point out that Jews are successful in getting such questioning declared unlawful in countries without a First Amendment. Many in Western European nations and in Canada are jailed—for years—for questioning the subject.[316] If

---

[316] Ernst Zundel, German citizen living in Canada for forty years, serves five years for "inciting racial hatred" through holocaust denial. Larry Keller, *Hatewatch* ("Keeping an Eye on the Radical Right"), 4 March 2010.

someone does not buy your view of history, and you jail him for it, just who has committed the "hate crime"?

Is discussing the "holocaust" the modern equivalent of imprisoning Nicolaus Copernicus for life because his explanation of planetary movement contradicts the beliefs of those controlling the populace? The uncomfortable truth of legalized bigotry somehow escapes the attention of those who profit from it.

One idea is central: Something, if factual, does not need criminal laws to defend it. "Free speech" is intended to protect unpopular speech. The truth, however unpopular, needs no protection!

The Jews learn many things from the Nazis. Perhaps Conservative columnist Charley Reese says it best: "The Israelis learned from the Holocaust that it is better to be like the Germans than to be like the Jews."[317] Knesset member Uri Avnery points out the Israeli government is "undemocratic" and includes "openly fascist elements."[318]

NOTE: During the German-Soviet invasion of Poland, German General Heinz Guderian and Jewish-Soviet General Semyon Krivishkin jointly review their tank units at Brest-Litovsk. As with photographs of Jewish soldiers in German uniforms, it is a picture "organized Jewry prefers to forget."[319]

The Jewish community "sees everyone outside the community as a potential enemy....Jews have prayed to God for centuries, year on year, on Pesach eve: 'Pour your wrath upon the goyim....'"[320]

Rabbi Oradia Yosef, head of the Shas' Party "Council of Torah Sages," declares, "Goyim were born only to serve us, without that, they have no

---

[317] Reese, *Conservative Chronicle*, 1 August 2001 (Vol. 16, No. 31), p. 28.

[318] Avnery (Self-described, "Witness to the collapse of German democracy"). "Weimar Revisited," *Media Monitors Network*, 18 November 2011.

[319] As many as 150,000 Jews serve Hitler in uniform! Bryan Mark Rigg, *Hitler's Jewish Soldiers* (2004). Rigg identifies himself as Jewish and serves in the Israeli army and USMC.

[320] Avnery, "The Second Herzl," *Media Monitors Network*, 14 October 2011. Theodor Herzl is the Hungarian founder of Zionism and the "Zionist World Congress" in 1897.

place in the world—Only to serve the people of Israel."[321] (I'm crossing Yosef off my Christmas card list.)

I confess to being somewhat uncomfortable writing this chapter. The fear of condemnation keeps many from speaking about things that need to be said—especially regarding a country that regularly attacks America and has a stranglehold on both political parties. I refuse to allow "sensitivity" to overrule free discussion and common sense. Why is vilifying Muslims "free speech" but insulting Jews "hate speech"? These are things we are not supposed to discuss. When Carl Cameron of Fox News reported (December 2001) that Israeli spies filming the 9-11 attacks were arrested and deported, the story sank like a stone. How did the Israelis know to be there?

Former CIA station chief Philip Giraldi writes ("It Is All About Israel," 17 January 2013), "Every nominee to a senior defense, intelligence, or security council position must be vetted and judged by whether or not they are completely committed to support the Israeli government, no matter what it does and no matter what the impact would be on American interests." Which country do you support? "Both" is not an option, especially for those of us in the military.

Myopic Americans unable to see the source of our disastrous foreign policy are deserving of its consequences. Why are we not outraged when presidential and congressional candidates say they will obey and support a foreign state over the interests of America? Those Americans who believe Israel is a "friend" have a lot of explaining to do....

---

[321] Johah Mandel, "Yosef: Gentiles Exist Only to Serve Jews," *The Jerusalem Post*, 18 October 2010.

Chapter XXXII

SUZIE'S GOT A GUN

"Pay No Attention to the Man Behind the Curtain!"
— *Wizard of Oz* (1939)

The "Man Behind the Curtain" in L.A. is Thomas J. Bradley, a former lieutenant in Wilshire Division who is active in politics while on the job. His California Democratic Council, a group of largely West-end liberal, white Jews, supports him through five terms as mayor. This puts him in open conflict with poor all-black areas.

Bradley implements his first "Affirmative Action" program in 1973, the year I transfer to the Police Commission. It is intended to bring blacks and women on the LAPD in balance with their percentage of the population—then about 18 percent black. Its preferential treatment, lowered standards, and quotas create a backlash that demoralizes the department. "Affirmative Action" becomes code for "discrimination and unfairness."

An "Affirmative Action Cultural Awareness" course is implemented in city hall for us middle managers. Opposition comes from black officers who (correctly) foresee that lowered standards will adversely impact them. They come on the job with the same qualifications as the rest of us, but cut-off dates are soon forgotten and everyone assumes they, too, are Affirmative Action hires, recruited in the apparent belief that blacks cannot succeed unless standards are adjusted for race.

Crime escalates and it is discovered that over 9,000 current officers are making 100,000 fewer arrests a year than are the 5,500 of us a few years earlier. There are several reasons for this. But, first, it is helpful to note the background leading to this conflict.

Discrimination, Prejudice, and Slavery

Discrimination. Discrimination is not a crime in my youth. We laud a man for discriminating tastes. "Discrimination" involves making choices: eat a hamburger and you discriminate against a chicken sandwich.

Marry and you discriminate against other potential partners. Discrimination based upon color is wrong; discrimination based upon behavior is called the law.

Prejudice. "Prejudice" is prejudgment. It refers to irrational judgments formed without consideration of available information or contrary to observations of reality. Judgments made in willful ignorance of available facts are in themselves prejudiced. To make observations about group behavior and characteristics—realizing there can be exceptions—allows us to make decisions without becoming paralyzed for fear of being "prejudiced."

Many stereotypes are the distilled wisdom of the empirical judgments of millions of people and represent valid inductive inference. To say, for example, "Most Irishmen are drunks," is to say—with the doomed enthusiasm of a child trying to fly—that drunkenness is substantially higher among the Irish.[322]

Diversity. One definition of nation is, "a people who share common customs, origins, history, and frequently language."[323] Diversity divides and destroys a nation. The parable of the Tower of Babel in the book of Genesis explains the multiplicity of languages. God intentionally confuses the common language of the time to force people apart so as to create new countries and separate societies—the very opposite idea central to American diversity.

Humans are tribal; too many tribes and you lose your nation. The heads of Germany, France, and Great Britain recently denounce multiculturalism as disastrous for their countries.

---

[322] "Ireland has a strikingly high prevalence of binge drinking and alcohol-related harm." Mats Ramstedt and Ann Hope (National Alcohol Policy Advisor, Dublin), *The Irish Drinking Culture* (2004), p. 10.

[323] "The Free Dictionary," taken from *The American Heritage Dictionary of the English Language*, Fourth Edition (2004).

Minorities

Blacks, the most obvious minority, are perhaps the most sensitive and demanding. In my lifetime, they insist on being called colored, Negro, African-American, then black.[324]

Barak H. Obama, in *Dreams from My Father* (1995), displays his ignorance of slavery in quotations as of white men going to Africa to "drag away the conquered in chains."[325]

Africa is ruled by Africans in the era of the Atlantic Slave Trade. Blacks sell slaves to whites. Conquest of Africa must wait until Europeans find how to survive lethal African diseases. Europeans enslave other Europeans centuries before the first African is brought in bondage to the Western Hemisphere.

Slavery

Noah curses the descendants of his black son, Ham, with servitude (Genesis 9:18–27). The division of humankind into three major races is related to tales of Noah's sons repopulating the earth after the Deluge. Southern whites use this to justify slavery.[326] An estimated 12 million Africans come to the Americas as slaves from 1492 to 1888 ("Black People," Wikipedia). Their descendants now number over 150 million.

The patriarchal nature of Arab society and the Koran permit sexual relations with slaves, and many mixed-race children result. The child is born free and given rights of inheritance. The term *"abd"* (as in Abdullah—

---

[324] Many Asian and African words to describe whites use their words for "ghost": Cantonese (phonetic) *"guey-lo"* (evil spirit people); Mandarin *"yang-guey tzu"* (foreign devil) or *"hong mao guey-ze"* (red fur devil—my wife's name for me when my hair was still red). Chinese funerary colors are white, not black. Chinese words towards Japanese and Koreans are even more colorful. Japanese "self-defense forces" translates as *"zi wei dui"* ("self-comforting forces" as in "masturbation").

[325] Quoted in Dr. Thomas Sowell, "Obama's Dreams," LewRockwell.com, 4 September 2012.

[326] Felicia R. Lee, "Noah's Curse is Slavery's Rationale, Race-matters.com, 1 November 2003.

"Servant of God") means "slave" and remains a common term for blacks in the Middle East.

Blacks, enslaved across cultures, have given modern ones an inferiority complex. A black is now in the White House and Oprah Winfrey is once the world's only black billionaire. (One wonders what their lives would be like had they or their ancestors remained in Africa?)

"The American colonies were mostly peopled with indentured servants."[327] Some indentured servants are volunteers on four to seven-year contracts. Most are slaves: "Children and adults seized by force, packed into ships tightly and, every two weeks given an allowance of bread." [328] Indentured servants could not vote, marry, travel, leave their houses, or buy or sell anything….Females were often raped by their master without legal recourse. They were whipped and beaten and put to work in the fields of Virginia and Maryland under the grueling hot summer sun….The large number of servants who ran away or committed suicide suggests that the conditions of life may not have been so different for servant or slave. (These references are to white people, not black.)

The European ancestors of many Americans are slaves: "Dublin, one of the largest Viking centers in the British Isles, became a major European slave trading center, where, historians estimate, tens of thousands of kidnapped Irishmen, Scotsmen, Anglo-Saxons, and others were bought and sold."[329]

Anglo-Saxons conquer Britain from the fifth century AD through the Norman invasion. "The laws of King Ine of Wessex (West Saxony) specify six social levels for Britons, five of which refer to slaves."[330] The very word "slav" means slave. Slavs are the most numerous ethnic and linguistic body in Europe. Asian coolies are similarly kidnapped and enslaved in the Pacific

---

[327] John Crandall, "Indentured Servants; Settling Early America," *American History*, by Suite 101, 27 August 2007.

[328] "Indentured Servant's Experiences, 1600–1700." Multicultural Activities for the American History Classroom. *Teacher Vision*, 2010.

[329] David Keys, "A Viking Mystery," *Smithsonian*, October 2010 (Vol. 41, No. 6), p. 66.

[330] Mathias Schulz, "Britain Is More Germanic Than It Thinks," *Spiegel International*, 21 June 2011.

trade and die in huge numbers. Slavery remains a problem in much of the world to this day.

So why are immense entitlements given to blacks because they are "oppressed" centuries before? Do any blacks in the States have lash marks on their backs? Have they forgotten the nation that sacrificed 650,000 dead in a war to (in part) eliminate slavery? Have they heard of the Thirteenth Amendment?

Affirmative Action Wonders

Changes to police applicant qualifications and consent decrees are not greeted with the expected enthusiasm by the rank and file. Considerable resistance is generated by field sergeants and watch commanders—those who oversee field performance. These "complainers" are ordered to be "identified and counseled" on their six-month "Performance Evaluation Reports."

Qualifications. The college entrance examination is tossed out in favor of a simple pass/fail written. A five-foot (five eight to six eight in my time) height requirement is abolished so "little people" can be hired. "Midget" (a term now considered offensive by those with dwarfism) means a short person with body proportions similar to other humans. The issue, of course, is the ability (or inability) to perform the job.

The "Physical Abilities Test" degenerates into the following:[331]

* Stability Platform (Balance). Ten seconds of balancing on a seesaw.

* Side-Step (Agility). Ten seconds of stepping back and forth across a line.

* Cable Pull (Strength). A five-second cable pull. Perform three times.

* Stationary Bicycle (Endurance). Two minutes of stationary bicycling.

---

[331] Sergeant Mike Arminio (Rampart Division), "Do We Really Need to Measure Up?" *Thin Blue Line*, April 1997 (Vol. 52, No. 4), p. 55.

The psych exam is tossed, but reinstated a few years later when it is discovered that psychopaths and killers-for-hire are joining. (One might be surprised to learn how many applicants answer the question, "Why do you wish to become a police officer?," with variations of, "I like to hurt people!") Background investigations no longer disqualify many drug users and various criminals, including some arrested-but-not-convicted felons and gang members.

LAPD recruiting decisions are prioritized for diversity and gender goals. Women and minorities gain entrance into the next academy class by scoring 70 or better on their oral exams. A Caucasian male must score close to 100 or higher (possible because of a 10-point veteran's credit). Many otherwise well-qualified men lose their careers because of this discrimination. Good officers are still hired, but it is *in spite of* rather than *because of* these unfair practices.

The "Academy ceases being a stressful experience designed to 'de-select' recruits and becomes a kinder and gentler program designed to graduate as many people as possible."[332]

Officers recently off probation are given choice assignments to specialized units previously requiring five or more years of varied experience. Less-experienced police officers lead to less-experienced supervisors. "Red flags" of improper conduct and procedures go unnoticed. This causes a "cauldron of corruption…that has boiled over and scalded this once magnificent police department."[333]

Deputy Chief Stephen Downing writes of LAPD going "full-cycle in corruption" with the elimination of selection standards: "The result: *3,600 police officers, including Rafael Perez, David Mack, and others of their ilk, meet the new, marginal character standards, make it thorough the accelerated hiring process, and graduate from the police academy to the streets of Los Angeles, armed with a badge and a gun….Perez fails their (Chino PD) background investigation while Mack becomes a bank robber.*"[334]

---

[332] Bob Baker, "The Decline of LAPD!" *Thin Blue Line*, July 2000 (Vol. 55, No. 7), p. 6.

[333] Ibid.

[334] Stephen M. Downing, "Reasons for Police Corruption," *Los Angeles Fire and Police Association Newsletter*," Spring 2000, pp. 14–15.

Steve, a friend and fellow policeman in Planning and Research Division, also notes the following: "The Rampart scandal is about the corruption of well intentioned affirmative action programs. It is about a dangerous numbers game and quota system brought to us by the DOJ in the form of a consent decree in the early 1980s."[335]

100,000 Fewer Arrests

"It was vexing and surprising to learn that the LAPD is now making 100,000 fewer arrests, issuing over 200,000 fewer citations, and conducting over 20,000 fewer field interviews per year," writes Mayor Richard Riordan to the Police Commission.[336]

This is because of three changes: women in law enforcement, a race-based disciplinary system, and work slowdowns in response to a lack of public support in the Rodney King incident leading to the second (1992) Watts Riots.

Assistant Chief Bayan Lewis tells the Police Commission, "Officers are afraid of confronting suspects—a fear that has bred a new, divisive definition of police work, 'driving and waving' (waving back and continuing on—to a citizen desperately waving for the help of a passing police car)… (this follows) the Rodney King incident (and) indictments of the officers, the attacks in the press, and the political pressure."[337]

The department blames "community policing" for less emphasis upon enforcement. This is disputed by Criminologist James Q. Wilson who notes that additional measures of productivity are also dramatically down. Field interviews, expected to increase under community policing, fall by over 172,000.[338] Officers riding about in their black-and-whites are taking

---

[335] Downing, Letter to the Editor, *Thin Blue Line*, November 2000 (Vol. 55, No. 11), p. 15.

[336] Jim Newton, "Riordan Orders Report on Plunge in LAPD Arrests," *Los Angeles Times*, 13 March 1996, pp. B-1 and B-3. See also, Attorney Gary Ingemunson, "Warning Bells," *Thin Blue Line*, July 2005 (Vol. 60, No. 7), p. 13 (and) Roger Director, "City of Angels—The Barney Wave," *Los Angeles*, May 1996 (Vol. 41, No. 5), p. 17.

[337] Jim Newton, "LAPD Admits It's Less Assertive," *Los Angeles Times*, 29 January 1997.

[338] Ibid.

inordinate amounts of time off the air to write reports. One officer tells me, "You don't get complaints if you don't contact anyone. If the public won't back us, why should we back them?"

"Although I had arrested thousands of career criminals, junkies, felons, and drunks before 1994, I successfully avoided criminal suspects and arrested no one between 1992 until I retired in 2000....As far as I was concerned, L.A.'s residents would get the gangs, crime, and declining quality of life they deserved....I smiled, waved, and became the model of the new LAPD—an all-American patriot who did everything except the job he was sworn to do."[339]

Escalation of Force

The "Escalation of Force Continuum" is taught early in the Academy:

1. Physical/Uniformed Presence,
2. Verbalization,
3. Pain Compliance Holds,
4. Control Holds[340]: Bar Arm, Carotid, Chancery, and Front Headlock,
5. Baton,
6. Deadly Force.

NOTE: By the time of the Rodney King incident in 1991, levels 3 and 4 are replaced with: "3. Swarming" and 4. TASER ('Tom A. Swift Electric Rifle')." The baton changes from a straight hickory stick to a metal or plastic "side-handle" Monadnock model (which is believed will minimize head injuries and lawsuits—as it is swung sideways with less force).

---

[339] Clark W. Baker, "Ex Liberal in Hollywood" Blog, 20 May 2005 (Updated 25 July 2011).
[340] Chief Edward M. Davis, *Training Bulletins*: Vol. IV, Issues 16, 17, and 18 of 31 July 1972; "Control Holds, Parts I, II, and III." Pp. 6.

Women in Law Enforcement

Most females lack the size and upper body strength of males. The fire department complains women cannot drag victims from fires or carry hose up ladders. The police department sees women escalating directly from verbal to deadly force, as they lack the strength to confront violent offenders or those who simply resist capture. This results in more shootings and increased lawsuits (which are not publicized, as such politically incorrect commentary endangers jobs and promotions).

It is known by almost every officer that women are more likely to shoot a citizen than is a policeman. They simply perceive threats and run out of options in situations men do not consider threatening.

Women are often hesitant to grab a suspect and take him down to the ground to control him. (Females rarely engage in contact sports in school and are reluctant to do battle with violent suspects.) They make fewer arrests and wait longer for backup of male officers while the situation escalates. Part of this problem is that the department (i.e., Mayor Bradley and his Police Commission) eliminates the control-holds portion of the force continuum.

There is no "nice" way to arrest a dangerous and combative suspect. Swift, aggressive, and violent action is sometimes required. A suspect, confronted by a small female and realizing she cannot hurt him, resists.

A Bowie County, Texas, female deputy is overpowered by an inmate in the courthouse and killed with her own gun (18 April 2011). A prisoner in the chapel of the Monroe Correctional Complex, Washington, strangles to death a five-foot-three-inch female deputy (from the front) on 29 January 2011. She bites and scratches her attacker, but this fails to deter him. Governor Christine Gregoire's solution: hire thirty-seven more guards and counselors (mostly female), install more panic alarms, and buy more pepper spray.[341] (Cost: $11 million a year.) No thought to simply hiring physically capable guards and not mixing genders in jails.

Femi-Nazi and NOW (National Organization for Women) Gangs. "The consensus of opinion *[sic]* is that women not only can do the job of policing

---

[341] "Prison-Guard Bill Will Add $11M. to State Budget," *Seattle Times*, 26 March 2011, p. B-9.

equally as well as men, but in fact hold the key for substantially decreasing police violence and its cost to taxpayers...physical strength has never been shown to be related to public functioning."[342]

A sensible approach to hiring female police officers is to accept those meeting the time-tested qualifications for the job. Instead, equal outcomes—numbers wearing the uniform without consideration for an ability to accomplish the basic job—become the standard. Do away with qualifications and hire by gender and race... Then sue the taxpayers when the results of your folly get people injured and killed.

The struggle of pioneer policewomen to gain a foothold in Los Angeles is described by Professor Janis Appier.[343] LAPD has, in fact, been too tough on women in some instances. Captain James McDowell states, "The State should pass a law prohibiting women driving automobiles....Twenty per cent of the automobile drivers in this city are women...and over 30 per cent of the accident fatalities are due to them."[344] (This must mean, conversely, that 80 percent of drivers are men who kill 70 percent of the victims.)

God Is a Woman

Legend is that when L.A. evangelist Aimee Semple McPherson dies in 1944, she is buried with a connected telephone so as to alert the world to her resurrection.[345] So maybe feminists are right and God IS a woman. (This explains a lot.)

---

[342] "Police Use of Excessive Force: Taking Gender into Account." Report by: The National Center for Women and Policing, Division of the Feminist Majority Foundation, June 1999, 8 pp.

[343] Appier, *Policing Women—The Sexual Politics of Law Enforcement and the LAPD* (1998), Philadelphia, 227 pp.

[344] "Auto Deaths Set New Records. Traffic Chief Would Bar Women Drivers...Los Angeles Now Leads in Killings," *Los Angeles Times*, 23 February 1920, front page.

[345] Ted Gup, "The Last Page," *Smithsonian*, October 2010 (Vol. 41, No. 6), p. 100. McPherson rests in a large flat marble monument on the "Sunrise Slope" below the Great Mausoleum, Glendale Forest Lawn. (Find-a-Grave Memorial #700).

Women can be tough. A female detective is convicted of gunning down the girlfriend of her ex-boyfriend.[346] Gladys Ingles, member of the barnstorming troupe, "The Thirteen Black Cats," is seen in a 1920s film "rescuing" a Curtiss JN-4 "Jenny" biplane over L.A. that has lost a wheel.[347] She climbs the top wing, spare wheel strapped to her back, and leaps to a second disabled biplane. She assembles the wheel within several feet of the spinning prop. All without a parachute or safety straps!

"When Adele Freeman fired five .38-caliber bullets into her boyfriend in 2000, she contributed to an often-overlooked statistic—more than one-third of all homicides each year connected to domestic violence are perpetrated by women."[348] There is also the woman who murders, cooks, and eats her husband.[349]

"Two high-explosive bombs wrecked a part of the (department store), collapsing a section of the ground floor. An oil-container bomb set fire to the debris....11 bodies. Hundreds of women hopped over hose lines and detoured around wreckage...elbowing to buy perfume and cosmetics (about to be) hit by a new sales tax, while firemen and air raid rescue squads dug through tons of debris to save 200 people trapped in the (burning) store's basement."[350]

A friend in the Royal Thai Border Patrol Police sends me an interesting clipping on their problems with policewomen. Two hundred BP women are deployed to confront the (largely) female Peoples' Alliance for Democracy (the "Dharma Army") marching on government house in the Big Mango.[351]

---

[346] Steve Huff, "Veteran LAPD Detective Stephanie Lazarus Arrested for Cold Case Homicide," *True Crime Report*, 5 June 2009.

[347] "Los Angeles—Air Crash Averted," *Pathe(scope) Gazette*, 9.5 mm film. Undated.

[348] Jon Aerts, "Male Victims Get Lost in Domestic Abuse Data," *Seattle Times*, 26 December 2010, p. A-23.

[349] Diane Marcum, "Parole Denied for Woman Who Cooked, Ate Husband," *Los Angeles Times*, 5 October 2011.

[350] The Luftwaffe bombs the hell out of London for seventy-six consecutive days during the "blitz," blowing up 43,000 civilians. Clerks man their posts while the ladies shop for bargains! "London Women Buy Bargains as Bodies Taken from Store," *Los Angeles Times*, 24 October 1940, front page.

[351] Wassayos Ngamkham, "Nasty Start for Female Officers," *Bangkok Post*, 22 June 2008.

P.W. Suphaporn Duangkanya, twenty-three, is confronted by a male demonstrator: "As he was about to throw a punch, she ducked and shouted she was a woman....'My colleagues who have pretty faces were spared the wrath of the protestors...I came close to receiving a blow because I have a tomboy look.'" Her sergeant major, Jutharat Panchagorn, "...maintained that most female border policewoman (parachute and weapons trained) were not Lesbians as many people believe."

Pregnant Police

A detective working for me in CID announces she is pregnant and has a doctor's note stating she requires three months off before giving birth and six months off for "recovery." She has several children and apparently experiences no previous medical problems. City physicians challenge her doctor to document her extraordinary needs. He writes a note of apology stating he is merely carrying out the wishes of his patient and that she is otherwise in good health. She then resigns in a huff. A taxpayer investment of several hundred thousand dollars—and years of experience—are lost.

Absences are difficult for large and small departments. Training a replacement can take years, even if such a budget item exists. If the absence is temporary, the replacement is eventually out of a job. This places stress and a burden upon other officers. The work simply does not get done, and the public suffers.

Female officers of the Metropolitan (D.C.) Police Department and Fraternal Order of Police complain that the department's female chief is making "war against pregnant and lactating officers" by requiring them to work patrol. They demand light duty jobs and special "lactating rooms."[352]

Pregnant police officers successfully sue small departments that refuse light-duty positions or have none available. The ladies refuse work "involving stress, firearms, loud noises, and toxic chemical exposure (defined as cleaning their duty firearms)."[353] They cannot work traffic

---

[352] Paul Clinton, "D.C. Chief, Police Union at Odds Over Breast Feeding Policy," *Police—Women in Law Enforcement*, 28 June 2011.

[353] Lori Connelly, "Pregnancy and Policing," *Police—Women in Law Enforcement*, 24 June 2011.

because of potential exposure to the fumes of burning flares. Ignored are the concerns of fellow officers about backup and safety issues of women unable to perform their duties. How is the public served by officers unwilling or unable to engage in routine, dangerous, or life-saving situations? How many competent men have lost their careers so these frauds can draw on the dole?

Lowering the Bar

A retired LAPD officer writes:

> "When some women couldn't vault walls, the walls were lowered.
> Written tests are made simpler. Some recruits even lacked the finger strength to fire their pistols. Another complained that her heavy badge hurt her shoulder and back and took a desk job. Officers who questioned the fitness of these useless officers were sternly warned about workplace harassment rules. Some field training officers (FTOs) were forced to pass dangerously incompetent rookies or lose their rank and merit pay….Some (female officers) have unnecessarily shot and killed unarmed (and) naked teenagers.
> Despite some outrageous (but secretly settled) excessive force lawsuits, no female officer has ever been charged criminally for using excessive force."[354]

Home on the Range

"Motor Sergeant Jackie Boyer…went to qualify on the Combat Range one night. She loaded her magazines and prepared to shoot. She had a jam immediately that she couldn't clear. Apparently she loaded the bullets in her magazine *backwards* and one of them jammed in the chamber."[355]

---

[354] Clark W. Baker, Blog: "Ex Liberal in Hollywood:" 20 March 2008.

[355] Roy Langheld, West Traffic Division, LAPD, "Westside Story," *Thin Blue Line*, July 1999 (Vol. 54, No. 7), p. 36. Sergeant Jacqueline Boyer, 24829, is arrested in San Dimas on 16 December 1989 for "domestic violence" against her female police officer roommate and "admitted to two psychiatric wards and held for 72 hours." She then sues an LAPD

Oh, What a Tangled Web We Weave. Are consent decrees—hiring women until they total 50 percent of the force—suitable only for police departments? How about national sports teams? Why are there different standards for men and women in football, boxing, and other sports? Why separate restrooms? Social engineering should not take place in positions where the public and other officers are endangered by inadequate physical capabilities. The Fourteenth Amendment "equal protection" clause is not about socioeconomic or physical equality; it is about equal protection under law.

Not all female police officers are pleased. A female sergeant (currently a commander) writes, "....most disturbing is the fact that the City of Los Angeles is not hiring the 'best person for the job.' They are obsessed with gender, race, ethnicity and lifestyle. Large numbers of qualified candidates are 'de-selected' simply because they are white males."[356]

A detective writes, "Years of affirmative action, multiculturalism, and other politically inspired policies have only served to promote anger, resentment, and division throughout the Department."[357]

The "Los Angeles Women Police Officers and Associates" (LAWPOA) complain, "...only Hispanics were being promoted to the rank of sergeant and detective in accordance with the goals of the consent decree."[358] (Translation: Hispanic women officers are being favored over white females.) This same article also complains that, although taxpayers build a child care center for female officers, three more are needed. "Hire me over better qualified candidates because I am a woman. As I can no longer care for my kids, I demand free day care!"

The late Sergeant Joseph J. Farrell writes me (29 February 1996), "I am afraid the LAPD is over. I have a son on the job and when he tells me some of the things that are going on it makes me sick. No more police work."

---

commander for approving her detention: Leslie Burger, "Profile: Mark A. Kroeker," *Los Angeles Times*, 22 December 1991.

[356] Sergeant Jeri Weinstein, Letter to the Editor, *Thin Blue Line*, March 1996 (Vol. 51, No. 3), p. 14.

[357] C. Wetzel, Letter to the Editor, *Thin Blue Line*, December 1995 (Vol. 50, No. 12), p. 13.

[358] Lita Abella, "LAWPOA News," *Thin Blue Line*, December 1995, p. 47.

Detective Leon Smith comments (31 August 1989), "The Department we knew and the Department that exists at this time are not the same." Police Commission Secretary William Cowdin pens (23 November 1991), "The scandals and problems in the Department can not be believed.... Affirmative action and social problems have made it hell to work there."

"There don't appear to be any vestiges of humor left in the old alma mater," corresponds Captain Jack I. Eberhardt on 4 July 1995. "My heart aches that an institution and its people whom I deeply loved has fallen into the depths of despair." Long-time LAPD press relations officer Lieutenant Daniel N. Cooke writes me (President's Day, 1996), "It's so sad to see what has happened to our Department over the years....I would give special emphasis to affirmative action. When you lower standards, you lower the status of the entire Dept."

I treasure a letter (21 May 1994) from the late deputy chief Charles D. Reese describing the "Golden Era" of LAPD: "I knew that something monumental had happened but I didn't have the depth of experience to recognize just what profound effort and insistence that Bill Parker must have had to alter the old, corrupt organization and make it not only an example for honesty and integrity but also for administrative genius for every other police outfit in the world...bar none."

The public is taking notice of poorly manned[359] and disciplined police departments. John Brennan comments on "women-men": "You know what I mean. Rough gals. You see them everywhere in law enforcement; females out to prove something....They are unattractive, masculine creatures you see acting like tough guys....The type we made fun of as kids. They were the misfits, the bullies, and are now wearing the uniforms...angry people who have some insatiable need to control others."[360]

---

[359] "Manned—Performed by a human." Merriam-Webster On-Line Dictionary. Feminists have altered the language by insisting upon "person," "he or she," or other such gender-substitutions for "man." The definition of "man" remains: "An adult human; humankind."

[360] Brennan, "The New Breed of Hero," LewRockwell.com, 21 December 2011.

Babes in Arms

Amazons are a tribe of warrior women living in Scythia (ancient Iran). Amazons, unfortunately, do not exist in sufficient numbers to form military units. So our politically-correct generals and politicians must invent them:

* Private First Class Jessica Dawn Lynch. Born in Palestine (West Virginia). Joins the Quartermaster Corps as a supply clerk. Her female supervisor makes a wrong turn and their convoy is ambushed near Nasiriyah, Iraq. Lynch, a female Rambo—full of knife and bullet holes—fights off the evil terrorists until she runs out of ammo. Our brave Rangers and SEALs fight their way into the hospital, where she is held captive, and airlift her out.

Jessica is an honorable soldier. She reveals she is actually injured in a vehicle accident. Iraqi doctors speed her to an American checkpoint in an ambulance—which we then fire upon. Hospital personnel are amazed by the arrival of a film crew and soldiers firing blanks and setting off explosives in a filmed phony rescue.[361]

* Private First Class Lynndie R. England. Military Police guard and scapegoat for prisoner of war scandals. Photos of her holding a leash around the neck of naked and tortured prisoners in Abu Ghraib Prison, Baghdad, provide one of the best recruiting tools for the insurgents and proof to the world of American atrocities.[362]

* Lieutenant Kara S. Hultgreen. First female pilot cleared for combat, crashes into the sea while attempting to land on the USS *Abraham Lincoln* in 1994. The navy goes to extraordinary means to show this is an engine failure when it is a series of pilot errors. She is an incompetent pilot who is not washed out because of her CO's threats to instructors

---

[361] John Kampfner, "The Truth About Jessica," *The Guardian* (UK), 15 May 2003.

[362] "England Sentenced to 3 Years for Prison Abuse," Associated Press, 28 September 2005.

following feminists demands after the "Tail-hook Scandals." [363] So who kills Lieutenant Hultgreen?

NOTE: Allegations of sexual harassment and misbehavior at "Tailhook 35" in 1991 at the Las Vegas Hilton result in 14 admirals cashiered and 300 naval aviator careers terminated. If females cannot fend off a few frisky airedales, how can they possibly confront a determined enemy soldier?

* <u>CBS News</u> (6 November 2009) hails "Female Cop and Fort Hood Hero" Kimberly "Mighty Mouse" Munley with shooting Major Nidal Hasan, army psychiatrist who guns down forty-four, killing thirteen.

Feminists screech their joy with toothache-inducing levels of condescension at this woman who does what a base full of armed male soldiers cannot. Only problem is that it is another civilian police officer, Senior Sergeant Mark Todd, who shoots the suspect, saving the downed "Mighty Mouse."[364]

Girls with Guns

Common sense and thousands of years of evolution tell us women should not be in combat. Men go out in packs and hunt; women care for the kids, gather fruits and vegetables, and shop. Women fight only when all their men are dead. Permitting them to fight is an affront to feminine dignity and simple decency.

---

[363] "Double Standards in Naval Aviation" (April 1995, 125 pp.), quoted in, "CMR Attorneys File Response in Support of Motion for Summary Judgment," Center for Military Readiness, May 2002.

[364] Chris Ayres (Los Angeles), *The Sunday Times* (London), 13 November 2009. See also, Fox News.com, 13 November 2009.

Female dominance in society is contrary to human nature. Matriarchies exist in the past, but are short-lived. The industry that creates the new world is built by male brawn and daring—not the usual attributes of the "fair sex."

Fitness is essential for combat readiness. Women can fire an artillery piece but cannot load the ammunition. They can drive a deuce-and-a-half but cannot change its tire. They can parachute into battle but haven't the stamina to carry their weapons and gear off the drop zone.

One report quotes a West Point study revealing P.T. sex-norming schemes where women receive "A" grades for the same performance that earns a man a "D."[365] The U.S. Army Physical Fitness Test requires fewer push-ups and other exercises for women. (Women also test from a kneeling push-up position instead of prone.) Navy women pass this test with 53 percent fewer push-ups than required for men.

Williams cites an army study reporting that only *12 percent* of female recruits can throw a hand grenade beyond its burst radius.[366] (Think about this.) At a woman's physical peak (ages twenty to thirty) she has the aerobic capacity of a fifty-year-old male. Her medical non-availability is twice that of male soldiers. The strongest woman recruit is typically only as strong as the weakest man.

Secretary of the Navy James Webb reports 51 percent of single Air Force and 48 percent of single navy women stationed in Iceland are pregnant. (They appear to be burning more rubber than gunpowder.) Replacements for pregnant personnel are not available, which increases the workload for the rest.

"The 'women in combat' demands of feminists are seen as 'empowerment, rights, respect, and entitlement' with no concern for military effectiveness."[367] Such nonsense forces military leadership to attend to the unique needs of women rather than to their mission. One first sergeant reports ten percent of his company—the females—take up 90 percent of his problem-solving

---

[365] Walter Williams, "Race and Sex in the Military," *Conservative Chronicle*, 14 October 1998 (Vol. 13, No. 41), p. 30. See, also, *Jewish World Review*, 8 October 1998.

[366] Ibid. Also, R. Cort Kirkwood, "The Military's War on Nature," *Chronicles*, April 2013 (Vol. 37, No. 4), pp. 5 and 6.

[367] Dr. Mackubin T. Owens (Professor, Naval War College), "Mothers in Combat Boots," *Human Rights Review*, Spring 1997 (Vol. 23, No. 1), pp. 35–45.

time.³⁶⁸ Instead of a "Band of Brothers," you get constant squabbling and rivalries among the men for the women's favors. Women are on prowl for the slightest hint of objection to their presence—so they can run to their unit's commissar, the "equal opportunity" rep.

The U.S. no longer fights wars to win. Our goal is to enrich special interests and to use war to frighten Americans into accepting a security state. Posing women and minorities in various action scenarios, thus, makes political sense even as it discards common sense.

Women in the Israeli Defense Force

Feminists unleash banshee-like wails when the mission of the military—carrying arms and ammunition, moving the wounded, killing the enemy—is enhanced by excluding females. "Look at women in the Israeli army," they insist.

Early Zionists in the collectivist *kibbutzim* treat girls and boys alike. As children, they receive toilet training together, and, as adolescents, they shower together. Never in modern history have male and female been so equal. The "War of Independence" in 1948 throws women soldiers into the line beside the men. At the first clash with the Arab legion, the women break and run, soon followed by the men. All women are immediately pulled out of combat.³⁶⁹

"Women have been barred from combat in Israel since 1950, when a review of the 1948 Arab-Israeli War showed how harmful their presence could be. The study revealed that men tried to protect and assist women rather than continue their attack (which) jeopardized the survival of their entire unit."³⁷⁰

Feminists are also active in Israel. Word is that IDF women are involved in field operations during the 2006 Lebanon War (which the Israelis lose).

---

[368] Charles W. Sasser, "Women in Combat?" *Soldier of Fortune*, March 1992, p. 41.

[369] Richard Grenier, "Equality's Downside," *The Washington Times*, 8 December 1996 (Vol. 3, No. 49), p. 29.

[370] Jon Dougherty, "Debunking the Israeli 'Women in Combat' Myth," *World Net Daily*, 2 August 2001.

I am unable to confirm if females still serve in the IDF Minorities Unit (Unit 300), which in my day is heavy with Druz, Bedouins, and American and European Jews not considered of "pure blood." (Shades of the Waffen SS.) It is now quiet and may be disbanded and integrated with other units. The Caracal (Thirty-third Infantry Brigade), formed in 2004 for duty on the Egyptian border, however, is of mixed gender.

The World of Suzie Wong

A biologically ironclad rule is that 105 boys are born for every 100 girls. Societies where men greatly outnumber women (China, India, Korea) are often violent and unstable. Unmarried men with limited incomes tend to make trouble.

Chinese men now bid to secure a bride. This enforced savings drives the Chinese demand for U.S. treasury bills, increasing U.S. debt.[371]

My Chinese wife adds that a rural girl will sometimes be married, and, upon arrival at her new husband's home, find she has three or four additional husbands—usually brothers of the groom. Bad things may happen to her if she complains....This gender imbalance encourages young women to become chattel to provide income for their families or pimps. Villages (or countries) will go to war to capture wives. This is a genuine threat to China's neighbors.

Men and women have their own characteristics and agendas. These differences have worked for thousands of years. The Billy Wilder comedy, *Some Like It Hot* (1959), closes with multimillionaire eccentric (Joe E. Brown) being told by his fiancée (Jack Lemmon, disguised as a woman) that she is really a man. Brown replies with a smile, "Nobody's perfect!"

Stand and Deliver

No warrior culture respects women who soldier or hold command, a matter that runs deeper than training standards. Natural law is not going to

---

[371] Jonathan V. Last, "The War Against Girls," *Wall Street Journal*, 18 June 2011.

change from any amount of diversity or sensitivity training. Soldiers know the more a woman is like a man, the less she is like a woman.

A device issued to females in Iraq and Afghanistan, known as a FUD (Feminine Urinary Device), permits women to urinate standing up. (The civilian brand is Go-Girl.) This is how women in the military are viewed: those who must act, as best they can, as men.

EPILOGUE

"Non, Je Ne Regrette Rien."[372]

I am the wanderer and vagabond. The spirit of my colonial ancestor, Private Thomas Hurlbut, touches me lightly over the span of centuries. [He infects, roughly, every other generation with this gypsy gene. Only time slows us down.]

I retire from the Big City to escape the heat, SMOG, crime, traffic, and aliens (not necessarily in this order). I swear to never work again in a town with a stop light. We head as far north as possible to troubleshoot "problem departments." A decade of five months of darkness and fifty-below-zero temperatures, alternating with 200 inches of summer rain and giant mosquitoes, convince us a compromise is best for retirement.

"City Marshal of Tombstone" caps my police career as a reform mayor tries to clean up a department run amok. The corruption in this corner of Arizona runs deep and is something to behold. Half of my department become "Cochise County Suicides."

Bellingham, Washington, has mild winters and cool summers. It rains a lot. Mildew is the state flower. We are twenty miles south of Canuckistan. (Eh? They call us "Upper Mexicans.") How can you take a country seriously when they call their dollar a "loonie" and dump raw sewage from Victoria, their British Columbia capital city, into the Strait of Juan de Fuca to float our way?

Canadian shoppers swarm south and drive our gas prices to the highest in the nation. Remember, northern neighbors, we invade countries for less. Do you think we provide for your defense over the decades just so you can spend your dollars, er…loonies, on social programs? Your land and resources are our future Manifest Destiny!

---

[372] "I regret nothing." Edith Piaf (La Mome Piaf—"The Little Sparrow") dedicates this song to the 1er REP following the 1961 Algerian putsch. The legionnaires sing it as they disband and march from their barracks, never to return.

My years in the army and assignments to every inhabited continent give me an overview of the "American Empire" and how we are seen by the rest of the world. It is not pretty. It becomes clear that little changes, whether Republicans or Democrats are in power. Our political parties are two wings of the same bird; a fat bird who feeds from special interests foreign to the will and desires of most Americans. There are promising signs that Americans are catching on and reaching for their torches and pitchforks.

Both parties fight sham battles and occasionally join forces to combat the latest bogeyman: Indians (it is no coincidence the code name for Osama Bin Laden is "Geronimo," as today's Redskins are the Muslims), Spain, the Kaiser, the Red Menace, Iraq, Iran, and "Islamo-Fascist" terrorism. When it becomes obvious the latest enemy is a hoax or just a minor nuisance, the same lies and false-flag operations begin against the next—Iran, China, or India will do nicely. The supposed mission is to bring our version of "American democracy" to all nations.

Neo-cons wish to accomplish this by warfare and liberals by welfare.

The president assumes control over the powers of Congress and his position trumps the Bill of Rights. He claims the power to assassinate anyone, including American citizens, on a secret "kill list." Our Constitution is trashed, and we become a security state. There is no outrage. The president and his minions are *above the law* and free to torture and jail without cause.

One courageous man reveals our private conversations and electronic communications are secretly recorded by the government. Does anyone seriously believe this will "make us safer?" I assure you, as a former counter-intel officer, this is to uncover little indiscretions so as to blackmail journalists and politicians for control over their stories and votes. Our basic Fourth Amendment right to be left alone no longer exists….thanks to Presidents Bush and Obama!

We invade/attack countries that do not threaten us. Our foreign policy is set by a small rogue nation of paranoid but influential Zealots on a suicide mission. Keep in mind that victory is not the goal of our wars; it is the conflict itself—along with the profits and domestic control through a state of permanent emergency. Overlooked is the retaliatory violence by victims seeking to restore control. The American Revolution at home is repealed without a shot being fired.

Our military spending exceeds that of the rest of the world combined and bankrupts us. False patriots, a fundamentalist Right, a cheerleading media, and two socialist parties turn our treasury over to hordes of foreign invaders intent upon the doom of Western civilization and our way of life. This scenario destroys empires before us, but the voices of reason are lost in the clamor for bread (welfare) and circuses (wars against weak, third world countries). The Great American Experiment is over! Americans plod along in a state of denial, not blinking at the militarization of law enforcement, loss of rights and privacy, and expanding government surveillance.

I have a good run. I grow up in an America so changed it is a lost civilization. If you never experience what goes before, however, it is difficult to miss or to appreciate it.

I do not visit Tibet until the Han invasion and Russia before the Soviet Union falls. I see the "Hanoi Hilton" (*Maison Centrale*) and Lubyanka Prison—KGB/FSB HQ—from the OUTSIDE. (It is said to be the tallest building in Moskwa, as you can see Siberia from its basement!) "Red Square" comes not from the Communist army (named after colors), but from the word *"kraznaya"* (red), also meaning "beautiful." This is the original meaning for Saint Basil's Cathedral, but it becomes lost. I find that Spetsnaz (special purpose forces) have much in common with U.S. Special Forces. But these are stories for another time.

My final words include a personal note from Horace [Quintus Horatius Flaccus (65–8 BC)], lyric poet and officer in the Republican army crushed at the Battle of Philippi (the one in 42 BC, not AD 1861). Horace is a witness to Rome's change from republic to empire, as you and I are witnesses to the same in America: *"Natales grate numeras?"* (Do you count your birthdays with gratitude?)

Horace, Book II, Epistle ii, line 210.

And a final toast dating back to the U.S. Indian Wars: "To lost trails, lost comrades, and lost causes...."

Soviet Sputnik—first artificial earth satellite. Card sent to author for his short-wave radio observations of a decaying orbit.
4 October 1957.

Max driving "Bower's Ambulance" Car 19—a 1959 red Cadillac. 430 East Pacific Coast Highway, Long Beach, CA. December 1959.

First official LAPD photo of author as police applicant. July 1960.

Max K. Hurlbut

Certificate of Appointment as Los Angeles Policeman signed
by Chief William H. Parker. 1 August 1960.

Vagabond Policeman

Policeman Max K. Hurlbut, 10603. Hollywood Division, LAPD.
January 1961.

Max K. Hurlbut

Author's 1959 Ford overturned by Memorial Day 1961 "Freedom Rider" rioters in the Merry-Go-Round area of Griffith Park.

Vagabond Policeman

Officer Max Hurlbut (left), Sgt. Willis J. Gough, and Clarence F. Corbitt capture a barricaded Jack C. Bradner who fires shots though the door of his 5200 Hollywood Boulevard apartment, wounding an officer.
12 August 1961.

Army Private Max directing traffic at the Provost Marshal General's (Military Police) School, Fort Gordon, GA. 17 July 1962.

Max working FT (Freeway Traffic) 88, in 1961 Plymouth "Freeway Interceptor." 13 March 1964, 0300 hours.

Max K. Hurlbut

Polaroids of Hollywood Vice: Working the brush above "Ferndell No. 9" outhouse, Griffith Park, and goofing-off in the Vice Office. 24 June 1964.

Active Duty Training with 316th Criminal Investigation Division, Fort MacArthur, CA. Honda "Trail 90." 3 November 1965.

Max K. Hurlbut

MSG Edward A. "Bud" Harper in T-10 'chute headed for target on Tatu Drop Zone (141 feet below sea level), Naval Parachute Test Range, El Centro, CA. Photo by SSG Max, in another parachute, of 12th Special Forces Group. Note approaching C-141 "Starlifter" at 1,000 feet and its shadow on the desert floor.
28 October 1967.

Vagabond Policeman

Special Weapons & Tactics (SWAT) Team 8 (Wilshire Division) in water tower night training exercise above the Police Academy. Clockwise from top left: Sgt. Max (Team Leader), Angelo M. Scotillo (Sharpshooter), Warren B. Carlson (Scout), & Benjamin J. Rendahl (Rear Guard/Shotgun). 21 March 1968.

Max K. Hurlbut

SWAT in storm drain beneath Wilshire Station. Photo by author.
2 May 1968.

Sgt. Max demonstrating Station Wagon Command Post at LAPD "Staff & Command School." 14 March 1968.

Sgt. Max deploying security at Command Post for "Operation Century '67." Visit of President Lyndon Johnson to the Century Plaza Hotel. Officers David N. Burton & Donald W. Perkins to author's right. Others not identified. 23 June 1967.

SSG MAX, "Jungle Expert" certified at the Jungle Warfare School, Fort Sherman, Canal Zone (Panama). July 1969.

Max K. Hurlbut

"Crevasse Rescue." SSG Max using Prusik knots to inch out of crevasse while team climbers are "On Belay." Gulkana Glacier. Northern Operations School. Fort Greely, Alaska. 17 June 1969.

Author leading intel-gathering patrol. Southeast Asia, 1968.
Note the selection of M-14 rifle over lighter M-16.

Max with "mbogo" after thorn-bush tunnel encounter. Block 57 (Masai), Kenya. Rigby .470 double rifle. 11 December 1969.

Selel (the Masai who knee-caps mbogo, saving the author) drying strips of cape buffalo biltong. Somewhere in Kenya, 1969.

Lieutenant Max presenting Series-6 LAPD badge to Chief R. Lee Heath (1904-26) for his 93d birthday. Tujunga. 16 June 1972.

Max with Baramba trackers. Browning .458 Magnum. Northeast Congo. July 1973.

Max K. Hurlbut

Max & tracker with forest elephant downed in Aka Swamp, Zaire (Congo), with Browning .458 magnum. 10 July 1973.

Baramba hunter with with caplock trade musket converted to a matchlock. Loincloth is of ficus bark. Aka Swamp, Zaire. July 1973.

Captain Max jumping from barrage balloon over Queen's Parade Drop Zone.
Depot the Parachute Regiment & Airborne Force.
Aldershot, Hampshire. 15 June 1976.

Man-trap, before and after burning off leaf cover. Ezo area,
the Sudan. February 1978.

Max & Katanga soldier, Hapana Fikiri, near Bambuka River, Nagasi, the Sudan. February 1978.

Max before departing to Kolwezi, Zaire, as observer. Ecole des Troupes Aeroportees. Pau, France. May 1978.

Royal Thai Border Patrol Police scout with crossbow. 1980.

Max with French MAT-49 submachine gun. Thai-Cambodian border. 1980.

Major Max (far right) in audience with His Majesty King Bhumibol Adulyadej (Rama IX)—near elephant tusk on left. Grand Palace, Bangkok. 23 December 1981.

Oberst (Colonel) Dieter Seebeck awarding Captain Max the German "Expert Infantry/ Efficiency" badge. Major Heinz Henn, center. Lechfeld Air Base, Bavaria. June 1978.

General Arturo Durazo Moreno, Mexican Federal Police, commissioning Max as Coronel of the Ranger-Parachute Brigade. Mexico, D.F. 26 September 1978.

Max K. Hurlbut

General Pablo Alfonso Rosas Guarin, Head of the Columbia National Police and International Police Association Region 6 (U.S.) Chairman Max, signing protocols. LAPD Det. Nathan D. Johnson, CID (standing, left), & Mayor Alvaro Blanco Noriega. Bogata.
28 September 1979

Chief Daryl F. Gates presenting First Place Award (Color) to Max for "In Focus" LAPD Photographic Contest. Chief's Office, Parker Center. 13 February 1980. [Photo is "Midnight Sun"—Dog sled on ice during Canadian Army North Pole Expedition].

Max K. Hurlbut

Troopers of 2d Battalion, 7th Special Forces Group (Airborne), jumping from tailgate of C-130 at 500 feet over Holland D.Z., Ft. Bragg, NC. 14 August 1981. Photo by author, the last jumper & Acting CI Chief of the JFK Center for Military Assistance.

Senator & former LAPD Chief Edward M. Davis congratulating American Legion Police Post 381 Commander Max. Palm Springs Convention. 25 June 1983.

Max & Hueih-Hueih ("Way-Way") with 1985 Kawasaki KZ-1000P.
Team Captain of L.A. Police Motorcycle Drill Team.

President Chun Doo-Hwan and First Lady Rhee Soon-ja at Cheong Wa-Dae (the Blue House), Seoul, Korea. Left-to-right: Max, Homer Gainer, Pepperdine Chancellor Norvel Young, President Chun & Rhee. 8 November 1984.

Max, OIC of CID Enforcement Section. 1981 Plymouth on Grand Avenue, Bunker Hill, Los Angeles. 16 January 1985.

William Shatner (as "T. J. Hooker") and Hueih-Hueih at
LAPD Academy Athletic Field. 8 July 1982.

Max & Hueih-Hueih on a sand bar. Shuyak Island, Alaska.
19 June 1986. USCG Sikorsky HH-3F Pelican No. 1473. It crashes on
Ugak Island, 2 Nov 1986, with no survivors.

Max & fellow Adventurers' & Explorers' Club member, John M. Goddard. Cape Chiniak, Kodiak Island, AK. 31 July 1987.

Max K. Hurlbut

Max & Hueih-Hueih in front of "Three-Saints" Russian Orthodox Church. Old Harbor, Kodiak Island, AK. 23 July 1987.

Max & Hueih-Hueih hunting bison for Winter meat. Cape Chiniak, Kodiak Island. Rifle is Model 1886 .45-70. 13 Dec 87.

Max & Corporal Richard C. Perkins with K-9 "Igor." Kodiak.

Max K. Hurlbut

Volunteer Fireman Max, serial 111, Bayside Fire Department, Kodiak Island. Engine 12, 1984 Western States 3,500 gallon Pumper. 9 April 1988.

Max (Director of Public Safety) & Hueih-Hueih, Rail-Ambulance Drivers and EMTs. 1981 Chevrolet Rail-Ambulance in front of Whittier Tunnel, Alaska. 2 November 1992.

MAX & HUEIH-HUEIH implement VPSO (Village Public Safety Officer—Native Police) Program on St. George, The Pribilof Islands, Bering Sea. "Saint George the Great Martyr" Russian Orthodox Church. 1990 Chevrolet "Scottsdale" Public Safety truck. February 1993.

Max K. Hurlbut

Max & Hueih-Hueih patrolling through brash off Blackstone Glacier in two-hatch kayak where Cheechako killed by calving ice. June 1993.

Part-time Deputy Dan G. Jewell with a burglar's compressed footprints in snow, isolated by winds blowing away surrounding loose flakes. Whittier, Alaska. 20 November 1993.

Max K. Hurlbut

Patrolling Portage Pass on snowshoes. H. & K. Model 91 rifle in 7.62 x 51mm. 23 January 1994.

Dog-sledding near Mile Post 66, Parks Highway,
Willow, Alaska. 17 March 1994.

Max K. Hurlbut

Tombstone City Marshal Max & Hueih-Hueih on Bell Ranch stage-coach in front of "O. K. Corral," 308 East Allen Street. Drawn by "Lilly" (left) & "Bay Rum." 16 October 1997.

Marshal Max with 1992 Mercury "Grand Marqis L.S."
Schieffelin Monument off West Allen Street about two miles west of
Tombstone, Arizona. 6 March 1998.

Max K. Hurlbut

"Northern Exposure" (Max patrolling Prince William Sound) and "Tombstone Territory." Caricatures by Chad Carpenter, "Tundra" artist and friend.

Tombstone Marshal's Office. (Left-to-right): Deputy Francisco D. "Frank" Hidalgo, Dispatcher Judith K. Miller, Marshal Max K. Hurlbut, Deputy Duane "Ray" Hudson, & Deputy Dennis J. Wahlen. 315 East Fremont Street next to "O. K. Corral" gun-fight site. 17 August 1998. Hidalgo and Hudson found shot-to-death in their vehicles.

Vagabond Policeman

Max riding "Homer" for "Helldorado '98" in front of "Campbell & Hatch Billiard Parlor" where Morgan Earp murdered on 18 March 1882. 400 block of Allen Street, Tombstone. 16 October 1998.

Max K. Hurlbut

Painting by author's amigo, Western artist
MIKE SCOVEL of the "Y-Me Ranch."

Max & Hueih-Hueih in Tombstone jail-cell office. 7 August 1998.

Max greeted by Thomas C. Christian at the Landing on Pitcairn Island. Tom, a fellow member of the Adventurers' Club, is the great-3d grandson of Fletcher of "Mutiny on the Bounty."
25 April 2006.

Max K. Hurlbut

Max after complaining of food on Russian icebreaker "Ortelius."
Whaler's Bay. Caldera of Deception Island (an active volcano).
Antarctica. 1 December 2012.

Chief of Police Max K. Hurlbut. Kodiak, Alaska. 1987.

Max K. Hurlbut

Female skeleton of possible murder victim washes up on Near Island, Kodiak, Alaska.
11 July 1987. Sea lice, crabs, & other marine life can reduce a body to bones
in a day or two....

www.ingramcontent.com/pod-product-compliance
Lightning Source LLC
Chambersburg PA
CBHW052007070526
44584CB00016B/1657